Zuma's Own Goal
Losing South Africa's 'War on Poverty'

Contents

Contributors

Franco Barchiesi is with the Department of African-American and African Studies, Ohio State University.

Patrick Bond is with the University of KwaZulu-Natal Centre for Civil Society and School of Development Studies.

Jackie Cock is a Wits University Professor Emeritus of Sociology.

Ashwin Desai was formerly with the University of Johannesburg and Rhodes University.

Andries du Toit is with the University of the Western Cape Programme in Land and Agrarian Studies.

Ben Fine is in the School of Oriental and African Studies at the University of London.

Mary Galvin directs Umphilo waManzi, a South African non-profit organisation.

Leonard Gentle is with the International Labour Research and Information Group.

Gillian Hart is with the University of California-Berkeley Department of Geography and UKZN Department of Sociology.

Fred Hendricks is Dean of Humanities at Rhodes University.

Mark Heywood is Director of SECTION27, incorporating the AIDS Law Project, and an executive of the Treatment Action Campaign.

Brij Maharaj is a geographer in the School of Environmental Sciences at the University of KwaZulu-Natal.

Hein Marais is an independent writer based in Johannesburg.

Enver Motala is associate researcher at the University of Johannesburg Centre for Education Rights and Transformation.

Prishani Naidoo is based at Wits University's Department of Sociology and is doing a PhD at the UKZN Centre for Civil Society.

Trevor Ngwane is a Masters student at the UKZN Centre for Civil Society.

Lungisile Ntsebeza is NRF Research Chair: Land Reform and Democracy in SA, University of Cape Town.

Anshu Padayachee is Chief Executive Officer of SANPAD.

Greg Ruiters is Matthew Goniwe Chair at the Rhodes Institute for Social and Economic Research.

Carol Anne Spreen is visiting professor at the University of Johannesburg.

Salim Vally is a senior researcher at the University of Johannesburg Centre for Education Rights and Transformation.

Foreword
Anshu Padayachee

It is with great pleasure that we present this book, originally a collection of papers presented in their initial form during the SANPAD-organised 2007 Poverty Conference that took place in Durban.

This Conference was characterised as seminal by those who attended, because it brought together large numbers of academics, researchers, senior politicians, analysts, opinion--makers, senior students, and representatives of civil society and the poor under one roof.

It elicited a wide variety of stimulating, occasionally heated debates on the challenges facing our country. And it provided a unique opportunity to all sectors of our society to be heard and noticed on issues such as economic policy, HIV/AIDS, social security, housing, basic services and education.

The result is an intellectually rigorous, meticulously researched and politically suffused book that is different, mostly because thorough analysis is complimented by advocacy for innovative and tangible alternatives. Thus it enhances and enriches one of the key objectives of SANPAD, that of providing developmental alternatives to the problems and challenges facing South Africa.

It is a book highly recommended for all citizens, policy makers, researchers, journalists, academics and all those who are deeply interested in the future of our country.

Introduction:
Poverty eradication as Holy Grail
Ashwin Desai, Brij Maharaj and Patrick Bond

One of the most abiding stories of all time is the quest for the Holy Grail. The twentieth century witnessed the return of this symbol time and again, in order to make sense of upheavals that accompanied industrialisation, the horrors of war and the erosion of the influence of Christianity.

It was the theme of probably the most popular English-language book of the 20th century, *Lord of the Rings* by Bloemfontein-born J.R.R. Tolkien. But in Frodo's hands, the Grail is not the "healing, heavenly talisman" but "powerful, corrupting and malevolent" (Morgan, 2005: 131). Poets, too, got in on the act. TS Eliot's masterpiece, The Waste Land, drew from the Grail legend as Eliot responded to the Great Transformation of the 1920s that saw the destruction of a system reliant on hierarchy and tradition, and replaced by a sense of despair and foreboding. No wonder, since Eliot was a Conservative and a Royalist.

Movies followed. John Boorman's *Excalibur*, George Lucas's *Star Wars*, the Indiana Jones series, and Monty Python's *Holy Grail* were obviously re-tellings. And there were many others in which the Holy Grail was less a literal artefact and more a religiously redemptive state of being, to be found in a place, a person or a way of life (see Barber 2004, for a review of the Grail's many incarnations).

And with the release of the last of the *Star Wars* episodes and the amazing popularity of Dan Brown's *Da Vinci Code*, the Grail continues to re-invent itself as representing personal struggle, collective journeying and the need to achieve the ultimate goal which when found will reveal a deeper level of truth and meaning to a dispiriting post-industrial society.

No matter how exotic the locale, however, the search tends to occur across social terrain that has been carefully laid by ruling groups. Whatever poverty-alleviating fruit is found along the path reminds those missionaries who consume it, that legitimising the earthly garden market is, ultimately, a worthy substitute for the elusive Grail. 'The perfect is the enemy of the good,' say some who give up the search, content to eat what's available; even if that means others go hungry. If you don't like this terrain, you might survive on the margins. But moving onto a more revolutionary terra incognita is, for rulers who define our narratives, strongly discouraged.

In economics, the quest for poverty eradication often represents the struggle to find one magic solution to bring an end to unnecessary worldly sufferings. Merlin-like characters abound, peddling various potions and expounding all manner of sage-like advice. The last century led to a host of approaches that ranged from colonialism (civilise the natives), the United States (bomb the natives), Pol Pot (exterminate the natives), the Bolshevik Revolution (that ran from permanent revolution to Stalin's socialism in one country to Castro's socialism on one island), home-grown forms of state-led African socialism (Nyerere's ujamma), the hybrid of state and market (the Asian Tigers), and shock therapy economics (post-communist Russia and post-Allende Chile).

As journalists en route with the Grail search party, social scientists tried to explain the growing gap between the first world and the rest - through modernisation (Rostow's take-off), dependency (Frank's development of underdevelopment), combined and uneven development (Bond and Desai) and the articulation of modes of production (Wolpe). The search for not only accurate analysis but also the magic bullet that would kill poverty ran the full gauntlet of experiments.

And so what of South Africa? A great many of these theories – highlighting race-class interactions – were attempted here from the 1960s-80s, even if theorising poverty has been far less common since. Most academics took on consultancies to become more relevant, and in such a milieu, asking bigger questions about the mode of production is plainly useless. The resulting state of intellectual sloth has compelled us to ask, both in our practice and our thought: *are we uprooting or re-rooting poverty in post-apartheid South Africa?*

It is indeed an old question. To close their book published at the end of the 1980s, Francis Wilson and Mamphele Ramphele posed the following issues:

> Will political liberation necessarily be accompanied by a significant improvement in the material conditions and the quality of life of the very poor? The fact that the answer to the latter question could be and has been 'no' for a number of African countries is a measure of the extent of the challenge in South Africa. There is nothing inevitable about the economic consequences of redistributing political power. Everything will depend on the capacity of the new society, not least of its leadership and of the variety of organisational structures available at the time, to move in that the right direction within the limits of what is feasible. It is not impossible, as the recent history of Latin America makes all too plain, that the hard won-gains of a long political struggle be lost in a few months or years either by provocation (for example through unnecessary hyperinflation) or a revolutionary counter-coup or by the

sacrifice of the claims of the poor to the selfishness of a new elite
(Wilson and Ramphele, 1989: 355).

Sixteen years after the coming of democracy and four national
democratic elections later, it is safe to say that right-wing coups or
hyperinflation are not on the horizon. However, that the poor remain as
large a group as ever, while a selfish new elite runs rampant, seems an
intractable feature of post-liberation South Africa. The United Nations
Development Programme (UNDP) revealed in its 2004 report that the
poverty rate in South Africa stood at 48 per cent (UNDP, 2004). The
Taylor Commission reported a poverty rate of between 45 and 55 per
cent. Charles Meth holds that there were some 19.5 million people living
below the poverty line in 2002, up from the 1997 figure of 17.2 million.
Of these people somewhere between 7 and 15 million are living in utter
destitution (Meth, 2004: 9). A government agency, Statistics South
Africa, reports that households earning less than R670 a month
increased from 20 per cent of the population in 1995 to 28 per cent in
2000 (SSA, 2002).[1]

Did matters improve thanks to the post-2000 'developmental state'
agenda and relaxation of fiscal constraints? It is hard to be certain, but
the most recent available analysis - by the SA Labour and Development
Research Unit, published in early 2010 - suggests that while rural
poverty has been reduced mainly through expanded welfare transfer
payments and emigration of poor people to the cities, urban poverty
actually increased from 1993-2008. As Leibbrandt et al. explain, "Over
the period poverty incidence barely changed in rural areas, while it
increased in urban areas. However, due to the large urbanisation of the
period from the high poverty rural areas to lower poverty urban areas,
overall poverty incidence declined" (Leibbrandt et al., 2010: 36).

In other words, what ordinary observers view as a manifestation of
dreadful policy failure – the peri-urban shack settlement stretching for
miles with dreadful living conditions – is in reality an improvement over
life in the depressed, hopeless rural periphery of South Africa.
Urbanisation increases, urban poverty increases, but overall poverty
decreases – leaving the South African Presidency and some
commentators to brag that progress is gradually being achieved, that the
War on Poverty is being won. How might we understand this narrative?

---

1. Perhaps the most upsetting statistic deals with levels of child poverty. Using a poverty
line of R430 a month (2002), 74 per cent of children between 0–17 years are poor, i.e. the
equivalent of more than 13 million children. Using R215 per month poverty line, 54.34
per cent are ultra poor; translating into 9.7 million children.

Losing the 'War on Poverty'

What, actually, is the status of the South African state's War on Poverty
(WoP)? We don't really know, because this is one of the most clandestine
operations in human history, with status reports kept confidential by a
bureaucracy that appears to be in rapid retreat from the front. A google
search of South African websites locates a mere 104 mentions (as of July
2010) in 2008, with a smattering in 2009 and 2010.

Initially the WoP appeared as a major national project. Early hubris
characterised the war, as happens in most. Imminent victory was
claimed even before then-president Mbeki officially launched the WoP
during his February 2008 State of the Nation speech. Trevor Manuel
bragged in his October 2007 Medium Term Budget Policy Statement,
"The number of South Africans living in poverty - based on a poverty line
of about R3000 per person per year in 2000 prices - has dropped
steadily from 52.1 per cent in 1999 to 47 per cent in 2004 and to 43.2
per cent by March this year."[2]

But such claims, initially devoured without questioning by a starving
press corps desperate for morsels of victory, would fall apart under
subsequent scrutiny, e.g., from the University of Cape Town research
team in January 2010 (Leibbrandt et al., 2010), showing virtually no
change from 1993-2008. The brag forewarned even the most moderate
NGOs - like the Global Call to Action Against Poverty (GCAP) – that the
WoP's first casualty could well be the Truth. From Johannesburg, a
cynical GCAP official chided,

> President Mbeki needs to be mindful of the gap between policy
> pronouncements and actions on the ground so this is not just
> more empty hype. He signed onto the Millennium Development
> Goals in 2000, and so far his obligations to the people of South
> Africa have not been fulfilled. Current levels of poverty and
> inequality in South Africa are unacceptable and we want to see a
> delivery plan to match the rhetoric.[3]

The plan to win the WoP was never unveiled, but six months after its
announcement, in August 2008, a national 'war room on poverty' was
established in the office of the Deputy President. From there, teams of

---

2. Benton, S., 2007. SA 'winning the war on poverty.' *BuaNews*, 31 October,
http://www.southafrica.info/about/social/minibudget-311007.htm
3. Global Call for Action Against Poverty, 2008. GCAP Africa welcomes MBEKI'S "war on
poverty" but warns of empty hype, Johannesburg, 8 February.

professionals would go 'from household to household' in thousands of identified areas where the enemy, poverty, was lurking.

Something akin to a 'Total Strategy', to borrow a 1970s phrase, was meant to include both low-intensity warfare techniques – such as welfare grants (old-age pensions, child and disability grants) and short-term Extended Public Works Projects jobs (usually no more than six months in duration) – as well as high-profile shock-and-awe tactics, such as delivery of water to schools, in what would become the equivalent of Protected Villages.

Although at that stage, newspaper references to the WoP became scarce, in late 2009, a new surge of WoP rhetoric emanated from Pretoria. As the government's SA Broadcasting Corporation headlined, "Motlanthe gets his hands dirty in helping the poor... pushing wheelbarrows and laying foundations for Reconstruction and Development Programme houses in Jacobsdal."[4] Small towns had some of the country's worst cases of poverty, and Motlanthe's ammunition included the Integrated Sustainable Rural Development Programme and presidential pilot projects aimed ostensibly at pacification of the enemy in hundreds of the country's poorest villages (demarcated politically, of course, as wards).

Motlanthe also unveiled a special weapon, namely self-help. Instead of soldier-bureaucrats doing the fighting, winning the WoP would be outsourced to the masses, thanks to:

> A pilot project aimed at ending grant dependency. The project identifies and helps individuals in poor households to either return to school or find a job. The project is expected to be rolled out countrywide and Motlanthe says the state believes such a project is the only way to fight poverty. He is of the opinion that such an approach will force people to help themselves out of poverty.[5]

But would the people 'help themselves' and join the state in the WoP, or instead would they continue to harbour the enemy in their houses? Would the masses fight dependency, or instead continue to nurture this psychological thug deep within their hearts, minds and homesteads?

Frankly, not enough is known about WoP to answer these questions.

4. *SA Broadcasting Corporation News, 2009*. Motlanthe gets his hands dirty in helping the poor. Johannesburg, 21 November.
http://www.sabcnews.com/portal/site/SABCNews/menuitem.5c4f8fe7ee929f602ea12
ea1674daeb9/?vgnextoid=fc16277225715210VgnVCM10000077d4ea9bRCRD&vgnextf
mt=default
5. *Ibid.*

Why do we have so little reliable information? After all, most contemporary wars feature extraordinary public relations offensives. It turns out that those who have been leading South Africa's WoP established a secret society, as can be discerned by checking in on the WoP's empty website or requesting research information directly from the webmaster.[6]

But the problem is deeper than a secrecy fetish. Unlike the old-style apartheid-era 'WHAM' (winning hearts and minds) strategy during the 1980s, in which Afrikaners maintained a lasting commitment to 'oil spots' and other pacification strategies in their War on Black South Africans, there really isn't enough action on the current WoP front to merit reporting, it would seem.

Reporting about the WoP had ceased nearly entirely by 2010, aside from SABC and *BuaNews* journalists hopelessly embedded amongst the bureaucrats and politicians. The WoP dropped off the media's radar screen, so the only information we have about the state's infiltration of enemy ranks with its new self-help artillery is a few filtered dispatches written by civil servants.

While genuine battles by the poor against the state were raging across the country, the next official siting of the WoP came again only in April 2010, when General Motlanthe returned to Ground Zero, to rally the troops and inspect the weaponry. According to Government Communication and Information,

> Deputy President Kgalema Motlanthe arrives in the Eastern Cape today on a two-day visit to assess launch sites for the War on Poverty Campaign and the roll-out of service delivery at Lubala village in Lusikisiki. The WoP Campaign was launched in Lubala village in September 2008 where commitments on service delivery were made.

---

6. Correspondence with a mercenary, aimed at unearthing WoP secrets, was truncated:
   Subject: RE: War on Poverty website
   Date: Fri, 26 Feb 2010 17:11:21 +0200
   From: Ian Houvet <IanH@dsd.gov.za>
   ... Apologies for the delayed response. I am afraid the War on Poverty web site is for government officials associated with the War on Poverty only and therefore access cannot be granted.
   To give a flavour of the qualifications of a leading WoP warrior, Houvet's online bio records "several years in IT and Management consulting where he served organisations such as Vodafone UK, Barclays and Cegetel in France. In moving to South Africa, Ian has continued his focus in the area of complex IT architectures and programme management in his work with Telkom SA and the Department of Social Development." http://www.govtech.co.za/http://wwwgovtech09/docs/speakers/IanHouvet_Govtech0 9_SpeakerInfo.pdf

The high profile visit also seeks to re-energise and re-focus the anti-poverty initiatives of government and to provide political leadership and mobilise all stakeholders. The campaign is also an instrument of coordination, alignment, support and supervision of anti-poverty initiatives to impact greatly on households and communities living in poverty in the short-term. Such initiatives seek to halve poverty by 2014 and eventually eradicate it in the long term.[7]

Another state journalist, Chris Bathembu, reported for Pretoria's BuaNews:

Mthatha - Government will explore every possible measure to ensure that poor people across the country are able to get assistance from the state, Deputy President Kgalema Motlanthe has vowed. Speaking at Lubala village near Mthatha on Saturday, Motlanthe said for as long as there were people still trapped in abject poverty, the country's hard won democracy was under threat.

Government launched the WoP campaign in the village in 2008 and Motlanthe's visit aimed at assessing progress made by the provincial government to meet the needs of the affected communities. Since the start of the WoP campaign, formerly headed by the then Deputy President Phumzile Mlambo-Ngcuka, government has implemented a number of programmes designed to eradicate poverty. Lubala, which had about 93 households in 2008, was chosen as a pilot site for household based integrated service delivery for the eradication of poverty. A survey conducted by Social Development pointed to high rate of unemployment, non-availability of quality drinking water, lack of primary health care services and high illiteracy rate as among the challenges facing this small Eastern Cape community.

After speaking to locals, BuaNews also established that most families were child headed as a result of the high mortality rate in the area and parents migrating to cities to look for work. The majority of people also depended on social grants to survive and some lacked the necessary documents to access these grants. Motlanthe, who undertook door to door visits before addressing

---

7. SA Broadcasting Corporation News, 2010. Motlanthe in E Cape to assess anti-poverty campaign. Johannesburg, 16 April.
http://www.sabcnews.com/portal/site/SABCNews/menuitem.5c4f8fe7ee929f602ea12
ea1674daeb9/?vgnextoid=5926d55755508210VgnVCM10000077d4ea9bRCRD&vgnext
fmt=default

more than 2000 people gathered in an open field, urged the
provincial government to move with speed in ensuring that all
government services were accessible to all people from where
they live. He warned officials to guard against corruption which
he said was contributing to the poverty experienced in most
parts of the province. "We must make sure that we give projects
to the right people and that monitoring takes place on a regular
basis," he said.[8]

Pledging that "rural people needed to be part of the economic
transformation taking place in the country and that government will
leave no stone unturned to ensure that poverty is tackled," Motlanthe got
back into the sedan and left Lubala. But before departing, Eastern Cape
Premier, Noxolo Kiviet, confessed that "lack of coordination and
integration of government services" meant that "only 30 percent of the
households surveyed received all the services needed." Those services
bravely endeavoured to hit the enemy, but were obviously too few and
far between to genuinely defeat poverty on home turf:

- the Departments of Agriculture and Rural Development assisted
  families with seedlings, and provided fencing "in more than 19
  households";
- the Department of Water Affairs had "undertaken" to provide
  water and sanitation to Lubala Primary School, and to give water
  tanks to 15 households; and
- there was skills upgrading: "about 15 young people have been
  trained in areas such as First Aid, chain saw operator, health and
  safety, personal finance and accounting."[9]

Bathembu concluded his report with a stiff upper lip: "The local
community has indicated that they have benefited in many respects from
the projects started in 2008."[10] But aside from such small incursions at
the first pilot site, this tiny Protected Village, the rest of the country was
going up in flames. Poverty was clearly winning the WoP.

Of course in any such war, those waging the Good Fight will suffer
faulty intelligence and troops will be lost to friendly fire. The most
obvious cases would be the seemingly ubiquitous 'service delivery
protests' that turn the state's attention from attacking poverty, to

8. Bathembu, C., 2010. 'Govt to intensify war on poverty,' *BuaNews*, 18 April.
http://www.buanews.gov.za/rss/10/10041814151001
9. *Ibid.*
10. *Ibid.*

attacking the poor themselves. The poor in turn react by burning down state buildings and councillors' houses in townships ranging from small Mpumalanga dorpies in the mountainous East, to the big-city ghettoes and highways on the plains of the Western Cape. The state's enemy, poverty, was by now bunkered in and heavily fortified. From time to time the enemy would suddenly emerge in the form of toyi-toying youth, who could manoeuvre with seeming ease around the desperately outnumbered local police forces and even the SA National Defence Force.

Amidst thousands of battles in the WoP, one was especially illustrative. Amongst the state's most feared symbols is an armoured vehicle, the Caspir, and on the auspicious date of 21 March 2010, Sharpeville Day, one found itself surrounded in the township of an Mpumalanga dorpie, Ogies. The SA Press Association's courageous reporter filed this story:

> Captain Leonard Hlathi, spokesperson for the Mpumalanga police said the Caspir was irreparably damaged when it was "outrageously attacked" by a mob who petrol bombed it several times. The protesters apparently led the Caspir into an ambush, by leading it over an improvised spike strip to puncture its tyres. Three of the heavy vehicles' puncture-proof tyres were blown out when it drove over the spikes, that were camouflaged with branches. "Nothing working remained in the vehicle," said Hlathi. "Only the steel hull remained."
>
> Hlathi said the protesters were targeting the 10 police members that were in the vehicle. The trapped police officers were forced to fight their way out, using live sharp point ammunition. "They had to get out of the vehicle. By that time it had been bombed several times," said Hlathi. "If they didn't fight back and if they weren't assisted by reinforcements who came to help, we would have been talking about a different matter entirely."
>
> Hlathi said it wasn't clear how many times the vehicles, which was used extensively by police during unrest before the 1994 elections, were bombed. He also couldn't say how long the spikes that were used to blow out the tyres were, or what they were made of. "They do have puncture proof tyres, but the spikes were too long," said Hlathi.
>
> One protester was injured during the violence, but Hlathi said there may have been more. "They [the protesters] carried the wounded away," he said. Sixty-one people have been arrested for public violence during service delivery protests in Mpumalanga over the long weekend. Twenty-nine of these were in Leslie near

Secunda after a municipal building and other property were burnt down. Another 32 were arrested in the Ogies protest. "Several cars were pelted with stones and 20 complaints have already been registered for malicious damage to property cases." Four civilian Toyota Quantum minibus taxis, a Condo, and two bakkies were also burnt down.

The Ogies protest started on Thursday, when a march was held to hand over a memorandum to representatives of the provincial government. "It is alleged the authorities did not turn up as requested. The people went on rampage, barricading the roads with burning tyres and burning down property." – Sapa[11]

Encountering these sorts of minefields across the country, the state had a choice at this stage: either rapidly intensify from the ongoing war of position (nice-sounding rhetorical speeches) to a serious war of movement against poverty, or simply retreat. Back in the War Room, it must have appeared that the WoP was now a fully-fledged class war, unwinnable under the country's prevailing economic conditions, given the motley coalition of power brokers in the Alliance and the continuing grip of neoliberal Treasury and Reserve Bank officials. A million jobs had been lost over the prior year, and the macroeconomic 'recovery' was accompanied by further job-shedding. The poor were advancing relentlessly, and the WoP looked like a US/Vietnam or Soviet/US Afghanistan story-line.

The state's forces were obviously confused and confounded. The older anti-poverty strategies were comparable to pre-1942 Maginot lines, easily broken through by a clever enemy. In this new terrain, trickle-down grants were simply not good enough to stem the broken dike. Poverty – and especially the poor themselves – fought back tirelessly, with sticks, stones and Molotov cocktails, retreating into the shack settlements and township alleyways before sallying forth for yet more outrageous attacks. Newer military techniques, such as aerial bombings or even US-style drones were either too high profile (an embarrassment when the state needed global legitimation during its other war – to carry off a World Cup in the face of global elite scepticism) or simply ineffectual. The late-apartheid regime's WHAM strategy looked impressive in comparison.

Finally in March 2010, the state took a new turn, a strategic repositioning of the WoP. In his March 24 budget speech to Parliament, Minister of Rural Development and Land Reform Gugile Nkwinti

---

11. SAPA 2010. Police Caspir burnt down in protest, 23 March.
http://www.iol.co.za/index.php?art_id=nw20100323154047240C790446

described both an advance and a retreat. On the one hand his department would 'roll out' its Comprehensive Rural Development Programme from the current 21 wards to a target of 181 within four years. But he dropped another bombshell: "As from 1 April, 2010 the War on Poverty, which has prioritised 1128 wards over the Medium Term Strategic Framework period has been relocated from the Presidency to the Department."[12]

Apparently, it was clear to the generals that one of their fronts had become too dangerous: the cities, and that the WoP was bogged down. After all, recall that the 2010 report of the Organisation for Economic Cooperation and Development prepared by Cape Town academics declared that, "poverty incidence barely changed in rural areas, while it increased in urban areas" (Leibbrandt et al., 2010: 36). So a crucial component of the new plan is, it seems, retreat.

Is the new rural-poverty general fit for the job? One report shows the kind of abuse of war funds that compares to the US Pentagon and Halliburton in Iraq, with similar results in the WoP:

> Nkwinti suggested that the government's land reform programmes had not been sustainable and confirmed that the target of transferring 30 percent of agricultural land to black farmers by 2014 would not be reached. He revealed that at least nine out of ten emerging farmers given land under the government's land reform policy had failed to make a commercial success of their farmland. A total of 5.9 million hectares had been redistributed since the end of apartheid but 90 per cent of that land was not productive.[13]

Oops. But there is a good reason this part of the WoP was failing, according to Nkwinti: the beneficiaries' own failure to "continue producing effectively and optimally on the land." The poor obviously wanted to remain poor. As a result, it seemed, the new WoP strategy to deal with this rural guerrilla army would be to financially starve the desperate landless:

---

12. Speech by the Minister of Rural Development and Land Reform, Mr G. Nkwinti, (MP), debate on the Budget Vote of the Department of Rural Development and Land Reform, National Assembly, Parliament, 24 March 2010,
http://www.politicsweb.co.za/politicsweb/view/politicsweb/en/page71654?oid=1678 97&sn=Detail
13. SAPA 2010. Land beneficiaries owed R34 billion, Pretoria, 25 July.
http://www.news24.com/SouthAfrica/Politics/Land-beneficiaries-owed-R34bn-Nkwinti-20100705

Cape Town - The government has failed to pay R3.4bn in post-settlement grants to beneficiaries of land reform with potentially damning consequences, Rural Development and Land Reform Minister Gugile Nkwinti said on Monday. Recipients in 389 cases had not received grants, the minister said in reply to a parliamentary question from the Democratic Alliance. He warned that this could lead to a change of land use on farms, a decline in crop production, an inability to maintain infrastructure, a lack of skills transfer to beneficiaries, community conflicts and even farm invasions. "Farm invasions could take place where beneficiaries cannot occupy farms as result of delays," he said. [14]

Then, in the wake of the apparent silent surrender on the urban front, another disaster emerged in the countryside: the colonel directing the troops apparently walked off the job. Nkwinti's director-general, Thozi Gwanya, resigned in July, but it happened secretly, like the WoP itself. Aside from WoP saboteurs in the Democratic Alliance who issued a press release about a mysterious but allegedly damning Auditor General's report, no one else breathed a word about this until days later. Then, the alleged departure was described as a 'malicious' report by the department, yet Gwanya was finally acknowledged as a real casualty four days later.[15]

The battlefield carnage was now too close to home. Just as Pretoria lost its last war against Cuban fighter jets on the outskirts of the Angolan city of Cuito Cuanavale in 1988, bodybags of high-profile WoP warriors (then it was younger white men, now older ANC politicians) could no longer be disguised. The state's inevitable defeat in the WoP war appeared, by now, just as hot a potato as Afghanistan had become to Stanley McChrystal, Barack Obama's top commander until indiscretions were revealed by a *Rolling Stone* reporter in July 2010. As Michael Hastings reveals, there are comparisons to the SA WoP, given SA state patronage systems and likewise, given that in Afghanistan,

> The massive influx of aid championed by McChrystal is likely only to make things worse. "Throwing money at the problem exacerbates the problem," says Andrew Wilder, an expert at Tufts University who has studied the effect of aid in southern Afghanistan. "A tsunami of cash fuels corruption, delegitimises the government and creates an environment where we're

14. *iAfrica News*, 2010. Land reform failing, 6 July.
http://business.iafrica.com/news/2519343.htm
15. *Business Day*, 2010. Denial, then department admits boss has resigned, 23 July.

picking winners and losers" – a process that fuels resentment and hostility among the civilian population. So far, counterinsurgency has succeeded only in creating a never-ending demand for the primary product supplied by the military: perpetual war. There is a reason that President Obama studiously avoids using the word "victory" when he talks about Afghanistan. Winning, it would seem, is not really possible. Not even with Stanley McChrystal in charge. [16]

Like Obama's imminent defeat in the Afghan war, part of the problem stems from corruption of the chain of the command - a core reason why McChrystal was fired. Other kinds of political corruption, patronage scandals, neoliberal logic in national policies, resistance to 'indigency' policies and service delivery protest by the ungrateful recipients, are indications of Zuma's imminent WoP defeat. And as Obama himself may learn in November 2012, extreme class conflict can go terminally sour even for two of South Africa's supreme leaders who, respectively, were fired and went Absent Without Leave: Thabo Mbeki and Phumzile Mlambo-Ngcuka. Motlanthe may yet push more wheelbarrows for SABC cameras, but where a fighting spirit is required – amongst generals like Nkwinti, colonels like Gwanya and especially ordinary bureaucrat-grunts – it has fizzled out.

Pretoria's last-gasp strategy, even if dangerously short-term and lacking the bread that comes with the old Roman circus (and we know what happened to that empire), was to welcome thirty-one squads of eleven soccer players and introduce millions of Chinese-made vuvuzelas in mid-2010, as a quaint distraction. It appeared effective, at first, and gave a boost to morale in the ruling party. But social protest soon returned at near the same pace as before.

Such analysis may yet be proven excessively pessimistic (after all, it's a secret war and there may be successes that are simply not being recorded, so as to keep the enemy off-guard, overconfident). However, since winning the WoP in South Africa now seems utterly impossible, given the balance of forces, the leadership, the chosen weaponry and the economic terrain upon which the battle rages, it's probably best for Pretoria to not even talk about this struggle any more. The war room is best located in the state's least effective ministry, one with an impressive record of failure, and the secret dispatches can be kept off the web too. If Pretoria is lucky, no one will really notice (and indeed no one else has).

---

16. Hastings, M., 2010. The runaway general. *Rolling Stone,* 22 June.
http://www.rollingstone.com/politics/news/17390/119236

Divine intervention

On 10 May 1994, Nelson Mandela was inaugurated as President. Before our eyes, the racial hierarchy of apartheid became the 'rainbow nation of god.' The twentieth century had come late to South Africa, but in this time of miracles, would not the last be first? While the right-wing threat, jittery investors and bureaucratic hostility could account for some of the state's inhibition - not opting for the most transformative outcomes – at least the ANC had set its sights, laudably, on a 'people-centred' strategy, the Reconstruction and Development Programme (RDP).

Government ministers (even Communists such as Slovo and Maharaj) and big business immediately distorted the RDP, saying that the original mandate did not pay sufficient heed to the god of the market. In the era of globalisation, capital moves. Fast. Greater cognisance would need to be taken of the 'outside' forces. By not abiding by the commandment: 'Thou shall make maximum profits', South Africa ran the risk of being abandoned in the wilderness for another forty years. And so the original social-democratic RDP became apocryphal, and a new gospel was preached, the more 'market-friendly' Growth, Employment and Redistribution (GEAR) strategy of liberalisation. More compatible with the prevailing neoliberal project, Thabo Mbeki nevertheless cleverly touted GEAR as an annexure to the commandments of the RDP, merely the macroeconomic accounting matrix.

It was widely believed, however, that in the land of small miracles, the negative effects of 'outside' forces would be mitigated. Here, neoliberalism would never lose its human face; it was trusted that the Merlinesque magic of Madiba would never allow this to happen..."the saviour from on high, an incarnation of public virtue... a demiurge of history to break the chain of fatalism... The Word is made flesh, the immense and uncontrollable forces of history are incarnate in a personified Higher Being" (Löwy, 2003: 14). Mandela's state, in the hands of the party, came to be seen as a "magnanimous sorcerer," to borrow from Coronil. It "acquired a providential hue" (Coronil, 1997: 1).

Mandela's emphasis on societal reconciliation, placating big business and paranoia about the right-wing threat, left him revealed as South Africa's saint, albeit a lame one. His successor, Thabo Mbeki was seen initially, as the 'Mr Delivery' of transformatory goals, such as the creation of jobs and alleviation of poverty. It was still a time when a once racially-stigmatised people basked in the defeat of apartheid and a belief in an almost divinely determined better future.

If it was (falsely) believed Mandela's long walk to freedom had illuminated the path to the Holy Grail, Mbeki felt he knew the real map. Edicts would be issued and the masses must follow directions. If things did not go according to plan, it was not the wrong policy, but the ignorance, impertinence and impatience of the masses. A document titled *The State and Social Transformation*, written by Mbeki and his close associates in 1996, laid out how the relationship between civil society and the state is to be viewed:

> The issue turns on the combination of the expertise and professionalism concentrated in the democratic state and the capacity for popular mobilisation which resides within the trade unions and the genuinely representative non-governmental popular organisations (ANC, 1996).

What is clearly implied in this is, in the words of Krista Johnson,

> To draw a clear distinction between the government or party experts who 'know' and the mass of the people who are supposed to apply this knowledge. He leaves no room for popular *political* participation outside of the state or the ruling class (Johnson, 2002: 228).

John Stuart Mill, writing disparagingly of the way the relationship between the ruling class and the poor was envisaged in the early days of modern English capitalism, elaborated:

> The lot of the poor, in all things which affect them collectively, should be regulated for them, not by them... It is the duty of the higher classes to think for them, and to take responsibility for their lot ... The rich should be *in loco parentis* to the poor, guiding and restraining them like children (Bauman, 2002: 31).

In the ANC's South Africa, the state and party blurs into one, and the president becomes the 'keeper of the chalice cup of wisdom.' Those who challenge the wisdom of the president, challenge the people. It is not a coincidence that the ANC comes to see itself as a broad church. But as Raymond Suttner, former ANC member of parliament and party enforcer, laconically commented, a church "also implies priesthood, often with superior powers of scriptural interpretation...Thabo Mbeki's interventions do not appear to be part of a broad debate. They are more in the nature of authoritative pronouncements" (Suttner, 2003).

All members of the broad church must show unswerving loyalty to the 'Leader' whose wisdom over time will be revealed and trickle down to the masses. Other leaders - false idols like Madikizela-Mandela, Ramaphosa, Sexwale and Phosa, for example, or a dozen others, who preached even slightly dissonant sermons, were swiftly excommunicated.

Mbekism represented a mixture of African nationalist neoliberalism that rails against colonialism and racism, while simultaneously imposing an economic trajectory drawing the country into a global capitalism notorious for its highly unequal terms. At a continental level too, the conditionalities and oversight mechanisms of the West – sugar-coated with ideas like good governance - were incorporated into Mbeki's African Renaissance economic bible, the New Partnership for Africa's Development (NEPAD).

Like the late 1990s Highly Indebted Poor Countries (HIPC) initiative of the World Bank, NEPAD would,

> Support existing poverty reduction initiatives at the multilateral level, such as the Comprehensive Development Framework of the World Bank and the Poverty Reduction Strategy approach linked to the HIPC debt initiative... Countries would engage with existing debt relief mechanisms-the HIPC and the Paris Club - before seeking recourse through the New Partnership for Africa's Development (NEPAD, 2001: 118, 149).

This approach was proposed despite the fact that – or perhaps precisely because - HIPC deals are fundamentally committed to maintaining existing power relations and the neoliberal economic philosophy because they entail only very slight adjustments to debt loads, and in return require lowest-income countries to liberalise their economies even further. By the late 2000s, low-income African countries realised that the cost of servicing external debt would actually rise by 50 per cent (in 2009) because although the overall outstanding debt was diminished, that was credit which would never be repaid in any case. The crucial matter was the cost of servicing debt year in and year out, and the 2005 'debt relief' of the G8 in Gleneagles was structured in such a way that Africa ended up making large downpayments on debt and paid a higher servicing cost.

Moreover, with debt relief and HIPC came yet more neoliberal conditionalities. In the main southern African pilot of HIPC, Mozambique's conditionality requirements included quintupling cost-recovery charges (user fees) at public health clinics, the privatisation of urban and rural water supply systems, and the simultaneous liberalisation and privatisation of its largest agro-industry, cashew nut processing, which destroyed the industry (Bond, 2002: 65, 79).

At a local level, the call for an African Renaissance and the need for us to be masters of our own destiny is negated by Mbeki's claim that the transformation of South Africa cannot include "solutions which are in discord with the rest of the world... which can be sustained by virtue of a voluntarist South African experiment of a special type, a world of anti-apartheid campaigners, who, out of loyalty to us, would support and sustain such voluntarism" (ANC, 1996: 5). Quite the opposite: the liberated South African state is opposed to the mass mobilisations that seek to challenge the architecture of global finance from the 'outside.' As ANC policy director Michael Sachs explained:

> We don't oppose the WTO. We'd never join a call to abolish it, or to abolish the World Bank or the IMF. Should we be out there condemning imperialism? If you do those things, how long will you last? There is no organisational alternative, no real policy alternative to what we're doing (Bond, 2004: 29).

The ANC ensured that the post-apartheid state is open to serving the interests of global capital, especially financiers, and to legitimating the power of the International Monetary Fund, World Bank and World Trade Organisation. To do this, according to Castells: "Nation-states must ally themselves closely with global economic interests and abide by global rules favourable to capital flows, while their societies are being asked to wait patiently for the trickle-down benefits of corporate ingenuity" (Alexander, 2002: 163).

Or, as Michael Hardt and Toni Negri explain,

> States conform to and even anticipate the needs of capital for fear of being subordinated in the global economic system. This creates a sort of race to the bottom among the nation states in which the interests of labour and society as a whole take a back seat to those of capital (Hardt and Negri, 2004: 279).

In this regard, Michael Neocosmos's arguments on how state rule is legitimised merit reflection. On one hand, the

> post-apartheid state attempts to secure its legitimacy around a state-defined consensus centering on liberalism (economic and political), human rights discourse and a nationalist discourse (for example, overcoming poverty among the previously disadvantaged racial groups, equalising access to economic resources between races, economic leadership in Africa) (Neocosmos, 2002: 11).

On the other hand, "a neoliberal economic discourse has presented the solution to poverty as a particular kind of technical intervention by both capital and the state." The liberal and nationalist "discourse relegates questions of political entitlements to the juridical sphere of the state, where claims to rights can be settled by an apparently impartial and technical juridical system." The neoliberal discourse:

> Relegates other political entitlements to an economic or managerial field where they are exclusively reduced to objects of state policy, again devised by apparently impartial experts. In either case, these issues are removed from an arena or domain of legitimate independent political intervention (and often even contestation) by society itself, and placed within the confines of a state-controlled domain where they are systematically 'technicised' and thus made out to be politically neutral and thus should be handled exclusively by apolitical experts. They are effectively de-politicised in form while still remaining highly political in context (Neocosmos, 2002: 11).

But while this is important, it is crucial to understand how the ANC government wields state power as a disciplinary power. One can discern it through the way the ANC government has approached the issue of poverty. This requires us to try to understand the state as a disciplinary power over its subjects, which is exercised in part as a regulating gaze aimed at what Deveaux has called "self-regulating docile bodies" (Deveaux, 1994). This of course is a conclusion famously arrived at by Foucault, when he showed how under the present system,

> there is no need for arms, physical violence, material constraints. Just a gaze. An inspecting gaze, or gaze which each individual under its weight will end by interiorising to the point that he is his own overseer, each individual thus exercising this surveillance over, and against himself. A superb formula: power exercised continuously and for what turns out to be minimal cost (Foucault, 1980: 155).

Employment

The literature on the state of unemployment in South Africa is riven with what appears at first glance to be scraps over issues of definition. Government made extravagant claims that anything between 1.6 million net new 'jobs' were created between 1995 and 2002, and 2.1 million by February 2004. These gains, Terry Bell argued, were almost exclusively in the precarious informal sector and are also the result of some ingenious 'accounting':

> Homemakers who help sustain themselves and their families out of backyard vegetable plots or who keep a few chickens are part of the new employed class. In fact, that vast army of the barely hidden jobless who stand forlornly on street corners for hire or who sell coat hangers, rubbish bags or handful of sweets at traffic lights or railway stations in the hope of making a few rand all add to this two million jobs figure. According to the latest statistics, in September 2001, 367,000 workers earned nothing for their labour, while a further 718,000 were paid between R1 and R200 a month.[17]

There is the official definition, ranging between 23 and 30 per cent (during the 2000s), which tallies active job-seekers who cannot find work. On an expanded definition that also counts those who have given up seeking employment, the figure during the late 2000s hovered around 35-40 per cent. The South African Reserve Bank put the unemployed (expanded) at 46.6 for males and 53.4 per cent for females. In order to survive, 79.2 per cent relied on other persons in the household (SARB, 2003:28). In 1995, 69 per cent of the economically active African population was employed full-time. By 2001 this figure had fallen to 49 per cent. At the same time, informal or atypical occupations rose from 13 per cent to 31 per cent (Altman, 2003). By late 2008 there were improvements in these data, but over the subsequent year and a half, roughly a million jobs were lost.

There is no denying the extent of joblessness in South Africa and that unemployment figures continue to mount. The economic effects are devastating, according to Hein Marais:

> Given that black workers' wage packets tend to be shared extensively within the family and kin circles, each job lost diminishes consumer demand-hitting sales of semi-durable goods (especially furniture and appliances), groceries, shoes and clothing...low income families spend up to 75 per cent of income on these categories...the sacking of an average semi-skilled miner costs the economy R83 000 a year: for a skilled miner the figure climbs to R132 000. The calculations measure the social burden created by the loss of the miner's consumption

---

17. Bell, T., 2004. How 'Non Jobs' come to the Aid of Government Election Propaganda. *Sunday Independent*, 15 February.

expenditure (that supports businesses and creates demand through a multiplier effect), as well as lost tax payments and the disappearance of remittances that support dependants (Marais, 2001: 176).

Why has the ANC government zealously contested the employment figures? One of the reasons, of course, is that governments the world over need to show that macro-economic policies are job-creating especially were unemployment figures are high. A central reason in post-apartheid South Africa is that the ANC's discourse is premised on the idea that social inclusion comes from access to formal employment. This position is captured in the RDP's position of how wage labour is the remedy for welfare dependency:

> Although a much stronger welfare system is needed to support all the vulnerable, the old, the disabled and the sick who currently live in poverty, a system of 'handouts' for the unemployed should be avoided. All South Africans should have the opportunity to participate in the economic life of the country (RDP, 1994).

Still, the government policy insists that social inclusion is about getting a job. This insistence came against the backdrop of two pillars of attack by the ANC government. Firstly, the inability of the existing social grants system to be financially viable as de-racialising took place. Secondly, the language of the threat of welfare dependency became increasingly shrill.

The National Department of Welfare published its White Paper for Social Welfare in 1997. At the centre of its objectives, it placed the building of human capacity and self-reliance: "South Africans will be afforded an opportunity to play an active role in *promoting their own well-being* and in contributing to the development of our nation" (Department of Welfare, 1997: 2). This gets concrete expression in the section that links macro-economic policy and welfare:

> While sound economic policies and a well-functioning labour market are essential for growth and employment generation, by themselves they are not sufficient. To reap the benefits, South Africa must invest in people; that is, to develop the human capital, which is essential for increasing productivity and moving people out of poverty...Social development programmes are investments, which lead to tangible economic gains and in turn lead to economic growth...Since resources are limited, trade-offs must be made between investment in economic growth and

human resources, and investment in a social safety net. Welfare expenditure will only be able to expand as higher economic growth targets are achieved...This means that the high expectations of many people for the new democratic Government to deliver welfare services cannot be fully met in the short-term (Department of Welfare, 1997: 4-5).

There are keywords to discern here: investments, tangible economic gains, trade-offs and a position that welfare expenditure will grow as a result of higher growth targets. In terms of the latter, there is very little consideration of how higher growth rates can be predicated on job losses and 'poverty wages' increasing the need for social security. Any form of decommodification is to be held hostage to market forces. 'Community development' and ubuntu are insinuated to replace the responsibilities of government.

The logic of the financing policy released in 1999 made more explicit the trend started in the White Paper (Department of Welfare, 1999; cf. Sewpaul and Hölscher, 2004). Vishanthie Sewpaul and Dorothee Hölscher have shown how the policy is replete with

> managerial terms and market metaphors...the Financing Policy talks of business plans, contractual agreements, affordability, effectiveness, efficiency, output and outcome orientation, financial sustainability, quality assurance and performance audits. Outsourcing, venture financing and service purchasing are new terms borrowed from the world of commercial interactions (Sewpaul and Hölscher, 2004: 82–83).

The emphasis is on how to shift money from institutional care to community-based models:

> The state is an entrepreneur of its own. It must make profit where it can. People don't understand the developmental debate, and they can't see that everything anybody does must be developmental. The state must be minimalist. It really must do the least and last. Civil society, empowered civil society is to do the most, and I don't know it will ever get there, the state must just give the money. Because of the bureaucracy, it becomes inefficient. So when it comes to service provision, it must be become the funder and let others do (Sewpaul and Hölscher, 2004: 84–85).

Privatisation, commodification and poverty

Government has made much of the delivery of basic services. A recent government publication highlighted the claim that

> more than 10 million people have access to clean water since 1994. Free basic water reaches three-quarters of those in areas with water infrastructure. Two million housing subsidies have been allocated to the poor since 1994 (Government Communication and Information System, 2005).

While it should have led to a Gini coefficient reduction, it was counteracted by other forces, leading to a rising Gini. Nevertheless, the optimistic position was taken to an extreme stand by Stellenbosch University professor Servaas van der Berg, who argued that between 1993 and 1997, social spending increased for the poorest 60 per cent of households, especially the poorest 20 per cent and especially the rural poor, and decreased for the 40 per cent who were better off, leading to a one-third improvement in the Gini coefficient (Bond, 2004). Hence the overall impact of state spending, he posited, would lead to a dramatic decline in actual inequality. Unfortunately, van der Berg (a regular consultant to the neoliberal Treasury Department) made no effort to calculate or even estimate state subsidies to capital, i.e. corporate welfare. Such subsidies are enormous because most of the economic infrastructures created through taxation – transport, industrial districts, the world's cheapest electricity, R&D subsidies – overwhelmingly benefits capital and its shareholders, as do many tax loopholes. It is hard to take the work of van der Berg seriously, and the ambitious claims by the Mbeki-era Government Communications and Information Service if apples (for poor people) are not compared with apples (for capital), but instead with simply nothing.

Steven Gelb, on the other hand, questioned the effectiveness of government's redistributive programmes,

> Where a service has to be delivered in an ongoing fashion to build assets (such as in education) or an asset has to be transferred (such as housing or land reform) ... addressing the unequal legacy of apartheid and enabling more effective participation in, and returns from, factor markets has been less extensive than would appear from an examination of expenditure only (Gelb, 2003: 57).

Pointing to the great strides in the delivery of housing, for example, Gelb argues that the government's focus has been on quantitative aspects, yet subsidies are low compared to other developing countries,

> and housing quality undervalued, while diversity of housing demand is overlooked together with the need to locate housing development in the context of broader processes of community development. These points are strikingly similar to those made about education in the sense that apparently successful current expenditure programmes have not produced the sought-after improvement in outcomes, for reasons which may well lie in the inability (or unwillingness) of government to address the wider context of inequality (Gelb, 2003: 58; Rust, 2003).

Delivery has also been overshadowed by the marketisation of basic service delivery, the institution of cost recovery mechanisms and a rash of disconnections and evictions. The numbers of disconnections have been the arena of dispute between researchers and government. But there is no doubt this occurs on an on-going basis and is a constant threat to poor people.

The reason for the disconnection epidemic was obvious. Notwithstanding deeper poverty, the South African government – ranging from municipalities to water catchment agencies to Eskom - raised water and electricity prices dramatically from the mid-1990s. By 2002, they accounted for 30 per cent of the income of those households earning less than R400 per month. One cause of higher municipal utility prices was that central-local state subsidies designed to cover operating/maintenance expenses suffered dramatic declines during the 1990s (85 per cent in real terms, according to the Finance and Fiscal Commission) (Bond, 2005).

The government responded to the wave of protests about water cut-offs with the introduction of a free basic minimum of water. A very small lifeline (6000 litres per household per month) was followed by very steep increases (along a convex tariff curve), such that the next consumption block became unaffordable. The free 6,000 litres represent just two toilet flushes a day for a household of eight, for those lucky enough to have flush toilets. It leaves no additional water to drink, to wash with, or to clean clothes or the house (Bond, 2005).

The UNDP 2003 Report also pointed to the issue of affordability:

> Eskom's full cost recovery approach has made access to electricity unaffordable to many Sowetans. The 'free services' policy has not been a particularly effective strategy for the urban poor because of the household density of many low-income

households and their need for larger volumes of electricity. The number of electricity disconnections has increased drastically, especially since 1996: On average, disconnections increased from over 22 000 per month in 1996 to almost 100 000 by 2001 (UNDP, 2003: 105).

In thinking through this process, David Harvey has written about the continuing centrality of primitive accumulation. In these times new forms of accumulation through dispossession have emerged. This involves in the main, privatisation. In South Africa, Harvey holds that, for example, "total cost recovery by municipal owned utilities" has meant that, "unable to afford the charges, more and more people were cut out of the service, and with less revenue the companies raised rates, making water even less affordable to low-income populations" (Harvey, 2003: 159).

But inscribed also in the commodification of basic services is the development of new forms of control and self-regulation. Veriava and Ngwane have shown how the installation of water meters affects this purpose. Once you get your free six kilolitres it will cut you off unless you feed the machine. Water meters

> are celebrated as tamper-proof and work in a very specific way to limit your possible options. They foreclose any negotiation or institutional mediation. The only option becomes feeding the device. They are in a sense a pedagogical tool, teaching the new laws of the economy - Pay as you go or go. As such they define the new condition of the citizen, that of the consumer (Veriava and Ngwane, 2004: 134).

Here we have, at microlevel, Foucault's

> mechanisms of power...its capillary form of existence, the point where power reaches into the very grain of individuals, touches their bodies and inserts itself into their actions and attitudes, learning process and everyday lives (Foucault in Chambon: 1999: 59).

In many cases, as Ferguson has pointed out, Foucault helps us understand "how the outcomes of planned social interventions can end up coming together into powerful constellations of control that were never intended ... " (Ferguson, 1990: 19). As Foucault argues,

For the observation that prison fails to eliminate crime, one should perhaps substitute the hypothesis that prison has succeeded extremely well in producing delinquency, a specific type, a politically or economically less dangerous, on occasion, usable-form of illegality; in producing delinquents, in an apparently marginal, but in fact centrally supervised milieu; in producing the delinquent as a pathologised subject...So successful has the prison been that, after a century and a half of 'failures', the prison still exists, producing the same results, and there is the greatest reluctance to dispense with (Ferguson, 1990: 20).

If one looks at the installation of water meters, the indigency policy, the technical details to be filled in to get any form of state support, it is not difficult to see how the emphasis on the second economy can lead to an emphasis on control and surveillance.

The political economy of AIDS

The literature on the impact of AIDS in exacerbating poverty is chilling. According to Jonathan Lewis,

A wave of sickness and death is already sweeping through South Africa, and its impact will be felt throughout this decade and beyond by the millions of households that will be directly affected. Beyond the widespread personal and human costs created by the pandemic lies a second level of effects. South Africa's economy, which has been struggling for two decades, is another indirect victim of the pandemic. HIV/AIDS adds one more 'tax' on South African firms trying to compete in a global market and burdens a government already facing pent-up demand for services that lie beyond its means. Just as society needs more resources to confront HIV/AIDS, the adverse impact of the epidemic on human capital, on productivity, and on government finances could impose a macroeconomic cost which would run as high as 1 per cent or more of the growth in GDP per capita, which is already too low to create enough jobs and alleviate widespread poverty (Lewis, 2004: 117).

Much more work is needed on the impact of AIDS on companies in different sectors – both direct and indirect. One significant attempt is that of Rosen et al., (2003) who try to discern the cost of a worker getting infected today and found that, "workers who tend to be at high risk of HIV infection, are not eligible for most of the benefits provided to permanent employees, nor do the companies invest substantial resources in training them (Rosen et al., 2003).

Very little work has been done on the effect of AIDS on households. One study by Booysen et al., found that besides the increased prevalence of illness in affected households, the difference between affected and unaffected households had an impact on economic outcomes. As Lewis, relying on the figures of Booysen et al., argues:

> For affected households, the average household that utilised savings spent the equivalent of twenty-one months of savings, whereas unaffected households using savings spent only five months' worth. How affected households used their savings differed as well. For affected households, the largest uses were funeral expenses (40 per cent) and medical expenses (24 per cent). In other words, nearly two-thirds of savings went for AIDS (or at least illness) related costs. For unaffected households, the pattern is more 'normal.' There was some spending for funerals (8 per cent), but the largest shares went to asset maintenance (31 per cent) and education (30 per cent), which did not appear at all in the affected households' spending (Lewis, 2004: 111).

In the face of this disaster, some argue that the spread of AIDS has potential benefits. Allister Sparks writes that economic and other forecasters have not

> taken sufficient account of the possible impact of this pandemic on the other doomsday scenario we heard so much only a few years ago - the population explosion...Well AIDS is not going to reduce South Africa's overall population, but it is going to slow its growth rate...a smaller population can be better educated, and better education, especially of women who are then in a stronger position to determine their own choices, is by far the more effective method of birth control (Sparks, 2003: 302–303).

Lazarus like Malthus has risen from the dead.

Mbeki's AIDS denialism was cloaked in an outrage against racism and westernisation. Yet his economic policies demand integration into the circuits of global capital on terms set out by the West. Alongside fiscal stinginess comes a set of new codewords: home-based care, self-reliance, community support. This strategy draws on old traditions of *ubuntu*. Hein Marais shows how a confluence occurs between two apparently contrary ideologies: *ubuntu* and neoliberalism. The guiding principles of communitarianism, mutual assistance and the bonding sense of shared destinies that underpin ubuntu provide a bedrock for the anticipated community-level resilience and solidarity that is expected to animate and sustain home-and community-based care...This is surprisingly compatible with a central thrust of neoliberalism, which is to absolve or at least excuse the state from its encompassing responsibility for social reproduction. On the one hand there is the disintended faith in 'coping' capacities at community and household levels; on the other, government strategies are marked by an overarching obeisance to the market and its organising principles. Around AIDS, these two apparently contradictory, value patterns emerge (Marais, 2005: 66–67).

The impact of AIDS is devastating. But in a country with South Africa's extent of inherited inequalities, Marais points out

these miseries are not distributed indiscriminately. The glacial crush of the epidemic exaggerates the social relations that constitute society. In that, AIDs unmasks the world we live in and reiterates the need to transform it. In South Africa, it specifically underscores the need for an encompassing social package as part of an overarching programme of redistribution and rights realisation (Marais, 2005: 109).

Poverty as crime

In the context of spiralling poverty, people must resort to desperate measures often merely to access life-saving support. Many hope to be able to be classified as disabled. Some even prefer to fall pregnant to be eligible for a meagre child support grant of less than R300. A 2003 study by the Planned Parenthood Association put the number of teenagers doing this as one in ten. The argument is that if you are not old, disabled or a vulnerable child, you have to look after yourself. "For salvation, this perspective looks toward increased employment opportunities (as a product of economic growth) and a surge in small-scale entrepreneurial activities" (Marais, 2005: 108). Both of these 'solutions' are completely unrealistic.

One of the shortcomings of 'poverty studies' in South Africa is the absence of the issue of Power. The result is much like the outcome of Percival's failure to ask the crucial question, "whom does the Grail serve?", thus denying him the chance to grasp the Holy Grail.

Ralph Miliband contends that in looking at the question of poverty one should focus

> first and foremost on the respective strength of conflicting forces operating in society, some making for the persistence of poverty, and others working against its persistence; and the trouble, for the poor, is that the forces operating against them are very much stronger than those working in their favour. What is involved here is not recognition, or the discovery of the right policies, or the creation of the right administrative framework, or even the good will of the power-holders. The matter goes deeper than that, and concerns the distribution of power in society (Miliband, 1974: 187).

Yet this is an area sorely lacking. Gillian Hart and Ari Sitas allege that there is "remarkably little critical, sustained research and reflection on the changing power relations and processes of acquiescence and opposition that are emerging in the post-apartheid era" (Hart and Sitas, 2004: 56; 31).

In a poem delivered at the opening of the KZN parliament, Sitas spoke about the House passing a Bill abolishing poverty.

> *On the first day*
> *Of the 11th year*
> *Of our democracy*
> *The provincial house*
> *Unanimously*
> *Unambiguously*
> *Famously*
> *Promulgated a Bill*
> *Abolishing Poverty*
>
> *At night*
> *As the moon made us*
> *All jazzhappy*
> *The subversives*
> *Who still claimed to be poor*
> *Were rounded up*
> *And sent to other provinces*
> *Provinces that deserve them.*

This was meant to be tongue in cheek. But regularly – e.g., before the big annual Tourism Indaba in the city of Durban, and as recently as February

2010 in advance of the World Cup - street-kids were rounded up and sent to shelters out of the city, or simply dumped miles from town. Reality catches up with parody.

In surveying the response of the South African state to the alleviation of poverty we see various attempts at what Foucault called govermentality. Central here is "Discipline...a type of power, a modality of its exercise, comprising a whole set of instruments, techniques, procedures, levels of application, target; it is a 'physics' or an 'anatomy' of power, a technology." This discipline is meant to constitute a "process of normalisation" that "not only restricts or erases unwanted behaviour, it also shapes wanted behaviour" (Chambon, 1999: 66).

For discipline to be effective, civil society must not simply be demobilised, it must become a conduit for decisions of the party in order to counteract those opposed to change. According to then presidential spokesperson, Joel Netshitenze,

> mass involvement is therefore both a spear of rapid advance and a shield against resistance. Such involvement should be planned to serve the strategic purpose, proceeding from the premise that revolutionaries deployed in various areas of activity at least try to pull in the same direction. When 'pressure from below' is exerted, it should aim at complementing the work of those who are exerting 'pressure' against the old order 'from above' (ANC, 1998: 12).

In the aftermath of the 2004 elections, the Minister of Public Service and Administration, Geraldine Fraser-Moleketi, stated that the election results showed that the mass of South Africans have "declared that no amount of sophistication or camouflage by the opposition can make them lose sight of *their* liberators" (Sunday Times, 2 May 2004). (Yet she and her husband – long an SACP power couple exiled until 1990 - were amongst the highest-profile victims of the Polokwane palace coup, agh shame.)

The class character of this approach, Frantz Fanon (1976) attested,

> is reflected most clearly in the relegation of the political and civil life of the people to being flag-waving supporters for those in power who speak of the 'people'... the masses are depoliticised, they are made to be 'unpolitical', only to be brought back at scripted events to legitimate the political élite. The party becomes administrative, encouraging an administrative mentality rather than a humanist programme... And in practice, when the civil rights come in conflict with the political life of the

country, they are trumped. The loyalty of the opposition is decided in advance (for in the end loyalty to the party trumps opposition) and mass action becomes, by definition, disloyalty to the 'nation', the 'revolution', and so forth. And as the administration sees threats everywhere, the by-word becomes, those who are not for us are against us (cited in Gibson, 2004: 12).

The party presents itself as the only legitimate agent of change. It "expels the people from history" and, through nationalist rhetoric, claims that the party incarnates the will of the people and therefore, to oppose it is to oppose the nation. So "these men who have sung the praises of their race... proclaim that the vocation of their people is to obey, to go on obeying and to be obedient to the end of time (Fanon, 1976: 135–138).

What happens when people stop obeying? Of course, if you ban poverty, then those who protest poverty are breaking the law.

Criminalisation. Like magic, the wand becomes a sjambok. Third Force. Misled by opportunists. The National Intelligence Agency is called upon to investigate the reasons for protest. Often, the poor find their quest for justice ending in the same way that the Monty Python quest for the Holy Grail was subverted: with the entire cast arrested.

Alas, there is no Holy Grail at the back of a police van.

A book, not a Holy Grail

We have no thoroughly convincing solutions to the problems we and our colleagues will now proceed to discuss. If the tone of independent critical thinking is set, the evidence must be assembled in such a way that the big, sweeping arguments we prefer about economic neoliberalism and political nationalism – joined by crony capitalism and 'tenderpreneurship' - can be validated by concrete data. And to do so, we must scan the broadest possible set of fields of policy and practice in post-apartheid South Africa.

This is not to support an epistemology of hypothesis-proof in positivistic ways. We readily confess the fluidity and conjunctural character of many features we have described, and the need for inter-relational (dialectic) thinking by which ingrained contradictions drive forward social processes.

For example, the society's most powerful post-apartheid Polanyian 'double-movement' – popular resistance to the commodification of life - may well be the backlash against Mbeki's refusal to provide AIDS medicines. And yet, whereas the Treatment Action Campaign is widely celebrated for its achievement in defeating Mbeki (2003) and before him the Bush (2001) and Clinton (1999) administration's property rights fetish, as well as Big Pharma's profits via monopolies on branded drugs (2001), still we dispute two aspects of the accounts you will read later. Firstly, we would want to question the 'rights talk' that sets up delivery of state services in terms of effective advocacy (albeit in this case there is a strong argument given the 2001 Constitutional Court victory which changed policy on access by pregnant women to nevirapine). And secondly, we are unconvinced by the Campaign's inordinate proximity to the ruling party, which gave its members confidence that their attack on Mbeki was merely an attack on a specific person or policy – not on the neoliberal-nationalist perspective that underlays Mbeki (and Zuma as well). This, in turn, probably explains why the struggle to get AIDS medicines never overlapped and interlocked with struggles to access clean water and free electricity (both vital components of AIDS prevention), as each of the major rights campaigns were locked within the silos of NGOist issue-area specialisations. By *not* connecting the dots, the activists and strategists in each of these excellent social movements did the society, and themselves, a disservice.

The point we would make from this example, is simply that the critiques you will read, in coming pages, of neoliberal post-apartheid economics, of nationalist rhetorics, and of crony-capitalist practices are tough, but they are measured and well deserved. They include autocritique. Moreover, latter chapters show how open the society is to a variety of bottom-up political influences. No one has a vanguard party formula that will take society forward, and no one believes anymore that the 'new social movements' are the agents of change that some of us (Desai and Bond especially) might have advertised a decade ago.

Of special importance here, is that the conjunctural forces associated with the trade union movement – mainly corporatist in orientation, seeking policy deals between big government, big business and big labour – are fragile. We are unable to confidently predict whether a Congress of SA Trade Unions (Cosatu) break from the Alliance is feasible in coming years, say before the next national election in 2014. If not, there is no reason to think that the present hegemonic block within the ANC, shorn of a few relatively conservative personalities in the Congress of the People party, will not continue to take society down a slippery slope. If the centre-left Communists and labour activists fend off the young rightwing populists (and their financial sponsors) and maintain the current fairly solid relationship with the KwaZulu-Natal regional powerbase, 'the centre can hold.' But we do know that if Cosatu does not break, we will need deepened independent-left thinking about social movement, environmentalist and community oppositionalism, of the sort that many of our writers see as the vehicle for their own critiques.

How are these critiques organised? The first chapter captures the long debate about the first and second economy, as Ashwin Desai and Brij Maharaj make the case that Mbeki's discursive framing strategy, enthusiastically re-articulated by Zuma, sets back our understanding of the challenges ahead. In the next chapter, evidence of both macroeconomic degradation and rising social tensions is presented by Patrick Bond. In the third chapter, on 'Provocations of neoliberalism,' Gillian Hart investigates some of the deeper meanings that relate economic orthodoxy to nationalist ideology. The fourth chapter considers another distracting concept, the 'developmental state,' which Ben Fine has long been sceptical about. Finally, by way of broad introductions, Andries du Toit's fifth chapter considers the different ways to enter the narratives of poverty and inequality, making the case for the latter.

The next chapters consider several more detailed topics. The question of whether 'Free Basic Water' does its beneficiaries more harm than good is raised by Greg Ruiters in Chapter Six. Prishani Naidoo uses the seventh chapter to debunk another discourse of poverty, namely its 'feminisation.' In the field of labour and social policy, the concept of citizenship is compared to state interests in social discipline by Franco Barchiesi in Chapter Eight. Moving to rural South Africa, the ninth chapter, by Fred Hendricks and Lungisile Ntsebeza, covers questions of race, class and the Zimbabwe precedent for land reform. In the tenth chapter, education and training are reconceptualised as the reconstitution of dominant power and privilege, by Enver Motala, Salim Vally and Carol Anne Spreen. For an eco-ethnographic account of a major environmental problem, golf courses, Jackie Cock uses Chapter Eleven to link the social relations that produce both 'caddies and cronies.'

The most challenging social problem, AIDS, is treated in terms of structural inequality by Hein Marais in Chapter 12, and in terms of Treatment Action Campaign (TAC) rights-based activism in Chapter 13 by Mark Heywood. While TAC is the most successful of civil society single-issue campaign challenges to state power, matters are far more complicated in the rural grassroots settings. In Chapter 14, Mary Galvin shows how generalisations about community-based organisations require rethinking if strategies emerge to take them from 'survival' to a more 'revolutionary' role. The subsequent two chapters, 15 on 'Poverty and social movements' by Lenny Gentle, and 16 on 'Political strategies of township social movements' by Trevor Ngwane, tell the story of civil society organising, mobilising and advocacy from the standpoint of uneven urban strength. A final chapter, by James Ferguson, addresses the ways that he believes post-neoliberal social policy and economic strategies might develop, in conjunction with momentum established through local agency. And an Afterword by the editors draws further lessons about elite hegemony from South Africa's experience hosting the World Cup in mid-2010.

Yet capitalist hegemony as reflected in commodification, corporate power and periodic displays of state repression, all displayed prominently in mid-2010, is bound to decline, in part because so many aspects of poverty and inequality – amplified as they were by the World Cup, its preparations and its aftermath – will be looked back upon as a collective Own Goal by South Africans. The tragedy, of course, is that this was a time when a very different outcome to the game was possible had the players in Pretoria stayed and fought onside with their constituents, not wandered offside with capital.

Zuma's Own Goal of worsening poverty and inequality is comprehensible only by considering the elite's War on Poverty as lost from the outset, given their ineffectual market weaponry. It was the policy equivalent of searching for a Holy Grail but returning home with only neoliberal-nationalist, corrupt, patriarchal, crony capitalism. Crowing about this sort of trophy, we see Mbeki, Zuma and their successors hoisting it as high as they may reach.

But they are being drowned out by a new vuvuzela din, 'service delivery protests.' For as ideologically chaotic and leaderless as they presently are, it is from discontent of this sort that, as we have witnessed in several Latin American countries, an alternative 'war on poverty' can at least be waged in coming years: for state power, new policies and a very different approach to grassroots and shopfloor constituents.

References

African National Congress. 1994. *State and Social Transformation.* Johannesburg: ANC Discussion Document.

African National Congress. 1994. *Reconstruction and Development Programme: A policy framework.* Johannesburg: Umanyano.

African National Congress. 1996. *The State and Social Transformation.* Johannesburg: ANC Discussion Document.

African National Congress. 1998. The State, Property Relations and Social Transformation. Johannesburg: ANC Discussion Document.

Alexander, N., 2002. *An Ordinary Country.* Pietermaritzburg: University of Pietermaritzburg Press.

Altman, M., 2003. State of employment and unemployment in South Africa. In J. Daniels, A. Habib and R. Southall. eds., *State of the Nation: South Africa 2003-2004.* Pretoria: HSRC Press.

Barber, 2004 R., 2004, *The Holy Grail,* London: Allen Lane and Morgan.

Barchiesi, F., 2005. *Social citizenship and the transformations of wage labour in the making of post-apartheid South Africa, 1994–2001.* Ph. D, Johannesburg: University of the Witwatersrand.

Bauman, Z., 2002. *Community.* Cambridge: Polity Press.

Bhorat, H. and Liebbrandt, M., 1999. Correlates of Vulnerability in the South African Labour Market. DPRU Working Paper, No.99/27.

Bond, P., 2002. Thabo Mbeki and NEPAD. *Thabo Mbeki's World*. Pietermaritzburg: University of Natal Press.

Bond, P., 2004. *Talk Left, Walk Right*. Pietermaritzburg: University of Natal Press.

Bond, P., 2005. *Elite Transition. From apartheid to Neoliberalism*. Pietermaritzburg: University of KwaZulu-Natal Press.

Bond, P., 2005. *Fanon's Warning*. Trenton, NJ: Africa World Press.

Bond, P. and Desai, A., 2006. Explaining Uneven and Combined Development in South Africa. In B. Dunn, ed. *Permanent Revolution: Results and Prospects 100 years on*. London: Pluto Press.

Booysen, F. Van Rensberg, H. Bachmann, M. Steyn, F. and Meyer, K., 2002. The Socio-Economic Impact of HIV/AIDS on Households in South Africa. Pilot study in Qwaqwa, Free State province. Report for USAID on economic impact of HIV/AIDS in SA. Available at:
http://www.uofs.ac.za/faculties/humanities/chrsd/research.asp

Chambon, A.S., 1999. Foucault's approach: Making the familiar visible. In A.S. Chambon, A. Irving, and L. Epstein, eds. *Reading Foucault for Social Work*. New York: Columbia University Press, pp.51-82.

Coronil, F., 1997. *The Magical State*. Chicago: University of Chicago Press.

Department of Welfare. 1997. *White Paper for Social Welfare. Principles, Guidelines, Proposed Policies and Programmes for Developmental Social Welfare in South Africa*. Pretoria: Government Printer.

Deveaux, M., 1994. Feminism as empowerment: A Critical Reading of Foucault. *Feminist Studies*, 20(2): pp.223-47.

Fanon, F., 1976. *The Wretched of the Earth*. London: Penguin.

Ferguson, J., 1990. *The Anti-Politics Machine*. Cambridge: Cambridge University Press.

Foucault, M., 1980. *The History of Sexuality, vol. 1*. New York: Vintage.

Gelb, S., 2003. *Inequality in South Africa: Nature, causes and responses*. Johannesburg: The EDGE Institute.

Gibson, N., 2004. Fanon, Marx and the new reality of the Nation: Black political empowerment and the challenges of a new humanism in South Africa. Unpublished mimeo.

Government Communication & Information System. 2005. *Building a South Africa that belongs to all*. Pretoria: Government Printer.

Hardt, M. and Negri, A., 2004. *Multitude*. New York: Penguin.

Hart, G. and Sitas, A., 2004. Beyond the urban-rural divide: linking land, labour and livelihoods. *Transformation*, 56(31).

Harvey, D., 2003. *The New Imperialism*. Oxford: Oxford University Press.

Johnson, K., 2002. State and Civil Society in Contemporary South Africa: Redefining the rules of the game. In S. Jacobs and R. Calland, eds. *Thabo Mbeki's World*. Pietermaritzburg: University of Natal Press.

Leibbrandt, M. Woolard, I. Finn, A. and Argent, J., 2010. Trends In South African Income Distribution And Poverty Since the Fall of Apartheid. OECD Social, Employment And Migration Working Papers No. 101. Southern Africa Labour and Development Research Unit, School of Economics, University of Cape Town: Cape Town.

Leonard, P., 1997. *Postmodern Welfare*. London: Sage Publications.

Lewis, J., 2004. Assessing the Demographic and Economic Impact of HIV/AIDS in AIDS and South Africa. In K. Kauffman and D. Lindauer, eds. *AIDS and South Africa*, New York: Palgrave.

Löwy, M., 2003. The Theory of Revolution in the Young Marx. Boston: Brill.

Marais, H., 2001. *South Africa, limits to change: The political economy of transformation.* London: Zed.

Marais, H., 2005, *Buckling - The Impact of AIDS in South Africa*, Pretoria: University of Pretoria.

Meth, C., 2004. Ideology and Social Policy. *Transformation,* 56 (9), pp.1-30.

Miliband, R., 1974. Politics and poverty. In D. Wedderburn, ed. *Poverty, inequality & class structure.* Cambridge: Cambridge University Press.

Morgan, G., 2005. *The Holy Grail.* Hertfordshire: Pocket Essentials.

Neocosmos, M., 2002. Democracy, Rights Discourse, National Healing and State Formation: Theoretical Reflections on the Liberation Transition in Southern Africa. In H. Melber, ed. *Political Cultures in Democratic South Africa.* Uppsala: Nordiska Afrikainstitutet.

New Partnership for Africa's Development (NEPAD), 23 October 2001. http://www.nepad.org

Rosen, S. Simon, J. Fox, M. Macloed, W. Vincent, J. and Thea, D., 2003. AIDS is your business. *Harvard Business Review*, February, 323.

Rostow, W., 1960. *The Stages of Economic Growth.* Cambridge: Cambridge University Press.

Rust, K., 2003. No shortcuts to progress: South Africa's progress in implementing its housing policy, 1994-2002. Johannesburg: Institute for Housing in South Africa.

Sewpaul, V. and Hölscher, D., 2004. *Social Work in Times of Neoliberalism: A Postmodern Discourse.* Pretoria: Van Schaik Publishers.

South African Reserve Bank. 2003. Labour Markets and Social Frontiers. 4(28).

Sparks, A., 2003. *Beyond the Miracle.* Jeppestown: Jonathan Ball.

Statistics South Africa. 2002. *Earning and Spending in South Africa.* Pretoria: Statistics South Africa.

Suttner, R., 2003. The Character and Formation of Intellectuals within the ANC-led South African Liberation Movement. Paper presented to African Studies/History Seminar, Durban, University of KwaZulu-Natal, 3 March.

United Nations Development Programme 2003. *South Africa Human Development Report 2003.* Oxford: Oxford University Press.

United Nations Development Programme 2004. *South Africa Human Development Report 2003.* Oxford: Oxford University Press.

Veriava, A. and Ngwane, T., 2004. Strategies and Tactics: Movements in the Neo-liberal Transition. In D. McKinley and P. Naidoo, eds. Mobilising for Change. *Development Update*, 5(2).

Wilson, F. and Ramphele, M., 1989. *Uprooting Poverty – The South African Challenge.* New York: W.W. Norton and Company.

Wolpe, H., 1980. Introduction. In H. Wolpe, ed. *The Articulation of Modes of Production.* London: Routledge & Kegan Paul.

1.
Debating the first and second economy
Ashwin Desai and Brij Maharaj

Introduction

There has been a great deal of debate about the division of South Africa into 'two economies.' It is noteworthy how the notion of the second economy "has become stump material for politicians, journalists, activists and academics alike and an integral component of contemporary political jargon" - key elements of a rhetoric that now informs "a substantive framework of policy and programme of action with tangible effects on the roll-out of services and societal interventions," as John Faull explains (2005: 10). This approach is, at times, even presented as being a radical divergence from classic neoliberal or trickle down economics, in that it provides for substantial state intervention.

However, despite the ubiquitous use of the term second economy – as much in the narratives of Jacob Zuma from 2009 as from Thabo Mbeki in the prior decade - there is little clarity about exactly what comprises the second economy. What particular interventions are to be made in the second economy are just as hazy, leading to a series of questions neatly summarised by Faull:

> Is the so-called 'Second Economy', and its contingent underdevelopment, a necessary consequence of the dynamics of the 'First Economy'? Is the concept of two parallel economies an appropriate basis for conceptualising policy and its implementation? To what extent is it desirable, efficient, or sustainable, to pursue two distinct, but related, macroeconomic policies on the basis of this separation of economic activity? Will government intervention, in this context, reinforce or ameliorate existing schisms in the economy and society? To what extent are the immediate needs and aspirations of the poor, as articulated by these constituencies, addressed through these interventions? (Faull, 2005: 9).

The main contention of this chapter is that the South African government yearns to solve its 'two economies' problem by marrying efficient managerialism at the microeconomic level and neoliberalism with a human face at the macroeconomic and social policy levels, exemplified by the extended public works programmes (EPWP), access to microcredit, and an expanded social wage. We consider the argument within four sections. The first focuses on the debates relating to the second economy. The second presents an assessment of two state-led approaches: the extended public works programmes, followed by the social grants debate. Turning to more entrepreneurial considerations, the third section considers micro-credit as a potential ladder out of the second economy. The final section highlights the brutal realities of survival in the second economy.

Mbeki dichotomies

Mbeki liked dichotomies. He characterised South Africa as two nations: one white and privileged and the other Black and poor. And politically, he adopted an approach that says if you are not for me, you are against me, much like George W. Bush after September 11, 2001. No middle ground for him, even while he adopted a befuddled middle road of Western neoliberalism tied to paranoid nationalism.

In 1998, then Deputy President Thabo Mbeki defined South Africa in this way during a debate on national reconciliation in Parliament:

> South Africa is a country of two nations. One of these nations is white, relatively prosperous, regardless of gender or geographic dispersal. It has ready access to a developed economic, physical, educational, communication and other infrastructure... The second and larger nation of South Africa is black and poor, with the worst affected being women in the rural areas, the black rural population in general and the disabled. This nation lives under conditions of a grossly underdeveloped economic, physical, educational, communication and other infrastructure... This reality of two nations, underwritten by the perpetuation of the racial, gender and spatial disparities born of a very long period of colonial and apartheid white minority domination, constitutes the material base which reinforces the notion that, indeed, we are not one nation, but two nations. And neither are we becoming one nation.

Mbeki here was describing how he saw South Africa, but he provided little of how he envisaged redressing this state of affairs. Building on this analogy, Mbeki followed the two nation thesis with another dichotomy, but this one – two economies - provided more substance to how he proposed to deal with the two separate worlds of South Africa. His argument about the first world and third world components of the economy bears closer examination:

> The first economy is the modern industrial, mining, agricultural, financial, and services sector of our economy that, everyday, become ever more integrated in the global economy. Many of the major interventions made by our government over the years have sought to address this 'first world economy', to ensure that it develops in the right direction, at the right pace... the successes we have scored with regard to the 'first world economy' also give us the possibility to attend to the problems posed by the 'third world economy', which exists side by side with the modern 'first world economy'... Of central and strategic importance is the fact that they are structurally disconnected from our country's 'first world economy'. Accordingly, the interventions we make with regard to this latter economy do not necessarily impact on these areas, the 'third world economy', in a beneficial manner (Mbeki, 2003).

Mbeki argued that the solution depended upon tweaking the neoliberal approach. For Mbeki, "those who benefit from the growth and development of the 'first world economy' will benefit even more from its expansion, resulting from the development of the 'third world economy' to the point that its loses its 'third world' character and becomes part of the 'first world economy'. To get to this point will require sustained government intervention" (Mbeki, 2003).

This, to some, appeared to lay the groundwork for a state-led attack on poverty. Progressive economist Sampie Terreblanche holds that Mbeki's admission that there was no staircase between the first and second economy confirms

> that the 'trickle down' effect is nothing but a myth... The acknowledgement that the government will have to play an entrepreneurial role in the 'second economy' is rather promising. Unfortunately, the government's ability to intervene in the 'second economy' is very much hampered by the lack of capacity in the public sector. But what is perhaps of greater importance, is that it will become contra-productive to intervene in the 'second economy' while the 'structure', the macroeconomic policy and the neoliberal privileges granted to the corporate sector remain intact in the 'first economy'. It is highly necessary to move towards a *truly developmental state system* in South Africa. But this cannot be created in the second economy only. It will have to be created in the South African economy as an undivided entity (Terreblanche, 2005: 10).

That was apparently not Mbeki's intention, though. And despite the transition from Mbeki to Zuma the first/second economy approach became the prevailing discourse in government circles, and is still, in 2010, seen as the framing strategy for addressing poverty and inequality. This approach has, at times, been presented as a divergence from classic neoliberal or trickle-down economics because of the implied state intervention. On the other hand, this is disingenuous, as we have come to know that neoliberalism relies on state intervention, especially its financial bailout mechanisms and repressive apparatus. Indeed, the emphasis on the second economy is trespassed with an agenda of control, as it is from here that the most sustained confrontation against the country's neoliberal transition has taken root.

Extended Public Works Programme and the BIG debate

One of the key areas of intervention is a programme known as the Extended Public Works Programme (EPWP). Here we can find the devil in the detail associated with using 'two economies' as a framing device. Melanie Samson has made an in-depth study of two EPWP's in the waste management sector. Her study shows that,

> rather than forging a pathway from the 'second' into the supposedly distinct 'first' economy, *the public works projects minimised the need for the generation of new jobs within the formal waste management sector*, and created new, inferior jobs which bear characteristics associated with the so-called 'second' economy. The public works projects therefore contributed to the production of the very problem that they were meant to overcome, belying both the myth that the two economies are separated by a structural divide, and the policy claims that the EPWP will be an effective way of bridging this divide (Samson, 2007: 245).

The EPWP entrenches the notion of a two-tier labour market. Interestingly, this was a position proposed by the Deputy Finance Minister, Jabu Moleketi, at the 2005 ANC National General Council, when he wrote in his paper for the conference that: "An increase in investment is only likely to result in an increase in employment if the cost of labour is reduced relative to capital" (ANC, 2005: 8). It was vigourously argued against on the floor by ANC members and the position of a two tier labour market roundly rejected. But as Samson explains, the EPWP allowed it to be introduced through the back door:

The framing of the EPWP as a mechanism to assist the 'unemployable' relegated to the 'second' economy disciplines those employed on the projects to accept their marginalised status as 'nonworkers'. As significantly, it also disciplines organised labour by getting labour to accept the de facto creation of a two tier labour market and defining the 'beneficiaries' as falling outside of organised labour's constituency. Once the EPWP workers with their minimal rights, wages and benefits become an entrenched reality, the EPWP will also limit and circumscribe labour's ability to negotiate wages and conditions of employment for full-time public employees (Samson, 2007: 254).

So the very mechanism promoted by Mbeki to act as a ladder out of the second economy in practice only serves to entrench and broaden its ambit.

For social welfare advocates with a desire for more straightforward income distribution in what became, under Mbeki, the world's most unequal major economy, a different approach emerged a decade ago, the Basic Income Grant (BIG). In 2000, the government appointed a Committee of Inquiry chaired by Vivian Taylor to recommend measures to streamline and rationalise the system of social assistance. The Taylor Committee advocated the much vaunted Basic Income Grant (at R100 a month). A coalition of liberal/progressive (Black Sash and the SA NGO Coalition), church (SA Council of Churches) and labour (Cosatu) forces emerged in support, although BIG advocacy never had the feel of a grassroots or shopfloor-led campaign, rumbling on the ground with urgency.

In spite of support from a welfare minister, Zola Skweyiwa, the ANC government rejected the recommendation, largely due to hostility from Trevor Manuel's Treasury. The ANC's 2002 National Policy Conference instead showed its preference for public works programmes to facilitate "pride and self-reliance of communities" (ANC, 2002). Mbeki, in his 2003 State of the Nation address, insisted that the task of his government was to "reduce the number of people dependent on social welfare, increasing the numbers that rely for their livelihood on normal participation in the economy" (Mbeki, 2003). Likewise, a vocal ANC MP, Ben Turok, argued that BIG "contains the risk of fostering a culture of dependency and entitlement which could bring major social strains if the funding should not be available in future years" (Turok, 2004: 7). This harks back to an old-fashioned 'culture of poverty' analysis, so common to the debate that wrecked the welfare system in the United States, and to hear it not from

Ronald Reagan Republicans but South Africans, who in exile three decades earlier were Muscovite communists, is extraordinary.

For those with faith in the sturdy ladder between second and first economies, R100 would act as a disincentive for people to look for work. Charles Meth disagreed:

> What cannot be called into question is the welfare improvement in, for example, workerless households, among whom the slightest risk (eg, job search requiring some expenditure) threatens an already precarious existence. Their menu of choices could be considerably expanded by the existence of a secure income source, be it ever so small (Meth, 2004: 22).

Many in the ANC camp have countered advocates of BIG and social grants in general with the alternative of public works programmes and the development of an 'entrepreneurial culture.' A government spokesperson explained that the government's approach had a different philosophical bent from the Taylor Report:

> It is a kind of approach that motivates against an income grant. We would rather create work opportunities... Job creation proposals to be considered include a 'massive expanded public works programme', which would include partnerships with the private sector... only people who were disabled or ill should get handouts.[1]

In 2002, the government allocated R15 billion for public works programmes over the next three years: "It is hoped that young work-seekers will gain experience of formal employment, and that older skilled men and women will have employment recourse in an economy where unskilled jobs are dwindling" (McCord, 2004: 69). In general, as Anna McCord points out:

> A public works programme cannot reduce the number of people living in poverty or ensure workers will find alternative formal-sector employment, but if designed sensitively, it can reduce the depth of poverty... In the context of mass poverty and unemployment that characterise South Africa in 2004, public works programmes are of limited impact, since the scale of such

---

1. *Sunday Times*, 28 July 2002.

programmes is modest in relation to the size of the problem (McCord, 2004: 71).[2]

The Taylor Committee noted that high unemployment, the loss of jobs in the formal sector and the rise of 'atypical' work together reduced the incomes of the poor, saw no change to the shift away from formal employment: "In developing countries, where stable full-time waged formal sector labour was never the norm, it is increasingly unlikely that it will become the norm...The reality is that in the developing world formal sector employment may never become the norm that it is in Europe (Department of Social Development, 2002: 38; 154, cf: Sewpaul and Hölscher, 2007).

Wage labour for the government remains the answer to poverty, despite the fact as Barchiesi points out, deteriorating

> material conditions... confirm a growing body of research according to which, far from being a vehicle of social advancement and emancipation, wage labour is turning in South Africa into a reality of poverty and social exclusion. The economic inadequacy of wages is compounded by the uncertainties generated by the increasingly commodified access to healthcare, housing, retirement income, transport and municipal services (Barchiesi, 2006: 31).

Marais points out that it is,

> not that job creation is not desperately needed - it is - not that joblessness doesn't constitute a national crisis - it does. But given the surfeit of working poor, the porous division between formal and informal employment, and the resolute grab-back of workers' benefits by employers, a job often does not ensure the rudiments of well-being, a secure living income, affordable access to essential services and insurance, food security, etc (Marais, 2005: 104).

For Marais, in the context of this and as the AIDS epidemic peaks, the real debate is not about jobs, but "about social rights and about the various ways of realizing them in a society in which millions are impoverished in the midst of abundance" (Marais, 2005: 204). Barcheisi goes further, arguing that one cannot conceptualise "the South African

---

2. *Ibid.*, 71. Some estimates have indicated that this programme will create 200 000 jobs. Some 8 million people are unemployed.

'social question' based on the simplistic dichotomy of employment and unemployment...." Barcheisi insists upon the urgent need for research "into the ways in which wage labour itself reproduces poverty and social marginalisation (Barchiesi, 2006: 31).

For the advocates of the Taylor recommendations, the solution to making unemployment productive lies in the very thing that was seen as the problem: the informal sector. BIG is not a temporary solution while people search for formal employment, but an incentive to release entrepreneurial energies in the informal sector:

> The informal urban economy, long understood as intrinsically resistant to, if not completely outside of, a state power conceived of as essentially regulatory is here imagined in a very different relation to a very different state. Having recognised the charismatic power of the dynamic, bustling netherworld of the shanty, reformers now envisage harnessing it, and bringing it into a new relation both with the national economy and with the project of government...the informal economy is not to be overcome or incorporated, but enhanced and expanded (Ferguson, 2007: 84).

This new relationship between the 'informal' and the 'formal' has come to be conceptualised as the first and second economy. James Ferguson sees in the 'adoption' of the informal sector narrative a strategy for informality "not to be overcome or incorporated, but enhanced and expanded." Moreover, Ferguson holds that a careful reading of the Taylor report illustrates a language entirely compatible with the neoliberal trajectory of the government:

> The BIG would provide not a 'safety net' (the circus image of old-style welfare as protection against hazard) but a 'springboard' - a means of risky (but presumably exciting) neoliberal flight (Ferguson, 2007: 81).

Micro-credit and micro-enterprises

The ideas of property-rights economist Hernando De Soto and microfinancier Muhammad Yunus have become increasingly popular amongst South African policy commentators (De Soto, 2000; Yunus and Jolis, 1998). For De Soto, according to Ferguson, the Holy Grail of ending poverty lies in the very shacks that slum-dwellers live in...if only they could be properly titled and registered. Simple reforms in property law, he imagines, have the potential to almost magically bridge the gap between capitalist rich and poor by even making the 'poorest of the poor' into capitalists themselves (Ferguson, 2007: 74).

Yet as Kate Philip has pointed out in her case studies of rural enterprises,

> Rural local economies will not kick-start development from their own resources, nor will the poor capitalise their way out of poverty... In an economy such as ours, which is not poor in absolute terms but where inequality rooted in social injustice is deeply structurally embedded, there is both an economic and social imperative to address this inequality through a range of redistributive measures. Effective social protection, including social grants, is a key instrument in this respect (Philip, 2005: 385).

Yunus's reputation has grown since winning the Nobel Peace Prize in 2006, and this led to renewed interest in his ideas in South Africa. This is understandable, as his approach serves to depoliticise poverty and indeed it often cuts off attempts to focus on the causes of poverty by positing that somehow all that is missing is credit, for which people really should exercise their 'human right.' This is exactly the approach of Mbekism with its mantra of not creating a 'dependency culture' and the 'poor must help themselves.' It is quite ironic that this approach is tied to an orientation that sees the need for a leg-up for black business from white corporates in Black Economic Empowerment, where among top ANC leaders, the dreaded culture of entitlement and black people's dependency on handouts are together given legitimacy and legislative sanction, as well as preference in state outsourcing contracts.

In contrast to the traditions of crony capitalism and intra-capitalist handouts, at the dawn of the industrial enterprise, 'Taylorism' was all the rage. It sought to measure the output of every worker scientifically. In this way the worker was also atomised and discouraged from attempts at collective organisation. The neoliberal South African version of Taylorism may appear welfarist in intent, but in reality our Taylorism would turn every unemployed person into a 'micro-enterprise,' atomising each household and inculcating a sense of self-reliance, and then, inevitably for most, self-failure.

Unpacking the idea of access to capital, with its multiple mentions in the 'post-GEAR' Accelerated and Shared Growth Initiative for South Africa (Asgisa), we quickly wonder how facilitating the poor to get mired in credit is a positive step. Patrick Bond points out some of the ways microfinance suffuses the Asgisa document:

- One key mechanism is to use the leverage of the First Economy to address the Second Economy. There are two key examples in Asgisa. The first is to leverage the increased levels of public expenditure, especially investment expenditure, to promote small businesses and broad-based empowerment addressing such issues as access to finance...
- Expanding women's access to economic opportunities...
- Ensuring they have access to finance (micro to mega bucks); Fast-tracking them out of the Second Economy... Leveraging components of BBBEE: Provisions for access to finance for women and youths; Funding commitments for housing and small business loans...
- The National African Chamber of Commerce has committed to establish 100 000 new small and medium enterprises per year, and government will support these efforts. A key challenge in this regard is to address the gap in loans between R10 000 and R250 000. One such effort is a new partnership between Khula and Business Partners in a R150-million fund for business loans of this size. Another is a planned fund for women entrepreneurs, which is the result of a collaboration between the DTI, Eskom, Umsobomvu and the Women's Development Bank...
- A commitment in the Financial Services Charter of R5 billion to small business loans is still to be finalised as a programme, but we expect progress shortly under the new leadership of the Charter. We also plan to accelerate the roll-out of the Apex (SAMAF) and Mafisa programmes of loans under R10 000... A final set of Second Economy interventions is centred on the challenge of realising the value of dead assets - land, houses, livestock, skills, indigenous knowledge and other assets that have intrinsic value not currently realised (cited in Bond, 2007: 216 – 230).

Though subsidies are certainly involved, what these strategies ultimately do is absolve the state from genuine, durable second-economy support. Failure to progress is seen as an individual issue. As Hein Marais notes, "microfinance schemes distil neoliberal ideology quite pithily, by presenting a household-level analogy of international finance institution emergency loans with deeper integration into the household economy and adherence to its strictures and conditions" (Marais, 2005: 108).

The problem is not only ideological, but in a society with the income disparities of South Africa, practical. Who can afford to repay the credit? The same issue arose in Bangladesh, where Yunus was actually a failure on his own terms, at least as judged by peers a decade ago when his generous Ford Foundation subsidy was removed, interest rates rose and the inevitable rise in defaults (and women's resistance to Yunus) began in earnest. As Bond argues in his survey of South African microfinance,

> On the one hand, when the *Wall Street Journal* profiled Yunus on its front page in 2001, it started in a celebratory manner: "To many, Grameen proves that capitalism can work for the poor as well as the rich," having "helped inspire an estimated 7,000 so-called microlenders with 25 million poor clients worldwide." Yet looking more closely, the *Journal's* reporters conceded the prevalence of Enron-style accounting. A fifth of the bank's loans in late 2001 were more than a year past-due: "Grameen would be showing steep losses if the bank followed the accounting practices recommended by institutions that help finance microlenders through lowinterest loans and private investments."
>
> Indeed by 2001, Grameen itself conceded a 6.9 per cent default rate, up from 0.1 per cent in 1997. According to the *Journal*, a typical Grameen gimmick was to reschedule short-term loans that were unpaid after as long as two years, instead of writing them off, letting borrowers accumulate interest through new loans simply to keep alive the fiction of repayments on the old loans. Not even extreme pressure techniques - such as removing tin roofs from delinquent women's houses, the *Journal* reported - improved repayment rates in the most crucial areas, where Grameen had earlier won its global reputation amongst neoliberals who consider credit and entrepreneurship as central prerequisites for development...
>
> Leaders of the microfinance industry expressed their sense of betrayal. "Grameen Bank had been at best lax, and more likely at worst, deceptive in reporting its financial performance", wrote World Bank microfinance promoter J. D. von Pischke. "Most of us in the trade probably had long suspected that something was fishy." Agreed Ross Croulet of the African Development Bank: "I myself have been suspicious for a long time about the true situation of Grameen so often disguised by Dr. Yunus's global stellar status" (Bond, 2007: 219).

Bond observes that after the 1998 financial crisis, which brought down many Black Economic Empowerment ventures as well as most of the higher-profile microfinance institutions in South Africa, a growing suspicion about the model was even registered – if not acted upon – in the ruling party's own ranks:

> The state's deregulatory orientation created severe microfinance problems, as acknowledged even by the African National Congress Economic Transformation Committee: "Rather than promoting asset creation, an unregulated micro-lending industry can promote the liquidation of assets to support consumption. Rather than promoting employment and economic security it could promote unemployment and economic insecurity by thriving on the extension of unsustainable debt burdens among low-income workers, thus generating economic disempowerment... The commercial micro-lending sector has rapidly reached the limit of its expansion. The nature of its business model is such that it can only extend financial services to the salaried workforce. The vast majority of the 'unbanked' fall outside this category. Furthermore, the objectives and institutional culture of the high street lender can hardly be considered appropriate for the implementation of an asset-based community development strategy" (Bond, 2007: 223).

Why, then, did Mbeki rely so heavily on microfinance ideology?

> The highest-profile South African proponent is probably Zanele Mbeki, but her Womens Development Banking not only finances rural women, according to the oil company BP, a supporter. It has also made "investments in high-growth businesses" such as Ceasars Gauteng casino and "Siza Water Company, the first privatised water company" in KwaZulu-Natal Province – both of which are counter-examples of poverty eradication (Bond, 2007: 226).

In the same spirit of privatisation, Taylorism was a management technique honed for the factory floor. It was here that 'new' workers had to be disciplined into 'work hours' and 'output,' and it was here of course that workers had to be cut-off from a collective challenge to the bosses, for it was trade unions that were seen as the central plank of resistance. In South Africa, suffering from large-scale unemployment and jobs that do not serve as a launch-pad out of poverty, and a trade union movement that is caught in the quagmire of the 'Alliance' and corporatism, community movements became a militant challenge to the ANC government. They have been at the forefront of struggles to defend the elements of 'bare life' and to reverse the state's attempts to commodify basic services. And so it is here that the state has turned its attention, instituting policies that have the net effect of dividing the poor from the very poor. This process takes place within an overarching ideology that places responsibility on the individual for their future. Policy prescriptions are received from on high as the 'scientific way', and the role of the citizen is to obey.

Providing credit as a launch-pad into entrepneurism is one example. The other is the implementation of devices such as prepaid meters for electricity and water. As Ahmed Veriava points out, they are

> introduced as a way of circumventing the problems associated with a system in which the onus for delivery is still on the state or a service provider. With a prepaid meter, the onus of delivery is on the individual paying citizen and the individual is forced to cut her/himself off from supply or employ 'self-inflicted' punishment for 'poor budgeting' (Veriava, 2006: 58).

Especially in the context of the renewed focus on the 'second economy', the significance "of this refocus of cost recovery practices through prepaid technologies is that it points to the close relationship between cost recovery initiatives and community struggles...in which each successive twist in the state's strategy is aimed at addressing the creativity and tenacity of communities in struggle," Veriava argues. The introduction of prepaid meters reaches deep into disciplining the household, so for example Johannesburg township water delivery is accompanied by a plethora of brochures that advise "daily regimes for (conservative) water usage in the observance of every day practices (including alternative daily hygiene regimens)" (Veriava, 2006: 58–59). The SA Water Caucus 'People's Voice' process in conjunction with the Durban and Cape Town municipalities was similarly aimed at cutting poor people's consumption, notwithstanding objections from Chatsworth leaders.

The Taylorism of the factory has moved address. The household as commodity, as entrepreneur, as a site of discipline, Taylorism for the twenty-first century. NeoTaylorism if you like. And neoTaylorism gels with the broader project of Mbekism: neoliberalism. But, just as at the scale of the factory, Taylorism met its opposition in trade unionism, neoTaylorism in South Africa also runs into severe potholes when it travels too quickly along the dirt roads of the second economy.

Inside the second economy

Mbeki described the challenge as follows:

> The second economy (or marginalised economy) is characterised
> by underdevelopment, contributes little to the GDP, contains a
> big percentage of our population, incorporates the poorest of our
> rural and urban poor, is structurally disconnected from both the
> first and the global economy and is incapable of self generated
> growth and development.[3]

To expose the duplicity of Mbeki's approach, one needs to first take
cognisance of how the very success of the first economy that Mbeki
heralds is predicated on the progressive underdevelopment of the
second economy which he wanted to rescue. Andries du Toit's research
on shack dwellers and farm workers in the Western Cape shows
graphically why the notion of 'structural disconnection' does not capture
the complex actual relationships that exist between the wealthy core of
the South African economy and its underdeveloped and impoverished
periphery:

> Shack dwellers in Khayelitsha, seasonal workers in Ceres and
> villagers in Mount Frere cannot be meaningfully described as being
> 'disconnected' from the South African economy. Their
> impoverishment, on the contrary, is directly related to the
> dynamics of 150 or more years of forcible incorporation into
> racialised capitalism; on disadvantageous terms. Indeed, it may
> well be that many of the obstacles to accumulation from below
> among poor people are at present linked to the depth of corporate
> penetration of the South African economy as a whole. The issue is
> not that there are 'not enough linkages' but the nature of those
> linkages, and the extent to which they serve either to empower
> poor people or simply to allow money to be squeezed out of them
> (Du Toit, 2004: 29–30).

Du Toit's research in the Ceres valley, the heart of wine and food
production illustrates the consequences of new global competitive
pressures and the effects of being all too well sutured into the first
economy. Employers responded by restructuring the labour market:

---

3. Address by President Thabo Mbeki to the National Council of Provinces, August 2003.

For many, this meant the restructuring of their businesses to reduce their exposure to the risks, costs and administrative burden of employing permanent labour...temporary and seasonal workers were supplanting permanent workers, and large numbers of farmers...were opting to use third-party labour contractors. In addition, there was a significant move away from the provision of tied housing to farm workers ... (Du Toit, 2004: 994).

Du Toit argues that labour on the farms of the Ceres Valley,

> are not people trapped in a second economy, unconnected from the first economy. Farm workers in Ceres, far from being excluded, are thoroughly incorporated into the first economy. Their poverty is produced and created by the normal operations of the market in that economy. This should give us cause to think twice about the simplistic notion that all South Africa needs to end poverty is growth. What matters is the kind of growth and the kinds of power relationships that shape the terms of economic exchange. [4]

Moving further from the major urban centres, Du Toit and Neves show in haunting detail how the poverty, unemployment and lack of a secondary economic sector in the former Transkei and in Mount Frere in particular are linked to the strength of the region's association with the formal economy. After 1990, deregulation of Bantustans meant the quick entry of large national supermarket chains into places such as Mount Frere. Building on the back of cheaper goods, these chains have dramatically changed the rural economy. One of the first causalities was the often inter-connected rural trading stores that in many ways comprised local centres in the district's agrarian economy:

> Although these stores enjoyed a statutory protection from competition that saw their white traders, and later the homeland elite, benefiting from a captive market, they were also important centres of local exchange. Rural trading stores were where migrant labours took 'the join' (labour recruitment); stores milled local farmers' maize, bought and sold local agricultural surpluses, and were hubs of postal and telephonic communication. The local credit economy on which these stores depended has made way for a cash economy in which supermarkets are central. These stores are in part what gives Mount Frere its centrality in the district: its limited importance

---

4. Du Toit, A., 2005. Hungry in the valley of plenty, *Mail&Guardian*, April 15 to 21.

as a centre of local government is of far less significance that the five large wholesalers and supermarkets it is home to. The national supermarket chains of Shoprite, Spar, and Boxer (a subsidiary of the Pick n Pay group) have shop frontage within a few hundred metres of the town's main road (Du Toit and Neves, 2007: 158).

The consequences of the entry of national supermarket chains for local production have been disastrous. The supermarkets all source their goods from further afield and this includes perishables like milk and meat. The only local owned of the five largest retailers in Mount Frere (by a long-resident Cypriot Greek family) does purchase locally. But this is done under one prerequisite. The producers cannot sell their products locally:

> The store's enterprising owners turn their local expertise and decentralised management into a competitive advantage; surplus or bruised fruit and vegetables are peddled directly on the pavement. Thus this store — a franchise of a major global supermarket chain, with 14 500 stores in 33 countries — competes head-to-head with the informal vendors on the dusty sidewalks of Mount Frere (Du Toit and Neves, 2007: 159).

The starkest signpost of the changing nature of the local economy is the machinery of retail banking:

> In less than a kilometre of main street there are three automated teller machines (ATMs) — and the way they are positioned says much about cash flows in the local economy. Each one is positioned in close proximity to one of the three major supermarkets: the Standard Bank ATM is in a new facebrick edifice across the road from the local Spar, Mount Frere's oldest supermarket. The ABSA ATM is grafted onto the side of a steel shipping container, on the pavement alongside the local Shoprite. One of the FNB machines illustrates the symbiosis between retail banking and food retail even more dramatically. A compact device no larger than a modest television set it sits *within* the lobby of the local Boxer supermarket — and contains no money. Instead, the machine dispenses printed slips which can be redeemed for cash or goods from the store cashiers, thereby eliminating the need for superfluous duplication of the cash infrastructure. A similar arrangement exists in respect of the pension pay-out machine situated inside the local Spar. The

machine bears a handwritten sign indicating that pensions can be drawn from the machine — on condition that they spend 10 per cent of their payout, immediately, in the shop (Du Toit and Neves, 2007: 159).

Tracing the flow of cash into Mount Frere and its subsequent journey provides clues as to connection and inter-connection with the 'first economy':

> cash comes into Mount Frere in armoured transit vans; is deposited into the ATMs; is drawn by local people – often against funds deposited there by distant relatives or drawn down as social grants – it typically moves five or ten metres across the street or lobby of a store, and then leaves again: repatriated as profits to South Africa's retail giants. Mount Frere is neither a local economic hub nor a neglected, economically irrelevant hinterland: rather, it is a small node in a larger network. Although the links into the national and mainstream economy appear direct and strong, what is lacking is a network of *internal* interconnections and meaningful local multipliers to constitute a functioning *local* economy (Du Toit and Neves, 2007: 159).

Mbeki's quaint idea of 'structural disconnection' – leaving the first economy blameless - does not meet these realities on the ground. The consequences of this are quite revealing for the connections are already there, but the terms on which they are connected actually exacerbate underdevelopment. The irony of the two economy thesis is that it is predisposed to integration but fails to recognise the importance of the terms on which this is done.

The idea of the second economy being absorbed by the first economy is, simply, old-fashioned modernisation theory, namely, to quote Mbeki, that "the 'third world economy' ... loses its 'third world' character and becomes part of the 'first world economy'."[5] Instead of distributing social goods by means other than the market (or imposing the sort of serious social and regulatory constraints on the profit motive that even Adam Smith had in mind) so as to integrate the two economies, Mbeki's apparent task was simply to complete the modernisation process.

But this is a version of the old Rostowian model in which Europe was what Africa should be judged by. Europe was the future. Now this Rostowian model has been repackaged so that we have an internal modernisation project of a special type, in which the first economy

---

5. Mbeki, *op cit.*

(Europe) is the future sans any cognisance of how the first economy is predicated on the underdevelopment of the second. The old Wolpian language of (internal) colonialism of a special type with its attendant two-stageism now mutating into two economies, has been dressed up for these neoliberal times.

The potential adverse effects of the Rostowian project remain. Writers on development have pointed to the 'unintended consequences' of Mbeki's approach to the informal economy, a large part of which is denoted by the second economy. As Serge Latouche warns:

> The normalisation of the informal tends to destroy the social ties existing at intra-national levels, on which the informal's dynamism rests. It introduces, indeed, the most destructive ingredients of outdated modernity: egoism, individualism and unchecked competition, which actually eat away at the social underpinnings of endogenous creativity, the tissues of social solidarity and networks with clients...the informal is already a synthesis of modernity and tradition. It becomes a question of somehow conserving the dynamic and original quality of this creative activity while simultaneously coming to take the form of mimetic development. These are rather long odds!... Formalising the informal boils down to asphyxiating it (Latouche, 1993: 151-158).

South Africa has a long history of trying to make 'improvements' in the second economy. In the 1930s, we had 'betterment schemes' whose aim was to ostensibly improve 'native agriculture' and reduce the pace of migration to urban areas. Betterment schemes under apartheid mutated into Bantustans and became a pillar of National Party policy under the rubric of separate development. Ferguson reminds:

> As the grim process of 'separate development' proceeded, it became more and more clear that 'betterment' was functioning less as a means for boosting agricultural production in the 'homelands' than as a device for regulating and controlling the process through which more and more people were being squeezed on to less and less land, and through which the dumped 'surplus people' relocated from 'white areas' could be accommodated and controlled. As the *bantustans* assumed their contemporary role as dumping grounds, 'betterment' schemes, as one source puts it, 'lost almost entirely any aspect of improvement or rationalisation of land use and became instead principally instruments of coercion (Ferguson, 1990: 262).

By the 1980s, as Deborah Posel pointed out, "large areas of state control are depoliticised by being depicted in technical terms which disclaim their political contestability. The legitimation of such policies devolves around 'proving' their effectiveness, rather than demonstrating their 'democratic' basis (Posel, 1987: 421). Similarly, Gill Hart argues that Mbeki's shift should be seen as part of dealing with challenges from social movements protesting a myriad of issues, from the non-provision of anti-retrovirals to the slow pace of land redistribution:

> What is significant about this discourse is the way it defines a segment of society that is superfluous to the 'modern' economy, and in need of paternal guidance - those falling within this category are citizens, but second class. As such, they are deserving of a modicum of social security, but on tightly disciplined and conditional terms (Hart, 2007: 59).

How prescient was Ashis Nandy when he warned of how the new ruling class borrowed the old elites' civilising mission of development:

> When, after decolonisation, the indigenous elites acquired control over the state apparatus, they quickly learnt to seek legitimacy in a native version of the civilising mission and sought to establish a similar colonial relationship between state and society (Nandy, 1992: 269).

At its core, then, the language of development wants to play precisely the role of what Ferguson calls an Anti-Politics Machine:

> the 'development' apparatus...is not a machine for eliminating poverty that is incidentally involved with the state bureaucracy; it is the machine for reinforcing and expanding the exercise of bureaucratic state power, which incidentally takes 'poverty' as its point of entry (Ferguson, 1990: 255).

Conclusion

Writing of the apartheid state's trajectory in the 1980's, Stanley Greenberg reflected on the attempt to diffuse protest by "negating the racial character of the state, diminishing the direct and visible role of the state in the labour market and workplace and shifting the locus of prestige to the private sector" (Greenberg, 1987: 391). Chris Tapscott argues that this strategy "rested heavily on discursive efforts to depoliticise the social order, to transmute the racial character of the state and to argue that social life should be governed by the market (Tapscott, 1995). This was basically the essence of Mbekism: to depoliticise the social order, to transmute the class character of the state and to spread the market into the very life of the poor through the commodification of basic services, and the turning of the poor into micro-entrepreneurs relying on micro-credit.

In the face of the dominance of Mbekism and its handmaiden neoTaylorism, to talk of the developmental state and South Africa's 'War on Poverty' is as Orwellian as calling the war waged by the United States in Iraq a weapon of peace and democracy. It takes appearance for its essence and takes the changing language of Mbekism as genuine intent. The proponents of the developmental state present it as a revelation but it obscures the main trajectory of the transition, the entrenching of crony capitalism dressed up in the language of nationalism. The effects of the pincer of commodification and the abrogation of state responsibility for the promised massive investments in education, health and infrastructure alongside the push away from welfare has had catastrophic effects on the poorest of South African society.

And herein lies the conundrum with the ascent of Zuma to power, first at Polokwane in December 2007, then with Mbeki's ouster as president in September 2008, and again in April 2009 when Zuma won his electoral mandate. The left within the Alliance initially trumpeted this process as a decisive victory. But it is now self-evident that they confused style with content, and mixed up who was playing in what uniform. If South Africa is a soccer pitch, the economic game played by Zuma includes some left-feint exhibitionism: dribbling a 'new' (more bouncy, shiny and slippery) Jabulani ball, playing to the gallery. After more than a year in power, it is clear that for Zuma's regime, the neoliberal nationalist fundamentals of Mbekism remain in place. Passes always go right, from Zuma, Trevor Manuel and former Reserve Bank governor Tito Mboweni, to their ideological twins, Pravin Gordhan and Gill Marcus.

Zuma's failure to reverse the course on poverty policy, including adopting a new narrative frame, is a world-historic Own Goal.

References

Barchiesi, F., 2006. Wage Labour and social citizenship in the making of post-apartheid South Africa. *Journal of Industrial Relations,* 48, pp.257-278.

Bond, P., 2007. 'Two Economies', Microcredit and the Accelerated and Shared Growth Initiative for South Africa. *Africanus,* 37 (2), pp.216-230.

De Soto, H., 2000. *The Mystery of Capital: Why Capitalism triumphs in the West and fails everywhere.* New York: Basic Books.

Du Toit, A., 2004. Why Poor People stay poor: The challenge of Chronic Poverty. *New Agenda,* 16.

Du Toit, A., 2004. Social Exclusion Discourse and Chronic Poverty: A South African Case Study. *Development and Change, 35,* pp.987-101.

Du Toit, A. and Neves, D., 2007. In Search of South Africa's Second Economy. *Africanus, 37,* pp.145-174.

Faull, J., 2005. Tracing the Two Economies: The Politics, Policy and Practice of Pragmatism. *ePoliticsSA,* 01, IDASA.

Ferguson, J., 1990. *The anti-politics Machine.* Cambridge: Cambridge University Press.

Ferguson, J., 2006. *Global Shadows: Africa in the Neoliberal World Order.* Durham, NC: Duke University Press.

Ferguson, J., 2007. Formalities of Poverty: Thinking about Social Assistance in Neoliberal South Africa. *African Studies Review, 50,* pp.71-86.

Greenberg, S., 1987. *Legitimating the Illegitimate: State, Markets and Resistance in South Africa.* New Haven: Yale University Press.

Hart, G., 2007. Changing Concepts of Articulation. *Africanus,* 37(2).

Latouche, S., 1993. *In the Wake of the Affluent Society.* London: Zed Books.

Marais, H., 2005. *Buckling - The Impact of AIDS in South Africa.* Pretoria: University of Pretoria.

Mbeki, T., 2003. State of the Nation address to the joint sitting of the Houses of Parliament. Cape Town, 8 February.

McCord, A., 2004. The Zimbabele Public Works Programme: Using Public Works to Address Poverty. In S. Brown and A. Fölscher, eds. *Taking Power in the Economy.* Cape Town: Institute for Justice and Reconciliation.

Meth, C., 2004. Ideology and Social Policy. *Transformation,* 56, pp.1-30.

Nandy, A., 1992. State. In S. Wolfgang, ed. *The Development Dictionary: A Guide to Knowledge and Power.* London: Zed Books, pp.264-274.

Philip, K., 2005. Rural Enterprise. In E. Webster and K. van Holdt, eds. *Beyond the Apartheid Workplace.* Pietermaritzburg: University of KwaZulu-Natal Press.

Posel, D., 1987. The Language of Domination. In S. Marks and S. Trapido, eds. *The Politics of Race, Class and Nationalism in Twentieth Century South Africa.* London: Longman, pp.419-444.

Samson, M., 2007. When Public Works Programmes create 'Second Economy' conditions. *Africanus,* 37, pp.244-256.

Tapscott, C., 1995. Changing Discourses of Development in South Africa. In J. Crush, ed. *Power of Development.* London: Routledge, pp.176-191.

Terreblanche, S., 2005. An Evaluation of Macroeconomic Policy in the Democratic Era. Paper presented at the Cosatu Conference on Ten Years of Democracy, 5-7 March 2005.

Turok, B., 2004. Overcoming Underdevelopment. *New Agenda,* 16.

Veriava, A., 2006. Unlocking the Present? Two Theories of Accumulation. In P. Bond, H. Chitonge and A. Hopfmann, eds. *The Accumulation of Capital in South Africa.* Proceedings of the Rosa Luxemborg Seminar and the Centre for Civil Society's Colloquium on Economy, Society and Nature, 58.

Yunus, M. and Jolis, A., 1998. *Banker to the Poor.* London: Aurum press.

2.
Limits to class apartheid
Patrick Bond[1]

Just as the world failed to shake the 'Washington Consensus' during the height of the September-October 2008 world economic crisis, South Africa could not shake 'Mbekism' at the same moment. Perhaps no South African talked left and walked right with more confidence and eloquence than former president Thabo Mbeki, who ruled not only from 1999-2008, but arguably also from 1994-99 as Nelson Mandela's deputy.[2] Reversals of his policies have long been promised, but aside from AIDS treatment, have not yet emerged in the Zuma administration.

Mbeki is of interest as a representative of the last quarter-century of Southern African ideological zigzagging. He was a star pupil not only of Keynesianism at Sussex during the mid-1960s but subsequently of what former SA Communist Party (SACP) theorist Raymond Suttner calls 'Brezhnevite Marxism' at the Lenin Institute in Moscow. Mbeki served in the SACP politburo until 1990, when the new SA president, FW De Klerk, liberalised politics as the Berlin Wall fell. From April 1990, Mbeki was crucial for drawing back the World Bank – whose last prior SA loan was 1967 – in part thanks to his old friend at Sussex, Geoff Lamb, a former SACP youth activist and then top Bank strategist credited with introducing the idea of homegrown structural adjustment to Africa during the 1980s.

The segue from racial to class apartheid could be read from more than a dozen World Bank 'reconnaissance missions' from 1990-94 in all the main sectoral areas, in which the ANC shoe-horned the more radical Mass Democratic Movement allies into cooperation rather than conflict. Intermediary agencies like Anglo American Corporation's Urban Foundation thinktank and the Development Bank of Southern Africa (a World Bank junior partner) were crucial in shaping the transition in hotly contested fields like housing, water, energy, land, healthcare and education. ANC functionaries, Thozamile Botha and Michael Sutcliffe, lubricated the Bank's re-entry for Mbeki in 1990. There was not a single aspect of social policy in which the 'Knowledge Bank' pilot function of the World Bank and its local consultant corps was not a powerful factor.

Even before liberation, an October 1993 agreement to repay the apartheid debt - $25 billion in foreign loans from commercial banks, and somewhat more domestically – prevented the subsequent ANC

1. A version of this chapter appeared in *Monthly Review* in 2010 and we are grateful for permission to republish. Thanks of a special type are due to Jeremy Seekings, Roger Keil, and Terry McBride for comments on an earlier draft.
2. The two leading studies of Mbeki are by Gevisser (2008) and Gumede (2007).

government from meeting social spending goals. An interim constitution in November 1993 assured property rights and an 'independent' (i.e. banker-biased, democracy-insulated) Reserve Bank. The International Monetary Fund had set the stage for other neoliberal economic policies – e.g. public sector wage and spending cuts - as a condition for a December 1993 $850 million loan, and the Fund's manager, Michel Camdessus, even compelled Mandela to reappoint the apartheid-era finance minister and central bank governor when the ANC took state power in May 1994. The General Agreement on Tariffs and Trade (soon to be the World Trade Organisation) hit South Africa hard in mid-1994, as fast-declining manufacturing protection reversed the anticipated gains of liberation for workers.

By early 1995, the dissolution of the dual exchange control system (a 'financial rand' used to deter international capital flight during the prior decade) and the encouragement of stock market investment by international finance meant first a huge inflow and then, on five separate occasions in the subsequent fifteen years, dramatic outflows and currency crashes of at least 25 per cent. The first of these runs, in February 1996, followed a rumour (unfounded) that Mandela was ill, and it left the president and his team so psychologically shaken that they ditched their last left vestige, the Reconstruction and Development Programme ministry, and within four months imposed the hated 'Growth, Employment and Redistribution' agenda of neoliberalism.

Slowly-deracialising class power had obvious macro manifestations of these types, but exactly the same dynamic was occurring in all the microdevelopmental arenas – one *White Paper* after another crafted by the World Bank and its proxies - as well as in provinces and municipalities. Water, for example, was priced at 'full cost recovery' by minister Kader Asmal, a populist social democrat, a policy that generated massive disconnections, a cholera epidemic and a steady flow of protest riots and illegal reconnections. Housing policy was constructed by Joe Slovo – then SACP chair and housing Minister – prior to his 1995 death, in a manner wholly consistent with the World Bank and Urban Foundation developer-driven, bank-centred philosophy.

The basis for a 'government of national unity' which included De Klerk's National Party and the Zulu-nationalist Inkatha party during the initial years of liberation was, of course, the reconciliation of several thousand elites in the liberation movement, white politics and white business. Due in part to the political-economic cowardice of Archbishop Desmond Tutu – who remains extremely strong on symbolic political and ethical matters but weak on social justice - the Truth and Reconciliation Commission he chaired ensured that reconciliation would not touch much, let alone penalise the vast majority of whites who were the main economic beneficiaries of apartheid. Successive Reserve Bank governors loosened exchange controls two dozen times from 1995 onwards, and finance minister Manuel let the capital flood out when in 1999 he gave permission for the relisting of financial headquarters for most of the largest companies on the London Stock Exchange. The firms that took the gap and permanently moved their historic apartheid loot offshore include Anglo American, DeBeers diamonds, Liberty Life insurance, Investec bank, Old Mutual insurance, Didata ICT, SAB Miller breweries (all to London), BHP Billiton metals (to Melbourne) and Mondi paper (to New York).

Although back in 1990, Mbeki had hurriedly quit the SACP to take advantage of the centering of mainstream SA politics, he never forgot how to deploy leftist rhetoric, as witnessed perhaps most publicly in his popularisation of the phrase 'global apartheid', first in mid-2000 when SA narrowly lost the hosting rights to the 2006 Soccer World Cup (to Germany thanks to a racist New Zealander's vote), and then again just prior to the 2002 United Nations World Summit on Sustainable Development in Johannesburg. That conference's main impact was the UN's reification of 'public-private partnerships' in areas as diverse as water, climate and environmental management, and represented another example of a potentially transformative analysis denuded by local/global corporatism. However, under neoliberal conditions, none of the global strategies – especially the New Partnership for Africa's Development, dubbed 'philosophically spot-on' by the US State Department - could and can deliver the goods (Gopinath, 2003). [3]

---

3. Others that occurred in the same spirit to the same ends, were the high rhetoric and low performance at the World Conference Against Racism in Durban (2001); the stunted New Partnership for Africa's Development (2001) and especially its disarming African Peer Review Mechanism (2002) strategy to canvas societies on how to fix problems caused largely by crony-capitalist ruling parties; the World Trade Organisation's Doha Agenda (2001); shakedowns of the G8 in exchange for photo opportunities, culminating in expansive (yet thoroughly broken) promises at Gleneagles (2005); the 'democratisation' of the International Monetary Fund and World Bank (2000-present); 'reform' of the United Nations including its Security Council (2006-08); and the Kyoto Protocol process with its carbon trade financing strategy (2006-present). These efforts have all come to naught. The more recent radical-nationalist critique of North-South power relations was often of a symbolic but relatively meaningless nature, e.g. SA's siding with the Myanmar junta and the Sudanese regime in Security Council votes and International Criminal Court proceedings respectively, or the post-Mbeki government's refusal in March 2009 to issue a visa to the Dalai Lama at the request of the Chinese government (a major ANC donor). For Zimbabweans, however, enormous damage was done by Mbeki's repeated inter-imperialist rivalries with the Brits, EU, Commonwealth and US. His objective seems to have been two-fold: forestall the dislodging of the liberation movement by a labour-led opposition party, and retain regional dominance for the sake of SA firms' penetration of Zimbabwe's potentially substantial resource base and consumer markets.

Degeneration set in within a year of Mbeki's ascent to the presidency, as witnessed in accusations that the Central Intelligence Agency and the industry known as 'Big Pharma' controlled the Treatment Action Campaign (TAC). TAC is a grassroots movement ultimately successful not only in combating AIDS stigma, but in getting anti-retroviral drugs to 750 000 South Africans today, albeit at the cost of 350 000 unnecessary deaths. TAC's victory was an extraordinary accomplishment given that the price for a year's supply of medicines when it started the campaign exceeded $15,000 (Cullinan and Thom, 2009). Other forms of delusion and schizophrenia characterised Mbeki's grip on power (e.g. a claim that three businessmen embarked on a 2001 conspiracy to unseat him). Mbeki's paranoid fear of leftists in and outside the Alliance reached a peak following the march of 30 000 social movement protesters against the UN environment summit on August 31 2002: 'They accuse our movement of having abandoned the working people, saying that we have adopted and are implementing neoliberal policies'.[4]

The neoliberal roll-out and results

Just as he refused to acknowledge the link between HIV and AIDS or that Zimbabwe faced a 'crisis', Mbeki and his ANC Political Education Unit would regularly deny critiques that his government served big business, e.g.: 'There are no facts that the anti-neoliberalism can produce to prove its accusations. Its statement characterising the policies pursued by the ANC and our government since 1994 as the expressive of a neoliberal agenda are complete falsification of reality' (sic).[5] Yet the evidence was overwhelming (Bond 2009):

- there was an immediate post-apartheid rise in income inequality, which was slightly tempered after 2001 by increased welfare payments, but which meant the Gini coefficient soared from below 0.6 in 1994 to 0.72 by 2006 (0.8 if welfare income is excluded), while absolute urban poverty actually increased,
- the official unemployment rate doubled (from 16 per cent in

4. Mbeki, T., 2002. Statement of the President of the African National Congress, at the ANC Policy Conference, Kempton Park, 27 September 2002.
5. African National Congress Political Education Unit. 2002. Contribution to the NEC/NWC Response to the 'Cronin Interviews' on the Issue of Neoliberalism. Johannesburg, September 2002; posted on the debate listserve, 25 September 2002. An edited version was published in the Mail&Guardian, 11 October 2002:
http://archive.mg.co.za/nxt/gateway.dll/PrintEdition/MGP2002/3lv00362/4lv00454/5lv00485.htm

1994 to around 32 per cent by the early 2000s, falling to 26 per cent by the late 2000s - but by counting those who gave up looking for work, the realistic rate is closer to 40 per cent) as a result of imported East Asian goods in relatively labour-intensive sectors (clothing, textiles, footwear, appliances and electronics) and capital-intensive production techniques elsewhere (especially mining and metals),

• the provision of housing to several million people was marred by the facts that the units produced are far smaller than apartheid 'matchboxes', are located further away from jobs and community amenities, are constructed with less durable building materials, come with lower-quality municipal services, and are saddled with higher-priced debt if and when credit is available,

• while free water and electricity are now provided to many low-income people, the overall price has risen dramatically since 1994, leading to millions of people facing disconnections each year when they cannot afford the second block of water consumption,

• the degeneration of the health system, combined with AIDS, has caused a dramatic decline in life expectancy, from 65 at the time of liberation to 52 a decade later,

• with respect to macroeconomic stability, the value of the Rand in fact crashed (against a basket of trading currencies) by more than a quarter in 1996, 1998, 2001, 2006 and 2008, the worst record of any major economy,

• South Africa's economy has become much more oriented to profit-taking from financial markets than production of real products, in part because of extremely high real interest rates (after a spike in 2008, consumer and housing credit markets were badly strained by serious arrears and defaults, although the 2009 cuts somewhat mitigated the problem),

• the two most successful major sectors from 1994-2004 were communications (12.2 per cent growth per year) and finance (7.6 per cent) while labour-intensive sectors such as textiles, footwear and gold mining shrank by 1-5 per cent per year, and overall, manufacturing as a percentage of GDP also declined,

• government admitted that overall employment growth was -0.2 per cent per year from 1994-2004 - but -0.2 per cent is a vast underestimate of the problem,

• overall, the problem of private sector 'capital strike' – large-scale firms' failure to invest - continues, as gross fixed capital formation hovered between 15-17 per cent from 1994-2004, hardly enough to cover wear-and-tear on equipment,

• where corporate profits were reinvested, returns were sought from speculative real estate and the Johannesburg Stock Exchange: there was a 50 per cent increase in share prices during the first half of the 2000s, and the property boom which began in 1999 had by 2004 sent house prices up by 389 per cent (US markets rose only by 64 per cent prior to the banking collapse),

• businesses also invested their South African profits abroad, for dating to the time of political and economic liberalisation, most of the largest Johannesburg Stock Exchange firms shifted their funding flows and even their primary share listings to overseas stock markets,

• the outflow of profits and dividends due these firms is one of two crucial reasons South Africa's 'current account deficit' has soared to amongst the highest in the world, and is hence a major danger in the event of currency instability,

• the other cause of the current account deficit is the negative trade balance, which can be blamed upon a vast inflow of imports after trade liberalisation, which export growth could not keep up with, and

• ecological problems have become far worse, according to the government's own commissioned research in the 2006 'Environmental Outlook' report, which according to the leading state official, 'outlined a general decline in the state of the environment'.

Countervailing claims of a 'developmental state' under construction hinged upon a series of vast white-elephant projects:

• the Coega industrial complex aimed at attracting a persistently elusive aluminium smelter (by early 2008 electricity shortages made this unlikely as it would add 3.5 percent demand to the stressed grid while creating only 800 jobs);

• the Lesotho Highlands Water Project mega-dams which permit hedonistic water consumption in Johannesburg while unaffordably raising prices for Soweto township residents;

• construction and refurbishment of ten soccer stadiums for the 2010 World Soccer Cup, which required a R24 billion capital subsidy and large operating subsidies in coming years;

• the $5 billion arms deal;

• until finally defunded in 2010, Pebble Bed Nuclear Reactors potentially costing tens of billions of dollars, alongside tens of billions more on coal-fired power plants notwithstanding SA's world-leading CO_2 emissions rate; and

• a $3 billion fast rail network allowing wealthy travellers easy, albeit expensive access between Johannesburg, Pretoria and the OR Tambo airport.

To finance state infrastructure spending and steady tax cuts for corporations (down from a rate of nearly 50 per cent in 1994 to less than 30 per cent today), Manuel engineered a parasitical growth process that looks impressive at surface level – a 5 percent GDP increase for much of the 2000s – but isn't when the downside is considered. The GDP growth fails to incorporate the depletion of non-renewable resources, and if such calculation is adjusted, SA would have a net *negative* per person rate of national wealth accumulation, according to even the World Bank.

Going into the Zuma era, in early 2009 South Africa had amongst the world's highest current account deficits and is the most economically vulnerable emerging market, according to *The Economist.*[6] After the ANC's huge victory on April 22, SA is not politically 'unstable' in the classical sense of potential government overthrow. But it is a society that is profoundly unstable in the Polanyian sense, i.e., with a powerful double movement operating, because experience has shown that anti-neoliberal resistance can make a genuine difference. The police measured more than 30,000 'gatherings' (15 or more people in some form of protest, for which permission is typically applied for a week ahead of time) from 2004-07. Of these, 10 percent generated 'unrest'. But many tens of thousands more spontaneous protests were not recorded, according to a survey by Johannesburg's two leading progressive research institutes (Freedom of Expression Institute and University of Johannesburg Centre for Sociological Research, 2009: 13).

Burst bubbles and socio-economic struggles

South Africa's wholehearted embrace of neoliberalism left its economic growth path especially fragile, relying on asset bubbles and subject to capital flight at the first sign of trouble. It is no surprise that in the second week of October 2008, the Johannesburg stock market crashed 10 per cent (on the worst day, shares worth $35 billion went up in

---

6. *The Economist*, 25 Feb 2009. The order of riskiness is as follows: SA, Hungary, Poland, South Korea, Mexico, Pakistan, Brazil, Turkey, Russia, Argentina, Venezuela, Indonesia, Thailand, India, Taiwan, Malaysia and China.

smoke) and the currency declined by 9 per cent, while the second week witnessed a further 10 per cent crash. Even the apparent death of South Africa's neoliberal project in September 2008, personified by former president Mbeki, whose pro-corporate managerialism was one reason for an unceremonious removal from power, is misleading. The 'populist' ruling party leader Jacob Zuma was intent on retaining Manuel as long as possible – he became overall planning minister in mid-2009, replaced at finance by the equally conservative Pravin Gordhan – even if that meant a collision course with his primary internal support base, trade unionists and communists. As Zuma put it to the American Chamber of Commerce in November 2008, "We are proud of the fiscal discipline, sound macroeconomic management and general manner in which the economy has been managed. That calls for continuity."[7]

A few days earlier, Manuel was asked by *The Financial Times* about the impact of the world crisis on South Africa, and told his constituents to tighten their belts:

> We need to disabuse people of the notion that we will have a mighty powerful developmental state capable of planning and creating all manner of employment. It may have been on the horizon in 1994 [when the governing African National Congress first came to office] but it could not be delivered now. The next period is likely to see a lot more competitiveness in the global economy. As consumer demand falls off there will be a huge battle between firms and countries to secure access to markets.[8]

Although as late as February 2009, Manuel claimed his policies would prevent a recession, he was proven badly wrong in May when government data showed a 6.4 per cent quarterly GDP decline, the worst since 1984 during anti-apartheid protests, the gold price's plummet and the tightening of sanctions. The economy shed close to a million jobs in 2009, especially in manufacturing and mining. January 2009 alone witnessed a 36 per cent crash in new car sales and 50 per cent production cut, the worst ever recorded, according to the National Association of Auto Manufacturers. Repossessed houses increased by 52 per cent in early 2009 from a year earlier.

The first quarter 2009 crash was, however, mitigated by the construction industry, which grew 9.4 per cent thanks to white elephant

---

7. Chilwane, L., 2008. Economic Policies to Remain, Zuma Tells US Business, *Business Day*, 27 November 2008.
8. Lapper, R. and Burgis, T., 2008. S Africans Urged to Beware Left Turn, *Financial Times*, 27 October 2008.

state infrastructural investments. The impact of all these public investments was to both maintain the expansive fiscal posture (at least through the Medupi power-plant when state-backed construction will probably grind to a halt), and to raise foreign debt dramatically given that these projects carry enormous import bills. From 7 per cent of GDP in 2003, the foreign debt rose to over 30 per cent ($85 billion) in mid-2010 to what First National Bank projected would be 45 per cent soon thereafter, a level last broached in 1985 when the apartheid leader P.W. Botha was forced into a $13 billion default and imposed exchange controls to halt capital flight.

Although South Africa technically left its downturn in late 2009, there is little doubt that further property recession, ongoing manufacturing stagnation, the credit squeeze and a return to dangerous current account deficits will create ever-sharper tensions, especially with labour demanding more concessions and increasingly angry about the macroeconomic policy *status quo*. Cosatu's mini-revolt included threats of a national strike to halt 25 per cent/year electricity price increases in the foreseeable future (with inflation hovering around 7 per cent), and anger that Gordhan's first budget in February 2010 not only ignored a promised National Health Insurance plan and the need to phase out 'labour brokers' (responsible for mass hiring/firing of casualised workers), but even introduced a 'dual labour market' by subsidising young workers at a cheaper entry-level wage.

In this context, some of the most important lessons of resistance come from deglobalisation and decommodification strategies used to acquire basic needs goods during the early 2000s, as exemplified by the Treatment Action Campaign and Johannesburg Anti-Privatisation Forum which have won, respectively, antiretroviral medicines needed to fight AIDS and publicly-provided water. The drugs are now made locally in Africa—in Johannesburg, Kampala, Harare, and so on—and on a generic not a branded basis, and generally provided free of charge, a great advance upon the $15,000/patient/year cost of branded AIDS medicines a decade earlier. In South Africa today, nearly 800,000 people receive them, representing one of the world's greatest victories against corporate capitalism and state neglect. Just as successful in the Constitutional Court was Durban's Abahlali base Mjondolo shackdwellers movement, which in 2009 won a major victory against a provincial housing ordinance justifying forced removals, though shortly afterwards they were uprooted from their base in Kennedy Road in vicious attacks attributed to the local ANC.

The water in Johannesburg is now produced and distributed by public agencies (Suez was sent back to Paris after its controversial 2001-06 protest-ridden management of municipal water). In April 2008, a major constitutional lawsuit in the High Court resulted in a doubling of free water to 50 litres per person per day and the prohibition of pre-payment water meters, but the Constitutional Court reversed this decision in September 2009 on grounds that judges should not make such detailed policy, leading activists to commit to illegal reconnections if required (Bond and Durgard, 2008).

The ability of social movements in the health and housing sectors to win major concessions from the capitalist state's courts under conditions of crisis is hotly contested, and will have further implications for movement strategies in the months ahead. Critics, however, consider a move beyond human rights rhetoric necessary on grounds not only that – following the Critical Legal Scholarship tradition—rights talk is only conjuncturally and contingently useful (Brand, 2005; Madlingozi, 2007; Pieterse, 2007). In addition, the limits of neoliberal capitalist democracy sometimes stand exposed, when battles between grassroots-based social movements and the state must be decided in a manner cognisant of the costs of labour power's reproduction. At that point, if a demand upon the state to provide much greater subsidies to working-class people in turn impinges upon capital's (and rich people's) prerogatives, we can expect capital to pot-hole the road to rights to the city.

The challenge for South Africans committed to a different society and economy is combining requisite humility based upon the limited gains social movements have won so far (in many cases matched by the worsening of regular defeats) with the soaring ambitions required to match the scale of the systemic crisis and the extent of social protest. Looking retrospectively, it is easy to see that the independent left—the radical social movements, serious environmentalists, internationalist activists and the left intelligentsia—peaked too early, in the impressive marches against Durban's World Conference Against Racism in 2001 and Johannesburg's World Summit on Sustainable Development in 2002. The 2003 protests against the US/UK for the Iraq war were impressive, too. But in retrospect, although in each case they out-organised the Alliance, the harsh reality of weak local organisation outside the three largest cities—plus interminable splits within the community—created major ideological, strategic and material problems that South Africa's independent left has failed to overcome, including divisions between its various currents.

By all accounts, the crucial leap forward will be when leftist trade unions and the more serious SA Communist Party members ally with the independent left. The big question is, when will Cosatu radicals reach the limits of their project within the Alliance? Many had anticipated the showdown in 2007 to go badly for unionists and communists, and they (myself included) were proven very wrong. There is probably no better national trade union movement in the English-speaking world than Cosatu, and the National Union of Metalworkers' regular bouts with neoliberal macroeconomic policy-makers are indicative of the soaring ambitions and harsh realities of life inside the Alliance.

These challenges are not particularly new nor unique, with many socialists in Latin America and Asia reporting similar opportunities during this crisis, but profound barriers to making the decisive gains anticipated. It is, however, in South Africa's intense confrontations during capitalist crisis that we may soon see, as we did in the mid-1980s and early 2000s, a resurgence of perhaps the world's most impressive urban social movements. And if not, we may see a degeneration into far worse conditions than even now prevail, in a post-apartheid South Africa more economically unequal, more environmentally unsustainable and more justified in fostering anger-ridden grassroots expectations, than during apartheid itself.

References

Bond, P., 2009. South Africa's 'Developmental State' Distraction. *Mediations: Journal of the Marxist Literary Group,* 24(1), http://www.mediationsjournal.org/toc/24_1

Bond, P. and Dugard, J., 2008. The Case of Johannesburg Water: What Really Happened at the Pre-paid 'Parish pump.' *Law, Democracy and Development,* 12(1) pp.1-28.

Brand, D., 2005. The Politics of Need Interpretation and the Adjudication of Socio-economic Rights Claims in South Africa. In A. Van der Walt, ed. *Theories of Social and Economic Justice.* Stellenbosch: Stellenbosch University Press.

Cullinan, K. and Thom, A., 2009. *The Virus, Vitamins and Vegetables,* Johannesburg: Jacana Press.

Freedom of Expression Institute and University of Johannesburg Centre for Sociological Research. 2009. *National Trends around Protest Action.* Johannesburg.

Gevisser, M., 2008. *The Dream Deferred.* Johannesburg: Jonathan Ball.

Gopinath, D., 2003. Doubt of Africa. *Institutional Investor,* May.

Gumede, W., 2007. Thabo Mbeki and the Struggle for the Soul of the ANC. London: Zed Books.

Madlingozi, T., 2007. Good Victim, Bad Victim. In W. le Roux and K. van Marle, eds. *Law, Memory and the Legacy of Apartheid.* Pretoria: University of Pretoria Press.

Pieterse, M., 2007. Eating Socioeconomic Rights. *Human Rights Quarterly,* 29, pp.796-822.

3.
Provocations of neoliberalism
Contesting the nation and liberation after apartheid
Gillian Hart[1]

Introduction

Deeply rooted in the current conjuncture in South Africa, this essay engages broader debates over neoliberalism. From a South African vantage point, I show how currently influential theories of neoliberalism cast in terms of class project, governmentality, and hegemony are at best partial. A more adequate understanding is not just a matter of combining these different dimensions into a more encompassing model of 'neoliberalism in general'. The challenge, rather, is coming to grips with how identifiably neoliberal projects and practices operate on terrains that always exceed them.

A crucially important dimension of what is going on in South Africa is that escalating struggles over the material conditions of life and livelihood are simultaneously struggles over the meaning of the nation and liberation, as well as expressions of profound betrayal. These processes underscore the analytical and political stakes in attending to interconnected historical geographies of specifically racialised forms of dispossession, and how they feature in the present. The chapter concludes with a call for a properly post-colonial frame of understanding that builds on the synergies and complementarities between a Gramscian reading of Fanon and relational conceptions of the production of space set forth by Lefebvre.

Let me start with a formative geographical moment. In 1965, the National Union of South African Students (NUSAS) invited Martin Luther King to deliver an address to mark the Day of Affirmation of Academic and Human Freedom. King agreed to come to South Africa – but the apartheid regime refused him a visa. He then helped to arrange for Bobby Kennedy to come in his stead. On June 6 1966, in the Great Hall at the University of Cape Town, Kennedy delivered what is widely regarded as his finest speech. Here is his introductory paragraph:

1. The essay was originally delivered as the Antipode Lecture at the Association of American Geographers conference in April 2007, and dedicated to the memory of my colleague Allan Pred who died earlier that year. A version appeared in *Antipode* in 2008 and we are grateful for permission to republish.

Mr. Chancellor, Mr. Vice Chancellor, Professor Robertson, Mr. Diamond, Mr. Daniel, Ladies and Gentlemen: I come here this evening because of my deep interest and affection for a land settled by the Dutch in the mid-seventeenth century, then taken over by the British, and at last independent; a land in which the native inhabitants were at first subdued, but relations with whom remain a problem to this day; a land which defined itself on a hostile frontier; a land which has tamed rich natural resources through the energetic application of modern technology; a land which was once the importer of slaves, and now must struggle to wipe out the last traces of that former bondage. {PAUSE} I refer, of course, to the United States of America.

The audience gave forth an audible gasp of recognition before erupting in riotous applause. In retrospect I realise that this was my first encounter with relational comparison, in the sense that grasping relations and connections between the US and South Africa enabled different understandings of both. I vividly recall excited discussions after the speech. For all the similarities and interconnections between the two settler societies that Kennedy had highlighted, at least some in my generation of South African students came to an understanding of what was profoundly different: unlike their North American counterparts, European settlers in South Africa had failed to decimate indigenous populations, and were still engaged in an ongoing struggle to subdue them. It is important to recall that 1966 was the height of apartheid repression, and at the time this insight seemed capable of punching at least a small hole in the armory of oppression.

Also in retrospect, what remains so important about this moment is that it placed interconnected global histories of racialised dispossession front and centre, forcing attention to specifically racialised forms of dispossession as ongoing processes – and disrupting situated ignorances and forgettings.

In this essay I return to the theme of racialised dispossession and to debates over socalled primitive accumulation as an ongoing process, as opposed to an historical event. My ambition is to move beyond an earlier Antipode essay that engages these debates (Hart, 2006a) to think about the contemporary salience of Fanon, and suggest the importance of a properly post-colonial frame of understanding that builds on the synergies and complementarities between a Gramscian reading of Fanon and relational conceptions of the production of space á la Lefebvre.

This framing grows out of my efforts to grapple with turbulent forces at play in South Africa over the past several years. They include, as we shall see, the collapse of what are labeled new social movements, the rise of what I call 'movement beyond movements', and the relationship of these shifting expressions of popular discontent to intense conflicts within and between the African National Congress (ANC) and its alliance partners, the South African Communist Party (SACP) and the Congress of South African Trade Unions (Cosatu). The key challenge, both analytical and political, is to produce concrete concepts that are adequate to the conditions with which they are seeking to come to grips.

Most immediately, these unfolding processes compel one to confront questions of 'neoliberalism', which functions in South Africa as a site of popular contention (and term of insult!), as well as a set of analytical categories informed by larger debates. My concern here is less with the question of what is or is not 'neoliberal' than with the analytical traction and political stakes in different conceptions of neoliberalism. Engaging debates over neoliberalism from a South African vantage point, I show how currently influential theories of neoliberalism cast in terms of class project, governmentality, and hegemony are at best partial. A more adequate understanding is not just a matter of combining these different dimensions into a more encompassing model of 'neoliberalism in general', as some have suggested. The challenge, rather, is coming to grips with how identifiably neoliberal projects and practices operate on terrains that always exceed them.

A crucially important dimension of what is going on in South Africa, I will argue, is that escalating struggles over the material conditions of life and livelihood are simultaneously struggles over the meaning of the nation and liberation, as well as expressions of profound betrayal. More generally, these struggles underscore the analytical and political stakes in attending to the interconnected historical geographies of specifically racialised forms of dispossession, as well as to the contemporary salience of Gramsci, Fanon, and Lefebvre.

Unfolding challenges in South Africa

After an absence of nearly 20 years, my re-engagement with South Africa in the early 1990s was through research on transformations in the first phase of post-apartheid order. Disabling Globalisation (Hart 2002) was an effort to engage with these transformations in two radically globalised sites in northwestern KwaZulu-Natal. A crucial moment came on June 30 1996, when the ANC government unilaterally inaugurated GEAR (an acronym for Growth, Employment and Redistribution), a home-grown version of structural adjustment. Strategically-placed government officials announced unequivocally that GEAR was nonnegotiable – because of globalisation there is no alternative.

Contrary to what I'd expected when I started out in 1994 in the afterglow of the first democratic election, an important part of my research came to focus on the devolution of massive responsibility to newly constituted local governments, concurrent with policies of fierce fiscal austerity that starved them of resources. I also witnessed the dramatic contraction of labour-intensive forms of production as the new government dismantled tariffs more rapidly than required at the time by the GATT, and cheap goods poured in from China. While GEAR had promised huge increases in employment, the 1990s saw the sharp contraction of jobs, especially in labour-intensive sectors.

My book came to an end with the Bredell land occupation in early July 2001 when thousands of impoverished settlers 'bought' plots of land for $3 – and were promptly thrown off the land by agents of the post-apartheid state who bore an uncanny resemblance to their predecessors. The moment was vividly captured in a declaration by Thoko Didiza, then Minister of Land and Agricultural Affairs, that "these people must go back to where they came from."

Bredell represented a profound moral crisis of the post-apartheid state (Hart 2002; 2006a). It also fed into and accelerated the rapid rise of oppositional movements such as the Landless People's Movement (LPM) protesting the snail's pace of land redistribution, the Anti-Privatisation Forum (APF) – an umbrella for widepread protests over electricity and water cutoffs – and the Anti-Eviction Campaign (AEC), among others. Two prominent international events - the World Conference Against Racism in Durban in early September 2001, and the World Summit on Sustainable Development in Johannesburg a year later – provided hugely important platforms for these movements, as well as opportunities for forging connections with related movements in other parts of the world, and with sympathetic donors. Of great significance at the close of the WSSD was the sharp contrast between the huge, rollicking March of Movements bedecked in red T-shirts, and the embarrassingly meager turnout for the simultaneous counter-march by the ANC and its Alliance partners, the South African Communist Party (SACP) and Cosatu, the Congress of South African Trade Unions.

Following the bitter disappointments of the 1990s, the rise of this first round of post-apartheid 'new social movements' (NSMs) renewed faith in South Africa as a site of hope for many on the left. What made these movements so compelling was their appearance as a 'bottom up' set of resistances to neoliberal capitalism, as well as their transnational connections. Widely heralded as embodiments of global civil society and counter-hegemonic globalisation, South African NSMs have pulled masses of researchers along in their wake. They have also provided grist for bigger theoretical mills. Both David Harvey (2005) and Hardt and

Negri (2004), for example, invoke South African movements in support of very different theoretical and political positions.

Recent developments have overtaken the celebratory accounts of NSMs. Many of the oppositional movements that burst on to the international stage in the early 2000s are in a state of decline. Some (like the LPM) appear to have imploded, and others are significantly weaker than they appeared in 2002.[2] State repression has undoubtedly played a role, but so too have internal conflicts and problems associated with donor funding – transnational connections are no guarantee of success.

At the same time, we have witnessed the emergence of what I call 'movement beyond movements' – vitally important processes taking place largely outside the scope of NSMs, about which most research focused on such movements has had very little to say. First is the massive outburst of angry protests that erupted after the national elections in April 2004, and spread throughout the country. In October 2005, the Minister of Safety and Security announced that his department had recorded 881 illegal protests during the 2004/5 financial year – during which period there were 5,085 legal protests.[3] The frequency of municipal revolts seemed to subside after local government elections in March 2006, but they re-emerged in early 2007 and are becoming increasingly violent. Many uprisings are directed at local government officials and councillors, and are framed in terms of failure to deliver basic services and housing. Yet they encompass a range of grievances and forms of politics that extend well beyond the technocratic language of 'service delivery', as well as the 'spontaneous' or 'non-ideological' labels that are often attached to them.[4] On a most general level, these protests exemplify the failure of the first round of post-apartheid NSMs to tap into huge reservoirs of popular anger and discontent – a point to which leaders of several of NSMs concede more readily than do many of those who study them.

Second, contrary to widespread expectations of massive boycotts of local government elections in March 2006, the ANC Alliance actually increased its share of the vote from 60 per cent in the 2000 local elections to 66 per cent, with a very similar turnout rate. These aggregates unquestionably mask significant shifts. Yet, as Susan Booysen (2007) has observed, it is also the case that many of the poorest South Africans have come to regard protest as a legitimate and necessary form

---

2. See for example Benjamin (2004), Desai (2006) and Pithouse (2006).

3. These figures are contained in an article entitled, '66 cops injured in illegal service delivery protests,' *Cape Argus*, 13 October 2005. I am indebted to Patrick Bond for this reference.

4. For a pointed critique of the language of 'service delivery' in relation to the Durban shackdwellers' movement (the Abahlali baseMjondolo), see Pithouse (2007).

of political action – at the same time that they continue to support the ANC vis-à-vis other political parties.

A third key dimension of what I am calling 'movement beyond movements' is popular support for Jacob Zuma, who stands at the centre of the 'succession debate' that is producing massive upheavals within and between the ANC, SACP, and Cosatu. Part of what is going on, no doubt, is opportunistic jostling for position in provincial, national, and local political arenas in the run-up to the ANC national conference in December 2007 that will elect a new party president. Yet the challenge to Mbeki and his followers has been made possible by powerful currents of popular support for Zuma, despite his having been charged with rape (for which he was acquitted) and threatened with charges of corruption. Indeed, for many of his followers, these charges are evidence of an anti-Zuma conspiracy.

On the left as well as the right, distaste for Zuma is authorising condescending, and at times, bizarre assertions of the reasons why millions of ordinary people throw their support behind him. The tendency on much of the left is to regard such support as false consciousness, or as an unpleasant populist resurgence of Zulu ethnic nationalism that the figure of Zuma is somehow capable of interpellating from above – an interpretation which fails to take into account support for him well beyond KwaZulu-Natal and isiZulu speaking populations.[5] Perhaps the most extravagant claim is that of Achille Mbembe (2006), who likens support for Zuma to a collective suicide impulse akin to the 1856-7 Xhosa cattle killings – "a populist rhetoric and millenarium form of politics which advocates, uses and legitimises self-destruction, or national suicide, as a means of salvation" (Mbembe 2006: 21).[6]

Yet 'populism' and 'millenarianism' are totally inadequate in coming to grips with multiple sources of support for Zuma, and the multiple manifestations of intense and seething popular anger within and beyond the ANC Alliance that far exceed the reach and organisational capacity of social movements – or the sort of liberal solutions proposed by Mbembe. Over the past several years, I have been able to witness the upsurge of this roiling discontent in the regions of KwaZulu-Natal where I have been engaged in research since 1994. Especially in areas of historically

---

5. A 2006 survey in Soweto by the Centre for Sociological Research at the University of Johannesburg found that Zuma support was strongest among relatively low income households, but that there were no marked differences between men and women, or among language groups (Terreblanche, 2007).
6. His recommendation is that fractions of the Communist Party, the trade unions, and the ANC Youth League should leave the Alliance to form their own political party: "What should emerge is a new political mainstream committed to a liberal constitution, to an explicitly social democratic agenda and to an Afropolitan cultural project" (Ibid).

strong ANC support, anger is palpable. Some of it has been channeled into a local chapter of the Umkhonto we Sizwe Military Veterans Association (MKMVA), with many 'non-veterans' clamoring to join. ANC Local Election Committee meetings in the second half of 2005 became increasingly contentious; on one notable occasion an infuriated man jumped up shouting, "The leadership must not privatise knowledge!" When Thabo Mbeki campaigned in the area shortly before the local government election, an angry crowd forced him to remove his ANC T-shirt and throw it into the crowd – and other dignitaries were compelled to follow suit.[7]

These uneven and changing forms of popular discontent pose urgent challenges, both political and analytical, precisely because they can potentially move in radically different directions. Most immediately, they call into question celebratory claims – often bolstered by invocations of Polanyi's (2001 [1944]) 'double movement' – of an inevitable, cumulative rising tide of progressive working class and popular opposition springing from below to challenge the devastation wrought by the top-down extension of neoliberal market forces into all forms of life and livelihood. One of the limits of this currently popular 'optimistic' reading of Polanyi is its neglect of the possibility – if not likelihood – that what he called 'enlightened reactionaries' may well become major forces in protective counter-movements, "seeking to re-embed neoliberalism in society, to make it more acceptable socially and politically, and to ensure that it is environmentally sustainable' as Jessop (2002: 467) puts it. One could argue that this is precisely what has been happening in South Africa and many other parts of the world under the guise of what Mohan and Stokke (2000) term revisionist neoliberalism, and Peck and Tickell (2002) dub the shift from roll-back to roll-out neoliberalism. Yet ideal-type categories run the danger of obscuring as much as they reveal. The imperative, rather, is to grasp the complex back-and-forth processes of contestation and acquiescence through which multiple, interconnected arenas in state and civil society have been remaking one another – and to the slippages, openings, contradictions, and possibilities for alliances.

Of necessity in a very schematic way, let me situate the changing shapes of popular discontent in relation to re-embedding strategies within and beyond the post-apartheid state. In 2001, at precisely the moment that the new social movements were gathering force, Padayachee and Valodia (2001) discerned signs of 'changing GEAR' – including a more interventionist stance in infrastructural investment,

---

7. The immediate source of popular anger was that the ANC leadership had replaced a popularly elected (male) candidate for ward councillor with a woman. She was elected, but died six months later.

industrial policy, and labour market interventions. These shifts, they argued, were the product of changing global conditions – including 'post-Washington Consensus' debates provoked by the Asian financial crisis – combined with growing pressures from within the ANC Alliance over the palpable failure to meet targets laid out in GEAR for growth, employment, social infrastructural development, and redistribution.[8]

This was also a moment in which biopolitical pressures were gathering force. The height of the Mbeki faction's denialism over the HIV/Aids pandemic coincided with a severe cholera epidemic in 2000/1 (Sitas, 2002). The spread of cholera was linked in turn to watercutoffs prompted by practices of cost-recovery. In September 2000 Ronnie Kasrils, then Minister of Water Affairs, announced a Free Basic Water policy that would provide a minimal free household allocation of 6 kilolitres a month, regardless of household size. This has since developed into a full-blown Municipal Indigence Policy that resembles in some ways the Poor Laws in early 19th century England (Hart, 2007a).

In the first phase of the post-apartheid era (1994 – 2000) local government emerged as a key site of contradictions, encapsulating in an intense form the tensions between stern rhetorics of efficiency, fiscal discipline, and responsibility on the one hand, and invocations of local participation, social justice, and democracy on the other. My recent research in northwestern KwaZulu-Natal makes clear how Municipal Indigence Policy embodies reconfigured but equally intense contradictions – but also how these tensions are constituted and fought over in locally specific ways. That townships in this region and beyond have not exploded in rage seems to have a great deal to do with the inability of municipal officials to impose water restrictions.

Municipal Indigence Policy has its counterpart in the invention of a First and Second Economy in mid-2003. In introducing the Second Economy, Mbeki pointed with disarming frankness to a relatively uneducated, unskilled, stratum of the population that is 'not required in terms of modern society', but in need of protection. Subsequent official statements embody fierce denials that the ANC government is neoliberal. For instance, a series of papers on the Second Economy published on the ANC website in 2004 launched a searing critique of the Washington Consensus in terms of how it serves the interests of the 'developed countries' and fails to address poverty:

---

8. Between 1996-9, fiscal restraint, tariff reduction and inflation control exceeded GEAR targets. At the same time, real private sector investment growth fell far short (1.2 per cent per annum in contrast to the 11.7 per cent projected by GEAR), as did GDP growth (2.4 per cent as opposed to a projected 4.2 per cent per annum). Formal non-agricultural employment is estimated to have shrunk by over 125,000 per year, in contrast to the project annual increase of 270,000 new jobs (Padayachee and Valodia, 2001: Table 1).

Contrary to arguments about minimal state intervention in the economy, we must proceed on the basis of the critical need for the state to be involved in the transformation of the Second Economy. This state intervention must entail detailed planning and implementation of comprehensive development programmes, fully accepting the concept of a developmental state.[9]

At the same time, leading ANC figures were quick to make clear that planned intervention in the Second Economy did not in any way reduce official commitment to rapid capital accumulation driven by market forces. The ANC government's embrace of the Second Economy needs to be understood in relation to pressures from the first round of social movements. In the second half of 2002, immediately following the World Summit on Sustainable Development, Mbeki and other strategically-placed figures in the ANC launched a vicious attack on 'ultra-leftists', accusing them of acting in alliance with 'real neoliberals' (i.e. the predominantly white Democratic Party) and foreign elements hostile to the national democratic revolution (Hart, 2006a). The ANC policy conference in December 2002 clamped down heavily on the left within the Alliance. Simultaneously, the government increased 'pro-poor' spending on the Child Support Grant, and funding going to local governments to finance Municipal Indigence. These strategies to identify and treat a 'backward' segment of society go a long way towards explaining the vehemence with which powerful figures in the ANC dismissed proposals set forth in 2002 for a modest universal Basic Income Grant (BIG) in favor of an Extended Public Works Programme: precisely because the BIG is universal, it lacks points of leverage for instilling 'correct' behavior (Hart, 2006b).

Yet the inadequacy of these responses - essentially strategies of containment - are evident in the escalating municipal protests. Deep tensions within the Alliance also burst into the open at the ANC National General Council conference in June 2005, when opposition to an additional set of Second Economy proposals to waive labour protections in the 'lower segment' of the labour market merged with anger over growing perceptions of 'second class citizenship'. The conference coincided with Mbeki dismissing Zuma as Deputy President, following the conviction on fraud charges of Zuma's financial advisor. This potent

9. http://www.ancorg.za/ancdocs/anctoday/2004/text/at47.txt Last accessed 19 December 2004.

combination of forces amplified popular support for Zuma and intensified powerful anti- Mbeki sentiment (Hart, 2007b).

Crucial to grasping these processes are resurgent forms of nationalism in South Africa today. On the left, there is a strong tendency to see the first round of post-apartheid social movements as embodying a post-nationalist cutting edge, capable of slicing through the ANC government's self-serving deployment of what is often termed 'exhausted nationalism'. In contrast, I suggest that we are witnessing the rise of diverse new forms of popular nationalism that are highly ambiguous, and can potentially move in very different directions. Struggles in multiple arenas over the meaning of the nation and liberation have become a key driving force in the remaking of state and civil society in relation to one another in the post-apartheid era – and will crucially shape the possibilities for something different to emerge. In short, the conjunctural moment in South Africa is radically open – which is why the analytical and political stakes in how we understand it are so high.

On one level these arguments are part of an effort to build a set of concrete concepts adequate to the dangerous conditions in which we find ourselves in South Africa today. At the same time, this effort to grapple with the current conjuncture in South Africa also speaks to broader debates around neoliberalism, and a more general imperative to focus on specifically racialised forms of dispossession.

Provocations of 'neoliberalism'

At the risk of oversimplifying complex and changing debates, it seems to me that a broad consensus has emerged over the past several years that an adequate analysis of neoliberalism entails joining understandings of it as a class project (and/or economic policy) with conceptions of neoliberalism as governmentality and as hegemony.[10] Advocates of this approach also seek to identify and deploy "the abstraction we might provisionally term neoliberalism in general" (Peck, 2004: 395), generated through a comparative synthesis of similarities shared by different variants of neoliberalism.

A provocative intervention by Clive Barnett (2005) is deeply critical of what he calls this trouble-free amalgamation of Foucault's ideas into a Marxist (or Gramscian) narrative of 'neoliberalism'. Conceptions of

---

10. Harvey (2003, 2005, 2006) offers the most comprehensive statement of neoliberalism as a class project. Claims about the relationships between neoliberalism as economic policy, governmentality and hegemony emerge from a set of back and forth engagements between Larner (2000); Peck & Tickell (2002); Larner (2003); and Peck (2004).

'neoliberalism-as-governmentality' and as hegemony, he asserts, suffer from the precisely the same problems – both are caught up in an account of subject-formation in which subject-effects are automatically secured. He recommends that we do away with the concept of 'neoliberalism' altogether, and focus instead on liberal democratic impulses springing up from below.

In addition to questions about melding Gramsci and Foucault, there are important methodological stakes in this debate. The attraction of 'neoliberalism in general', Noel Castree points out, is that it seems to allow us to link our 'local' research findings to a "much bigger and apparently important conversation" (Castree, 2006: 6; see also Castree, 2005). Yet trying to abstract neoliberal practices from what are always more-than-neoliberal contexts involves simply listing generic, albeit historically specific, characteristics found in multiple geographical contexts (Castree, 2006: 4).

Precisely what is important about in-depth historical geographies and ethnographies grounded in relational conceptions of the production of space is their capacity to illuminate constitutive processes and interconnections, and thereby contribute to the production of concrete concepts. Thus, while concurring with Castree's critique, I suggest that refusing to chase after the chimera of 'neoliberalism in general' does not simply consign us to the idiographic specificities of 'case studies'. Accordingly, in engaging debates over neoliberalism from a South African vantage point, I am not positing South Africa as a specific 'case' or variant of a more general or abstract genus of neoliberalism, but what Doreen Massey (1994) would call a nodal point of interconnection in socially produced space. Essentially I want to show how understandings of neoliberalism as class project, governmentality, and hegemony – either singly or in combination – are at best partial, and how the turbulent processes underway in South Africa sharply delineate their limits.

Let me start with the question of neoliberalism as a class project. Pressures emanating from the growing power and reach of finance capital undoubtedly played into the advent of GEAR in 1996, as did the negotiated end to apartheid that made major concessions to corporate white-owned capital. It is also indeed the case that IMF and World Bank emissaries along with South African capitalists moved quickly in the early 1990s to try to purge the ANC leadership of socialist (and indeed Keynesian) ambitions and understandings, and imbue them with appropriate knowledge. Yet arguments about a socialist-inclined ANC having been steamrollered by external forces into accepting neoliberal economic policies are totally inadequate. A far more useful understanding, spelled out most fully by Hein Marais (1998), attends to complex struggles in the ANC Alliance in which a conservative power bloc with increasingly close ties to domestic and foreign capital emerged triumphant.

From one perspective, GEAR can undoubtedly be seen as a wide-ranging class project that has been stunningly successful on its own terms. On July 9, 2006, the Johannesburg *Sunday Times* reported the Merrill Lynch World Wealth Report finding that South Africa had produced 5,880 new dollar millionaires during the previous year – the highest per capita rate of increase in the world. At the same time, the collapse of formal employment that has accompanied the opening up of the economy has devastated the livelihoods of millions of South Africans and severely weakened the labour movement.[11] The political stakes in understanding neoliberalism as a class project are laid out unequivocally by David Harvey:

> The more neoliberalism is recognised as a failed if not disingenuous class project masking a successful attempt at class power, the more it lays the basis for a resurgence of mass movements voicing egalitarian political demands, seeking economic justice, fair trade and greater economic security, and democratisation...The more clearly oppositional movements recognise...that their central objective must be to confront the class power that has been so effectively restored under neoliberalisation, the more they will likely themselves cohere (Harvey, 2006: 157-8).

In other words, the central task confronting the left is to rip away the mask that obfuscates neoliberal class power – and such an exposé will help pave the way for a coherent resurgence of mass movements. We must, in other words, move beyond race, ethnicity, gender, and other dimensions of difference in order to achieve class-based solidarity in an increasingly dangerous world.[12]

---

11. The following week, the *Sunday Times* carried results of research showing that more than 15 per cent of South Africa's 46.9 million people live on less than $1 a day. The report also cites figures published by Global Insight Southern Africa, indicating that the number of desperately poor people had risen from 1.9 million to 4.49 million between 1994 and 2002.

12. As Melissa Wright (2006: 101) points out, Harvey's claims rest on "the dual assumption that differences can be recognised as such and then that, through negotiation or agreement or some other enlightenment appeal to reason, these differences can be put aside for strategic purposes." Harvey is, she notes, susceptible to some of his own criticisms of Hardt & Negri's (2000; 2004) assertions that an amorphous multitude will, as he himself puts it, "magically rise up and inherit the earth." A recent volume devoted to critical appreciations of Harvey's work (Castree and Gregory, 2006) contains several

Pace David Harvey, the task confronting the left in South Africa and elsewhere is considerably more complex than that of exposing neoliberal class power. Nor is it adequate to posit a shift from race to class apartheid. Most immediately, the ANC government's embrace of GEAR constitutes a re-articulation of race and class that is also very much part of an activist project of rule. Elements of this project include the consolidation of conservative forces working in alliance with white corporate capital to create a black bourgeoisie nominally more responsive to 'development'; creating the conditions in which the coalition in control of the state can hold not only its agencies but also non-state bodies to its principles; and inciting not only the black bourgeoisie but the population more generally to embrace freedom and democracy by becoming 'entrepreneurs of themselves'.

How useful, then, are conceptions of neoliberal governmentality – strategic interventions exercised delicately and at a distance to transform citizens into consumers and entrepreneurial subjects who will take responsibility for themselves? In fact, increasingly influential claims about neoliberal governmentality derive less from Foucault's quite circumscribed observations on neoliberalism than from a self-described group of English Foucauldians who became disillusioned with Marxist theory – most notably Nikolas Rose (1996; 1999; 2006).[13] For the Anglo-Foucauldians, neoliberalism (or what Rose terms 'advanced liberalism') embodies a new rationality of government in the name of freedom that emerged as a sustained critique of the welfare state in the 20th century.[14] Whereas the 'state of welfare' entailed government through 'the social' – characterised by discretionary authority and defined in terms of the territorial space of the nation – neoliberalism works through individual allegiances to multiple, overlapping communities "whose vectors and forces can be mobilised, enrolled, deployed in novel programmes and techniques which encourage and harness active practices of self-management and identity construction, of personal ethics and collective allegiances" (Rose, 1999: 176). Hence his claim that neoliberalism entails 'the death of the social' – endorsing, in effect, Thatcher's declaration that "there is no such thing as society."

---

other incisive engagements with these sorts of claims - contributions by Castree, Gregory, and Katz are especially salient.

13. See also the collection edited by Barry, Osborne and Rose (1996).

14. "Like critics from the radical left, [neoliberal critics] regarded social government as generating government overload, fiscal crisis, dependency, and rigidity. Yet unlike those critics, they created another rationality for government in the name of freedom, and invented or utilised a range of techniques that would enable the state to divest itself of many of its obligations, devolving these to quasi-autonomous entities that would be governed at a distance by means of budgets, audits, standards, benchmarks, and other technologies that were both autonomising and responsibilising" (Rose et al., 2006: 91).

Viewing post-apartheid South Africa through an Anglo-Foucauldian lens undoubtedly brings into view some important dimensions that tend to be obscured by economistic understandings of neoliberalism. From this perspective, GEAR inaugurated not just a set of conservative economic policies that strengthened the hand of white corporate capital and a reinvigorated black bourgeoisie. In addition, it can be seen as having installed a new political rationality of rule that can contrast itself with apartheid precisely because it takes the market as its model, to which it can articulate freedom, democracy, and flexibility as opposed to apartheid state repression and rigidity.[15]

In South Africa today, one can easily come up with any number of instances of neoliberal rationalities of rule. In addition to prepaid water and electricity meters, they include the proliferation of NGOs heavily engaged in governmental practices; the 'responsibilisation' through new practices of audit of state education, health care and local government; privatised forms of security, and many other examples of the extension of market models into realms that were heavily bureaucratised under much of apartheid rule. [16] The revamping of parts of the bureaucracy along neoliberal lines and devolution of responsibility to non-state agencies also makes sense when one recalls that the negotiated end to apartheid included a 'sunset clause' for apartheid state employees whom the new ANC government inherited. In addition, as Jim Ferguson (2007) has noted, some proponents of a Basic Income Grant are deploying neoliberal logics in their efforts to pressure the Mbeki government to provide a minimum income to every South African.

At the same time, what one might identify as neoliberal rationalities of rule in themselves provide very little leverage into some of the most urgent and compelling forces at work in South Africa today – the ANC government's efforts to identify and cordon off the 'deserving poor' and the groundswell of popular anger that such strategies are unable to contain. These processes throw into sharp relief the limits of Anglo-Foucauldian explications of neoliberal (or advanced liberal) governmentality more generally. Several critics of such notions (including some quite sympathetic ones) have pointed out that it is one thing to identify a project of rule, and quite another to presume that it is accomplished in practice.[17] In a revealing recent response to their critics, Rose et al., (2006) explicitly reject attention to 'messy processes of

---

15. Elsewhere (Hart, 2002: 25), I have made broadly similar points within a Gramscian framework.

16. It is important to note, however, that some moves in this direction were underway in the later phases of apartheid.

17. See for example O'Malley et al., (1997); Li (1999, 2007); Larner (2000); and Moore (2000). This is also the thrust of Barnett's (2005) critique.

implementation' – their focus, they insist, is precisely on diagnosing rationalities and technologies of rule.[18] They are not, in other words, concerned with the question of whether or not subject-effects are secured.

The methodological limits that the Anglo-Foucauldians themselves concede, undermine some of their key claims. John Clarke (nd: 6), for instance, punctures a large hole in Rose's sweeping assertion about the death of the social in 'advanced liberal' Britain:

> Governmental technologies – and their conceptions – represent specific attempts at mapping (and institutionalising the maps), but they have to negotiate both pre-existing and emergent mappings. They do not, so to speak, have the social all to themselves...The social remains a conflicted and contested terrain – with struggles to mobilise collective identities taking place alongside, at the same time as, and in conflict with political-cultural projects that aim to 'de-socialise' ... contested inequalities.

Significantly, Clarke's insistence on a richer conception of 'the social' is simultaneously spatial; indeed, he draws his metaphor of mapping from Catherine Hall's (2002) focus on 'mapping difference' in her study of metropole and colony in nineteenth century England and Jamaica. A related point is not just that projects of rule are congenitally failing operations that continually generate new and revised projects, as the Anglo-Foucauldians maintain; it's that Anglo-Foucauldian conceptions of neoliberal governmentality are congenitally incapable of coming to grips with the constitutive role of contestation.[19] What also falls out of sight in Anglo-Foucauldian formulations is Foucault's own emphasis on liberalism as the effective practice of security.[20]

Let me turn now to the question of hegemony, and underscore that what Barnett (2005) and others gloss as Gramscian theories of

---

18. In response to the charge that the Anglo-Foucauldian governmentality approach is limited to studies of the mind or texts of the programmer, Rose et al., (2006: 100) respond as follows: "If the alternative is thought to be the sociological study of how programmes are actually implemented, or the proportions and numbers of subjects who adopt or refuse governmental problematics or agendas, or whether or not according to their own criteria programmes succeed or fail, then there is a limited truth to the statement. Governmental analysis does not aspire to be such a sociology."

19. Rose et al., (2006) complain that the tripartite division of liberalism, welfarism and advanced liberalism was initially a heuristic device, but that it has become formalised as a set of chronologically-arranged ideal types into which everything else is fitted. Yet the resolute focus on diagnosis encourages precisely the latter interpretation.

20. I develop this argument more fully in a forthcoming book provisionally entitled *The Government of Freedom*.

neoliberalism-as-hegemony in fact refers to interpretations of neoliberalism cast in terms of regulation theory. There is a fundamentally important difference between these regulationist accounts, and a fully Gramscian conjunctural analysis of the terrain on which identifiably neoliberal policies and practices take hold, along with the multiple, contradictory trends and tendencies that such policies and practices reflect and reconfigure. This Gramscian conception of hegemony is also closely attentive to the cultural politics of articulation in the sense laid out by Stuart Hall. As I have argued more fully elsewhere (Hart, 2007b), Hall's concept of articulation was honed through his engagement with the race/class debate in South Africa in the 1970s and 1980s as well as with Thatcherism, and remains powerfully salient.

Crucial to any understanding of the contested terrain on which GEAR was launched are issues of popular mobilisation – both in terms of the fierce opposition to apartheid that gathered force during the 1980s, and the intense contests within the liberation movement in the early to mid-1990s over the role of popular mobilisation in what is widely termed the National Democratic Revolution (NDR).[21] Reflecting the dominant position of conservative elements within the liberation movement following the assassination of Chris Hani in 1993, GEAR can be seen in part as a fundamental redefinition of the NDR that embodies a powerful drive to contain popular mobilisation, as well as a re-articulation of race and class. More than just a neoliberal rationality of rule or a narrowly defined class project, it is part of a vanguardist project to exercise a new form of activism defined in technocratic and hierarchical terms, and to assert the dominance of a transnationally-connected technocratic elite over mass mobilisation and action.[22]

This broader project also works in and through articulations of the nation and liberation. To grasp the hegemonic power and limits of official articulations of nationalism, we also have to attend carefully to ongoing invocations of 'the national question'– a profoundly evocative term in South Africa that conjures up struggles against colonialism and imperialism, the indignities and violence of racial injustice and dispossession, the sacrifices and suffering embodied in movements for

---

21. I discuss the NDR more fully in Hart (2007b). For a fascinating set of reflections on debates over popular mobilisation within the liberation movement in the early 1990s, see Helena Sheehan's interview with Jeremy Cronin, available at http://webpages.dcu.ie/~sheehanh/za/cronin02.htm. Last accessed 8 December 2007.
22. Johnson (2003) argues that Mbeki and his followers have found the reorganisation of the state along conventional (neo)liberal lines quite compatible with their Leninist understanding of the primacy of vanguard party leadership over mass action.

national liberation, and the visions of social and economic justice for which many fought and died.

Articulations of national liberation are not just cynical manipulations from above; they carry powerful moral weight and connect with specific histories, memories, embodied experiences and meanings of racial oppression, racialised dispossession, and struggles against apartheid. Precisely because official articulations of nationalism tap into popular understandings of freedom, justice, and liberation from apartheid racial oppression, they bolster the ANC state's hegemonic project in crucially important ways. At the same time, because such articulations of nationalism are linked to histories, memories, and meanings of freedom struggles, redress for the wrongs of the past, and visions of a new nation, they are vulnerable to counter-claims of betrayal – which is exactly what has been happening.

In other words, the capacity of the ruling bloc to tap into deep veins of popular understandings of 'the national question' has been simultaneously the lynchpin of its hegemonic power and a key source of vulnerability. Thus, for example, what are ostensibly 'service delivery' protests over housing, water, sanitation, electricity and so forth are simultaneously expressions of betrayal – intensified and sharpened by obscene and escalating material inequalities, and the crisis of livelihood confronting many in South Africa today. At the same time, my recent research highlights some of the contradictory processes through which the capacity of Municipal Indigence Policies to produce governable subjects are severely limited in practice (Hart, 2007a).

The double-edged character of official deployments of nationalism in the context of escalating inequality and persistent deprivation is also crucial to grasping popular support for Jacob Zuma. As I have argued more fully elsewhere (Hart, 2007b: 97-8), part of what Zuma represents is a move to seize the mantle of the liberation struggle, and present himself as its rightful heir. Positioning himself as the hero of national liberation is the key to Zuma's capacity – at least for the time being - to articulate multiple, often contradictory meanings into a complex unity that appeals powerfully to 'common sense' across a broad spectrum. They include his asserting himself as a man of the left (much to the chagrin of many on the left who point to his support for GEAR, as well as his links to certain fractions of capital); as a traditionalist who dons leopard skins on key occasions; as a peace-maker who helped to end the violent civil war in KwaZulu-Natal in the early 1990s; and as an anti-elitist (as displayed in his regular reference to himself as 'not educated' - but, by implication, extremely smart).

Together, they constitute a direct attack on the technocratic elite surrounding Mbeki, often portrayed by Zuma supporters as arrogant and self-serving, and as not having served in the trenches of the revolutionary struggle. These rearticulations of race, class, and nationalism are also shot through with gender and sexuality – overtly, as in the phallic symbolism of Zuma's signature song about his machine gun, as well as in some more of the more complex ways that Mark Hunter's (2007) important analysis of the Zuma rape trial makes clear.

Recent fascinating developments underscore the importance of different contemporary expressions of nationalism, and their relationship to one another and to neoliberalism. Early in 2007, folk rock singer Bok van Blerk issued a music video entitled De la Rey, an ode to the Anglo-Boer War general Jacobus de la Rey, which captivated white Afrikaans-speaking South Africans and quickly became a spectacular hit.[23] With its chorus "De la Rey, De la Rey, sal jy die Boere kom lei [will you come and lead the Boers]," the song sparked widespread speculation of a right-wing Afrikaner call-to-arms. Yet it can also be read as an insistent recollection of white Afrikaner struggle for liberation from British imperialism at the turn of the last century. Sung by a young Boer soldier in the blood and mud of the battle field, De la Rey depicts courageous Boer men confronting the overwhelming might of British forces, their farms burnt to the ground by the 'khakies', and their women and children dying in concentration camps.[24]

The English language press and the liberal opposition Democratic Alliance were quick to draw parallels between De la Rey and Zuma's theme song, Awaleth' umshini wami (Bring me my machine gun), debating which of the two nationalist (and hypermasculinist) anthems was more dangerous. When Zuma invited Bok van Blerk and several other prominent white Afrikaners in the popular culture industry to a braai (barbeque) in March 2007, the Mail & Guardian responded with the telling headline Generaal Jacobus Zuma?[25] The irony intensifies when one recalls that rapprochement between British and Boers at the end of the war came about through the political exclusion, economic exploitation, and further dispossession of black South Africans – and that the ANC has its origins in demands for inclusion in the post-war order by an African landholding class, many of them groomed in Protestant mission schools and imbued with a tradition of liberal politics stretching well back into the 19th century.

---

23. See http://www.youtube.com/watch?v=fAhHWpqPz9A. Last accessed 30 July 2007.

24. The visuals are very precise about the number of British (346,693) and Boer (82,742) forces – but make no mention of the very large numbers of black South Africans directly entangled in the war.

25. http://www.mg.co.za/articlePage.aspx?articleid=303365&area=/insight/insight_nat ional/. Last accessed 30 July 2007.

In other words we are confronting resurgent popular nationalisms, both African and Afrikaner, in which historical geographies of colonialism and imperialism are insistently being inserted into the present through struggles over the meaning of the nation and liberation. What makes these struggles so urgent and compelling is that articulations of nationalism have no necessary class belonging; they can potentially be linked to multiple projects, and move in many different directions. While these struggles are unquestionably bound up with identifiably neoliberal projects and contestations in the post-apartheid era, they also exceed understandings of 'neoliberalism' as class project, governmentality, or hegemony either individually or in combination. Further, any effort to abstract from such excesses to identify a more generic model of 'neoliberalism in general' is analytically untenable and politically dangerous.

Instead of a generic model to which we link our 'local' research, what we need are properly post-colonial understandings of interconnected processes unfolding in different regions of the world. In elaborating what seems to me a more productive way forward, I want to return to questions of primitive accumulation, and attend closely to the stakes in focusing on specifically racialised forms of dispossession.

Revisiting racialised dispossession

One of the most important debates of recent years turns around efforts to understand what Marx termed 'so-called primitive accumulation' as an ongoing process, as opposed to an event that can be relegated to the past. In a comprehensive review of unfolding debates, Jim Glassman (2006) calls attention to the political implications of different conceptions, both in terms of how they have operated in the past and in relation to the imperatives of the present. He notes how, historically, the focus by many Marxists in the Global North on the vanguard role of the urban-industrial working class in effect pushed primitive accumulation into the theoretical background while forefronting its status as an historical event. In the Global South, by contrast, the focus historically has been on far more heterogeneous popular nationalist movements.

Part of what is at stake in focusing on specifically racialised forms of dispossession is bridging this sort of divide. In laying out what I mean by a properly post-colonial understanding, let me start with Henri Lefebvre's ([1974] 1991) observations on the limits of a binary model that opposes capital to labour. This framing makes it possible to grasp their conflictual development in a formal manner, he pointed out, but presumes the disappearance from the picture of the figure Marx called Madame la Terre in the 'trinity formula' that he sketched out at the end of Volume III of Capital. In speaking of the earth, Lefebvre reminds us, Marx did not simply mean agriculture. Nor was he only concerned with natural resources, but also with 'the national state confined within a specific territory, and hence, ultimately, in the most absolute sense [with] politics and political strategy' (Lefebvre, 1991: 325).

Fernando Coronil (1996; 1997; 2000) has made an enormously important contribution in elabourating Lefebvre's arguments, and extending them in a post-colonial direction: A perspective that recognises the triadic dialectic among labour, capital, and land leads to a fuller understanding of the economic, cultural and political processes entailed in the mutual constitution of Europe and its colonies, processes that continue to define the relation between postcolonial and imperial states. It helps to specify the operations through which Europe's colonies, first in America and then in Africa and Asia, provided it with cultural and material resources with which it fashioned itself as the standard of humanity – the bearer of a superior religion, reason, and civilisation embodied in European selves (Coronil, 2000: 357).

In other words, we have to attend closely to the complex and uneven reverberations and articulations in the present of much longer historical geographies of colonialism and imperialism, along with their specifically racialised – as well as gendered, sexualised, and ethnicised – forms. Relational conceptions of the production of space bequeathed to us by Lefebvre are crucially important in attending to specifically racialised forms of dispossession as ongoing processes, precisely because of their capacity to illuminate spatial interconnection and mutual processes of constitution at play in different regions of the world. Building on these conceptions, the first phase of my research drew on connections between South Africa and East Asia to suggest how methods of relational comparison and critical ethnography could be made to do analytical as well as political work (Hart, 2002; 2006a).

My efforts to grapple with the processes currently unfolding in South Africa reinforce the stakes in focusing on specifically racialised forms of dispossession as ongoing processes, while also suggesting new dimensions to what I am calling a properly post-colonial frame of understanding. Along with several others, I want to suggest the contemporary salience of a Gramscian reading of Fanon, and how this complements, extends, and enriches Lefebvrian understandings of spatial interconnection and mutual processes of constitution. [26] Indeed,

---

26. See also important recent work by Kipfer and Goonewardena (2007) and Kipfer (2007), who have drawn attention to key sections of the second volume of Lefebvre's *The Critique of Everyday Life* and De l'Etat that are deeply complementary with Fanon.

Lefebvre's own Gramscian provenance makes him a natural, as it were, for linking with Fanon in mutually enriching ways.

Let me start with one of many passages in *The Wretched of the Earth* that resonate painfully in South Africa today:

> During the struggle for liberation the leader awakened the people and promised them a forward march, heroic and unmitigated. Today, he uses every means to put them to sleep, and three or four times a year asks them to remember the colonial period and to look back on the long way they have come since then. Now it must be said that the masses show themselves totally incapable of appreciating the long way they have come. The peasant who goes on scratching out a living from the soil, and the unemployed man who never finds employment do not manage, in spite of public holidays and flags, new and brightly-coloured though they may be, to convince themselves that anything has really changed in their lives....The intellectuals who on the eve of independence rallied to the party, now make it clear by their attitude that they gave their support with no other end in view than to secure their slices of the cake of independence. The party is becoming a means of private advancement (Fanon, 1963: 169-171).

Not surprisingly, the chief use of Fanon in South Africa today is to excoriate a comprador national bourgeoisie.[27] This deployment of Fanon is often linked to claims that nationalism is rapidly becoming exhausted, and that oppositional movements embody a post-nationalist sensibility.

Yet Fanon did not just posit the first, most prescient – and to my mind still the most powerful – critique of the betrayals of post-colonial promises. *The Wretched of the Earth* is also a plea for a transformative new humanism and internationalism that has to be grounded in national consciousness forged in the struggle for liberation:

> National claims, it is here and there stated, are a phase that humanity has left behind...We however consider that the mistake, which may have very serious consequences, lies in wishing to skip the national period...National consciousness,

---

27. Patrick Bond (2005) extends what he calls 'Fanon's warning' to the New Partnership for Africa's Development (Nepad), a South African-led reform initiative which many see as entrenching neoliberal policies and economic dependence throughout the African continent.

which is not nationalism, is the only thing that will give us an
international dimension (Fanon, 1963: 247).

National consciousness for Fanon was a unifying force, essential to
bridging rural-urban, racial, ethnic, and other divisions produced or
reinforced by colonialism. At the same time, he insisted, "if nationalism is
not made explicit, if it is not enriched and deepened by a very rapid
transformation into a consciousness of social and political needs, in
other words into humanism, it leads up a blind alley" (Fanon, 1963:
204). Fanon's insistence on an international dimension, along with his
focus on the racialised spaces of the colonial city and connections
between the city and the countryside, resonate powerfully with
Lefebvrian understandings of spatial interconnection and mutual
processes of constitution. [28]

The contemporary salience of Fanon's work is elaborated in
important recent rereadings through a Gramscian lens by Ato Sekyi-Otu
(1996) and Nigel Gibson (2003).[29] Both are writing against
interpretations of Fanon as the prophet of violence. They are also
writing in critique of cultural discourse theorists like Homi Bhabha
whose "postmodernist commitments result in the evisceration of
Fanon's texts; they excise the critical normative, yes, revolutionary
humanist vision which informs his account of the colonial condition and
its aftermath" (Sekyi-otu, 1996: 3). Reading Fanon's texts "as though
they formed one dramatic dialectical narrative", Sekyi-Otu acknowledges
Fanon's debt to Hegel while making a powerful case that Fanon's
dialectic of experience is far closer to Gramsci: "So strikingly similar are
Gramsci's and Fanon's idioms and programmes – to say nothing of their
supportive concepts – that I am tempted to call Gramsci a precocious
Fanonist" (Sekyi-otu, 1996: 118).

At the same time, Sekyi-Otu shows how bringing Gramsci and Fanon
into relation with one another compels careful attention to the specific
historical-geographical conjunctures with which each was grappling –
and serves as a powerful warning against any mechanistic applications
of their insights. A key point of overlap between Gramsci and Fanon,
albeit with their own historically and geographically specific differences,
turns around engagements between intellectuals and ordinary people,

---

28. See Kipfer and Goonewardena (2007) and Kipfer (2007) for a useful elaboration of
these points.

29. Along with Richard Pithouse, Gibson has also written about how a shackdweller's
movement that emerged in Durban in 2005 embodies Fanonian understandings. These
and other articles (including Gibson's earlier work on Fanon in relation to Steve Biko) are
available on the websites of the Centre for Civil Society at the University of KwaZulu
Natal and the Abahlali baseMjondolo.

and the reciprocal processes through which they transform one another. Noting how realists and scientific analysts have ridiculed the romanticism of Fanon's account of the mutual embrace of urban intellectual revolutionaries and country dwellers, Sekyi-Otu (1996: 177) urges us to read the text "as a symbolic account of what is to be done if the nascent nation's disparate resources are to be gathered for its self-renewal."

Of necessity in a skeletal way, let me suggest some of the analytical and political leverage that Gramsci, Fanon, and Lefebvre together provide in South Africa and beyond. Most immediately, they sound a strong warning against presumptions that one can read political struggles directly off the structure of economic relations, or that top-down neoliberalism (or 'accumulation through dispossession') necessarily calls forth bottom-up resistance. By the same token, they are adamantly opposed to vanguardist understandings that define the role of intellectuals in terms of specifying the level of development of productive forces (or unmasking the class basis of neoliberalism), and supposing that progressive popular opposition will follow in some automatic fashion. Together they alert us to how there are always slippages, openings, contradictions, and possibilities for something different to emerge – but that these have to be grounded in what Gramsci called common sense, through a process of "renovating and making 'critical' an already existing activity" (Gramsci, 1971: 330-1).

A closely related set of points concerns the imperative of intellectuals' engaging deeply and seriously with popular understandings and the processes that produce them, recognising that "the educator must him(her)self be educated", and is also in part a product of these forces. This challenge is rendered all the more complex by the enormous diversity of historically and geographically specific conditions, as well as their interconnections with forces at play elsewhere. At the same time, understandings of space and place as actively produced, and of relational interconnections, mutual processes of constitution, and the ongoing reverberations of the past, are key resources. Let me end with the ideas of Allan Pred:

> In Sweden, as anywhere else, the connection between locally situated practices and locally occurring racialisation and racist relations ... is not to be confused with a purely local production and experience of 'race' [and racialised dispossession] ... Even under the most isolated of circumstances, 'local' social forms have always to some extent been synonymous with a hub of material and relational flows, with a more or less developed mesh of interactions and interrelations across multiple

geographical scales, with comings and goings that have made a virtual impossibility of the unselfconsciously 'local' (Pred, 2000: 23).

Postscript

I write this Postscript in South Africa in the immediate aftermath of the ANC's conference held in the northern town of Polokwane from December 16-20, 2007. Zuma and his supporters came sweeping into power on what some have called a Zunami, while the Mbekiites suffered a deeply humiliating defeat at the hands of delegates elected by ANC branches. Popular anger towards the ruling bloc was powerfully evident at the conference, especially on the first day when thousands of delegates hissed Thabo Mbeki, and broke into singing Mshini wam immediately following his speech that lasted for two and a half hours. Delegates then shouted down conference chair Mosiuoa ('Terror') Lekota – a strong Mbeki supporter, openly critical of Zuma – who was forced to cede the platform to Zuma's chosen deputy, Kgalema Motlanthe. On a national scale, these expressions of popular anger and discontent mirrored precisely the dynamics that I have been observing in ANC meetings in Ladysmith since the second half of 2005.

Not surprisingly, there is intense speculation about the direction in which the Zumaites will steer the ANC – and indeed the state. In his acceptance speech at the close of the conference on December 20, Zuma assiduously reassured domestic and international capital that nothing would change in terms of macro-economic policy – at the same time that he spoke of the importance of the SACP and Cosatu in the ANC Alliance, and the imperatives for redistributive policies.

Shortly before the Polokwane conference, Zuma travelled to India, the UK and the US to calm the jitters of nervous capitalists, and impress upon them his good intentions. I was able to observe one version of this performance at first hand on December 5, 2007, when Zuma addressed a small group of academics and business people at a lunch sponsored by the Institute for International Studies at UC Berkeley. [30] In his speech,

---

30. I was told that Zuma was interested in meeting academics, and a student in the Political Science department at UC Berkeley had connections with him. South African press reports subsequently explained that Zuma had been invited by Stratfor (Strategic Forecasting Incorporated), described by Fortune magazine as "one of the elite but low-profile private intelligence agencies that are increasingly relied on by multinational corporations, private investors, hedge funds and even the [US] government's own spy agencies, for the analysis of geopolitical risks" (reported in an article entitled, US intelligence firm sponsors Zuma trip, 6 December 2007 http://www.thetimes.co.za Last accessed 12 June 2007). George Friedman, the CEO of Stratfor, was favorably impressed by Zuma, according to this and other reports.

delivered with considerable élan, Zuma started out by emphasising the need for political stability and economic growth. He went on to outline the role of the ANC in bringing about the transition from apartheid, along with the inclusive, democratic process through which the constitution emerged: "This is not a country that depends on a leader," he insisted, going on to note that "we play in a framework determined by the constitution; no individual or party can take us in a different direction." Zuma then turned to the question of the economy – carefully separated in good liberal fashion from that of politics. Here are some of his comments, taken from my notes:

> We have established a political system that no-one can complain about. Our economic policies have been balanced up to now. They have withstood turbulences in different parts of the world. However we are still faced with a first economy and a second economy. The question is how to put them together. This goes with [the question of] the plight of the poor. Some say that the gap between the rich and the poor has increased. There has been a big increase in the number of people in the cities living in informal settlements. We need thinking people to say how to address the poverty issue. This is the issue we are debating within the Alliance and the progressive forces. What policies do we need? We are having this debate with the participation of the trade unions and the SACP. Where do we go? The challenge is to bridge the gap between the first and second economies to address the plight of the people. How to address this problem? We want scholars to help: how do we grow the economy and address the plight of the people? Education is critical. A high percentage of the unemployed people are unskilled. A big chunk of them are unemployable because they have no skills. The country cannot develop when people are not educated. Human capital is essential. We have not done enough to address this issue. Rural development is also very important – how do you do that? People are flocking into the cities because there is no economy in the rural areas. We do have policies in general terms. But how do we implement them? I come from a university situated in a rural area. I am the chancellor [an honorary position in South Africa]. I am running a pilot project of toilets in rural areas. You can't solve problems of sewage in rural areas in the same way as in the cities. I spoke to Billiton – they understand. They put in septic tanks in rural areas. [More generally] sewage, water and electricity must be put in rural areas. We want to establish a relationship with this university. Professor Vilakazi in

South Africa says that development must go from rural to urban. This is an issue we are debating all the time... We have a surplus while people are starving. The system has tried to do something – but we need to do more.

Zuma's appropriation of Mbeki's discourse of a first and second economy in this context is especially interesting and significant – and was notably absent from his crowd-pleasing acceptance speech at the ANC conference, where themes of social justice were far more overt. In the wake of the Zuma victory that caught many by surprise, intense debate is currently unfolding on the independent left about whether – and, if so, how – to engage with the left of the ANC Alliance. That this debate is happening at all represents a significant shift from the era of the new social movements, when the predominant position was to maintain a careful distance from Alliance politics.

Much of course depends on how one analyses the present conjuncture. One emerging line of argument, articulated most fully by Patrick Bond, is that the fall of Mbeki and the rise of Zuma is simply a smokescreen. [31] Bond argues that, for all his left-leaning talk, Zuma represents neoliberal business-as-usual, and class apartheid will rapidly reassert itself. Since grassroots protests are directed primarily against the ANC's neoliberal economic policies we can expect them to continue, and the independent left represented by the new social movements should position itself to capture this discontent: "Only then," he says, "will South Africa enjoy the possibility of a fully liberatory, post-Mbeki set of politics, not personalities, as the far-sighted left-left makes common cause with serious comrades in labour and the Communist Party, egged on no doubt by increasingly angry feminists and other democrats."

My argument throughout this chapter has been that the challenges confronting the left are far more complex. The drama that exploded at Polokwane was as much about contesting the meaning of the nation and liberation as it was about the fallout from a neoliberal class project and socio-economic structure, and we ignore these sentiments and struggles at our peril. It is useful here to recall Gramsci's warnings about the complexities of grasping the dialectical nexus between organic and conjunctural movements, along with his observation that "if error is serious in historiography, it becomes still more serious in the art of politics, when it is not the reconstruction of past history but the

---

31. Bond, P., 2007. 'Zuma, the centre-left, and the left-left.' 21 December 2007, distributed on the debate listserve (debate@lists.kabissa.org).

construction of present and future history which is at stake" (Gramsci, 1971: 178).

Polokwane also stands as a profound warning against the dangers of vanguardism. When the news of Zuma's victory broke, a friend in Ladysmith turned to me and said, "You must understand, Gill, that this is about the masses versus the intellectuals." It seems to me that those of us who occupy the formal position of 'intellectuals' need to take very seriously the subtext of this statement. What it suggests, among other things, is that we should be attending far more carefully to the complex dynamics unfolding in 'ordinary' places.

References

Barnett, C., 2005. The consolations of 'neoliberalism.' *Geoforum* 36, pp. 7-12.

Barry, A. Osborne, T. and Rose, N., eds., 1996. *Foucault and Political Reason: Liberalism, Neoliberalism, and Rationalities of Government.* Chicago: University of Chicago Press.

Benjamin, N., 2004. Organisation building and mass mobilisation. *Development Update*, pp.73-93.

Bond, P. ed., 2005. *Fanon's Warning: A Civil Society Reader on the New Partnership for Africa's Development*, Trenton NJ: Africa World Press.

Booysen, S., 2007. With the ballot and the brick: The politics of attaining service delivery. *Progress in Development Studies*, 7, pp.21-32.

Castree, N., 2005. The epistemology of particulars. *Geoforum* 36, pp.541-44.

_2006. From neoliberalism to neoliberalisation: Consolations, confusions, and necessary illusions. *Environment and Planning A*, 38, pp.1-6.

Clarke, J., (nd). Consumerism and the remaking of state-citizen relationships. Unpublished paper.

Coronil, F., 1996. Beyond occidentalism: toward nonimperial geohistorical categories. *Cultural Anthropology*, 11, pp.51-87.

_ 1997. *The Magical State: Nature, Money, and Modernity in Venezuela.* Chicago: University of Chicago Press.

_ 2000. Towards a critique of globalcentrism: speculations on capitalism's nature. *Public Culture*, 12, pp.351-374.

Desai, A., 2006. Vans, Autos, Kombis and the Drivers of Social Movements. http://www.ukzn.ac.za/ccs/default.asp?3,28,10,2680 (last accessed 4 April 2007).

Fanon, F., 1963. *The Wretched of the Earth.* New York: Grove Press.

Ferguson, J., 2007. Formalities of poverty: Thinking about social assistance in neoliberal South Africa. *African Studies Review*, 50, pp.71-86.

Gibson, N., 2003. *Fanon: The Postcolonial Imagination.* Cambridge: Polity Press.

Glassman, J., 2006. Primitive accumulation, accumulation by dispossession, accumulation by 'extra-economic' means. *Progress in Human Geography*, 30, pp.608-625.

Gramsci, A., 1971. *Selections from the Prison Notebooks.* Edited and translated by Q. Hoare and G. Nowell Smith. New York: International Publishers.

Hall, C., 2002. *Civilising Subjects: Metropole and Colony in the English Imagination 1830-1867.* Chicago: University of Chicago Press.

Hardt, M. and Negri, A., 2000. *Empire.* Cambridge, Mass.: Harvard University Press.

_ 2004. *Multitude: War and Democracy in the Age of Empire.* New York: Penguin Press.

Hart, G., 2002. *Disabling Globalisation: Places of Power in Post-Apartheid South Africa.* Berkeley: University of California Press.

___ 2006a. Denaturalising dispossession: Critical ethnography in the time of resurgent imperialism. *Antipode,* 38, pp.977-1004.

___ 2006b. Post-apartheid developments in historical and comparative perspective, in V. Padayachee, ed. *The Development Decade? Economic and Social Change in South Africa 1994-2004.* Pretoria: HSRC Press, pp.13-32.

___ 2007a. The New Poor Laws and the Crisis of Local Government. *Amandla* 2, pp.5-6. Available at: http://www.amandla.org.

___ 2007b. Changing concepts of articulation: Political stakes in South Africa today. *Review of African Political Economy,* 111, pp.85-101.

Harvey, D., 2003. *The New Imperialism.* Oxford, New York: Oxford University Press.

___ 2005. *A Brief History of Neoliberalism.* Oxford, New York: Oxford University Press.

___ 2006. Neoliberalism as creative destruction. Stockholm: Geografisker Annaler, 88B(2), pp.145-158.

Hunter, M., 2007. Left behind in a KwaZulu-Natal township: Thinking about state, gender and class after the Zuma rape trial. Paper for the Development Dilemmas workshop, Durban, University of KwaZulu-Natal, 16-18 November.

Jessop, B., 2002. Liberalism, neoliberalism and urban governance: A state-theoretical perspective. *Antipode,* 34, pp.452-472.

Johnson, K., 2003. Liberal or Liberation Framework? The Contradictions of ANC Rule in South Africa. In H. Melber, ed. *Limits to Liberalism in Southern Africa: The Unfinished Business of Democratic Consolidation.* Pretoria: HSRC Press, pp.200-223.

Kipfer, S., 2007. Fanon and space: Colonisation, urbanisation, and liberation from the colonial to the global city. *Environment and Planning D: Society and Space,* 25, pp.701-726.

Kipfer, S. and Goonewardena, K., 2007. Colonisation and the new imperialism: On the meaning of urbicide today. *Theory and Event,* Spring.

Larner, W., 2000. Neoliberalism: Politics, ideology, governmentality. *Studies in Political Economy,* 23, pp.5-25.

___ 2003. Neoliberalism? *Environment & Planning D-Society & Space,* 21, pp.509-512.

Lefebvre, H., 1991 [1974]. *The production of space.* Oxford: Blackwell.

Li, T., 1999. Compromising power: Development, culture and rule in Indonesia. *Cultural Anthropology,* 14, pp.295-322.

___ 2007. *The Will to Improve: Governmentality, Development, and the Practice of Politics.* Durham: Duke University Press.

Marais, H., 1998. *South Africa Limits to Change: The Political Economy of Transition.* London and New York: Zed Books.

Massey, D., 1994. *Space, Place, and Gender.* Minneapolis: University of Minnesota Press.

Mbembe, A., 2006. *South Africa's second coming: The Nongqawuse syndrome.* http://www.opendemocracy.net/author/Achille_Mbembe.jsp (Accessed 4 June 2007).

Mohan, G. and Stokke, K., 2000. Participatory development and empowerment: The dangers of localism. *Third World Quarterly,* 21, pp.247-68.

Moore, D., 2000. The crucible of cultural politics: reworking 'development' in Zimbabwe's eastern highlands. *American Ethnologist* 26, pp.654-89.

O'Malley, P. Weir, L. and Shearing, C., 1997. Governmentality, Criticism, Politics. *Economy and Society,* 26, pp.501-517.

Padayachee, V. and Valodia, I., 2001. Changing Gear? The 2001 budget and economic policy in South Africa. *Transformation,* 46, pp.71-83.

Peck, J. and Tickell, A., 2002. Neoliberalising space. *Antipode,* 34, pp.380-404.

Peck, J., 2004. Geography and public policy: constructions of neoliberalism. *Progress in Human Geography,* 28, pp.392-405.

Pithouse, R., 2006. The necessity, promises and pitfalls of global linkages for South African movements. In N. Gibson, ed. *Challenging Hegemony: Social Movements and* the *Quest for a New Humanism in Post-Apartheid South Africa*. Trenton, NJ: Africa World Press.

__2007. The University of Abahlali baseMjondolo. http://www.abahlali.org/node/2814. (Accessed 27 December 2007).

Polanyi, K., 2001 [1944]. *The Great Transformation*. Boston, MA: Beacon Press.

Pred A., 2000. *Even in Sweden: Racisms, Racialised Spaces, and the Popular Geographical Imagination*. Berkeley: University of California Press.

Rose, N., 1999. *The Powers of Freedom*. Cambridge: Cambridge University Press.

Rose, N. O'Malley, P. and Valverde, M., 2006. Governmentality. *Annual Review of Law & Social Science*, 2, pp.83-104.

Sekyi-Otu, A., 1996. *Fanon's Dialectic of Experience*. Cambridge MA: Harvard University Press.

Sitas, A., 2002. Love in the time of cholera? Unpublished paper.

Wright, M., 2006. Differences that matter. In N. Castree and D. Gregory, eds. *David Harvey: A Critical Reader*. Malden, MA: Blackwell, pp.80-101.

4.
The developmental state?
Ben Fine

Introduction

My contribution is in part a tale of the murder of the developmental state in those dark days of the Washington Consensus.[1] But is not the world of development economics now illuminated by the light shed by the more progressive post Washington Consensus? Does this not offer the prospect of a revival of the developmental state?

With minor exceptions, the answer is in the negative. Whilst there is a limited degree of reform in thinking attached to the post Washington Consensus, it is appropriate to view the notion of developmental state with a degree of circumspection. As I have emphasised elsewhere, scholarship, ideology or rhetoric and policy in practice, especially of the World Bank, are mutually supportive if inconsistent in different and shifting ways (Fine 2001a and 2010a). Much the same is true more generally for development in terms of scholarship, policy and ideology - or 'advocacy', as it has now become more gently known (see Deaton et al., 2006 and Bayliss et al., forthcoming for critique). We have to be careful in negotiating intellectual autism in the dark, and not to be blinded when emerging into the bright lights of alternatives.

This, though, is a chapter primarily concerned with some aspects of the developmental state paradigm. Nonetheless, I am acutely aware of why I have been solicited to address these topics. It is a result of the recent prominence of the developmental state in political discourse in South Africa to which I will turn my attention in the final section. Its sudden and unexpected appearance means that I will be more than normally, if selectively, attentive to the history of the developmental state as an idea, as covered in the next section. I have on and off been concerned with both the developmental state and South African economic policymaking for twenty years or more. Possibly it is my age and the revisiting of fond and familiar topics that has induced me to be more than normally, even acceptably, self-indulgent in reviewing my

---

1. This is a shortened version of Fine (2007), the lengthier title indicating in part what has been omitted. See also Ashman et al., (2010) and Fine (2010b). For continuing critical work on the developmental state, visit:
http://www.iippe.org/wiki/Beyond_Developmental_State_Working_Group
and for the South African minerals-energy complex, see below, visit,
http://www.iippe.org/wiki/Minerals_Energy_Complex_and_Comparative_Industrialisati
on_Working_Group

own contributions. Immodesty aside, this also has the effect in practice of giving an unattractive air of 'I told you so' to the proceedings. In these respects, I simply beg your indulgence, as well as exercising my own, as the price to be paid for shedding some light on why the developmental state has not been deployed to address South Africa in the past, why it is being used now, and how it might best be used.

The developmental state is dead – long live the developmental state

This is the third occasion on which I have sought to examine the extent to which the developmental state approach can realise its promise of offering solutions to the problems of development.[2] In the early 1990s, the influence of the developmental state was at its height for a number of reasons, and it seemed appropriate to draw out lessons for the South African economy on which I was working at the time in both academic and policy arenas. First and foremost, the developmental state offered an explanation for the East Asian Miracle, and the sorts of policies that made it possible. Second, it was one of the two main pillars of criticism of the Washington Consensus, the other being adjustment with a human face. Third, it combined contributions from across the social sciences, economics, politics, sociology and history if the latter only to a limited extent.

I returned to the developmental state a decade or so later, by which time its influence was probably at an all time low. Again, there are three reasons for this. Following the sudden and generally unanticipated Asian crisis of 1997/98, the perspective of miracle was rapidly turned over, and all that had been perceived to underpin it was cast aside or reinterpreted as negative. For Lee (2004: 11), "the 1997 Asian financial crisis triggered suspicion by many scholars about the utility of the developmental state model".[3] Second, the Washington consensus had given way to the post Washington consensus, and the positive lessons of the developmental state had been both absorbed and diluted down. Third, the academic literature had itself evolved to suggest that the developmental state brought about its own dissolution. Development itself, brought about by the state, is perceived to undermine both the conditions and need for the developmental state.

There is then a curious incidence of the developmental state by virtue of its sharp shift in influence over time. No doubt, this reflects its

---

2. See Fine (1992) and Fine and Rustomjee (1997) for first occasion, and Fine (2004c and 2006) for the second. Here I seek predominantly to cover the literature not discussed in these earlier contributions.

3. Zhu (2002) also sees the end of the Cold War as leading to the erosion of threat as a galvanising factor in promoting the unity underpinning developmental states.

own analytical strengths and weaknesses as well as the changing material conditions that it seeks to address and within which it is situated. But it also, as already indicated, is more or less prominent by virtue of its alter ego, the developmental thinking deriving from the World Bank that has always distanced itself from this approach. This was, of course, overt during its commitment to the Washington Consensus which set the analytical, ideological and policy agenda of market versus the state in which the developmental state situated itself on the opposite to the pro-market side. This conflict came to a head with the East Asian Miracle Report of the World Bank (1993). It was motivated and funded by Japan, not least in light of its dissatisfaction with the Washington Consensus for the denial of its own history and in seeking to serve its policy needs in undertaking direct investment in the Asia-Pacific Rim, Wade (1996) and Rigg (2002) for more recent view.[4]

In substance, though, far from the Report serving to promote the state in general and the developmental state in particular, it represented the death throes and not the death of the Washington Consensus, drawing the conclusion that the miracle or, more exactly, miracles were market-conforming, when attached to state intervention, and non-replicable. By this is meant that there was extensive state economic intervention but it was only successful when it did what the market would have done had it been working perfectly. Even within its own terms of reference of market versus state, this is vacuous in content, unlike the implication drawn that this perfection of the market through state intervention could not be emulated in other countries.

As a result, the developmental state did not emerge triumphant from the demise of the Washington Consensus. Instead, it was ignored or outflanked by the post Washington Consensus, not least through a remarkable rewriting of intellectual history although one that is far from rare in the practices of the World Bank, as it partially incorporates longstanding ideas in opposition to it and claims them as due to its own originality. Thus, whilst the developmental state literature was one of the major intellectual driving forces behind the rejection of the Washington Consensus, and in prompting the East Asian Miracle Report that denied the salience of the developmental state, the Report is perceived to have initiated a turn in the Bank's thinking.

Such is the view of Stiglitz himself. Literally in a half-truth (first sentence right, the second wrong), the creator of the post Washington

---

4. Crucially, Japan had also become a leading source of aid and so had some muscle in determining how its role should be perceived. But see also Hirata (2002) for the idea that the death of the developmental state in Japan has also opened up growing influence of NGOs on Japanese policymaking.

Consensus launches it with the following claim of East Asia, "Their industrial policy, designed to close the technological gap between them and the more advanced countries, was actually contrary to the spirit of the Washington consensus. These observations were the basis for the World Bank's East Asian Miracle study (WB 1993), and it stimulated the recent rethinking of the role of the state in economic development."

On the contrary, the rethink long preceded WB 1993 and was denied by it. What this allowed is for the developmental state literature to be denied its intellectual significance as a killer of the Washington Consensus and for its substance to be watered down if not ignored. As I was to write a few years later, it was a case of 'The Developmental State Is Dead - Long Live Social Capital?', Fine (1999) although, now in retrospect, this was to exaggerate the influence and role of social capital in commanding the World Bank's continuing antipathy to substantial state intervention. This is to point, however, to how little social capital had to be promoted in order to outflank the developmental state, buttressed as it was by notions of governance, empowerment and so on – anything other than the developmental state.

The subsequent rise, and fall, of social capital within the Bank's thinking has proven to be a misconceived and failed attempt by its social scientists to have themselves taken seriously by its economists, as opposed to them being successfully used by the economists to legitimise their appropriation of the 'non-economic' intellectual, ideological and policy terrain. I have discussed this all at inordinate length elsewhere, most recently Fine (2010a). But, to return to my two earlier forays into the developmental state literature, they offered both continuities and change in thinking.

The most important continuity is the division of the literature into two schools, the economic and the political as I have termed them. They are complementary and mutually exclusive with remarkably limited overlap between them. The economic school focuses on the economic policies that the state needs to adopt in order to bring about development, and identifies how this has been done in the past, most notably from Latin American ISI through the variety of interventions associated with the East Asian NICs, especially protection, export promotion, targeted investment and finance, and so on. Inevitably, explicitly or otherwise, this involves an economic theory that breaches with laissez-faire, drawing for example on the notion of static or dynamic economies of scale and scope. The political school, on the other hand, is more or less free of economic analysis, and vice-versa for the economic school, addressing the issue of whether the state has the capacity and motivation to adopt developmental policies without really interrogating what these might be. In particular, the focus is upon whether the state has the autonomy in some sense both to adopt policy independent of special interests and to deploy that independence for developmental aims.

If the first continuity across the evolving developmental state literature is that it has been divided into two mutually exclusive parts, the second continuity is one of difference in how it has been able to accommodate empirical evidence, as its sphere of application has been extended over time and by time itself. In general, the economic school has not suffered any discomfort in this respect. It is simply possible for it to interpret any case of successful development as the consequence of the right policies having been adopted and failed development otherwise. Wherever there is or has been development, there must have been a developmental state, with Ha-Joon Chang the leading proponent of this view.

The situation with the political school has been entirely different. For, it seems that the autonomy of the state has to be refined to take account of each new case study, both in terms of the nature of the state and the conditions which allow it to be so or not. Within the literature, there has been a proliferation of terminology to fill this empirical credibility gap, relative and embedded autonomy, weak and strong states, the role of culture, institutions, bureaucracy, and so on. As Howell (2006: 275) puts it, "the notion of the developmental state, too, has become vulnerable to semantic overload, ideological appropriation and empirical amorphousness." It leads him to adopt the notion of "a polymorphous state that reveals contradictory features of developmentalism and predation, rivalry and unity, autonomy and clientelism, efficiency and inefficiency, across time and space" (Howell, 2006: 278).[5]

With this portfolio of opposites, anything becomes explicable. This does not mean the developmental state literature is without content because it focuses upon the role of the state in development and on particular mechanisms and pre-conditions. As a result, as already indicated, change is possible within the literature, and is discernible with my second review finding the literature to be much less upbeat than the first, reflecting the Asian crisis, the intellectual climate of more state-friendly post Washington Consensus (undermining and sidelining the status of developmental state as opposition), increased concern over the sustainability and/or the feasibility of late-comer developmental state in

---

5. Note that Doner et al., (2005) seek to roll back this polymorphism by reducing presence of developmental state to the presence of systemic vulnerability, itself induced by the constraint of building internal coalitions, scarce resources and external threat. Their casual claims to the contrary, Africa would appear to be replete with counterexamples!

light of globalisation,[6] and, if only implicitly, an evolving recognition of lack of integration across the two schools. The latter took the form of bringing class back in, an economic and political category, in suggesting that the East Asian developmental states had brought about their own demise by creating forces more powerful than itself, a capitalist class for example or democratisation in case autonomy had been seen as a consequence of authoritarianism.

In retrospect, the developmental state literature now appeared remarkably and paradoxically static as a portfolio of economic policies or as a political structure, each separately divined but together wroughting fundamental economic and social change, eroding their own conditions of existence. In addition, the developmental state had now been round long enough that it can now be used casually and in passing without acknowledging its theoretical and empirical complexities.[7] This is important and, in a sense, paradoxical. For, as the developmental state literature has grown in theoretical and empirical complexity to the point of overburdening itself with refinement and exceptions, so it can become its opposite, something emptied of content, to be flagged in passing, or to mean whatever any contributor cares to make of it, see below in case of South Africa.

There were a number of conclusions that I drew from these literature surveys. First, it is inappropriate to seek a simple synthesis across the two literatures. Rather, second, it is necessary to reintroduce class and economic and political interests more generally at a higher analytical level in order to examine how these are represented through both the market and through the state (and rather than starting from a stance of state versus market). Third, this combination of interests will be attached to a particular system of accumulation of capital with differences that need to be identified in ranging from one country to another and, almost inevitably, from one sector to another within a country. Fourth, this also applies to what are liable to be the specific relationships between industrial and financial systems, as well as the presence and influence of international interests.

In this light, what does my third turn at the developmental state literature reveal? Most important is that there has been something of a revival of the developmental state in the literature, although I have not

---

6. For Painter (2005: 336), if unduly homogenising, but in the context of the Hong Kong neo-administrative state: "The combination of a powerful bureaucracy, incomplete democratic institutions, limited political freedoms, and a dynamic capitalist economy typifies the so-called East Asian developmental state ... A common challenge ... is to adapt these institutions and roles to the changing nature of the global economy."

7. As for two studies for Singapore as city developmental state, the term only effectively appears in Ooi's (2005) title and similarly for Hee and Ooi (2003) and Jha (2004).

prepared any hard and fast evidence in support of this assessment. Its renewal comes in three forms. First is business as usual with the developmental state, and the pre-conditions for it, being recognised wherever any development has taken place. This is most notable for China, unsurprising in view of its most recent growth record.[8] More generally, as Boyd and Ngo (2005: 1) put it, with more than a degree of exaggeration if not error, "for more than twenty years the theory has captured and held the imagination of researchers working across East Asia. It has extended its scholarly empire far and wide to embrace the political economies of Asia, Latin America, and Africa. The theory has been taken up as much by planners, policy-makers, and international organisations such as the World Bank as by academics." They see it as a convenient intermediary between command and market economies, a challenge both to neoclassical and dependency theory.

Indeed, "it has become a stylised fact: the thing itself, a fixity in real-world politics in a trope that makes it possible to assert that 'State X *is* a developmental state'" (Boyd and Ngo, 2005: 2). It might have lost some of its 'gloss' with the Asian crisis, for "Recipes for success were now said to be the ingredients of failure," and sound empirical foundations have been lost with refined contributions from regional experts. They appropriately observe, at least for the economic if not the political school, that the developmental state literature has adopted a partial Weberianism that emphasises "legitimacy, rationality, and instrumentality at the expense of monopoly, violence, and domination."

It is, in short, a state-led theory of economic growth that lacks a theory of the state other than primarily as an independent variable promoting growth, rather than examining the politics of the state that make it the way that it is. This assessment is both rare and late in recognising the limited integration of economics and politics within the developmental state literature, and how the corresponding theory of the state is underdeveloped in terms of underlying classes and the forms taken by them in the state apparatus (as opposed to taking the state apparatus as developmental bureaucracy or ministry for example).[9]

---

8. There has been almost no work on the transition economies of Eastern Europe as developmental states, not surprising in view of their perceived failure. An exception is provided in a comparative study of Hungary and Romania by Negoita (2006) whose emphasis is upon the absence of a capitalist class that, accordingly, needs to be created. For Africa, sample Lockwood (2005), Sindzingre (2006), Shaw (2006), Edigheji (2005) and Nabudere (2006). See also 'The Democratic Developmental State in Africa: Conceptual and Methodological Workshop', Centre for Policy Studies, Johannesburg, July 24-25, 2006, http://www.pidegypt.org/africa/jnb.html.
9. See also Jessop (2005) and Pirie (2006 and 2007).

These themes of a proper theory of politics, the state, class interests, the consequences of change, etc, do, however, recur in milder form in the latest literature, reflecting at least implicit dissatisfaction with division between economic and political schools. To a large extent, this is inevitable as any new literature has to negotiate the charge of death, and can only do so by claiming life after death or despite the crisis, changed global circumstances, and the consequences of development itself.

Second, then, revival of the developmental state is notable in the literature that suggests that reports of its death in its classic locations have been exaggerated. It is hardly surprising, under the assault of crisis, neoliberalism and globalisation, that the developmental state should take something of a battering. But the state does remain crucially important, not least in industrial policy, both in riding and restructuring in the wake of the crisis, albeit in changed circumstances. In South Korea, for example, as revealed by Cherry (2005), it has brokered Big Deals amongst the chaebol, or large-scale conglomerates. This has often been against their individual and collective resistance, especially in coordinating investments and restructuring capacity to avoid undue duplication, but equally in a context in which foreign MNCs have now made substantial inroads into the industrial base as a result of the opening up of the economy in the wake of the crisis. This is not so different from the policies adopted by the state in the classic period of the developmental state, although the creation of the chaebol and the absence of, if cooperation with, foreign capital was more to the fore. Is this, then, the death or the continuing evolution of the South Korean developmental state?

Third, though, the life of the developmental state is no longer confined to the nation-state but has been extended to the local or sectoral developmental state. Thus, Ahmed (2006: 97) sees electricity policy in India as a challenge to the clean sweep of neoliberalism imposed by the IFIs, with "the changing nature of state-society ... as new coalitions representing [a] different set of interests come to occupy positions of power at different points of time." Alcañiz (2005) examines how nuclear professionals proved capable of resisting privatisation of the Argentine nuclear energy sector, against the more general dismantling of the welfare-developmental state. Jacobs (2003: 620) suggests that the developmental state view of Japan has been over-centralised, neglecting the role of prefectures so that, "the term 'centralised' no longer appropriately describes the Japanese developmental state." Lim (2003: 233) describes how the internet has allowed popular resistance to the media representation of Indonesia as a "progressive 'developmental state' ... bolstering civil society in its resistance to state and corporate dominance".

For Thun (2006: 4), as admiration for the developmental states of East Asia spread, "China was no exception, and there were many early indications that Chinese policymakers sought to emulate the example of its neighbours: from plans for 'pillar industries' beginning in the mid-1980s to formal industrial policies in the mid-1990s." He offers three ideal types for decentralised state-led development - the local developmental state, the laissez-faire local state, and the centrally controlled state-owned enterprise - arguing for the need to focus on the needs attached to a specific sector, the car industry in his own case study, to locate it within a specific institutional and local context, and highlighting the importance of local government and inter-firm relations. Whilst there are strong first mover advantages to be derived from the local developmental state, it becomes necessary to neutralise the vested interests created in moving to more competitive but resisted external relations, for sources of supply for example, the temporary infant industry argument within the nation as it were.[10]

Further, Howell (2006) provides some account of the differing ways in which the Chinese local developmental state has been broached, and Pieke (2004), an anthropology of the local Chinese developmental state in which the state is seen as part of society and not just as its regulator. For Zhu, J. (2004: 47), "In its transitional phase, China is changing from a centrally controlled economy to a market oriented one. The forces of decentralisation, marketisation and political legitimisation have transformed China's local government into local states with a strong interest in development ... China's local state is a developmental state of its own kind."[11] Zhu (2005) sees the Chinese local developmental state in terms of its command of land and regulation of emerging land markets. Zhu, Y. (2004) raises the issue of the Chinese developmental state in light of labour migration. But Keeley (2003) offers a sectoral variant in terms of the Chinese biotech developmental state, emphasising how first and foremost, there is a need for the state to create an indigenous bio-tech corporation that negotiates across different agencies from foreign corporations through its own ministries to scientists, etc – with the prospect if not guarantee of pro-poor outcomes.

Fascinatingly from a comparative perspective, Wong (2006) offers a study for the same sector for Taiwan, focusing on how the developmental state needs to move beyond catch-up and to play a dual facilitative and coordinating role, the latter having been eroded – "Gone

---

10. For an alternative view, dedicated to Samuel P. Huntington, see Pei (2006) who argues that the Chinese authoritarian but decentralised developmental state will inevitably degenerate into a non-performing predatory state.
11. See also Edin (2005).

are the days when government policymakers in Taiwan could play a 'big' leadership role in guiding industrial transformation, mobilising public and private resources, and know-how around certain targeted technologies," (Wong, 2006: 668). Is this the prospect for the Chinese developmental state too, whether relative to localities or sectors? The explicit treatment of innovation itself is an innovation in the developmental state literature, having previously been presumed to be a consequence of other factors (such as involvement of foreign capital). Nonetheless, treatment of agriculture has remained more or less absent.

A fourth area in which the developmental state literature has made some progress in the most recent period is in paying attention to welfare provision. This has been neglected in the past. On the one hand, the decline of the Latin American developmental state is perceived to be a consequence of the destructive claims made upon it by strengthening the labour movement in particular and populist demands in general. On the other hand, the success of the East Asian developmental states is explained in part by a conventional wisdom of low priority to welfare provision relative to developmental goals and the subordination of labour and broader demands to the requirements of capital. Kasza (2006: 3) offers ample evidence, for example, that Japan has been considered to be a 'welfare laggard.' Indeed:

> The mainstream view is that (1) Japan adopted welfare programmes comparatively late in its economic development; (2) its policies are less generous than those of the major western European nations, if still more open-handed than those of the United States; and (3) company and family play greater roles in welfare provision than they do in other developed countries, and the state a lesser role.

Further, "This half-hearted character of Japan's welfare state is one of the few points on which leftish and non-leftist scholars of Japan seem to agree ... owing to capitalist greed or to developmental [state] priorities," respectively (Kasza, 2006: 4).

Kasza pinpoints this conventional wisdom in order to debunk it. As he concludes, not only in Japan, but also in East Asia more generally, and Taiwan and South Korea in particular, the need for an educated, healthy and highly motivated workforce, "reads the priorities of the developmental state into health [and other] policy" (Kasza, 2006: 124). He demonstrates this both empirically and by critical reference to the welfare state literature. As he correctly observes, "Most leading figures in welfare scholarship today accept Esping-Andersen's basic contention that several distinct types of welfare regime exist" (Kasza, 2006: 6).

Esping-Andersen's (1991) approach is one that identifies three different types of welfare regime – the social democratic, the liberal and the authoritarian (with Scandinavia, UK and Germany as illustrations) – this itself derived from a more general resources-power approach to welfare provision, "the different degrees of control that class-based political parties have exercised over governments." So dominant has this approach been that it has inevitably been extended from a few developed countries to the world as a whole, including East Asia and developing countries. Equally inevitably, such extrapolation of ideal types has floundered as case studies fit more or less uncomfortably within the hypothetical scheme of three welfare regimes, whether across or within countries across different programmes of welfare provision.

These anomalies have been more neglected than observed, not least because they have been subordinated to two other concerns. The first is the response of the Asian developmental states to the crisis of 1997/98. The presumption is that welfare provision would come under assault from the presumed initially low levels of provision. This also explains why, and when, welfare has come within the orbit of the developmental state literature. Second, though, is the impact of the globalisation literature, suggesting much the same conclusion in its neoliberal, and some radical versions, that welfare provision through the state is liable to be undermined by the free international movement of capital and its squeeze upon the nation state's room for manoeuvre in this respect.

The empirical evidence, however, suggests otherwise with expansion of welfare programmes in response to the crisis in some East Asian NICs, most notably South Korea, although this can be explained in terms of the greater need for support prevailing over greater constraints with uncertain outcomes from one country to another (Haggard 2005 and Kwon 2003: 2005), for example. As a result of these theoretical and empirical developments, the conclusion can be drawn, as emphasised by Kasza, that divergence in welfare provision has predominated over convergence. Thus, in looking at the literature on welfare policy in comparative perspective, divergence has carried the day, and this has reinforced the status of the welfare regimes approach and the notion of Japan and east Asia as a distinct regime (and backward for its level of development). For Kasza (2006: 133-34), however, there is no evidence for an East Asian welfare model, since welfare policies are not regionally based there any more than they are across (western) Europe. In contrast, Kasza suggests that a more appropriate conclusion is that the provision of welfare in Japan and more widely in East Asia is not exceptional compared to elsewhere, nor homogenous within.

To a large extent, this conforms with my own critical take on the Esping-Andersen and the welfare regime literature, Fine (2002 2005).

Leaving aside an analytical convergence upon the new welfare economics, in which the state and individuals play games with one another in a context of asymmetric information, my dissatisfaction with the approach is because of its undue generalisation across different welfare programmes within and across countries. This critique has two elements. First, account must be taken of the differences in the nature of what is provided – health, education, water, unemployment benefit, pensions, housing, etc, are all distinctive in what they constitute and how they are provided. There can be no presumption that one, or other, or a mix of three welfare regimes will address their particularities. Second, by the same token, provision will be both country and programme specific, reflecting economic, political and ideological factors as well as the nature of the service itself.[12]

As a result, in lieu of the welfare regimes approach, I have suggested what I have termed a public service system of provision approach, pssop, to welfare and social and economic infrastructure more generally, one that focuses on the material culture attached to welfare across specific programmes and countries, Fine (2002; 2009a; b) and (Bayliss and Fine, 2008). In a sense, this is to push against an open door since there is a longstanding tradition of examining the health, education, housing and water systems, etc. To a large extent, though, such a systemic approach has been squeezed out by the pincer movement furnished by neoliberalism (and a one market-delivery model fits all) and the welfare regimes approach which is almost as insensitive to differing programmes of delivery as opposed to the diverse balance of politics and resources that is supposed to underpin them.

Significantly, then, there is the welcome prospect of the developmental state literature critically interrogating the welfare regime approach as it begins to address welfare provision more fully and accurately. China, the latest developmental state, offers a significant case study. Guan (2005), for example, points to the tensions involved in Chinese welfare policy, a previous duality between urban and rural provision, with state-owned enterprises serving as a pillar for the former. But state-owned enterprises are being displaced and Guan concludes that, "two decades of social policy reform can be summarised as a transition from the traditional state enterprises model to a 'societalised' model, form a pure welfare service system to a marketisation service model and from a universal welfare to a selective welfare model" (Guan, 2005: 252). But, in his conclusion, he is forced to qualify these generalisations since, "for political stability social welfare

---

12. A third element concerns the context-specific construction of the meaning of welfare itself both to those who provide and to those who are provided.

decline cannot go too far, and needs to be strengthened in some specific fields ... a slowing down in welfare reduction and even some policy reversal after the late 1990s" (Guan, 2005: 255). Yet, partly prompted by the SARS crisis from 2003, the Chinese government is already proposing a total reform of the health system, the leadership potentially choosing to adopt the UK National Health Service model in the National People's Congress of March, 2007, certainly to undertake provision based on the ultimate responsibility of the central state.[13] Similar moves are on the agenda for education but outcomes are liable to depend on the nature of each service involved and the continuing tensions within Chinese development, rather than to follow from a given model derived and imposed from study of best international practice.

South Africa as case study

At this point, across developmental state, industrial policy, welfare provision and growth, a single conclusion is being drawn concerning the need for country and sector specific analysis. This does, however, need to be located within an understanding of an evolving system of capital accumulation with its attendant configuration of shifting economic and political interests. Yet, South Africa had not attracted much attention from those seeking to pin the label of developmental state upon it. It did not really hit the radar of my last previous review of the literature even though it has only just been published. Interestingly, the most recent academic literature has offered some exception to the rule of neglect of South Africa as developmental state but it still remains, as yet, limited by search of academic journals alone.[14] A search by Google offers disproportionately greater rewards, with my downloading being brought to an end on the two-hundredth entry or so that at last had reached developmental state as an element in the research of South African child psychologists, a syndrome I have previously encountered in literature searches.

The reason for this pattern in the literature is that the developmental state has sprung into South African discourse from the political arena. Trevor Manuel (2004), for example, cites Sen extensively and in grasping the developmental state can even be seen as groping towards the pssop approach in lecturing senior public sector managers on their

---

13. 'We will phase in a basic health care system that covers both urban and rural areas,' Report on the Implementation of the 2006 Plan for National Economic and Social Development and on the 2007 Draft Plan for National Economic and Social Development, Fifth Session of the Tenth National People's Congress, 5 March 2007.
14. See also Luiz (2002) and Lemon (2005) and Tsheola (2002), the latter deploying the concept casually.

responsibilities in delivering through increased public (welfare) expenditure.[15] Manuel's text is heavily quoted verbatim in President Mbeki's Budget Speech for 2006. And the developmental state has appeared in speeches from a range of Ministers over the last couple of years.[16] Further, in opening its next edition, Southall (2006: xvii) reports that:[17]

> In the introduction to the *State of the Nation: South Africa 2004-2005*, the editors noted that 'the African National Congress (ANC) is in the throes of shifting from the Growth, Employment and Redistribution (GEAR) strategy to a more interventionist, developmental state'.

Further, they later reveal how the developmental state in principle is to be complemented by plans to launch a massive public sector investment programme, with state-owned enterprises to become, citing Mbeki (2005: xix) 'drivers of growth and development'. I cannot resist the temptation to observe what a remarkable if belated acceptance this is of the MERG (1993) programme, see below, and also to quote my own commentary of almost ten years ago, Fine (1998a):

> Currently, GEAR is generally and rightly, if not openly, admitted to be an empty shell as far as policymaking and judgement of performance are concerned. The only interesting questions in this respect are how long can GEAR hold out as official ideological talisman and what will replace it in substance and rhetoric. These will be open to dispute for which clarity on the nature and dynamic of the South African economy is of crucial importance for progressive outcomes.

---

15. See also Soobrayan, B., 'Reflections on SA's Perspective on Capacity Development for the Developmental State', Director General, South African Management Development Institute, Presentation to the CAPAM High Level Seminar, In Pursuit of Excellence: Developing & Maintaining a High-Quality Public Service.
http://www.capam.org/pdfs/Soobrayan_SAMDI.pdf.
16. For example, for education,
http://www.chet.org.za/issues/PandorAcademicFreedom05.doc; for science and technology, http://www.dst.gov.za/media/speeches.php?id=208&print=1; for public service and administration,
http://www.info.gov.za/speeches/2004/04052714151001.htm; and for the Presidency, http://www.progressive-
governance.net/uploadedFiles/Events/Events/Pahad%20speech.pdf.
17. But note that the developmental state hardly appears at all in the rest of the volume.

The developmental state, at least in part, seems to be the answer to the first question but what of the nature and dynamic of the South African economy?

For this, we are not liable to find answers from the politicians. Inevitably, the posture they adopt is one within the economics school, of the appropriate balance and redirection of policy with little or no critical assessment of capacity or willingness to deliver, bureaucracy and administration apart, in light of underlying economic and political interests. Equally inevitably, and commendably, COSATU and the CPSA have both welcomed the shift in rhetoric but with some suspicion, given experience of the last decade or more, of what will be delivered and how, Makgetla (2005) for COSATU. Southall (2006: xxvii) quotes Jeremy Cronin, Deputy General Secretary of the SACP, "there is now a growing inter-ANC alliance consensus on the need for a strong, developmental state" but observes that, the latter's "present popularity may well be that it can serve as an ideological glue to hold the Alliance together."

In short, when it comes the developmental state, how long or thick is such a piece of string and how long does its glue remain sticky. The notion might be abandoned as rapidly as it has been taken up, given that the fluidity between political and academic (and other) discourses in South Africa is remarkably extensive and rapid, possibly uniquely and troublingly so, in so far as politicians may then set scholarly agendas (and selectively vice-versa) and intellectual independence and dissent is heavily squeezed if not circumscribed.

There has been a flush of workshops, conferences and academic papers on the developmental state and South Africa.[18] For Swilling et al (2004), South Africa even aspired to be a developmental state from the mid-1990s (although no evidence is presented for this and I suspect there is little) but failed to realise this ambition. But nor did it degenerate in this account to the opposite extreme of a "corporate-led globalisation plus the need to accommodate a new black elite [that] resulted in neoliberal economic policies that conformed to the global 'Washington Consensus' about 'best practice'" (Swilling, 2004: 17).

This view is also questionable since no adjustment under the Washington Consensus let alone the post Washington Consensus, then waiting in the wings, has ever conformed to the neoliberal template in its pure form. Rather, discretion and local 'ownership' to a greater or lesser degree have always been present in the interventions dictated by the IFIs in practice. What is apparent is that in a few years, the ANC-led

---

18. See especially Gelb (2006), Freund (2006) and Hassim (2005) the latter only pegging gender and welfare to the developmental state. See also Akoojee and McGrath (2005) in context of education and training.

Government of National Unity had, through GEAR, adopted policies that were more or less indistinguishable from those being proposed by the IFIs and even from those put forward by the previous apartheid government as its New Economic Model.

Swilling et al suggest that the last decade or more has been marked by an interregnum lying somewhere between, or adrift of, developmental state and Washington Consensus for the "priority was to dismantle the uniquely configured *apartheid state system* that was deeply rooted in South Africa's economy of racial capitalism" (Swilling et al, 2004: 16). Most important, they suggest that the foundation has now been provided for greater integration and coordination of policy in the future, for a developmental state to emerge, so that with black empowerment "it remains to be seen whether ... [such] strategies, coupled to state-funded investment strategies, will manage to break white control of investment decision-making quickly enough to ensure private sector investment levels climb back up over the 15 per cent of GDP mark" (Swilling et al, 2004: 74). Further, in terms of social expenditure, they suggest, "The results have been mixed, with disappointingly low levels of expenditure due mainly to a failure to adequately manage the institutionalisation of these various strategies and approaches. A shortage of funds was never the problem" (Swilling et al, 2004: 75).

In a companion piece, Swilling and Breda (2005) assess the record of such institutionalisation more closely, concluding that a 'developmental state' (their own inverted commas) is seen to be in operation over the first ten post-apartheid years, not least in proliferation of "innovative institutional experiments aimed at capturing and directing funds into developmental and anti-poverty programmes ... [but] the most important contribution that many of these experiments may have made is to institutional learning about what it takes to build institutions that can make a lasting developmental impact on the ground" (Swilling and Breda, 2004: 88). Thus, the benefits that might have been gained are to learn about institutions, institutionalising trade-offs between welfare and development, and institutional capacity itself (Swilling and Breda, 2004: 130).

Nit-picking aside, there is much to commend these analyses other than that they are at least ten years too late, without explaining why. For much longer, the power of South African corporations has been highlighted in the literature. My own take on this, from almost twenty years ago, was to characterise the South African economy as a mineral-energy complex, MEC. Here is an account taken more or less verbatim from an unpublished paper of ten years ago, Fine (1998a).

What is the MEC and what are its current structure and dynamics?

As discussed in detail in Fine and Rustomjee (1997), the MEC is to be understood as a system of accumulation specific to South Africa and its history. At the simplest level, it comprises a core set of activities organised in and around energy and mining. Contrary to majority opinion, these core sectors continue to carry a, if not the, major determining role in the economy. Further, they have been attached institutionally to a highly concentrated structure of corporate capital, state-owned enterprises and other organisations such as the IDC which have themselves reflected underlying structure and balance of economic and political power.

In the 1930s, there was what has been termed a disjuncture between the economic power of mining capitalists and the political power of Afrikaners. The post-war period has witnessed the erosion of this disjuncture in a particular way. During the 1950s, Afrikaner finance capital was built up. In the 1960s, it incorporated ownership of productive capital, not least in mining itself. Until this point, industrialisation only proceeded on a piecemeal basis according to limited diversification out of the MEC core sectors and import-substituting industrialisation for consumer goods under heavy protection. Notably absent was vertical integration of and between the two. This reflected a lack of commitment on the part of the mining houses, lack of resources on the part of Afrikaner capital, and the political impossibility of the state adopting industrial policy to support large-scale capital along a programme of industrialisation.

In the 1970s, with the creation of large-scale Afrikaner capital and its integration with the corporate sector as a whole, coherent economic policy became possible for the first time. However, the decade was marked by oil and gold price increases. Economic policy became heavily oriented around a state-sponsored investment programme to expand the core sectors. At the same time, South Africa's conglomerate structure was further consolidated as profits from mining were deployed through the financial system to gain ownership across many sectors. By the 1980s, with the decline both in oil and gold prices, the apartheid system was in crisis, and investment stagnated, precluding a programme for industrialisation.

The current structure and dynamic of the MEC has changed again. For it is heavily dependent upon the globalising strategies of South African conglomerates.[19] They are little prepared to commit their

---

19. Note that between 1994 and 1999, South Africa's (legal) outflow of foreign direct investment was R77 billion compared with an inflow of R55 billion, placing the GEAR

financial resources to domestic investment in industry, and they are
equally concerned to integrate their domestic operations with their
international interests. There is no reason why these should coincide
with the imperatives of generating viable domestic industry, given the
age of capital stock, lack of vertical integration, lack of intermediate and
capital goods, and a general pre-disposition to oppose interventionist
policy in case it becomes more radical. By the same token, there is
extreme pressure for the removal of exchange controls on domestic
corporations in order to be able to engage in capital flight. The ethnic
divisions between white capitalists have been resolved. It would be
unfortunate if those with black capitalists focused primarily on
promoting small business and creating a share for a minority of blacks
within big business without unduly affecting the scale and scope of
domestic industrialisation.

The macroeconomic policy associated with GEAR for stabilising the
economy had the effect of underpinning the capacity for capital flight,
exposing the economy to vulnerability however well or badly it
performed, since success would prompt pressure for relaxation of
controls and failure for increased austerity on government expenditure
and intervention (often excused by appeal to responsible management
and/or lack of capacity). This account was complemented in another
paper by specifying detailed strategic considerations for formulating
industrial policy, Fine (1997), the summary of which appears as an
appendix to Fine (2007).[20] If South Africa was to become a
developmental state, at least in the industrial arena, this suggested how.

Further, in the field of welfare, I was responsible for the social and
economic infrastructure section of the MERG Report (1993), covering
health, housing, electrification and schooling as pssops (although the full
term was not yet in use then).[21] Whilst Swilling et al make no reference
to this report, it fully anticipates their conclusions arguing that the
greatest constraint on welfare provision would be institutional capacity
to deliver. This is unless, as has indeed occurred by a more circumspect
interpretation of the evidence of a decade of institutional learning, other
constraints were unnecessarily imposed such as the imposition of user

---

focus on attracting FDI into perspective. Further, of the inflow, two-thirds was for
acquisition as opposed to new investments, one third alone for the purchase of privatised
energy and telecom facilities, Heese (1999). Further, even this poor record has been
based upon the unusual contribution made by Malaysia which came second in volume
behind the United States but ahead of the United Kingdom! This is due to political and
economic motives that are not liable to be sustained, Padayachee and Valodia (1999).
20. See also Fine (1998b) for a case study of the steel industry.
21. I find it amusing to point out that this Report, published in the same year, also took
the same title as Putnam's (1993) study of Italy that launched his career as a leading
social capitalist.

charges, and market- and finance-led imperatives in provision more generally. Once again, these perspectives from my earlier work are available from an unpublished contribution of more than ten years standing, again reproduced as an appendix to Fine (2007).

As has been recognised within South Africa, what will be made of the developmental state remains open and to be contested but that the notion has arisen at all reflects both progress and potential although, in returning to the theme of the complex and shifting reactions between ideology, scholarship and policy, these have to be negotiated and are not guaranteed. With a sense of déjà vu, I am reminded of the rise of the notions of globalisation and of social capital, Fine (2004d). The first has been won away from neoliberal dogma, that the state is withering away under market forces and this is to be welcomed. The rise of the developmental state in South Africa is in part testimony to this victory. Social capital, heavily promoted by the World Bank and highly influential within South Africa, if not so much for Africa more generally, is much less amenable to broader, progressive capture.[22] Indeed, it has now been abandoned by the World Bank social capitalists, accepting the criticisms made in retrospect but justifying themselves in having shifted the social content of the Bank's economic agenda. Whether the developmental state in South Africa turns out more like globalisation or more like social capital remains to be seen and negotiated, but my own personal inclination and perspective is one in which scholarly integrity should not be sacrificed for political opportunism with South Africans particularly susceptible to swings in thinking in conformity to political and economic imperatives, from Freedom Charter, through RDP and GEAR to the developmental state.

I fear I have cast myself into a Cassandra-like figure, a dog that did bark in the night but was only murdered in the sense of not being heard. On the other hand, in South Africa, the creation of a developmental state is, to coin a far from subtle reference to Sherlock Holmes, a dog that did not bark in the night. This silence in the past offers an admirable clue to a deeper understanding of the country's predicament and the failure to address it. It remains to be seen whether the shift in rhetoric to the developmental state in South Africa will shed bright light where there was night and offer a more dogged attempt to address the deeply entrenched inequality and inequity inherited from the past.

But I want to close on an empirically humbling note for all concerned in the developmental state debate. Three features stand out from the experience of the successful east Asian NICs, although they are rarely observed and I exaggerate them. First, they had no economists. Second,

---

22. On social capital and (South) Africa, see Fine (2001b, 2004a and b and 2011).

they had no notion that they were developmental states until they were told so by western social scientists. And, third, the east Asian melt-down hit at the point when returning American-trained economists reached critical numbers and influence. I leave you to draw your own conclusion, although replicability does not seem to be on the agenda in these three respects.

References

Ahmed, W., 2006 Global Discourses and Local Politics in the Production of Power Policy in India. *Development*, 49(3), pp.94-100.

Akoojee, S. and McGrath, S., 2005. Post-Basic Education and Training and Poverty Reduction in South Africa: Progress to 2004 and Vision to 2014, no 2, October, Centre of African Studies, University of Edinburgh.

Alcañiz, I., 2005. Defeating Welfare Retrenchment: Privatisation and Conflict in the Argentine Nuclear Energy Sector. *New Political Science*, 27(3), pp.331-44.

Ashman, S. Fine, B. and Newman, S., 2010. The Developmental State and Post-Liberation South Africa. In J. February and N. Misra, eds. 2010. *Testing Democracy: Which Way is South Africa Headed?* Cape Town: IDASA Publishing.

Bayliss, K. and Fine, B. eds. 2007. *Whither the Privatisation Experiment? Electricity and Water Sector Reform in Sub-Saharan Africa.* Basingstoke: Palgrave MacMillan.

Bayliss, K. Fine, B. and van Waeyenberge, E. eds., 2011. *The World Bank and Neo-Liberalism and Development Research.* London: Pluto Press, forthcoming.

Bebbington, A., 2004. Social Capital and Development Studies 1: Critique, Debate, Progress? *Progress in Development Studies*, 4(4), pp.343-49.

Bebbington, A. Guggenheim, S. Olson, E. and Woolcock, M., 2004. Grounding Discourse in Practice: Exploring Social Capital Debates at the World Bank. *Journal of Development Studies*, 40(5), pp.33-64.

Bebbington, A. Woolcock, M. Guggenheim, S. and Olson, E. eds., 2006. *The Search for Empowerment: Social Capital as Idea and Practice at the World Bank*, Bloomfield: Kumarian Press.

Boyd, R. and Ngo, T., 2005. *Emancipating the Political Economy of Asia from the Growth Paradigm.* In R. Boyd and T. Ngo, eds. 2005. *Asian States: Beyond the Developmental Perspective*, London: Routledge Curzon.

Boyd, R. and Ngo, T. eds., 2005. *Asian States: Beyond the Developmental Perspective*, London: Routledge Curzon.

Buhlungu, S. et al., 2006. *State of the Nation: South Africa, 2005-2006*, Cape Town: HSRC Press.

Cherry, J., 2005. 'Big Deal' or Big Disappointment? The Continuing Evolution of the South Korean Developmental State. *The Pacific Review*, 18(3), pp.327-54.

Deaton, A. et al., 2006. *An Evaluation of World Bank Research, 1998-2005.* http://siteresources.worldbank.org/DEC/Resources/84797-1109362238001/726454-1164121166494/RESEARCH-EVALUATION-2006-Main-Report.pdf.

Doner, R. et al., 2005. Systematic Vulnerability and the Origins of Developmental States: Northeast and Southeast Asia in Comparative Perspective. *International Organisation*, 59(2), pp.327-62.

Edigheji, O., 2005. A Democratic Developmental State in Africa? A Concept Paper. Centre for Policy Studies, Research Report 105, Johannesburg.

Edigheji, O. ed., 2010. *Constructing a Democratic Developmental State in South Africa: Potentials and Challenges.* Cape Town: Human Sciences Research Council Press.

Edin, M., 2005. Local State Structure and Developmental Incentives in China. In R. Boyd and T. Ngo, eds. 2005. *Asian States: Beyond the Developmental Perspective,* London: Routledge Curzon.

February, J. and Misra, N. eds., 2010. *Testing Democracy: Which Way is South Africa Headed?* Cape Town: IDASA Publishing.

Fine, B., 1992. Linkage and the State: The Case of South Korea. SOAS Department of Economics, Working Paper, no 2.

Fine, B., 1997. Industrial Policy and South Africa: A Strategic View. NIEP Occasional Paper Series, no 5, Johannesburg: National Institute for Economic Policy.

Fine, B., 1998a. Industrial Policy Revisited – An Exercise in Self-Indulgence. TIPS Conference, September, mimeo.

Fine, B., 1998b. Vertical Relations in the South African Steel Industry. NIEP Occasional Paper Series, no 13, Johannesburg: National Institute for Economic Policy.

Fine, B., 1999. The Developmental State is Dead - Long Live Social Capital? *Development and Change,* 30(1), pp.1-19.

Fine, B., 2001a. *Social Capital versus Social Theory: Political Economy and Social Science at the Turn of the Millennium.* London: Routledge.

Fine, B., 2001b. It Ain't Social, It Ain't Capital and It Ain't Africa. *Studia Africana,* 13, pp.18-33.

Fine, B., 2002. *The World of Consumption: The Material and Cultural Revisited.* London: Routledge.

Fine, B., 2003. Social Capital: The World Bank's Fungible Friend. *Journal of Agrarian Change,* 3(4), pp.586-603.

Fine, B., 2004a. Social Capital for Africa? *Transformation,* 53, pp.29-52.

Fine, B., 2004b. Contesting Social Capital: A Response to Elke Zuern. *Transformation,* 55, pp.113-15.

Fine, B., 2004c. Beyond the Developmental State: Towards a Political Economy of Development. In Hirakawa et al., eds. 2004. *Beyond Market-Driven Development: A New Stream of Political Economy of Development,* Tokyo: Nihon Hyoron Sha (in Japanese, with English version in Lapavitsas and Noguchi. eds., 2005.

Fine, B., 2004d. Examining the Idea of Globalisation and Development Critically: What Role for Political Economy? *New Political Economy,* 9(2), pp.213-31.

Fine, B., 2005. Social Policy and Development: Social Capital as Point of Departure. In T. Mkandawire, ed. 2005. *Social Policy in a Development Context.* UNRISD, Basingstoke: Palgrave MacMillan.

Fine, B., 2006. The Developmental State and the Political Economy of Development. In K. Jomo and B. Fine, eds. 2006. *The New Development Economics: After the Washington Consensus,* Delhi: Tulika, and London: Zed Press.

Fine, B., 2007. State, Development and Inequality: The Curious Incidence of the Developmental State in the Night-Time. Paper presented to Sanpad Conference, Durban, June 26-30.

Fine, B., 2009a. Social Policy and the Crisis of Neoliberalism. Prepared for Conference on 'The Crisis of Neoliberalism in India: Challenges and Alternatives', Tata Institute of Social Sciences (TISS) Mumbai and International Development Economics Associates (IDEAs), 13-15 March 2009.
    http://www.networkideas.org/ideasact/jan09/ia27_International_Conference.htm

Fine, B., 2009b. Financialisation and Social Policy. Prepared for Conference on 'Social and Political Dimensions of the Global Crisis: Implications for Developing Countries', Geneva, UNRISD, 12–13 November 2009.
https://eprints.soas.ac.uk/7984.

Fine, B., 2010a. *Theories of Social Capital: Researchers Behaving Badly.* London: Pluto Press.

Fine, B., 2010b. Can South Africa Be a Developmental State? In O. Edigheji, ed. 2010. *Constructing a Democratic Developmental State in South Africa: Potentials and Challenges.* Cape Town: Human Sciences Research Council Press.

Fine, B., 2011. Social Capital and Health. In Bayliss et al. eds. *The World Bank and Neo-Liberalism and Development Research.* London: Pluto Press, forthcoming.

Fine, B. and Rustomjee, Z., 1997. *South Africa's Political Economy: From Minerals-Energy Complex to Industrialisation,* Johannesburg: Wits University Press.

Freund, B., 2006. South Africa: A Developmental State?
http://www.nu.ac.za/ccs/files/Freund   per   cent20Developmental   per cent20State.pdf.

Gelb, S., 2006. A South African Developmental State: What Is Possible? Presented at the Harold Wolpe Memorial Trust's Tenth Anniversary Colloquium.
http://www.wolpetrust.org.za/conferences/colloquium/gelb.pdf.

Guan, X., 2005. China's Social Policy: Reform and Development in the Context of Marketisation and Globalisation. In Kwon, ed. 2005. *Transforming the Developmental State in East Asia,* Basingstoke: Houndmills.

Hassim, S., 2005. Gender, Welfare and the Developmental State in South Africa. UNRISD Project on Gender and Social Policy.
http://www.sarpn.org.za/documents/d0001335/index.php.

Hee, L. and Ooi, G., 2005. The Politics of Public Space Planning in Singapore. *Planning Perspectives,* 18(1), pp. 79-103.

Heese, K., 1999. Foreign Direct Investment in South Africa (1994-1999) – Confronting Globalisation. Paper presented to TIPS Annual Forum, Johannesburg, September.

Hirakawa, H. et al. eds. 2004. *Beyond Market-Driven Development: A New Stream of Political Economy of Development,* Tokyo: Nihon Hyoron Sha (in Japanese).

Hirata, K., 2002. Whither the Developmental State? The Growing Role of NGOs in Japanese Aid Policymaking. *Journal of Comparative Policy Analysis,* 4(2), pp.165-88.

Howell, J., 2006. Reflections on the Chinese State. *Development and Change,* 37(2), pp. 273-97.

Jacobs, A., 2003. Devolving Authority and Expanding Autonomy in Japanese Prefectures and Municipalities. *Governance,* 16(4), pp. 601-23.

Jessop, B., 2005. A Regulationist and State-Theoretical Analysis. In R. Boyd and T. Ngo, eds. 2005. *Asian States: Beyond the Developmental Perspective,* London: Routledge Curzon.

Jha, P., 2004. India: From Developmental to Predator State. In S. Munshi and B. Abraham, eds. 2004. *Good Governance, Democratic Societies and Globalisation.* New Delhi: Sage Publications.

Jomo, K. and Fine, B. eds. 2006. *The New Development Economics: After the Washington Consensus,* Delhi: Tulika, and London: Zed Press.

Kasza, G., 2006. *One World of Welfare: Japan in Comparative Perspective,* Ithaca: Cornell University Press.

Keeley, J., 2003. The Biotech Developmental State? Investigating the Chinese Gene Revolution. IDS Working Paper, no 207, Institute of Development Studies, University of Sussex.

Kwon, H-J., 2003. Transforming the Developmental State in the Republic of Korea, Economic and Social Commission for Western Asia. ESCWA, United Nations, Social Policy Series, no 6.

Kwon, H-J., 2005. An Overview of the Study: The Developmental Welfare State and Policy Reforms in East Asia. In Kwon, ed. 2005.

Kwon, H-J. ed., 2005. Transforming the Developmental State in East Asia, Basingstoke: Houndmills.

Lapavitsas, C. and Noguchi, M. ed., 2005. *Beyond Market-Driven Development: Drawing on the Experience of Asia and Latin America*, London: Routledge.

Lee, S., 2004. The Politics of the Asian Financial Crisis in Malaysia and South Korea', Journal of the Asia Pacific Economy, 9(1), pp.10-31.

Lemon, A., 2005. Shifting Geographies of Inclusion and Exclusion: Secondary Education in Pietermaritzburg, South Africa. *African Affairs*, 104(414), pp.69-96.

Lim M., 2003. From War-Net to Net-War: The Internet and Resistance Identities in Indonesia. *International Information & Library Review*, 35(2), pp.233-48.

Lockwood, M., 2005. *The State They're In: An Agenda for International Action on Poverty in Africa*. Bourton on Dunsmore: ITDG Publishing.

Luiz J., 2002. South African State Capacity and Post-Apartheid Economic Reconstruction. *International Journal of Social Economics*, 29(8), pp. 594-614.

MacLean, S. et al. eds., 2006. *A Decade of Human Security: Global Governance and New Multilateralisms*. Aldershot: Ashgate.

Makgetla, N., 2005. A Developmental State for South Africa? Discussion Paper for Cosatu's Central Committee.

Manuel, T., 2004. Budgeting Challenges in the Developmental State. Speech by the Minister of Finance at Senior Management Service Conference in Cape Town, 20 September. http://www.treasury.gov.za/speech/2004092001.pdf.

Mbeki, T., 2005. Address of the President of South Africa to the Second Joint Sitting of the Third Democratic Parliament. Cape Town, 11 February.
http://www.info.gov.za/speeches/2005/05021110501001.htm.

MERG. 1993. *Making Democracy Work: A Framework for Macroeconomic Policy in South Africa*. Cape Town: CDS.

Mkandawire, T. ed., 2005. *Social Policy in a Development Context*. UNRISD, Basingstoke: Palgrave MacMillan.

Munshi, S. and Abraham, B. eds., 2004. *Good Governance, Democratic Societies and Globalisation*. New Delhi: Sage Publications.

Nabudere, D., 2006. The Development State, Democracy and the Glocal Society in Africa. Presented to the Conference on 'Investment Choices for Education in Africa', Faculty of Education, University of Witwatersrand, 20 September.

Negoita, M., 2006. The Social Bases of Development: Hungary and Romania in Comparative Perspective. *Socio-Economic Review*, 4(2), pp. 209-38.

Ooi, G., 2005. The Role of the Developmental State and Interethnic Relations in Singapore. *Asian Ethnicity*, 6(2), pp.109-20.

Padayachee, V. and Valodia, I., 1999. Malaysian Investment in South Africa: South-South Relations in a Globalising Environment? Paper presented to TIPS Annual Forum, Johannesburg, September.

Painter, M., 2005. Transforming the Administrative State: Reform in Hong Kong and the Future of the Developmental State. *Public Administration Review*, 65(3), pp. 335-46.

Pei, M., 2006. *China's Trapped Transition: The Limits of Developmental Autocracy*. Cambridge: Harvard University Press.

Pieke, F., 2004. Contours of an Anthropology of the Chinese State: Political Structure, Agency and Economic Development in Rural China. *Journal of the Royal Anthropological Institute*, 10(3), pp.517-38.

Pirie, I., 2006. Economic Crisis and the Construction of a Neoliberal Regulatory Regime in Korea. *Competition and Change*, 10(1), pp.49-71.

Pirie, I., 2008. *The Korean Developmental State: From Dirigisme to Neoliberalism*. London: Routledge, forthcoming.

Putnam, R., 1993a. *Making Democracy Work: Civic Traditions in Modern Italy*. Princeton: Princeton University Press.

Rigg, J., 2002. Of Miracles and Crises: (Re)Intepretations of Growth and Decline in East and Southeast Asia. *Asia Pacific Viewpoint*, 43(2), pp.137-56.

Shaw, T., 2006. Two Africas? Two Ugandas? An African 'Democratic Developmental State'? Or another 'Failed State'? In MacLean et al., eds. 2006.

Sindzingre, A., 2006. Financing the Developmental State: Tax and Revenue Issues. Presentation at Overseas Development Institute, London. http://www.odi.org.uk/speeches/states_06/5thApril/Presentations/SindzingreDev elopmentalStateTaxationODI06.pdf.

Southall, R., 2006. Introduction: Can South Africa Be a Developmental State? In S. Buhlungu et al., 2006. *State of the Nation: South Africa, 2005-2006*, Cape Town: HSRC Press.

Swilling, M. and van Breda, J., 2005. Institutionalising the Developmental State: The Case of the 'Special Funds'. *Centre for Civil Society, Economic Policy and Poverty Alleviation Report Series*, Report no 4.

Swilling, M. et al., 2004. Economic Policy-Making in a Developmental State: Review of the South African Government's Poverty and Development Approaches, 1994-2004. *Centre for Civil Society, Economic Policy and Poverty Alleviation Report Series*, Report no 3.

Thun, E., 2006. *Changing Lanes in China: Foreign Direct Investment, Local Governments, and Auto Sector Development*. Cambridge: Cambridge University Press.

Tsheola, J., 2002. Basic Needs in the Northern Province and South Africa's Globalisation Agenda. *African Development Review*, 14(1), pp.48–74.

Wade, R., 1996. Japan, the World Bank, and the Art of Paradigm Maintenance: The East Asian Miracle in Political Perspective. *New Left Review*, 217, pp.3-37.

Wong, J., 2006. Technovation in Taiwan: Implications for Industrial Governance', *Governance*, 19(4), pp.651-72.

World Bank. 1993. *The East Asian Miracle: Economic Growth and Public Policy*. A World Bank Policy Research Report. Oxford: Oxford University Press.

Zhu J., 2004. Local Developmental State and Order in China's Urban Development during Transition. *International Journal of Urban and Regional Research*, 28(2), pp.424-47.

Zhu, J., 2005. A Transitional Institution for the Emerging Land Market in Urban China. *Urban Studies*, 42(8), pp.1369-90.

Zhu, T., 2002. Developmental States and Threat Perceptions in North-East Asia. *Conflict, Security and Development*, 2(1), pp.5-29.

Zhu, Y., 2004. Workers, Unions and the State: Migrant Workers in China's Labour-Intensive Foreign Enterprises. *Development and Change*, vol 35, (5), pp.1011-36.

5.

The proper subject for poverty research is inequality
Andries du Toit

Introduction

This chapter explores some key challenges facing poverty research in
South Africa today. Although there have been real advances in poverty
studies, important challenges lie ahead. In particular, it argues that a key
challenge for poverty researchers is the need to go beyond the limits of
what Alice O'Connor has called official American poverty knowledge: a
theoretically orthodox, politically circumscribed and institutionally
enforced 'normal science' — exported globally through the dominance of
institutions like the World Bank — which marginalises and ignores
other, more critical ways of looking at poverty (O'Connor, 2006).

This argument engages with the wider international, theoretical and
methodological issues in the field of poverty studies and development
research, but it is also concerned with local specificity. For although
South African poverty research is powerfully shaped by international
trends, buzzwords, paradigms and orthodoxies, it has also been
influenced by the local idiosyncrasies of the South African political
context. These idiosyncrasies have, among other things, ensured that
poverty studies in South Africa have an *ambiguous* nature: they are
unable *either* to satisfactorily address *or* to entirely evade politically
contentious questions about the nature of 'durable inequality' and
economic marginalisation.

This ambiguity means that mainstream South African poverty
discourse at the moment contains important opportunities for engaging
critically with orthodox theories of economic growth and development
— but at the time of writing this critical engagement is only happening
patchily. A key underlying thread in this chapter is an argument that
poverty studies in South Africa can be deepened and strengthened
through revisiting some debates from the recent past, and by being
reconnected with important earlier threads of scholarly enquiry into the
nature and sources of inequality in South Africa.

The chapter begins with a brief discussion of the ambiguous political
nature of dominant approaches to poverty studies in South Africa. This is
followed by a brief description of some of the ways in which dominant
poverty discourses work to depoliticise discourse about poverty in
South Africa, and the consequences of this dominance for the discursive
construction of poverty. This sets the scene for a brief discussion of the
state of 'poverty knowledge' in South Africa, and of the extent to which

South African poverty studies have managed to break with O'Connor's problematic 'normal science.' Here the focus will be to look at some of the more important ways in which poverty researchers have explored how structural factors, social relations and social process contribute to the perpetuation of deep and entrenched inequality. The chapter closes with a brief description of a research agenda by which these advances may be continued, to create space for a more critical approach to poverty studies in South Africa.

Depoliticising poverty research

Since the transition to democracy, research on poverty has expanded and deepened considerably in South Africa. South African scholarship on poverty has indeed moved far from the days when the state could not be bothered to collect data about the wellbeing or ill-being about the majority of its subjects (Seekings, 2002), and when concern about poverty, and about understanding its depth and scope, was the preserve of a small number of relatively marginal academics situated in the universities (Seekings, 2002; see also Wilson & Ramphele, 1989). Poverty now occupies a central place in the national political agenda.

A central role here has been played by an explosion in quantitative research described elsewhere by Jeremy Seekings (Seekings, 2002), starting from SALDRU's 1993/1994 Project for Statistics on Living Standards and Development (PSLSD); its elabouration into a panel dataset by Waves 2 and 3 of the Kwazulu-Natal Income Dynamics Study (KIDS); and official surveys such as the October Household Study (OHS) and the Incomes and Expenditures Survey (IES). In addition, the government has launched a range of additional data collection exercises specifically geared at better understanding the nature and dynamics of poverty. Thus, the South African Presidency has initiated a National Income Dynamics Study (NIDS) while Statistics South Africa has launched its own 'Living Conditions Survey' intended to provide detailed information about well-being and poverty indicators (Stats SA, 2008). In addition, there have been a number of smaller area-based academic studies, focussing in greater detail on one or other aspect of poverty in a particular region: prominent examples are the Cape Area Panel Study and the Agincourt Health Demographic Surveillance System.[1]

Useful as these advances are, they also involve some significant limits. Consider in more detail the centrality of poverty as an item on the

---

1. See the Agincourt Health Demographic Surveillance System.
http://www.caps.uct.ac.za
http://web.wits.ac.za/Academic/Health/PublicHealth/Agincourt/

national agenda, and the rise in the importance and productivity of poverty studies. This unquestioned centrality is in itself worth reflecting on. Given the highly divisive policies of the past and the great inequality in the distribution of wealth and incomes in South Africa, one might have expected discussions about the nature of poverty and about policies for addressing it and its consequences to be a matter of intense political division and disagreement. Instead, one of the more remarkable features of the post-Apartheid political scene is the breadth of the national consensus – stretching across most of the formal political spectrum, both on the need *to* address poverty and (for the most part) on the means by which to do so.

Part of the reason obviously lies in the emphasis on consensus and nation-building that characterised the years after 1994; and part of it on the way in which the tripartite alliance between the African National Congress, COSATU and the SACP has affected debate about key strategic alternatives. But it also lies in the nature of the discourse around poverty itself. In these debates, poverty is a concept that appears — on the face of it at least — to be without politics: it is usually presented as a form of unnecessary human suffering all citizens should be against. Though it carries a significant moral charge, the concept seems to be quite amenable to use in apparently value-free, technical discussions that do not require participants to subscribe to particular ideological and political positions.

Poverty discourse in South Africa thus seems to be characterised by a deep ambiguity: discourse analysts would say that poverty talk in South Africa has a 'double logic', or that it operates in two registers at once. On the one hand it draws its appeals to legitimacy, its demands for time, attention and resources — and, indeed, the motivations of many of its practioners — from a distinctive and historically specific moral, political and social context: poverty studies in South Africa need to be understood as a project informed by, and responding to, a plethora of politically charged issues relating to the structural violence of colonial settlement and Apartheid, the deeply entrenched forms of highly racialised inequality that it institutionalised in South African society, the broad based resistance that arose in response to it, and the incontrovertible and widely supported demands for political and social transformation and change articulated by this popular movement.

At the same time, the discourse about poverty in South Africa, as it is articulated by researchers and policymakers, has developed in ways that generally work to dispel and sublimate this political charge, framing poverty in managerial and modernist terms as a problem essentially available to technical solution.[2] Poverty discourse in South Africa, in other words, functions in some ways like an 'anti-politics' machine — the term famously coined by James Ferguson in his analysis of the ways in which development discourse acts to reframe political problems as if they can be understood and resolved in technical terms (Ferguson, 1990).

It is important to recognise that this depoliticising, technicising aspect of South African poverty discourse has had mixed consequences: some of them useful, and others less so. On the one hand, it must be acknowledged that this depoliticisation has allowed wide political co-operation in policy initiatives aimed at addressing poverty, and plays a key role in underpinning public support for anti-poverty initiatives that would otherwise be much more contentious. On the other hand, this depoliticisation vitiates the ability of participants in South African poverty debates to engage effectively with the underlying causal processes and political dynamics that underpin structural poverty and entrench inequality. Most importantly, mainstream poverty discourses, and debates about poverty reduction, often seem characterised by a difficulty in developing a *critical* argument that can relate discussions of poverty in South Africa to an analysis of social relations of power.

Variants of poverty discourse

To understand why, it is important to look more closely at the nature of South African poverty discourse and the frameworks that shape it, and to understand in more detail how the 'depoliticising' effect is accomplished. To begin with, a word is in order about poverty discourse more generally, and the essentially contested nature of poverty as a concept. This is something that is often not recognised — not even in contemporary discussions about the politics of poverty concepts: these discussions often proceed as if all that is at stake is a narrow range of competing technical 'definitions' ('monetary' poverty, capability poverty, and so on) (see, for example, Alcock 2006). Such discussions seem not to grasp the full implications of the notion that poverty is an *essentially* contested concept. Historically, the notion of poverty has always been deployed in ways that are informed by a wide range of highly specific —

---

2. The nature of poverty discourse is of course only part of the story. The development of institutionally invested poverty knowledge (and poverty management) fits within the much wider and complex discursive formations that dominate the new South African political order. Other important components which I will not touch on here include, of course, technicist discourses about 'delivery' and 'institutional transformation' within the state. Here I am much indebted to insights gleaned from Olajide Oloyede, Ciraj Rasool and Lionel Thaver, and to Oloyede's paper on the subject (Oloyede, 2007).

and often contested and contradictory — underlying ideological stories about the nature of society, the relationship between suffering, humanity and material lack, and the obligations of citizenship, community membership and solidarity. These discourses draw on and are informed by a wide range of diverse and sometimes contradictory religious, ideological, historical and cultural traditions about civic duty, social obligation, social solidarity and moral community (see, e.g. Iliffe, 1987).

This diverse and contested history gives the concept of poverty a protean diversity and breadth of meaning, and imparts to it a certain inherent 'messiness'. As it occurs in the wild, poverty is a broad and sprawling concept. It has no single, clear 'core' meaning; rather it functions in a *field* of meaning that includes objective material lack, experienced want, indignity, suffering, social standing, the nature of social expectation, social contracts and obligations, and moral desert; often in no particular order and related in no systematic manner. Indeed, this messiness is arguably one of the more important and valuable aspects of the notion of poverty as it has circulated in popular discourse in modernity, because it is this open-textured discursive nature that gives the notion of poverty its ability to play such a central role in hegemonic and counter-hegemonic social struggles in present day society. The notion of poverty is available for mobilisation in a wide range of different contexts and in the service of a multitude of agendas. Its flexibility and its open-textured nature means that discussions about what poverty is and what it is not play a key role in highlighting (or in hiding) all manner of contentious social problems, and in legitimating (or delegitimating) various political and economic arrangements.

In present-day South Africa, this complex legacy is available for public discourse in very particular ways. More work is necessary on this, and the remarks here should be taken as broad interpretive hypotheses and not as authoritative assertions. However, it seems reasonable to suggest that mainstream debates and discussions about poverty in South Africa are shaped by (inter alia) three dominant underlying traditions of poverty talk: firstly, a moral tradition focussing on desert and obligation; a technical and managerial discourse of poverty measurement, and lastly a radical tradition that is not so much concerned with understanding the depth of poverty itself, but rather sees it essentially as the symptom of deeper, underlying tensions and contradictions in society. These traditions are of course not neatly separable: any particular intervention or argument may contain elements of all three. At the same time, they involve very different ways of framing or approaching poverty.

Furthermore, it seems that since the transition to democracy, the first two have predominated. Radical discourse about poverty is still present, as we shall see later. But an understanding of the strengths and limitations of mainstream poverty discourse requires that we deal first with the underlying assumptions of the moral and the technical discourses.

Social solidarity and the deserving poor

Firstly, much popular poverty discourse – particularly in the media – focusses on poverty essentially in *moral* terms. The focus is not on *why* people are poor, nor on exactly *how* poor they are: other than vague and often (in the eyes of 'experts') quite poorly informed talk about 'breadlines,' poverty is most commonly unpacked in terms of fairly general and untheorised references to hunger, want, need, lack, indignity and social justice broadly conceived. Consider, for example, the words of two sixteen-year-old South Africans, interviewed in 2006 for a story about the persistence of poverty twelve years after transition (Nduru, 2006):

> I am a 16-year old white, middle class female. You may not find that relevant but it is sad how it affects my daily life,' [Laura] de Lange told IPS, noting that she saw poverty every day. 'When I climb into my parents' car and drive to school, when I walk to the nearest coffee shop with my friends, when I do community outreach work -- I see people living in the pieces of open ground where the wealthy developers have not built yet,' said the student at Sutherland High School in Centurion, near the capital of Pretoria. 'I see their houses made from plastic and rubbish. I hear their soft talking or animated voices as they wait for their turn to get soup from the big can. I feel their rough hands as I hand over the plastic cup filled with soup that probably means they will live a little longer,' she added. 'And I know this has to stop.

Her words were echoed by another campaigner, 16-year-old Sarita Pillay:

> It's not easy to simply close your eyes when the reality of poverty is everywhere. A child and mother begging at the side of a BMW at a robot (traffic light) is a common occurrence in South Africa,' said the pupil from Sagewood College in Midrand, near Johannesburg. 'It's unfair that we live in a country where a person living in a shack and barely making ends meet can live a few kilometres away from a person living in a mansion with three cars,' she added. 'Poverty shows an unequal distribution of

the world's resources, when it has been proven that it is an issue which can be addressed. The problem of poverty has to be tackled head on and not brushed aside.

Given the highly diverse and many-faceted nature of poverty discourse, it would of course be mistaken to take any single example such as this and offer it as 'typical': popular moral discourse on poverty in South Africa can take many different directions and contain very different emphases. At the same time, this example usefully highlights some key themes. Note, how here a focus on the *depth* or *level* of poverty takes second place to a concern with the *ethical standing* of the people involved, and the nature of the moral, social and political obligations faced both by 'poor' people themselves and society more generally. From an econometric point of view, some of those considered 'poor' by De Lange and Pillay may in fact be living above one or other poverty line: they could well be surviving on more than one or even two dollars a day. But here, this does not matter: in this discourse, particular signifiers of poverty (living in shacks, begging by the side of the road) are indicated as general signs of suffering – a suffering that is explicitly contrasted with the wealth of others.

In post-Apartheid South Africa, this moral discourse about poverty is of course closely linked to broader discourses about nation-building, reconciliation, and social justice. But they also often echo or draw on the pre-occupations of Victorian notions about the 'deserving poor'. As Jeremy Seekings has pointed out, in South Africa such notions are for example commonly present in discussions about 'desert', i.e. about who should and who should not, benefit from social welfare (Seekings 2005b; for an overview of these arguments in the development of poverty studies in Britain, see Alcock 2006).

But although these notions of poverty may draw their moral framework from religious discourse, they are not exclusively religious. When South African journalists, for example, draw attention to the persistence of poverty in post-Apartheid South Africa, and refer to poor people 'patiently waiting' for their lives to improve with changing political times, or to nuclear families threatened with dissolution by the depredations of unemployment, they are, just like Victorian writers on the 'deserving poor,' and like Laura and Sarita in the quote above, also drawing on an essentially moral framework for understanding what poverty is, what the presence of poverty obliges 'society' to do, and what is expected from poor people themselves if they are to benefit from social solidarity. What they have in common is that they are not so much concerned with precise judgements as to who is or is not poor, or with how poor they are, as they are with the nature of the claims and obligations arising from it.

Although scholars often dismiss or warn against Victorian 'deserving-poor' arguments and their present-day descendants, it can be argued that some kind of discourse about 'desert', however constructed, is essential for any project that tries to justify pro-poor interventions through some kind of broader discourse of social solidarity or humanitarian concern. As Seekings's arguments imply, South Africa's current welfare system would not draw the support it has — a support that, incidentally, cuts across racial lines — without being able to rely on often fairly moralising discourses around 'desert' (Seekings, 2005a, 2005b).

At the same time, these moralising discourses around poverty have their dangerous side. Popular moral discourse on poverty often proceeds in the absence of any real sociological and analytical understanding of the factors that actually cause and perpetuate poverty. Because it often focuses on the individual character of poor people themselves, it is often blind to structural and contextual factors. It is often available for quite conservative individualist and voluntarist ideologies that fall back on simplistic notions, for example of the need for a 'work ethic' among poor people. And, in the context of deeply entrenched patriarchal ideology, notions of 'desert' often end up leaving out, or actively demonising or blaming, some of the most vulnerable and marginalised groupings in South African society: this is most evident, for example, in the generalised notion that young women are abusing the South African child grant, either by spending it on alcohol or clothes, or by falling pregnant with the explicit aim of accessing this grant.

Measurement, management and the government of poverty

A second important and distinct discursive tradition is often found in approaches that frame poverty in *technical*, *managerial* or *economistic* terms. Again, this is a heterogenous tradition with a complex and internally contested history. One important strand in this tradition is the attempt to create a ground on which judgements about poverty can be held to be value-free, neutral, objective or scientific. Historically this has taken many forms, ranging from Rowntree's pathbreaking surveys (Alcock 2006), through the desire of the Save the Children Fund, the oldest of present-day relief organisations, to "elevate charity into an exact science" (Iliffe, 1987: 199), to the current tendency to frame poverty in biomedical terms — for example, the definition of food insecurity through reference to calorie requirements and the like (FAO, 2000).

A key characteristic of this is the tendency to frame poverty as a state that can essentially be defined in terms of some *concretely specifiable degree of objective and measurable lack*. (This, incidentally, is the case for *both* 'absolute' *and* 'relative' poverty; this approach is present when this lack is defined in terms of supposedly invariant human needs, *and* when it is defined in terms of a 'moving' threshold defined with reference to the distribution of resources in a particular society). Attempts to define poverty in terms of monetary poverty lines are only the most obvious example of this approach: 'multidimensional' and 'capability' approaches to poverty — often thought of as challenges to monetary definitions — are often operationalised in very similar ways, especially when they too are reduced to questions of measurement, or of the absence or presence of one 'poverty indicator' or another (du Toit, 2006).

This tradition plays a dominant role in present day scholarship around poverty in South Africa. The reasons for this are complex. One factor is undoubtedly the hunger for reliable quantitative information on the part of the newly elected government. In addition, as Jeremy Seekings notes (2003), the aversion of many left-leaning sociologists to quantitative analysis has meant that most of the current work on poverty has been done by economists. But developments in South Africa have also been shaped by the domination of econometric approaches in the international literature on poverty and development.

In the field of poverty research, the agent *par excellence* of this reframing has been the World Bank which, as Ben Fine has argued, has presided over the wholesale annexation by economists of questions that previously were the preserve of sociology and anthropology (Fine, 2001). The domination of econometric approaches to poverty in South Africa and elsewhere can, I have suggested elsewhere, be seen as aspects of what we might think of as a globalised project of the 'government of poverty' — a set of portable, widely adaptible strategies that help us conceive of poverty as an object avaialble for managerial intervention and 'neutral' scientific judgement (Du Toit, 2006).

The result is that the domination of poverty research by detailed large scale quantitative work has been accompanied by a theoretical monoculture, the underlying assumptions of which can be called the *econometric imaginary*. Key aspects of this monoculture are the centrality of economics as a privileged discipline in the field of poverty studies, of explanatory frameworks drawing on methodological individualism, 'rational-choice', and of underlying assumptions often tied to ideological neoliberalism. It is also central in very particular forms of institutional power and bureaucratic functioning, and therefore its scholarly and research preoccupations cannot be understood separately from the managerial need of government for targeting, budgeting, and 'monitoring and evaluation'. Very often in South Africa, it is closely linked to bureaucratic discourses and practices of 'service delivery' and the construction of poor people as 'clients' and 'targets' of various government departments.

Perhaps the most important aspect of the dominance of the econometric imaginary is that policy discussions of poverty almost universally proceed on the basis of the assumption that poverty needs to be 'defined' in some particular way (see, for example, SPII, 2007); that this definition has to be one that allows a systematic distinction between 'the poor' and 'the non-poor'; and that essentially the most useful way of doing this is on the basis of some kind of monetary poverty line (see du Toit, 2006 for a more detailed discussion). Even discussions that critically question 'poverty line orthodoxy' often simply amount to an attempt to derive a monetary poverty line in a different way — e.g. through the development of a more consensual approach to the determination of the 'socially accepted minimum necessities' without which a person can be deemed to be poor (Noble, Ratcliffe and Wright, 2004)— or through the development of some other dichotomous capability-based indicator on the basis of which people can be identified as either deprived or non-deprived (Barrientos, 2003).[3]

Like the moral discourse about poverty, this approach has both its strengths and weaknesses. On the one hand, the ability to approach poverty in this way is clearly a key prerequisite for modern bureaucratic or governmental action, and also helps sidestep political divides. At the same time, as I have argued elsewhere (Du Toit, 2006), the consensual, technicist aspects of this discourse come at a cost. The domination of mainstream poverty studies by the econometric imaginary has meant that key concepts and bodies of theory that can contribute centrally to the understanding of poverty have all too often tended to be marginalised or ignored. Above all, it makes it possible for us to discuss poverty without also discussing politics, and to talk about 'the poor' without discussing the wealthy.

Here, it is important to be clear about just what this means. Although I and others have extensively criticised the centrality of measurement-based approaches to the definition and understanding of poverty (Eyben, 2003; Bevan, 2004; du Toit, 2005; du Toit, 2006; Harris, 2006; O'Connor, 2006), these arguments should not be taken to be an objection

---

3. Even discussions of *relative* poverty often seem to lose sight of the close link between the relative concept of poverty and the critique of inequality, and thus conflate the *distributional* relativity of 'relative' poverty with the question of the social and temporal mobility and relativity of absolute poverty lines; or attempt to derive 'relative poverty lines'.

to the notion of measurement or quantitative knowledge about poverty as such. Clearly the detailed quantitative understanding of, for example, the distribution of income or access to social resources in South Africa is absolutely crucial. The problem arises when, rather than trying to understand access to income or other material resources as an important aspect of poverty, poverty itself is *defined* in terms of such an absolute lack.

This is not only true of monetary poverty indicators such as poverty lines: it holds as well for indicators of capability poverty, or for attempts to develop consensually derived poverty lines (Barrientos, 2003; Noble, Ratcliffe and Wright, 2004). It holds also for attempts to define structural poverty by way of asset poverty lines (Carter and May, 2001; Carter and Barret, 2005). These processes risk confusing poverty with its indicator: taking one aspect of a complex relational process, and to reify it as if it *is* poverty. To some extent, as James C Scott pointed out, this is a necessary aspect of the 'optics of governmentality' by which the modern state tries to make society 'legible' and available for systematic intervention: for the state to 'see' poverty and to be able to make juridical managerial judgements about it, it needs technologies of measurement and judgement that are acontextual and portable from one context to another (Scott, 1998). But very often, what is produced is a focus on poverty that disconnects it from an understanding of the social relations that produce and perpetuate it.

This point is perhaps worth expanding on. If the key issue in understanding poverty is not simply material lack, but also social and economic *agency* — people's ability to participate effectively in society as social and economic actors — this poses very specific challenges to poverty research. As Charles Tilly has pointed out (Tilly, 1998), social power is not something that is distributed in society in continuous gradations. Rather, there seem to be sharp discontinuities, 'tipping points' and 'state changes' that are linked to powerfully enforced and historically durable social dichotomies: white and black, master and slave, male and female, christian and barbarian. Inequality is not simply a matter of distributions, but rather of social relations and socially imposed categories. And if our focus is on the concrete implications of poverty — on the link between poverty and social agency —students of poverty should not simply consider it in terms of a particular threshold on a continuously moving variable like income, or nutritional intake, or years of education: attention should also be on social power relations in society.

This is why the econometric attempt to *define* poverty in a measurement based way is so important, and why its critique is not just trivial. Poverty lines can be useful constructs when their essentially arbitrary and indicative nature is recognised — and indeed most econometricians will be quick to acknowledge that any particular threshold is 'just a line', essentially arbitrarily placed, and useful mostly as a way of monitoring change. But in spite of this acknowledgement, the reality is that econometric analysis *at the same time* often proceeds as if such lines *do* indeed mark a significant 'tipping point' or state change.

Firstly, poverty lines are usually set and justified in terms of (often rather tendentious) arguments that do try to suggest (on the basis of arguments about the supposed behaviour of imaginary, ahistorical and decontextualised 'households' and 'individuals') that particular income or other thresholds are more significant than others.

Secondly, econometric analysis often proceeds as if poverty lines do indicate some kind of fundamental underlying state change. Such fetishisation of poverty lines occurs, for instance, when students of chronic poverty seek to construct a population called 'the chronic poor' – imagined to be significantly different from another group called 'the transitory poor' - based on the way in which people show up in a transition matrix around a poverty line. While it is clearly true that people who show up under a poverty line in repeated measurements are worse off than those who do not, imagining that this means they are a socially and economically distinct group is to mistake a statistical construct for a social reality.

And thirdly, despite scholarly acknowledgement that poverty lines are in essence necessary fictions, essentially arbitrary distinctions made for the purpose of monitoring, evaluation, political accountability and international reporting, the reality is that in policy discourse and in programme implementation, these notional distinctions are given political consequence and institutional weight. Consider the tendency of official discourse to refer to socio-economic programmes, 'graduating' people 'out of poverty:' a tellingly formal metaphor that constructs the transition out of poverty as a two-tailed, cut-and-dried and bureaucratic matter. Moreover, it is tightly linked to material consequences, because 'graduating' someone out of poverty is also about getting them to "graduate out of dependence on social grants" (Mbeki, 2007).

Understanding poverty as social and economic disempowerment requires that we do not simply measure the extent of people's access to or deprivation of a particular asset. We need to understand *process*. We need to explore the particular causal pathways and interactions by which access (or deprivation) of particular resources or goods interact with one another and with complex social processes to systematically produce social and economic disempowerment and marginalisation. This is one of the reasons why calls for the integration of qualitative and quantitative research in poverty studies is welcome (Kanbur, 2002;

Kanbur & Shaffer, 2007). The interactions involved are rarely linear, and are always mediated by locality, history, and a wide range of factors that may be unquantifiable, hard-to-quantify, or simply ignored in household surveys. Though they may be *partially* visible in large quantitative datasets, quantitative analysis of these factors needs to be supplemented and informed by forms of research that can explore these complex social processes in more detail.

But qual-quant integration is not simply about adding 'qualitative data' to the analysis of the smooth and continuous curves of econometric distributional analysis. If we want to understand the social processes that constitute and undergird poverty, this requires an analysis of the functioning of social relations; and because social relations cannot be understood outside the meaning-giving context of the discursive practices, local contexts and histories in which they are embedded, analysis has to grapple with the complexities of ideology, identity, 'culture,' practices, and all the other complex dynamics that contribute to what Tilly called 'durable inequality' in society. The econometric reification of poverty, in terms of its indicators, disconnects the study of poverty from the study of inequality; and by directing attention away from the structural factors and social processes that perpetuate 'durable inequality,' it marginalises the kinds of questions that would allow a critical and political engagement with its causes and with ways of changing it.

The ambiguity of poverty discourse in South Africa

My argument so far has traversed terrain that should be familiar to readers of Alice O'Connor, Tanya Murray Li, Ben Fine, Uma Kothari and other critical scholars of the development and poverty research industry more generally (Ferguson, 1990; Ferguson, 2007; Kothari, 2005; O'Connor, 2006; Li, 2006). These writers have argued that international development studies have been dominated by a theoretical monoculture, and this has meant, as Alice O'Connor (2006) has pointed out, that Anglophone scholarship and debate about poverty have increasingly been characterised by a deep disjuncture between two different ways of understanding poverty. On the one hand, there is what O'Connor calls the officially sanctioned 'Poverty Knowledge' institutionally situated in the World Bank — ideologically neoliberal, profoundly dominated by economics, and prone to what Pip Bevan and Ravi Kanbur have called 'policy-messaging' approaches (Bevan, 2005). On the other hand there is a much more marginalised and critical approach — 'knowledge about poverty', as O'Connor (2006) calls it — centred more in the disciplines of

sociology and anthropology, and often much less closely connected to
the machineries of policymaking.

These arguments clearly have important resonances in South Africa:
by reframing the contested, politically charged and explosive legacy of
racial inequality in terms of the rather more ahistorical consensus on the
need to 'eradicate' or 'reduce' poverty, the mainstream of post-Apartheid
discourse on poverty risks jettisoning the ability to critically understand
the power relations and social processes that perpetuate 'durable
inequality' and entrench social injustice. This risks marginalising or
excluding the political traditions of struggle for transformation and
change to which the present day political order owes at least some of its
existence.

At the same time, this is not all that can be said. It is not enough
simply to present this generic critique of managerial discourse.
Elsewhere, critics of the mystificatory aspects of development discourse
can sometimes present the operations of global capitalist ideological
hegemony as all but seamless and complete – Ferguson's analysis of the
way in which the discourse of community based natural resource
management subjugates local community interests to those of a
globalised tourist industry, for instance (Ferguson, 2006); or Kothari's
critique of the way in which participatory approaches amount simply to
a new 'ordering of dissent' that leaves colonial modes of power-
knowledge intact (Kothari, 2005).

But in South Africa, matters seem (for now at least) more
ambiguously posed. Firstly, in contrast to many other 'developing
nations,' where the study of poverty is almost entirely dominated by
distantly located 'development experts' who often work to a research
agenda narrowly contained within World Bank orthodoxy, South Africa
is in the fortunate position of being able to 'write back.' Although the
'poverty research community' is still rather small (and, it must be said,
noticeably white), it does constitute an important source of local
capacity. This means that quantitative research about poverty research
in South Africa is not as dominated by those whose engagement with its
social reality is limited to crunching datasets from distant places.
Secondly, poverty research in South Africa takes place within the highly
distinctive *political* context created by the aftermath of the struggle
against Apartheid. Even though moralising, technicist, managerialist and
consensualist tropes have a powerful hold, and play a central role in
regulating what can and what cannot be said, the ghost of the earlier
project of deeper social and political transformation cannot be entirely
exorcised. Most crucially, even the most abstruse and technicist debates
about poverty measurement in South Africa do not take place in a
political vacuum: in a context where the post-Apartheid government has

staked so much of its credibility on its promises to improve the lives of poor people – and in which a rising tide of service delivery protests signify the willingness of those poor people to challenge government to live up to those promises, debates about poverty measurement and pro-poor policy are necessarily shaped by an awareness of the presence, or at least the possibility, of a more contestatory politics.

The result is that poverty-related research and debate in South Africa have a crucially ambiguous nature. Although the depoliticising logic I describe here is present and real, the discourse on poverty in South Africa is not *simply* an 'anti-politics' machine; politics seems still to have a powerful, if occluded presence. The converse is also true: although debates and research about poverty often explicitly note the broader processes of political struggle and social inequality to which poverty is linked, these dynamics and processes are often only patchily explored. It is necessary to go further. In particular, it is important that the possibility of the political critique of technicist discourse does not lapse into the kind of romantic populism that explains poverty in terms of the simplistic dyad between virtuous poor victims and an oppressive, persecutory system. Compelling as such psychodramas are, we should resist the temptation to substitute their moral authority for more dispassionate, careful analysis. This section of the chapter considers some of the more important advances in poverty studies in South Africa, and (perhaps rather presumptuously) sets out some points on a research agenda that can take these advances further.

Understanding durable inequality in South Africa

The first set of challenges arise out of the notion that the proper study of poverty is inequality: that it is necessary to challenge the way in which some of the orthodox approaches described above make it possible to de-link the study of poverty from a concern with the *distribution* of resources in society. In this regard, it does seem that South African poverty studies seem to have done well. Research on poverty in South Africa since 1994 has been marked by a lively and detailed concern with the nature of inequality in South Africa. Poverty research has been thoroughly informed, for example, by an awareness of the ways in which inequality may in fact have been deepened since 1994 (to mention just a few examples, see e.g. Leibbrandt, Bhorat & Woolard, 2001; Seekings, 2003a; Seekings et al., 2003; McCord & Bhorat, 2003; Seekings & Natrass, 2005; Keswell, 2004).

However, with the exception of Seekings and Nattrass, poverty researchers in South Africa seem to have done less well in unpicking the *social* aspects of inequality in some detail. One of the more interesting aspects of poverty research in South Africa since 1994 is the virtual absence of any really coherent and systematic exploration of the dynamics of *class* in South Africa. For the most part, the discussion of inequality has tended to understand it narrowly in terms of *distributional* inequality, without considering the numerous other *sociological* and *relational* aspects of inequality – the power relations and the hierarchical orderings of society on which sociologists and anthropologists focus.

Given the centrality and importance of class analyses in earlier scholarship on South African inequality, this absence is quite remarkable. From a situation where Marxist analysis was virtually hegemonic in South African sociology and historiography, we have shifted to a situation where it is deeply marginalised. Not only is there relatively little mainstream South African scholarship that takes class seriously; it also seems that even when there are explicit attempts to take it up again, such attempts fall well short of anything that can be called class analysis.

The call to take social class seriously should not be taken for a call for a return to the forgotten verities of structuralist class analysis. Though the broader structural analyses of South African society are very useful, Marxist analysis has also often analysed class in reductionist and theory driven ways that serve not to organise or provide insights into empirical reality, but to ignore it and ride roughshod over it (see e.g. Bozzoli, 1983; Bradford, 1990). Neither is it enough simply to explain inequality in South Africa through a blanket reference to 'globalisation' and 'neoliberalism,' words that are used to explain everything in general, hence turning out to explain nothing.

A return to structural analysis of inequality, however, does not have to follow these reductionist or generalising and flattening paths. There is a rich tradition in South Africa of empirically nuanced analysis of social identity that looks carefully at the complex interrelations between class, 'racial,' gender and other identities. While in the 1990s, much of this analysis was articulated in a Marxist tradition, later work (e.g. Erasmus, 2001; Steyn, 2001; Habib & Bentley, 2008) have often however, remained confined to the analysis of the politics of identity – particularly race and gender. Although they are alive to the social dynamics of inequality, class in present-day South Africa is taken as a given; the perpetuation of durable inequality in South African society more broadly, is not itself explored head-on.

The most notable attempt to account in a systematic way for the structural underpinnings of inequality in South Africa is Seekings and Nattrass's searching exploration of the changing nature of inequality in South Africa since 1994 (Seekings and Nattrass, 2005). This study is unusual in that it goes beyond merely focussing on distributional curves and the stratification of population in terms of income percentiles, and tries to link the analysis of income inequality to an account of an (essentially descriptive and occupational) sociological account of class. Using an analysis that draws both on the strengths of recent quantitative household surveys and on insights from Weberian (Goldthorpe) and neoMarxist (Erik Olin Wright) class analysis, Seekings and Nattrass highlight important continuities between the 'distributional regime' of post-Apartheid South Africa and the key institutions that regulated the labour market and redistribution in late Apartheid society. In particular, their argument emphasises the ways in which these institutions, and the capital-intensive, skills-intensive 'productivity now' growth path adopted by the democratic government, have helped create an 'underclass' of increasingly marginalised landless and unemployed people. Going well beyond the simplistic appeal to 'neoliberalism' as a catch-all explanation for deepening inequality, their analysis argues that working class politics has contributed to the deepening divisions between this underclass and those who still have a foothold in the South African economy.

Seekings and Nattrass provide a powerful and wide-ranging account of the reasons for continuing and deepening inequality in South Africa. Their argument is sure to be controversial in some quarters, not least because of the emphasis they put on the role played by the high-wage, high-productivity policies supported by the mainstream trade union movement in accounting for deepening unemployment. At the same time, it is hard to fault their account of the differences that separate the 'core working class' from marginalised workers and the broader mass of the landless and structurally unemployed. Certainly their analysis poses important questions for accounts of change in South Africa that try simply to champion 'working class interests,' without considering the internally diverse nature of this working class, or that would absolve South Africa's industrial relations machinery from its part in the South African economy's flight from unskilled labour.

At the same time, important questions remain. Although their critique of labour market policy in South Africa is important, questions remain about its place in their analysis. In fact, they themselves seem to vacillate at times, arguing at some points that it is merely one of many factors contributing to South Africa's unemployment problems; and at other times giving it pride of place (Seeking and Nattrass, 2005: 376 ff). This is problematic on two counts. In the first place, one important problem with privileging labour market rigidity as a cause of inequality is the danger of ignoring the reality of poverty *among* the *presently* employed, and the existence of significant scope for the employment of low-waged, unskilled workers *within* the terms of South African labour law. Secondly, it's worth remembering that *both* the creation of a relatively privileged, skilled and waged 'core' *and* the processes of externalisation, casualisation and informalisation by which corporates pass risk and cost onto workers are aspects of a broader process of economic restructuring. It is true that the defense of the gains of the 'core working class' does not address the needs and interests of marginalised workers or the unemployed - but neither can it be entirely blamed for their exclusion.

This is related to another feature of Seekings and Nattrass's overall analysis: ambitious, detailed and sweeping as their account is, it tends more or less to ignore the questions posed by South Africa's insertion into a wider, 'global' economic order. As the authors note in their introduction, the book is an investigation primarily of South African labour market and welfare policies, and how these might need to be transformed to address the challenges of poverty and inequality. This it does well — but ultimately the analysis remains too limited. The result is an oddly parochial analysis which seems to omit the need to look at the transnational economic changes within which South African labour market and welfare policies had to take shape. Thus, the flight from labour intensive manufacturing is approached almost *sui generis*, a country-level capitalist strategy, as if it has only been happening in the Republic, rather than being recognised as the local variant of the complex re-articulation of an increasingly global and footloose capitalism internationally. To be sure, as Seekings and Nattrass point out, not much is contributed by analyses that simply and in blanket terms blame 'neoliberalism' and 'globalisation' for everything. But subtler and more nuanced approaches to the analysis of the impact of 'globalisation' are possible: the avoidance of tub-thumping anti-globalisation rhetoric should not lead to the failure to take into account the complex ways in which, alongside labour market and welfare reforms, international trading relations, value chains and commodity systems have themselves been restructured and re-regulated in ways that contribute powerfully to marginalisation and inequality.

Answering these questions requires us to go beyond positivist, rational choice and methodological individualism in the analysis of identity, and to look more closely at the ways in which discourse, identity and social meaning shape the ways both race and class are mediated. Such an account will have to be able to look carefully both at the level of the micro-politics of everyday life (because this is the level at which we have to understand the kinds of socio-economic agency, empowerment and disempowerment that should be one of the key concerns in poverty studies); but it should be able to connect and relate what happens at the micro-social level to an analysis of the broader political economy of poverty, and the macro-structure of South African society and economy.

From 'social capital' to identity, relationships and networks

The dominant way in which mainstream poverty discourse makes sense of questions of social process and interaction at the micro-level is through the now almost ubiquitous notion of 'social capital.' Discussion of the strengths and weaknesses of 'social capital' as a term is made somewhat difficult by the fact that it is in itself such a vague and open-ended term, and tends to be used in a wide range of more or less rigorous ways. Part of its centrality comes from the fact that it represents one of the (limited) ways in which mainstream poverty discourse (read: the World Bank) has attempted to recognise the role of social dynamics (Fine, 2001; Eyben, 2003). Although this may be an important achievement in that it may have won some space for considering the value of traditions of co-operations, solidarity and mutual aid among World Bank policymakers, it has serious disadvantages as an analytical concept. Above all, what 'social capital' discourse almost entirely obscures is that social capital is not a quantifiable resource; at best it is a kind of convenient shorthand for the various complex ways in which social networks work to shape, enable, undermine, facilitate or inform a wide range of social transactions, exchanges, encounters, contestations and negotiations. 'Social capital' exists nowhere except in particular social relationships and interaction; conceiving of it as a quantum that can be accumulated, dispersed, exchanged, stored or appreciated is to misunderstand it entirely: it can only be grasped by looking at the particular transactions in which people engage, and by analysing the resources and goods involved in their exchanges, the social relationships that shape the terms of those exchanges, and the meaning-giving discourses, ideologies and identities that lay down the explicit or unspoken rules of the game.

An analysis of how reciprocal exchange works in Khayelitsha and the Eastern Cape highlights the ambiguous and ambivalent nature of the practices and connections that constitute the phenomena usually referred to by champions of 'social capital.' Research recently done by PLAAS in the Eastern Cape and in impoverished suburbs of Cape Town's African townships (du Toit and Neves, 2008a, 2008b) highlights the important role social networks and practices of reciprocal exchange play in ameliorating the effects of poverty and inequality. But these practices have real limitations. For one thing, only those who already have access to some resources are able to participate in the practices of reciprocal exchange (Spiegel, 1996). Secondly, these practices work in highly uneven ways — while they ameliorate vulnerability for some, they worsen it for others. They often involve ways of passing on cost and risk to others — and the practices of exchange can be highly extortionate and exploitative. This is the dark side of 'social capital': those who are disadvantaged within the terms of patriarchal gender roles, the elderly and unemployed, those who defy local cultural norms of respectability, those who are excluded from local communities on the basis of identity, and those who have little leverage to begin with, are poorly positioned to transact effectively within the networks that constitute 'private social protection' (Sagner & Mtati, 1999; du Toit & Neves, 2008a, 2008b). This presents a very different picture from that conjured up by the notion of 'social capital' as a kind of universally beneficial lubricant for entrepreneurship and mutual aid. Looking at the ways in which social networks are constituted through particular transactions, negotiations, and practices of reciprocal exchange (and how they, in their turn shape these transactions) suggests a rather grimmer view of how social connections of various kinds impact on poverty and vulnerability.

The prevalence of the notion of social capital thus presents poverty analysts with a serious strategic conundrum. On the one hand, it is almost omnipresent in the discourse of government, policymaking and social movements as a kind of generalised shorthand for what armchair sociologists might call 'the fabric of society'; as such it is almost impossible *not* to use the term. On the other hand, it is seriously lacking as an analytical concept. Many of the more heated sociological discussions about 'social capital', indeed, are not about what the word means or how social capital itself should be understood; but rather the *strategic* merits and demerits of using it as a kind of conceptual 'trojan horse' by which some of the blindnesses of World Bank discourse can be somewhat addressed. At present in South Africa, it does seem as if we are stuck with 'social capital'; and as if the best that social scientists involved in use-oriented basic research or public sociology can do is not to discard it, but to try to use it in a way that is informed by a finer analysis of the logic of social networks.

From social exclusion and disconnection to adverse incorporation

One of the more interesting shifts in policy debates about poverty in recent years has been the increasing centrality of 'second economy' discourse in official and policymaking circles (Mbeki, 2003; PCAS, 2003; Faull, 2005; Bond, 2007). The rise of second economy discourse has marked an important break in official economic thinking, particularly in that it involved an explicit recognition of the limitations of 'trickle down' and put on the map not just the need for growth, but also questions about the nature of the growth path and the pattern of growth. Another important contribution of 'second economy discourse' is that it involves a serious attempt to recognise the segmented nature of the South African economy, and raises as a possibility the existence of 'structural disjunctures' which may systematically marginalise poor people, preventing them from benefiting from the opportunities arising out of increased rates of economic growth.

At the same time, as I and others have argued extensively elsewhere, these benefits are somewhat neutralised by the fact that second economy discourse typically tends to misrecognise and misrepresent the nature of these structural disjunctures. Like the liberal versions of 'social exclusion' discourse that are at present being assiduously imported into developing country contexts, second economy discourse locates the nature of the structural disjuncture in the idea that people are 'disconnected' from the formal economy, for instance because they do not have marketable skills and because they do not produce the kinds of goods the formal economy needs. This kind of analysis misunderstands the nature of the relationship between the informal and the formal economies in South Africa. For one thing, in many cases poverty seems entrenched in particular regions or communities not so much because people are disconnected from the formal economy, but because they are tightly integrated into it on disadvantageous terms. Part of the problem, indeed, may be the very high degree of corporate penetration deep into South Africa's rural economy, and the highly concentrated and anti-competitive nature of the South African formal sector (du Toit & Neves, 2007).

This is perhaps among the most important challenge facing researchers about poverty in South Africa. Rather than reifying a realm called 'the second economy', it is necessary to explore in much more detail the multifarious ways in which it is connected into the formal economy; and rather than disconnecting the study of poverty from the analysis of the formal economy, it is necessary to look in more detail at the structural composition of the South African economy as a whole and to explore the ways in which the entire formation of this economy, including the 'successful, globally integrated first economy' contribute to the patterns of marginalisation and disempowerment that perpetuate and entrench durable inequality in South Africa.

In a way this is not a new task – it is the kind of analysis that was the stock in trade of Marxist analyses of South African society in the late 1970s and the 1980s. No doubt many of the crucial insights developed *inter alia* by Legassick and Wolpe (Wolpe, 1972; 1980) can still be relied on and extended; and indeed some important steps in that direction are being undertaken (Arrighi, 2007). At the same time, more will be required than reiterating in a doctrinaire way the certainties of earlier ideological battles. More is required than simply explaining all of South African poverty by way of vague references to globalisation, international capitalism and neoliberal ideology. Comforting though it may be to answer neoliberalism with neopopulism, it does not help the task of an accurate analysis, and neither does it help with identifying more clearly the room for manoeuvre that is available in struggles for social justice.

References

Alcock, P., 2006. *Understanding Poverty*. Third Edition. London: Palgrave Macmillan.

Arrighi, G., 2007. Labour Supplies in Comparative Perspective: The Southern Africa Paradigm Revisited. Paper presented for SANPAD conference. Durban. The Poverty Challenge 2007: Poverty and Poverty Reduction in South Africa, India, and Brazil. 26-29 June 2007.

Barrientos, A., 2003. *Non-contributory Pensions and the well-being of older people: evidence on multi-dimensional deprivation from Brazil and South Africa*. Mimeo Manchester: IDPM, University of Manchester.

Baulch, B. and Masset, E., 2003. Do Monetary and Non-Monetary Indicators Tell the Same Story About Chronic Poverty? A Study of Vietnam in the 1990s. *World Development,* 31 (3), pp.441-454.

Bevan, P., 2004. Exploring the Structured Dynamics of Chronic Poverty: a sociological approach. WeD Working Paper 06. Bath: Wellbeing in Developing Countries, ESRC research group, University of Bath.

Bevan, P., 2005. Studying Multi-Dimensional Poverty in Ethiopia: towards a Q-Integrated Approach. Q-Squared Working Paper no. 15. Toronto: Centre for International Studies.

Bond, P., 2007. Introduction: Two Economies - or one system of super-exploitation. *Africanus,* 37(2), pp.1-21.

Bozzoli, B., 1983. Introduction: History, Experience and Culture. In B. Bozzoli, ed. *Town and Countryside in the Transvaal: Capitalist Penetration and Popular Response.* Johannesburg: Ravan Press, pp.1-47.

Bradford, H., 1990. Highways, Byways and Culs de Sacs: the transition to Agrarian Capitalism in Revisionist South African History. *Radical History Review,* 46(7), pp. 59 - 88.

Carvalho, S. and White, H., 1997. Combining the quantitative and qualitative approaches to poverty measurement and analysis. World Bank Technical Paper 366. Washington DC: The World Bank.

Carter, M. and May, J., 2001. One Kind of Freedom: Poverty Dynamics in Post-Apartheid South Africa. *World Development,* 29 (12), pp.1987-2006.

Carter, M. and Barrett, C., 2005. The Economics of Poverty Traps and Persistent Poverty: an Asset-based Approach. Unpublished Typescript. Basis CRSP. See http://www.cfnpp.cornell.edu/images/wp178.pdf.

Chronic Poverty Research Centre 2004 (CPRC). *The Chronic Poverty Report 2004 – 05.* Manchester: Chronic Poverty Research Centre.

Du Toit, A., 2005. The Sociology of Chronic and Structural Poverty in South Africa: Challenges for action and research. CPRC Working Paper #56. Bellville, Cape Town and Manchester: PLAAS, CPRC and CSSR.

Du Toit, A., 2006. Poverty Measurement Blues: Some obstacles to understanding 'Chronic' and 'Structural' Poverty in post-Apartheid South Africa. Paper Prepared for the Workshop on Concepts for Analysing Poverty Dynamics and Chronic Poverty CPRC, University of Manchester, 23-25 October 2006.

Du Toit, A. and Neves, D., 2007. In Search of South Africa's 'second Economy'. *Africanus* 37(2), pp.145-174

Du Toit A. and Neves D., 2008a. Informal Social Protection in post-Apartheid Migrant Networks: Vulnerability, Social Networks and Reciprocal Exchange in the Eastern and Western Cape, South Africa. Bellville: PLAAS Working paper No. 2. (forthcoming)

Du Toit A. and Neves D., 2008b. Trading on a grant: integrating formal and informal social protection in post-Apartheid migrant networks. Bellville: PLAAS Working paper No. 3 (forthcoming).

Erasmus, Z., 2001. *Coloured by History, Shaped by Place: Re-imagining Coloured Identities in Cape Town.* Cape Town: Kwela.

Eyben, R., 2003. Why Is Bolivia Different From India? How Can International Development Agencies Get To Grips With Social And Political Inequality? Discussion paper presented at the conference 'Staying Poor: Chronic Poverty and Development Policy' at the University of Manchester, 7-9 April 2003. Available at: http://www.chronicpoverty.org/pdfs/2003conferencepapers/eyben.pdf

FAO, 2000. *Guidelines for National FIVIMS: Background and Principles.* Rome: Food and Agriculture Organisation.

Faull, J., 2005. Tracing the 'Two Economies': the politics, policy and practice of pragmatism. *ePoliticsSA,* (01) Pretoria: IDASA.

Ferguson, J., 1990. *The Anti-Politics Machine: 'Development', Depoliticisation, and Bureaucratic Power in Lesotho.* Cambridge: Cambridge University Press.

Ferguson, J., 2006. *Global Shadows: Africa in the Neoliberal World Order.* Durham, NC: Duke University Press.

Fine, B., 2001. *Social Capital versus Social Theory: Political Economy and Social Science at the Turn of the Millennium.* New York: Routledge.

Green, M., 2006. Thinking Through Chronic Poverty and Destitution: Theorising Social Relations and Social Ordering. Paper Prepared for the Workshop on Concepts for Analysing Poverty Dynamics and Chronic Poverty CPRC, University of Manchester, 23-25 October 2006.

Habib, A. and Bentley, K., 2008. *Racial Redress & Citizenship in South Africa.* Pretoria: HSRC.

Harriss, J., 2006. Why Understanding of Social Relations Matters More for Policy on Chronic Poverty than Measurement. Paper Prepared for the Workshop on Concepts for Analysing Poverty Dynamics and Chronic Poverty, CPRC, University of Manchester, 23-25 October 2006.

Hulme, D. and Shepherd, A., 2003. Conceptualising Chronic Poverty. *World Development,* 31(3) pp.403:424.

Illiffe, J., 1987. *The African Poor: a History.* Cambridge: Cambridge University Press.

Kanbur, R. and Shaffer, P., 2007. Epistemology, Normative Theory and Poverty Analysis: Implications for Q-Squared in Practice. *World Development,* 35(2), pp. 183-196.

Keswell, M., 2004. Education and Racial Inequality in Post-Apartheid South Africa. Santa Fe Institute Working Paper 04-02-008, Santa Fe, New Mexico.

Kothari, U., 2001. Power, Knowledge and Social Control in Participatory Development. In B. Cooke and U. Kothari, eds. *Participation, the New Tyranny?* London: Zed, pp.139-152.

Kothari, U., 2005. Authority and Expertise: The Professionalisation of International Development and the Ordering of Dissent. *Antipode* pp. 425–446.

Legassick M. and Wolpe, H., 1976. The Bantustans and capital accumulation in South Africa. *Review of African Political Economy*, Winter 1976, pp.87–107.

Legassick, M., 2007. Flaws in South Africa's 'first' economy. *Africanus*, 37(2), pp.111–44.

Leibbrandt, M. Woolard, I. and Bhorat, H., 2001. Understanding Contemporary Household Inequality in South Africa. In H. Bhorat et al., eds. *Fighting Poverty: Labour Markets and Inequality in South Africa*. Cape Town: UCT Press.

Li, T.M., 2006. Neoliberal Strategies of Government through Community: The Social Development Programme of the World Bank in Indonesia. IILJ Working Paper 2006/2. New York: Institute for International Law and Justice.

Mbeki, T., 2003. Letter from the President.
    http://www.anc.org.za/ancdocs/anctoday/2003/at33.htm#preslet

Mbeki, T., 2007. State of the Nation Address 2007.
    http://www.info.gov.za/speeches/2007/07020911001001.htm

McCord, A. and Bhorat, H., 2003. *Employment and labour market trends. Human Resources Development Review: Education, Employment and Skills in South Africa*. Cape Town: Human Sciences Research Council Press and East Lansing: Michigan State University Press

Meagher, K., 2005. Social capital or analytical liability? Social networks and African informal economies. *Global Networks*, 5 (3), pp. 217–238.

Noble, M. Ratcliffe, A. and Wright, G., 2004. *Conceptualising, Defining and Measuring Poverty in South Africa: an Argument for a Consensual Approach*. Oxford: CASASP.

Nduru, M., 2006. The reality of poverty is everywhere. Inter Press Service News Agency, 16 October 2006. http://ipsnews.net/news.asp?idnews=35113

O'Connor, A., 2006. Global Poverty Knowledge and the USA: What It Has Been, Why It Needs to Change. Paper Prepared for the Workshop on Concepts for Analysing Poverty Dynamics and Chronic Poverty CPRC, University of Manchester, 23-25 October 2006. Available at:
    http://www.chronicpoverty.org/news_events/ConceptsWorkshop-Oct2006.htm

Oloyede, O., 2007. Social transformation: Anatomy of a concept. Unpublished paper presented at the South African and Contemporary History and Humanities Seminar at UWC, 5 June 2007.

Policy Coordination and Adivisory Service (PCAS). 2003. Towards a ten year review: synthesis report on implementation of South African government programmes. Pretoria: Policy Co-ordination and Advisory Services, Office of the President.

Ravallion, M., 1996. Issues in Measuring and Modelling Poverty. *The Economic Journal* 106, pp.1328-1343.

Sagner, A. and Mtati, R., 1999. Politics of pension sharing in urban South Africa. *Ageing and Society*, 19, pp.393-416.

Scott, J. C., 1998. *Seeing Like a State: How Certain Schemes to Improve the Human Condition Have Failed*. New Haven: Yale University Press.

Seekings, J., 2002. The uneven development of quantitative social science in South Africa. CSSR Working Paper No.6. Cape Town: Centre for Social Science Research.

Seekings, J., 2003. *Do South Africa's unemployed constitute an underclass?* CSSR Working Paper No. 32. Cape Town: Centre for Social Science Research.

Seekings, J. Nattrass, N. & Leibbrandt, M., 2003. *Inequality in post-apartheid South Africa: Trends in the distribution of incomes and opportunities and their social and political implications*. Report for Centre for Enterprise Development. Cape Town: Centre for Social Science Research.

Seekings, J., 2005a. The Mutability of Distributive Justice Attitudes in South Africa. CSSR Working Paper, No 125. Cape Town: Centre for Social Science Research.

Seekings, J., 2005b. The Colour Of Desert: Race, Class And Distributive Justice In Post-Apartheid South Africa. CSSR Working Paper No 126. Cape Town: Centre for Social Science Research.

Sen, A., 1999. *Development as Freedom.* Oxford: Oxford University Press.

Shepherd, A., 2007. Understanding and explaining chronic poverty – An evolving framework for Phase III of CPRC's research. Working Paper 80, Manchester: IDPM/Chronic Poverty Research Centre.

Spiegel, A., 1996. Introduction: Domestic fluidity in South Africa. *Social Dynamics,* 22(1), pp.5-6.

Spiegel, A. Watson, V. and Wilkinson, P., 1996. Domestic diversity and fluidity among some South African households in Greater Cape Town. *Social Dynamics,* 22(1), pp. 7-30.

Stats SA. 2008. Stats SA to carry out targeted survey to assess poverty battle. Originally published in *Business Report,* 15 February 2008. Available at:
http://www.statssa.gov.za/news_archive/15February2008_1.asp

Steyn, M., 2001. *Whiteness just isn't what it used to be: White identity in a changing South Africa.* Albany: State University of New York Press

Wolpe, H., 1972. Capitalism and cheap labour-power in South Africa: from segregation to apartheid. *Economy & Society*, 1(4).

Wolpe, H., 1980. Introduction. In H. Wolpe, ed. *The articulation of modes of production.* London: Routledge & Kegan Paul.

6.
Poverty research, oppression and 'Free Basic Water'
Greg Ruiters

Introduction

Recently in South Africa there has been an enormous amount of policy-oriented poverty research often driven by large-scale funding organisations and state agencies. This reflects commitments by the ANC and local pressures on the government, but also a larger development whereby poverty has been put at the centre of the development agenda on a global scale. According to the World Bank, about one person out of five in the world still lives in extreme poverty (less than US$1 a day), and nearly half of the world's population lives in poverty (less than US$2 a day; World Bank, 2006: 9). In September 2000, the United Nations Millennium Declaration made 'Eradicating Extreme Poverty and Hunger' the first of eight Millennium Development Goals (MDGs), with specific targets for 2015.[1] Globally, poverty was the top concern on all continents, and in 60 of the 68 countries recently surveyed (Noel, 2006). Poorer countries now produce Poverty Reduction Strategy Papers (PRSPs), with procedures from the International Monetary Fund (IMF) and the World Bank.

For the most part, the current fashionability of pro-poor state interventions has been welcomed by civil society organisations as a progressive move. Those enlisted as social partners in the 'war on poverty' are seen as 'partners'. For the first time in many decades poverty has been made a 'national' issue for public debate and contestation. A government can now be held to account by its own people and by international agencies for not meeting targets. The antipoverty consensus creates new opportunities for creative reformist politics. It "changes the terms of the debate between the left and the right and, in doing so, it redefines the world of policy possibilities" (Noel, 2006). By seizing on the poverty issue, governments have been able to define the terms of debate and continue to promote neoliberal policies. "Poverty became a new focal point because it is an issue closely tied to the dominant neoliberal agenda, an agenda that is supposed to be

---

1. United Nations. 2000. Resolution Adopted by the General Assembly: United Nations Millennium Declaration, A/RES/55/2, 18 September. New York: UN, accessed 8 August 2006. http://www.un.org. United Nations. 2001. Road Map Towards the Implementation of the United Nations Millennium Declaration: Report of the Secretary-General, A/56/326, 6 September. New York: UN, http://www.un.org.

effective in reducing poverty at home and abroad, through stronger economic growth" (Noel, 2006).

Why has there been a resurgence of interest in poverty alleviation? Have the pressures from social movements or the embarrassing gaps between the rich and the poor forced governments to step in? Have governments coopted social movements and their discourse or should we take the establishment of pro-poor commitments seriously and recognise a new beginning and possibilities for 'inclusionary partnerships' between governments, the private sector and civil society to fight poverty?

In this chapter, I suggest that the 'consensus against poverty' needs to be examined more critically. The state does not innocently solve social problems. The new poverty programmes are carefully tied to new discourses of responsibility and framed within what might be termed 'residual welfarism' that is largely consistent with ongoing neoliberal styles of governance. Residual welfare assumes that welfare is a temporary measure for selected poor groups, considered deserving (Patel, 2005). The state uses limited welfare concessions to extend its own administrative power over resources and people. Thus, any pro-poor programme also needs to be evaluated as an exercise in power. In addition, pro-poor policies are couched in the language of partnerships between 'stakeholders' and participation obscuring fundamental social antagonisms. The social and political conditionalities imposed on recipients need to be carefully researched. The chapter starts with a brief review of the critical social policy literature. We then move on to an examination of a few case studies of pro-poor programmes in South Africa to illustrate the general argument.

The issues commonly addressed in poverty research are most often cast in moral terms firstly and then in technocratic terms. The argument is that the state wants to help people but it needs to be able to measure social and demographic conditions. It needs a definition of poverty, its geographical spread, and this will inform how to target, design and evaluate anti-poverty programmes. In South Africa the poverty issue is also framed as a human rights issue, a constitutional imperative, and a means for lifting the poor out of the 'second' economy and into employment. In more populist versions, it is about 'helping our people... healing the nation etc.'

The politics of poverty and everyday needs

One of the major anti-development critics, Arturo Escobar has observed a relationship between poverty relief programmes and disempowerment; "while running water may mean real improvements in people's living conditions, these changes enter into an ongoing situation of power and resistance" (1995: 145). As James Ferguson has argued, state projects whether they fail or whether they 'succeed', produce a host of regular and unacknowledged effects, including the expansion of bureaucratic power and the translation of the political realities of poverty and powerlessness into 'technical' problems awaiting solution by development agencies and experts (Ferguson, 1999). In her critique of the World Bank, Payer suggests infrastructure services (like roads) bring benefits but can equally serve to exploit, pacify, integrate and reconstitute subjects and cultures (Payer, 1982: 90-91). It can bring about a change in social organisations, notions of citizenship and beliefs. Services therefore also serve to govern.

For Gramsci (1971), hegemonic state projects involve processes led by the state to win 'the active consent of those over whom it rules'. Gramsci's idea is that "every relationship of hegemony is necessarily an educational relationship" (1986: 350). In the exercise of hegemony, the state appears as an 'educator' in as much as it shapes and creates new forms of social organisation and citizenship (Gramsci, 1971: 244-247). State pro-poor projects might therefore be seen as partly an exercise in education. Services also function as means to socially integrate 'marginal' populations. But "hegemony is not possible if it is not plausible ... it has two sides" (Wood, 1988: 149). The problem for first-wave neoliberalism is that it has broadly lost credibility, both as a programme for reducing inequality and for producing economic growth and jobs (Harvey, 2004; Jessop, 2002). First-wave neoliberalism was punitive and deepened social polarisation, and it has been followed by a revised 'social neoliberalism'.[2] In second-wave neoliberalism, the active role of the state in educating civic-cultural values can be seen in social policy discourse. Local government and 'pro-poor' services thus need to be seen as politico-cultural interventions that do not question inequality or interrogate the political economy but instead strengthen the overall property regime of the post-apartheid settlement and post-apartheid social formation.[3] Benign interventions and concessions help to secure

---

2. Neoliberalism is most often understood as referring to the 'political preference for market mechanisms as a means of ensuring economic and social wellbeing' (Larner, 2004) and the privatisation of public assets. But neoliberal projects also attempt to create new forms of governable subjects and subjectivities in the form of entrepreneurial, self-responsible individuals (Jessop, 2002: 470; Newman, 2004). Citizens are re-articulated as customers or as on the way to becoming customers within a 'first economy'. More recently, what we might call 'Third Wayism' has articulated neoliberalism with social democratic aspirations.

3. For Gramsci, the state is not only within the 'public' domain (political parties, public administration etc.) but it also constitutes the 'private' domain: civil society (church,

popular complicity in new forms of marketised subordination and governance. If we look closely at pro-poor programmes' design we find it is broadly consistent with neoliberal notions of citizenship. Its pedagogic aims are to help the poor to cope within and 'graduate' into market society. It also has a strong rehab element (from the culture of non-payment to a culture of payment).

Hegemony includes the power to name a problem, to set an agenda and rules for policy, and exercise of material power. The decision to call South Africa's problems 'poverty' as opposed to exploitation or oppression has the effect of shifting the focus to the 'victims' and away from the underlying causes and perpetrators of poverty. Pro-poor social policies thus always have normative content, i.e, they seek to change or direct the behaviour of subject populations. The moral side of state social policy or welfare includes an image of how things ought to be, beliefs, ideologies about the state, society and the good citizen. These processes are mediated locally and are revealed in the ambivalent ways the 'target populations' view the state's efforts (see Desai, 2002; Egan and Wafer, 2006).

Policy makers invariably have underlying ideas about recipients' needs. In the third world context, the term 'basic needs' frequently occurs and there are vigorous disputes about how far the state should go in helping individuals or groups of people and who should be helped. The politics of how needs get decided is crucial: subjectively felt, and expressed needs, or 'objective' experts, a democratic consensual process, or comparing with others are examples of various approaches. Bare physical survival and human needs are not the same. Humans require autonomy, the ability to interact with other humans, take decisions and so on. Early welfare in Europe (Poor Laws) 'targeted' the really poor (paupers or indigents), who were given assistance in exchange for some of their freedoms. The Poor Law sought to develop the 'character' of the poor. The deserving and undeserving were separated; opportunists had to be weeded out. Any welfare concessions had to be carefully managed lest the demand for welfare exceeded public budgets.

Echoes of the Poor Law may be found in contemporary social policy debates, in neoliberal policy and, as we shall argue, in the FBW policy and its implementation. What also flows from this observation is a basic 'tension' in social welfare between the state's caring role and social control. Efforts to help the poor may be entangled, if not compromised, by efforts to control claimants and their behaviour (Ferguson, 1999). The state also imposes concepts of needs, and 'resources' creating

---

public opinion, media, education) through which hegemony functions (Gramsci, 1971: 261). The state is not a separate entity from society but itself a social relation.

struggles with communities about what these are and whose standards of needs and justice are being used (Harvey, 1996: 147). A stress on defining the 'needy' and weeding out unworthy or fraudulent recipients deeply affects the way welfare is experienced by recipients and perceived by the public at large (Walker, 1993: 146-7).

Welfare may be seen as a form of social control, a quid pro quo for social peace, a class or racial compromise, a way of co-opting opponents such as social movements, an insurance for the safety of the rich, a way of cementing social inequality and as a method for expanding state legitimacy and the state's reach (Elster, 1988; Painter, 1995). Titmuss devised three models of welfare (residual, mixed, work-based or redistributive). Residual welfare is welfare for those who cannot provide for themselves. Residual welfare assumes that welfare is a temporary measure for selected poor groups, considered deserving. It has been associated with neoliberal approaches that favour privatisation and community-based self-provisioning and work-fare (Patel, 2005: 24-5). Work-related welfare systems provide welfare that focuses on getting people back into the labour market.[4] Redistributive (universal welfare) aims for social equality and inclusive citizenship. Esping came up with a similar classification of welfare regimes; using a 'decommodification score' (Alcock, 1998: 18-19) he showed that there was both convergence and divergence. Implementing and administering welfare can be complex and expensive, and welfare regimes (conservative, liberal, social democratic) differ considerably.

The Left has also noted that certain welfare regimes often require, implicitly perhaps, a 'submissive recognition' by claimants of the superior morality of the capitalist order which created these needs (see Offe, 1983: 154-6; Desai, 2002). The welfare dispensed by the state becomes an 'exchange transaction' that harms the politico-ideological and dignity of claimants. Curiously these arguments are harnessed by both the Right and the Left although for different ends. The left both support and criticise welfare.

---

4. The conservative argument (sometimes expressed by the Democratic Alliance, Centre for Development Enterprise and even in the African National Congress) is that welfare (or the wrong kind and amount of welfare) will discourage the unemployed from looking for work and encourage dependency and discourage an entrepreneurial culture (see Trevor Manuel, Minister of Finance, in *Business Day*, 19 February 2004). According to a free market thinktank, 'The government's roll-out of electricity, telephones, water, and housing since 1994 is extremely impressive. But people do not have money to pay for these goods and services, and considerable roll-back is occurring. Unless economic growth improves dramatically and results in many more job opportunities, these services are unsustainable'. Centre for Development and Enterprise, Roundtable: Number seven, 2003.

State action in welfare and social infrastructure is a factor in socially constructing the needs of the poor and keeping people 'in place' (Harvey, 1996). A geographical perspective of social control as 'spatio-temporal ordering' is explored by David Harvey (1996: 230): "The fixing of spatiality through material building creates solidly constructed spaces that instantiate negotiated or imposed social values, spatial stigmatisation and spatial control of unwanted groups (vagrants, homeless, the poor) as well as complex processes of symbolic meanings and attacks on spatio-temporal orderings through, for example land-invasions, illegal 'squatting' and the like." Critical geographers stress a socio-spatial dialectic driven by capitalist uneven development that helps to situate welfare as part of the built environment of class reproduction. Housing, sidewalks, water-supply are social infrastructures that define residential property markets and place. According to Harvey, "Place functions as a closed terrain of social control that becomes extremely hard to break (or break out of) once it achieves a particular permanence" (Harvey, 1996: 312).

These introductory remarks might provide a useful critical standpoint for exploring the rollout of pro-poor services in South Africa and the politics of needs.

Keeping people out using 'free' water

Mainstream ANC leaders and government strategists insist that development should not be universal but 'targeted' at the needy. Poverty needs to be 'scientifically' and bureaucratically defined and the needy identified. The amount of benefit has to be carefully defined to maintain macro-fiscal discipline and economic sustainability. The poor should be geographically mapped, their conditions measured and resources 'directed' only at the qualifying poor. The immediate aim is the relief, not elimination of, the condition of poverty (hence the slogan 'some for all, for ever'). Universal welfare is seen as wasting resources, but crucially welfare should not be excessive to discourage work-seeking.

The ANC government has rejected services for all (for example as embodied in the Freedom Charter) in favour of selective provision (means tested delivery). The selective approach seems fair; it means benefits for the poor, better containment of costs to the fiscus and allows for cross-subsidies. The child support grant and municipal services packages (6 kl of free water and 50 KwH of free electricity) are examples of this.

Opponents of targeting point to the huge expense in administration, the risk of excluding the less poor (those who just earn above the poverty line), stigma and low take up. Lund shows that in the case of the child support grant, the decision was made to adopt a selective strategy:

> Much administrative effort is now being spent on finding ways of keeping some children out, rather than bringing all in. Even a sophisticated state would be hard pressed to devise and administer a means test which can finely discriminate income and asset levels in households on either side of the 50 per cent line (Lund, 2001: 235).

As Gillian Hart (2006) puts it, the shift to basic welfare and stepped-up poverty alleviation should be seen as,

> part of an effort to contain the pressures emanating from the rise of oppositional movements protesting the inadequacies of service provision, the snail's pace of land redistribution, failures to provide anti-retrovirals, and the absence of secure jobs-as well as pressures from within the Alliance... What is significant about this discourse is the way it defines a segment of society that is superfluous to the 'modern' economy, and in need of paternal guidance...they are deserving of a modicum of social security, but on tightly disciplined and conditional terms.

This observation applies to the entire gamut of social policy in South Africa.[5] Consider the case of Free Basic Water. In late 2000, after six years of unsuccessful cost recovery in urban services, a cholera epidemic and just before municipal elections, the South African government backed down from its hard-nosed cost recovery approach. Different stories have circulated about why it changed its mind. The Water Minister, then Ronnie Kasrils, claimed that FBW came about because of an epiphany. While visiting a rural village, he was appalled to see that despite having nearby communal taps from which water could be bought for a few cents, women and children were still walking to rivers to fetch unsafe water. He decided then that free basic water was the answer. The idea then started circulating in government and Mbeki later announced that government was giving all households a free ration of basic services (starting with free basic water to be followed by electricity and

---

5. Lund (2001) argues: 'Three main lessons: policy makers underestimated the time it takes to move from policy making, policy consultations to implementation. There is a trade off between public participation and rapid delivery. Policy makers underestimated the 'power of the old guard to undermine attempts at change.' New administrative leaders lacked insider knowledge of procedures. The lack of money is often not the problem in some services but the lack of human resource management.'

sanitation). Those using more than the basic amount (six kl of water per month) would still pay.

According to an ANC statement, "In October 2000 at the launch of the ANC's election campaign in Beaufort West, Mbeki announced that ANC controlled municipalities would provide free basic water and electricity to its citizens. This was central to the ANC local government Manifesto. The DA not to be outsmarted also adopted the idea."[6] During late 2000 and early 2001, a number of consultative meetings took place within government and with consultants and a task team headed by Macleod to decide on the best way or ways to deliver FBW was established. Macleod was credited with initiating free basic water in 1996-7 in Durban (Loftus, 2005). Of interest for this chapter's argument, however, are the administrative and legal conditions attached to FBW.

The FBW policy stipulated a free monthly supply of at least six kilolitres of water per property (not family). Unmetered communal standpipe supply in informal settlements was free (distance and drudgery instead of meters imposed limits and discipline on users). Households with in-house taps had to be metered and had to desist from meter tampering in order to get the free water ration. Urban households had to pay for any extra water used over the six kilolitre limit. Illegal connections disqualified the household, and failure to pay incurred being moved onto a limited service, instead of total cut-off (as in previous years). Residents could also request a prepaid meter.

The narrative was straightforward, according to Thabo Mbeki: "the provision of free basic amounts of water and electricity to our people will alleviate the plight of the poorest among us" (Mbeki, 2001). In February 2000, the Minister of Water Affairs, Ronnie Kasrils, further announced that government had decided that poor households could not be cut off from an assured basic free water supply. It was announced as a programme to uplift the poor, and especially women and children, who suffered because water was unaffordable and municipalities were disconnecting water on a large scale.

Subsequently, government's *Strategic Framework for Water Services* stipulated that no poor household could be deprived of basic supply. Kasrils insisted, "Users [are] entitled to their quota regardless of the state of their accounts. In no way have we ever indicated that they can cut water supply..."[7] The *Strategic Framework* document, adopted by Cabinet, feared that FBW would be misunderstood as free water in general. The document warned, "With the right to free basic water,

---

6. http://www.anc.org.za/ancdocs/pr/2002/pr0326.html (26 March 2002)
7. *Sunday Times*, 12 May 2002.

comes responsibility to pay for services over and above the basic service."

Indeed, government believed that FBW would 'enhance sustainability' since the "adoption of the free basic water policy has not negated this (user-pays) principle. On the contrary, the free basic water policy *strengthens the principle* in that it clearly requires consumption in excess of the basic water supply service to be paid for while enabling free access by the poor to a basic water supply service necessary to sustain life" -- a constitutional right. This is a very significant aspect of the policy in that free basic water would teach people the 'payment principle'.

In 2004, the government further clarified that "instead of total water cuts...*restriction valves* will be placed on meters, allowing for a trickle of water. However, anyone tampering with the valve will have a full-service cut."[8] Hence FBW signalled the end of full disconnections and the opening of new regimes of restricted water services of which the prepaid meter was one type.

In technical terms, a basic water supply facility was defined as "the infrastructure necessary to supply 25 litres of potable water per person per day supplied within 200 metres of a household and with a minimum flow of 10 litres per minute (in the case of communal water points) or 6 000 litres of potable water supplied per formal connection per month (in the case of yard or house connections)."

In many big cities *all* residents on the network were not charged for the first six kl, favouring smaller middle class households compared to multiple families on single plots in townships. Some urban households without metered supply (Soweto for example) could not get free water because they were still billed on a flat rate basis (i.e., 'deemed' consumption). As from 2004, to get free water, Sowetans were compelled to get a prepaid meter or be downgraded to yard taps. The typical strategy is for smaller municipalities to 'invite' the poor to register as 'indigents'. Indigents are those South African households with very limited property, unemployed, on pension and earning combined household income below a certain amount (typically in the order of R1500 per month). No uniform national indigent standard exists.

In 2003-4, Buffalo City had just under 40 000 registered indigent households (200 000 people) in a city of just under a million people. But 70 per cent of the municipality's households are poor (earning under R1500). In 2005-6, the number increased to 50 000. What is evident is that to register as an indigent, the householder (registered owner with title deed, or tenant) must appear in person with South African ID. An

---

8. *The Star*, 26 February 2004.

'indigent grant application' must be obtained and filled in. If unemployed, an affidavit signed at a police station is required. Furthermore, the IDs of husband, wife, a recent municipal account, and ward councillor signature are required. The applicant is screened and then later informed by post of their fate. Indigence status is valid for one year and has to be renewed every year. There is a R5 000 fine for giving false information and loss of all benefits[9].

The strategic political aims of Free Basic Water

In addition to the payment principle and generating an indigency registry, the implicit aims of state pro-poor policy are well illustrated in Kader Asmal's assessment of FBW which stresses free basic water as a separation strategy to 'sort out' certain groups:

> My successor, Minister Ronnie Kasrils, has pioneered a bold new policy, a difficult compromise between global imperatives and local realities. It aims to *sort out* those who for whatever reason won't pay for water services, and those impoverished millions who simply can't pay. It is South Africa's 'free basic water' policy, which allows a free quantity of 25 litres per person per day, and then charges a steeply graded price for consumption thereafter. When first introduced it seemed heresy to the World Bank and IMF, but has since been praised by liberals and conservatives alike, garnering favourable mention during the recent WSSD from unlikely supporters (Asmal, 2004: 23).

Interestingly, in 1998 Asmal himself – as Water Minister - had strenuously opposed implementation of FBW, writing to Patrick Bond (a FBW advocate),

> The positions I put forward are not positions of a sell-out, but of positions that uphold the policy of the South African government and the ANC ... The provision of such free water has financial implications for local government that I as a national minister must be extremely careful enforcing on local government.[10]

The free basic services 'strategy' (sic) was also justified within the state bureaucracy as "an innovative approach that will enable us to separate

---

9. http://www.buffalocity.gov.za/news2005/sep/sep30_benefits.stm
10. Asmal, K., 1998. Policy Directions of the Department of Water Affairs and Forestry. Letter to the author, Pretoria, 8 May, p. 1.

the can't pays from the won't pays or 'free-riders.'" Once the poor get their free water (through 'freepay' meters as Johannesburg Water called them), they simply won't be allowed to get into debt because they would have 'chosen' a restricted service (e.g., a self-disconnect prepaid meter, a yard-tank, standpipe or a flow restrictor). The poor would 'self-target' by accepting the FBW concession in exchange for lower, but free consumption.

Mike Muller (the DWAF director general) also openly articulated the deeper political rationales and strategic governmental advantages of FBW.[11] Free basic water, the tariff systems and cost recovery are strongly interconnected and have to be considered together. While different municipalities have different tariffs regimes, the state advised municipalities to adopt stepped tariffs. The more you use, the more you pay, so that overall people would learn to use less water. Muller reassured that free basic water was in fact the state's cost recovery strategy. Also stressing the cost-recovery aspect, the authoritative Department of Finance suggested, "To make it (FBW) work only the really proven poor should get these while anyone else should be forced to pay even at higher tariffs" (2001: 132). It was explicitly fashioned as a 'strategy' for distinguishing between the deserving and non-deserving (Muller, 2001: 14).

Since free basic water was introduced, most large urban municipalities began to use step tariffs to recover the cost of providing free water (Still, 2001: 17). In Durban, once households used above the extremely limited free amount, R32 extra per month was automatically added to the next tier's volume charges. In 2003, Johannesburg charged R5, 81 per kl in the 20 to 40kl range (this was R7, 75 in 2005-6) but Johannesburg has not proceeded without fixed charges (Dof, 2003: 223). The anomaly is that the *urban* poor use well over six kl a month, and in Durban, the effective doubling of water prices for poor people from 1997-2004 led to a 30 per cent decline in consumption, from 22kl per household per month, to 15 (while wealthier household consumption declined only 10 per cent). The state acknowledges that 20-30kl is the average for black urban townships (Dof, 2003). In many cases, to save themselves, households have had to 'voluntarily' downsize by having flow limiters fitted so that they can only access 6 000 litres per month and not get into a financial mess.

The politics of Johannesburg's special cases programme

---

11. Muller, M., 2001. Free basic water challenge. *Water Sewage and Effluent,* August/September, p.14.

The 'Special Cases Programme' in Johannesburg provides another illustration of how pro-poor policies are implemented as political strategies. A major concern in city government is the attitude and behavioural characteristics of the poor, specifically their civic duties to pay regularly for services and second, the dispositions of public servants towards discharging their duties. City of Johannesburg (CoJ) managers see 'rehabilitation' of defaulters and mobilising consumer-centred civic participation as one of the key tasks of good governance.[12] Some municipal managers still prefer 'strong rule', while many have come to see governance as a pedagogic task over the long-term, not to be imposed through rushed marketisation.

Alongside the educational dimension, municipal strategists have also debated the appropriate socio-technical infrastructure (such as prepaid meters) that can circumscribe consumption choices and assist pedagogically. The CoJ managers have, since 2001, utilised a sophisticated blend of neoliberal cost-recovery and paternalistic, residual welfare. This blend sought to develop the poor person into civic responsibility. 'Rehabilitating' the citizen involved new city-wide institutions and education programmes signalling a shift to more humane and at the same deeper marketised forms of delivery. Various schemes for 'meeting the poor halfway' but on new state terms such as prepaid meters were developed. Rather than exclude, it seeks to manage the poor and to provide technologies for the poor to increase their capacity to self-manage.

Smith and Vawda (2003: 35) caution against a too rapid "shift from the citizen to the customer," as this may alienate residents. The authors point out that because black South Africans lack consumer skills, it will take time before customer-citizenship can become feasible. The SCP was a multi-faced intervention to assist 'indigents', pensioners, the disabled, HIV-Aids patients, and all households with a monthly income of under R1401 ($200). It was also designed for the poor "to rehabilitate their municipal accounts and (to) create a culture of payment."[13]

Johannesburg Metro has a total of 3, 2 million residents (1 050 229 households) with a million people (300 000 households) classified as poor. It has a higher percentage of poor (32 per cent) compared to

---

12. The United Nations has considered 'good' governance as an essential component of the Millennium Development Goals [MDGs], because 'good' governance establishes a framework for fighting poverty and inequality (United Nations. 2007. *Public Governance Indicators: A Literature Review*, New York: UN).

13. Johannesburg extends helping hand, *City News,* 3 February 2006. Note that 'accounts', not people are singled out for rehabilitation in this document.

Tshwane with 28 per cent and Cape Town with 23 per cent.[14] By late 2005, one in six CoJ accountholders (or 92 000 households) were estimated as eligible.

Pensioners and the disabled needed to show their National Social Security Grant cards; 'indigents' were required to present ID documents, a copy of latest municipal account, a letter from the tax authority confirming tax status and, a police affidavit confirming their unemployed status. Concessions included FBW, FBE, free sewage and refuse collection, rates exemption for property if valued under R20 000, total write-off of arrears, conditional on accepting prepaid meters for water and electricity, agreeing to random 'home assessments for verification of information' and paying all current charges until the prepaid meters are installed. Cheating incurs a five year ban on re-applications.[15] "Although there is no cut-off date to apply for the subsidy itself, one feature of the scheme expires on 31 January 2005 – successful applicants will have their arrears debt written off."[16]

Prepaid meters in Johannesburg and the shift to self-disconnections

Johannesburg Water (JW), created in 2001 as an offshoot, in a radical restructuring of Johannesburg municipal administration, became a ring-fenced corporatised, independent private utility company, under a management contract with the French Suez Water company. Johannesburg Water is one of a few ring-fenced water departments in South Africa, and as an independent company, it has the City of Johannesburg as its only shareholder. Johannesburg Water claims that the reason for the formation of a private utility to control the water was to "introduce greater efficiency, professionalism, customer orientation and service delivery" (Johannesburg Water Corporate Profile, 2001). Johannesburg Water claims that there is greater accountability by separating the roles of governance and delivery (Johannesburg Water Corporate Profile, 2001). Johannesburg Water has implemented the FBW policy since July 2001. The first block (0-6kl) is zero-rated, thereafter steep tariff increases apply. JW's FBW policy is non-discretionary, i.e., it is applied throughout Johannesburg where there are

14. National Treasury. 2007. *Local Government Budgets and Expenditure Review*, 2001/2 – 2006/7. Pretoria: Republic of South Africa, p. 107.
15. Official Brochure, Municipal Services Subsidy,
http://www.joburg.org.za/services/municipal_subsidy.stm
also see Speech by Executive Mayor, 4 May 2005,
http://www.joburg.org.za/2005/may/may5_speech.stm, 15 March 2006.
16. Arrears write offs end Tuesday,
 http://www.joburg.org.za/2006/jan/jan30_revenue.stm

meters by simply zero-rating the first 6kl of metered water. Thus the FBW is nominally provided to all (who are already served with metered infrastructure) rather than to only the poor.

There are technical impediments to the delivery of 6 kl of free water in major townships where there are no meters. JW indicated that flat-rated areas (i.e., where meters were either not read or not installed) were not recipients of the FBW (Interview with J.P Mas, July 2004, cited in Deedat, 2002). In fact, in Soweto, which is flat-rated, prepayment has been marketed as a strategy to give the poor their allotted FBW. Areas where FBW is not yet supplied include Alexandra (350 000) and Soweto (1 million) except for prepaid metered households. For instance, Alexandra, one of Johannesburg's oldest townships, has 4 060 formal houses and 34 000 shacks with an average four households for every 40m². "Approximately 70 percent of households accommodate more than 10 people" (Jonews Agency, 16 June, 2005).

In 2003, the city provided 36 392 households in informal settlements with free water from mobile water tankers at a cost to the city of about R5 889 000 in the 2003/2004 financial year (Social Services Package, 2004: 19). Additionally 92 277 households (9 per cent) got water at the nearest stand pipe that is over 200 metres away.17 [Half a million residents in informal settlements around the province were serviced in this way.] Residents living in the informal settlements were not charged for these essentially emergency services. The tanker service and communal tap was also counted as FBW, although this is clearly not the same FBW that suburban households conveniently receive inside their homes.

FBW, nevertheless was a concession, it provided strategic space and legitimacy to pursue market and punitive strategies directed at the poor (such as restricted or full cut-offs if people were caught stealing services). But another possibility existed: installing the prepaid meter (PPM). Dubbed 'the way of the future' by town planners and leading politicians (Imeisa, 2001: 31), the installation of prepaid meters (PPM) in South Africa has taken place with an amazing speed. Already since 2000, the national electricity commission (Eskom) and municipalities had installed some 3.2 million prepaid meters. "Most went to new customers, i.e., previously non- electrified houses" in black areas (Tewari and Shah, 2003: 25-6). After 2002, all RDP houses with in-house or yard taps were meant to be fitted with prepayment water.

The City of Johannesburg (CoJ) saw the problem (of water management) as, "the effects of a much bigger problem of oversupply

---

17. http://www.joburg-archive.co.za/corporate_planning/package.pdf

and a lack of ownership of water consumption by residents."18 Poor residents (without meters and on flat-rated deemed consumption) were said to have bad attitudes, overused water, and many did not pay or were illegally connected.19 Jameel Chand, a city official portrayed Soweto as an area 'riddled with illegal connections'.20 Residents were implored to accept prepaid water meters, and in return Joberg Water would repair household leaks and install 'free-pay meters', to allow a monthly 6 kl of free water. With less water loss, JW projected savings of R158 million per year upon completion of the prepayment project.21 In 2003, therefore, Johannesburg Water spearheaded a major campaign to install prepaid water in 160 000 Soweto homes, although nothing prevented them from fixing leaks without PPM. By 2006, about 44 000 meters had been installed with all 160 000 to be installed by 2008.

Speaking optimistically of a 'new culture of prepayment' in South Africa which would make installing prepaid water more acceptable to the population, Johannesburg Water, the new corporatised utility that emerged out of restructuring in 2001, hoped PPM could be installed as a quid-pro-quo for arrear write-offs. In parts of Orange Farm, communities were promised sanitation.22 National government has supported prepaid meters: "The pre-paid meters are in fact designed and programmed to provide the basic amount for free. They have the added advantage of allowing households to monitor and control their water consumption... households appreciate this facility" (Kasrils, 2003). Since consumers 'self-disconnect' the PPM strategy is 'debt-proof' and convenient for councils as long as consumers do not tamper with the system.

Promoted as the 'ultimate solution' to non-payment, the PPM is less dictatorial, and conceals the penalty itself, as Foucault (1995: 10) would put it. The PPM does not have to be read by council workers, and no bills have to be sent out. Disconnections are self-imposed. The consumer bears the costs of buying prepaid units from the municipality or local vendors. This downloading of transactions and costs to the end-user may also be counted as a part of the logic of privatisation. Some consumers however, believe it at least provides them a measure of direct

---

18. Johannesburg Water Managing Director, Greg Segoneco, cited in Special Projects http://www.johannesburgwater.co.za/asp/catalogue, 16 May 2005.
19. See Egan and Wafer, 2006 for account of electricity and water 'theft' or popular illegalities in Soweto and the activities of the Soweto Electricity Crisis Committee.
20. Chand, cited in, 'Johannesburg Municipality, city gets cracking'. *Financial Mail*, 11 February 2005. For a detailed account of how illegalities become normalised, see Olukoju, A., 2004. Never Expect Power Always: Electricity consumers response to monopoly, corruption and inefficient services in Nigeria. *African Affairs*, 103, pp.51-71.
21. CoJ, Johannesburg Business Plan, May 2005.
22. *The Star*, 2 May 2003.

control over their expenditure and at the same time avoids billing errors, a common problem in Johannesburg.

The 'technical' literature on prepayment (see DBSA, 2001; WRC, 2003) showed a keen awareness of the political 'benefits' of prepaid water, in particular what managers call 'conflict avoidance' and cheap administration. Tewari and Shah (2003: 20) argue: "The social unwillingness to use prepaid primarily stems from the political power a society enjoys which gets translated in to rent-earning activity." [23] Prepaid meters change the structure of opportunities and discipline consumers through direct money power. The initial free amount on the prepaid meter is crucial as it provides the incentive for 'wise use' and legitimises self-disconnection.

As suggested recently by John Rabe, one of the architects of Johanesburg's PPM,

> Probably the biggest impact (newly created dimension) that prepayment can have on a service provider is the effective creation of customers…offering 'customer service' rather than continuing in a paradigm which considers the end-users as only a consumer.[24]

To make FBW and PPM more credible, the Johannesburg Water Company's 'customer services' division conducted an education campaign to show the poor that six kl is enough to survive in an urban setting. With six kl, a family could choose five body washes; six toilet flushes, two kettles of water, one sink-full of water for dishes (per day), and one clothes wash every second day.[25]

Prepaid meters are, to borrow from Foucault (1995: 23), 'political tactics'. As technologies they educate, they create 'modern' rational patterns of behaviour suitable for marketised social life. As Foucault insisted, modern forms of power such as evident in the FBW and prepaid meters are not prohibitions, but 'go right down to the depths of society' as 'fields of knowledge'.

---

23. Eskom had a difficult time managing the conventional meters. Eskom used to hire workers whose main task was to read meters and disconnect electricity of those whose payments were overdue. This entailed ensuring the transportation from house to house and the protection of its employees in the event of conflict with customers. 'The conventional metering, in the absence of proper social attitudes to electricity, became a system demanding very high maintenance. Prepaid metering reduced this cost tremendously'. (McGibbon, 2002, Eskom Manager).

24. Michael Rabe, Affidavit, 11 January 2007, p. 17, in the Case on prepaid meters, Centre for Applied Legal Studies. http://www.law.wits.ac.za/cals (20 May 2007).

25. http://www.johannesburgwater.co.za.

But as we have argued, they are also part of a wider project of new subject formation and new social attitudes: an ideal middle-class thrifty consumer transposed onto the poor. The liberal commodity discourse associated with households' use of prepaid meters is evident in the idea that the consumer 'takes ownership' of the service (Johannesburg Water, 2001) and that such ownership is 'empowering' and reinforces 'consumer sovereignty'.

Since there are no public records of how many times households self-disconnect, municipalities are also spared the political embarrassment of loud disconnections. Soweto, historic centre of the 1976 uprisings, owed R 506 million in electricity payments to Eskom over two years (2001/2), but payment rates fell from 61 per cent to 36 per cent in the same period (*Sowetan*, 14 March 2003). Since the early 1990s, some 65 000 or 45 per cent of township bondholders have had homes repossessed (*Financial Mail*, 30 August 2002: 34).

A national survey of municipalities revealed that municipal managers overstate the extent of community support for PPM and, "there is a tendency by water services providers to assume that technology will solve problems which are in fact social ones" (WRC 2003: 14). Pre-paid meters may weaken community solidarity with neigbours sometimes stealing water from one another or re-selling water to others (Deedat, 2002). Highly politicised communities, such as Soweto in Johannesburg, have perceived prepaid meters as racially discriminatory,[26] while more middle-class consumers have welcomed prepaid meters because they have been victims of wrong billing and mistaken cutoffs by the municipality[27]. As in Durban with its restrictors, "prepayment technology has reduced, not necessarily solved the problem of pilferage; revenue losses from pilferage are still high."[28] Angry Soweto residents have repeatedly ripped out electricity prepaid meters and dumped them at local council or Eskom offices.[29]

Conclusion

This chapter points to the need to research the ambiguities of neoliberal social development and the underlying political rationales of 'pro-poor' policy in South Africa and how these are woven into an attempted engineering of a market-based disciplinary society. The chapter concludes that service delivery has only to a limited extent addressed

26. *Business Day*, 16 March 2004 and 17 November 2004.
27. *Sunday Times*, 4 July 2004.
28. *Business Day*, 23 March 2001.
29. *The Star*, 14 March 2003.

absolute poverty, but more generally has become linked to negative outcomes such as isolating the very poor and imposing market citizenship on township communities in South Africa, the African National Congress's core constituency.

The critique of poverty alleviation research programmes needs three further comments. First, research needs to address the problem that poverty reduction policies have not shifted wider macro-economic orthodoxy, such as the priority given to fighting inflation through high real interest rates. Thus many pro-poor interventions are systematically undermined by pro-rich ones. South Africa's failure to reduce unemployment and insecurity must rank as one of its fundamental failures.

A second critique of existing research takes this further by suggesting that pro-poor policies are designed to promote market values and are specifically designed as selected or targeted programmes to deepen a prevailing neoliberal ethos. Poverty reduction has become both a symbolic and institutionalising politics for stringing the poor along and incorporating them into a market society. The project of reducing poverty may be seen as a component of a neoliberal idea itself. The focus on 'poverty' postpones speaking of the impediments to wider social change. Poverty reduction usually fragments into various fundable specialisms and programmes (child poverty, rural poverty, or 'extreme' poverty). It is less threatening as long as a holistic approach is avoided. The poverty consensus has become a discursive bridge uniting a more conservative clique of NGOs, the academy and the state.

Anti-poverty as an official state activity sets up a contractarian mode of accountability where once performance targets are met, the poor are meant to reciprocate with good behaviour and loyalty to the state. Poverty, and development offered by the government is also clearly a defensive response to waves of protests and a way of keeping various populations in their place. In SA, rather than abandoning the poor, poverty relief seeks to regulate the poor by 'meeting the poor halfway' in exchange for concessions but on strict terms.[30] Consequently, the tension between helping and regulating the poor needs to become a more central concern for research in welfare policy and governance.

---

30. For purposes of this chapter, 'the poor' may be defined as broad category households including the working poor that struggle to pay for services and fall into debt either periodically or chronically. Some 40 per cent of Johannesburg's municipal accountholders (or 290 000 accounts) earn less than R6500 per month and struggle to pay municipal bills (these are termed the less poor). Aside from these households, there are 32 per cent of the general population, who have less than R1500 income per month, the official poor.

References

Alcock, P., 1993. *Understanding Poverty*. London: MacMillan.

Asmal, K., 2004. *Water in civil society Arid African upstream safari: a transboundary expedition*. Unesco: Paris.

City of Johannesburg. 2005. Johannesburg Business Plan, May.

Deacon, A., 2002. *Perspectives on Welfare*. Open University Press: Buckingham.

Deedat, H., 2006. Free-Pay meters in Johannesburg, Unpublished Municipal Services Report.

Desai, A., 2002. *We are the poors*. New York: Monthly Review Press.

Department of Water Affairs and Forestry (DWAF). 2000. Delivery of Free Water. Pretoria.

DWAF. 2001a. Questions and answers, Free basic water. Pretoria. http://www.dwaf.gov.za/FreeBasicWater/.

DWAF. 2001b. Free basic water implementation strategy. Case study: Durban Unicity. Prepared by Palmer Development Group. http://www.dwaf.gov.za/FreeBasicWater/Docs/casestud/ .

DWAF. 2003. Strategic Framework for Water Services. Pretoria.

Egan, A. and Wafer, A., 2006. Dynamics of a Mini-mass Movement. In R. Ballard, A. Habib and I. Valodia, eds. *Voices of Protest: Social Movements in Post-apartheid South Africa*. Scottsville: University of KwaZulu-Natal Press.

Escobar, A., 1995 *Encountering development*. Princeton: Princeton University Press.

ESI Africa. 2002. Prepaid water and electricity dispensers. http://www.esi.co.za/last/ESI_3_2002/ESI132002_050_1.htm.

Ferguson, J., 1999. *The Anti-politics machine*. Berkeley: UC Press.

Gramsci, A., 1971. Selections from the *Prison Notebooks*. Translated and edited by Q. Hoare and G. Nowell Smith. New York: International Publishers.

Hart, G., 2006. Post Apartheid Developments in historical and comparative perspective. In V. Padayachee, ed. *The development Decade? Economic and Social Change inSouth Africa 1994-2004*. Pretoria: HSRC Press, pp.13-32.

Harvey, D., 1996. *Justice, Nature and the Geography of Difference*. Oxford: Basil Blackwell.

Harvey, D., 2005. *A brief history of Neoliberalism*. Oxford: Oxford University Press.

Jessop, B., 2002. Liberalism, neoliberalism, and urban governance: A State-theoretic perspective. *Antipode*, 34 (3), pp.451-72.

Larner, W., 2004. Neoliberalism in (regional) theory and practice: the stronger communities action fund. Research Paper 14, Auckland University, Dept of Sociology.

Lund, F., 2001. South Africa, Transition under Pressure. In P. Alcock and G. Craig, eds. *International Social Policy*. New York: Palgrave.

Newman, J., 2004. Modernising the state. A new style of Governance? In J. Lewis and R. Surrender, eds. *Welfare state change, towards a third way?* Oxford: Oxford University Press. Oxford Scholarship Online. http://dx.doi.org/10.1093/0199266727.001.0001>

Noel, A., 2006. The new global politics of poverty. *Global Social Policy*, 6(304), pp.304-333.

Offe, C., 1983. *Contradictions of the Welfare State*. London: Hutchinson

Painter, J., 1995. *Politics, Geography and Political Geography*. London: Arnold.

Patel, L., 2005. *Social welfare and social development in South Africa* Oxford: Oxford University Press.

Payer, C., 1982. *The World Bank, a critical analysis*. New York: Monthly Review Press.

Smith, L. and Vawda, A., 2003. Citizens vs. Customer: Different Approaches to public participation in service delivery in Cape Town. *Urban Forum*, 14(1), pp. 26-52.

Still, A., 2001. Free basic water, who pains, who gains. *Water, Sewage and Effluent*, 21 (4), p.17.

Tewari D.D. and Shah, T., 2003. An Assessment of South Africa's Prepaid Electricity Experiment, Lessons Learned, and their Policy Implications for Developing Countries. *Energy Policy*, 31, pp.911-927.

Walker, C., 1993. *Managing Poverty, The Limits of Social Assistance*. London: Routledge.

7.
'The feminisation of poverty' as disabling discourse
Prishani Naidoo[1]

'Help Eliminate Poverty.
Empower a woman and feed a family.
Make Mom proud. Help fight poverty!'[2]

Introduction

It has almost become a mantra that women are the worst affected by the growing poverty that characterises society today, and that any serious attempt at poverty alleviation or eradication needs to target women as a group. The statement quoted above is just one of the many adverts and slogans that appear on the sidebar of a google search results page when one types in the word 'poverty'. In fulfilling one's own desire for affirmation (by making Mom proud), one is urged to assist in eradicating poverty through the empowerment of one woman through whom an entire family, it is claimed, will be fed. In these undoubtedly nobly-intentioned sentiments, lie a number of moral judgments of men and gendered expectations of women, as well as a host of gendered (and other culturally-biased) assumptions about 'families'. The statement also falls into a growing trend that seeks to measure the lowest levels of poverty and to find interventions that cost the least and have the widest effect with regard to neutralising the potential volatility of the poor, most often reinforcing levels of vast inequality in society and confining large layers of society to extremely basic levels of services, and life on its margins (Naidoo, 2007). Here, women become the 'most cost-effective' and 'sensible' targets for intervention, allowing 'limited resources' to be spent in ways that are thought to guarantee 'good returns'. And, the underlying causes of poverty (which are deeply gendered) are left untouched. This article interrogates how such discourses of poverty, that seem to address the position of the most vulnerable in society, identified as women, often reinforce the very gendered stereotypes, beliefs, values, and practices that have allowed for inequality and poverty to exist.

The term 'the feminisation of poverty' appears within this context of woman becoming the global face of poverty and target of interventions,

---

1. This article began as a collabourative project with Gladys Mokolo, Nthabiseng Mahlangu, Christina Nthoroana and Nonhlanhla Ngwenya, to whom I am deeply indebted for sharing their time and life experiences so generously with me.
2. sponsored link on google search results page for <poverty> to
http://www.unitus.org/EmpowerWomen; accessed 12 March 2007

particularly in the research and policy documents produced by governments, the United Nations, donor agencies, parts of academia, and the growing number of non-governmental organisations (NGOs) comprising global civil society. It is most often used as a catch-all descriptive phrase for the growing vulnerability of women today, without much substantiation or argument (BRIDGE, 2001; Chant, 2003; 2006). Often it is just tagged onto discussions to give the impression that gender issues have been considered in an argument or set of recommendations about poverty. When the term is defined, it usually refers to the greater incidence of poverty amongst women (most often measured in terms of household income); the greater severity of the experience of poverty by women compared with that experienced by men; and a trend amongst women towards greater poverty, usually associated with a rising number of female-headed-households and growing female participation in the informal economy (BRIDGE, 2001).

However, theorists highlight the paucity of appropriate statistics and research to prove all of these claims, and look towards understanding to what ends this discourse works in different contexts. In particular, theorists problematise easy assumptions that are made about female-headed-households and the absence of gender disaggregated household data, and argue for the development of statistical models and indicators that consider the ways in which gender relations determine the nature of poverty and the success or failure of interventions designed to eradicate it (BRIDGE, 2001; Chant, 2003; 2006). Sylvia Chant (2006) argues that use of the term is also usually accompanied by some form of recommendation for the targeted relief of women when designing programmes to address poverty, in this way allowing for minimalist interventions to be crafted and sold by governments and donor agencies. This article will explore some of these critiques through the experiences of a group of women living in Orange Farm, a socio-economically disadvantaged part of Johannesburg.

Beginning with the experiences of women, described by the dominant discourse as 'poor', rather than with the discourse itself, this article attempts to offer an alternative way of approaching the question of poverty in society, a method that acknowledges the workings of power in the very act of speaking and writing about 'the poor'. Rather than examining the experiences of 'poor women' through the discourse of 'the feminisation of poverty', this article will evaluate the worth of the discourse in terms of the lived experiences of a group of women living in conditions of socio-economic disadvantage. In this way, the writing up of the experiences of 'the poor' is not mediated by the frame of the discourse, but is directed by the nature of the experiences themselves and the contexts in which they unfold.

On method

This article began as an attempt to initiate a discussion on 'the feminisation of poverty' with a group of four women living in Orange Farm, who would subsequently become co-researchers on this project. I came into contact with each of the women through my research, development and political work with community organisations in Orange Farm, in particular the Kganya Women's Consortium (a collective of thirteen women's projects) and the Orange Farm Water Crisis Committee (OWCC), and based my choice of participants on their different ages and experiences with regard to poverty. When, in the first group meeting, none of the women had heard of the term 'the feminisation of poverty', it was decided that discussions would focus rather on the experiences of poverty as felt by each of the women in the group, and a more qualitative exploration of the experience of poverty would be undertaken through discussions facilitated by me in this small group. I would feed information gleaned from a secondary research process on 'the feminisation of poverty' into group discussions, in this way facilitating a conversation amongst participants about the discourse. While the group discussions are by no means representative of the views of all poor women in Orange Farm, Johannesburg or South Africa, they do, however, speak to experiences of poverty and knowledge of experiences that go beyond those of the women in the group, that suggest the need for alternative approaches to the study and eradication of poverty in society today. They provide reasons for greater effort to be put towards more qualitative and participatory approaches to the study and attempted eradication of poverty.

In two separate discussions, the group met and shared experiences related to their lives as women in Orange Farm, in processes facilitated by me. Discussion was allowed to flow freely, with participants speaking about their individual life histories, relating their experiences to the overall theme of poverty, and steering of the discussion happening only when necessary, and feeding of the discussion from time to time with information from the secondary research process that was directly related to the discourse of 'the feminisation of poverty'. Participants also shared their experiences and knowledge of poverty in Orange Farm more generally. While this article is, then, based on the stories and experiences of the four women from Orange Farm, it also speaks to the stories of others known to them.

To facilitate openness, honesty, trust, and the absence of fear in group discussions, it was agreed that the names of participants would not be linked to the particular stories discussed in this article. In addition, specific stories would not be used to reach particular conclusions. Rather, there would be general discussion about the conclusions reached in group discussions, with some stories being used to illustrate some conclusions.

In this way, participants believed that they could speak about their lives and experiences without ignoring the very potential effects that this act of speaking could have on their lives and the lives of their loved ones who might come to recognise themselves in criticisms raised in this article. This article does not, therefore, contain names. It does, however, contain the views and experiences of four women living in Orange Farm about the lives of women generally in Orange Farm, mediated by my own views and experiences. While I acted largely as facilitator of discussions amongst the four other women, I did also, at times, become a participant by offering my own views and experiences, and sharing material collected from the secondary research process. My control of facilitation also allowed me to frame and direct discussions towards answering particular questions, and my own interpretation of secondary material undoubtedly had some effect on the nature of discussions. While the group attempted to maintain as democratic, horizontal and open a space as possible in which discussions could take place, the role of facilitator and writer would ultimately afford me much more power in the process of research, discussion, and writing. This was recognised at the outset, and the very limitations of academic writing problematised. While this discussion could be the subject of another article, the group felt that it would be important to signal here the need for greater resources (both human and material) to be dedicated towards more participatory and qualitative approaches to understanding and eradicating poverty being developed in which the traditional hierarchies set up by academic forms of writing and research are challenged. The method employed in the writing of this article must, then, be seen only as an initial step in developing an alternative way of studying and writing about poverty that is itself limited and limiting. It nevertheless highlights the importance and need for this alternative, and shows the potential for its development given greater resources and commitment in society.

Experiences and critique

Through the stories and experiences that flowed in the first discussion, participants began to make some of the assertions also made by proponents of the discourse of 'the feminisation of poverty' i.e., that the majority of the poor are women, that the majority of women are poor, and that rising female poverty corresponds with an increase in the number of female headed households. These assertions are borne out in statistics related to poverty when explored through a gender lens with regard to Orange Farm (Khanya College/Kganya Women's Consortium, 2002) and South Africa (Hassim, 2005). With Orange Farm being identified in official state policy documents as a socio-economically disadvantaged area, it would also be reasonable to expect the population of Orange Farm to reflect the gendered characteristics of poverty exhibited in national statistics related to households.

Orange Farm is a township located approximately 45 km south-west of the city of Johannesburg. It began as an area demarcated for the resettlement of black squatters by the apartheid government in 1987, as influx control laws were lifted and strategies were crafted to organise and regulate the urbanisation of black people. The few research projects that have been conducted in Orange Farm since 1994 have demonstrated the particularly precarious and vulnerable positions occupied by women in Orange Farm, many living in female-headed-households, often led by single mothers or grandmothers (Khanya College/Kganya Consortium, 2002; Coalition Against Water Privatisation et. al., 2003). These projects have also highlighted the widespread existence of income generation and other community projects, many of which have been initiated by unemployed women.

While existing statistics and the immediate experiences of the group seemed to support each other, participants agreed that such assertions and their implications for policy formulation and community struggles needed to be explored further to make them meaningful. What did it mean that poverty in Orange Farm was characterised by a large number of female-headed households? How did women experience poverty differently from men? Was this indeed the case or was poverty the result of more complicated sets of gendered relations in society that produced inequalities that allowed poverty to persist?

Female-headed households as Apartheid's gendered legacy

In the experience of participants, the majority of their neighbours in Orange Farm are single mothers, heading households without the presence of men. Each of them had been confronted with personal difficulties as well as the problems of other women and families in the community in their daily lives and work as the problems associated with rising poverty presented themselves. In a survey of 194 women in households in Orange Farm conducted in 2001, the majority of interviewees were single parents and widows (Khanya College/Kganya Consortium). In the small group constituted to produce this article, two participants were single parents, the oldest member of the group - a pensioner who had divorced twice due to the experience of domestic violence, and a widow who had recently lost her partner to HIV-AIDS and is herself HIV-positive. The youngest member of the group shared the experience and perspective of a young girl whose life had been adversely affected by the separation of her parents at an early stage of her life. Only one participant was happily married. In this group of four women, three had been directly affected by the phenomenon of female-headed households.

As the group tried to understand the reasons behind this phenomenon, participants began to talk about the experiences of women in male-headed households, that resulted in divorce, separation and the rise in the number of female single parents spoken about in mainstream discussions and apprehended in their own experiences. In many cases, domestic violence was a reason for separation. Experiences in the group going back as far as 1946, participants were able to explore some of the changing living conditions for men and women since the start of apartheid, and the effects that they produced in society. For most African women, life under apartheid was extremely difficult, with their survival almost completely dependent on their relationships with men.

While African culture and colonial society had already produced a highly gendered society, segregation and apartheid made further changes to the structure of gender relations, particularly through the regulation of the labour market. Migrant labour had profound effects on relations between African men and women, dividing families and separating husbands and wives (or partners) for most of their lives. Based on the notion that an African male worker was 'single' or 'responsible for' a wife and children living in the 'homelands' or 'bantustans' who were able to subsist through farming and support of extended family networks, wages were generally low, and living conditions harsh. Through the migrant labour system and influx control, apartheid legislated the separation of African men and women, and attempted to structure African life in such a manner that only the most basic needs of men and women would need to be provided for by the state and white employers. The welfare system was based on the notion that African life was cheaper than white life, with African needs requiring fewer resources than white needs. As life in 'the homelands' became increasingly difficult, many women would move to urban areas to seek employment or join their partners. (Parnell, 1992; Parnell & Mosdell, 2003; Ramphele, 2002). Stories shared in this small group focused largely on urban women as all participants had been born to parents already living in townships of the city of Johannesburg. But here too, African men and women experienced the effects of a system designed to (re)produce the deep lines of inequality of apartheid society.

Under apartheid, African women were not tolerated in urban areas unless they could prove that they were married to working men or themselves employed. The Natives Urban Areas Act (1923) and the Slums Act (1934) legislated these stipulations (Parnell, 1992). African women were also actively prevented from entering the formal labour market, with a minority gaining access to professions such as nursing and teaching, and the majority of employed African women in urban areas being found in domestic service, especially in white homes (and some Indian and coloured homes). The oldest in the group shared the frustrations she felt as a young African woman living under apartheid through her experiences of being prevented from buying furniture without her husband being present to 'sign for her', and not being able to buy a house without being married even when she could prove that she had a job. For her generation, choosing a life of independence as a single woman was difficult. In the urban areas, this was almost impossible without resorting to various forms of illegality e.g. the running of shebeens, spaza shops, and sex work. In order to have a roof over one's head, most women had to submit themselves to marriage or to domestic employment. The independence of women was also not generally accepted in African culture, and clearly defined roles were prescribed for men and women. Being accepted in society and gaining respect and affirmation from one's elders meant getting married (in most cases meaning to have a man pay 'lobola' for a woman) and assuming particular roles in a family and extended family. Participants agreed that these roles, across cultures, taught us that men should occupy the role of 'provider' and women that of 'caregiver', be it in the nuclear or extended family. Living up to these roles came to be defined by the restrictions placed on the lives of African men and women by apartheid.

Working with a group of African youth in the early 1990s in Crossroads, Cape Town, Mamphela Ramphele was able to record and try to understand the effects of the disruption of families through the migrant labour system on the lives of future generations. In the group of sixteen young people with whom she came to work, ten were raised by their mothers, two by their grandmothers, and one by his sister. Only one of the youth had been raised by both parents. And only six of the group did not have the experience of encountering problems related to parents having children from previous relationships. (Ramphele, 2002: 31). The lives of these children had been deeply affected by the nature of the relationships between men and women in their homes, in particular between their parents. Ramphele writes that men are, "disempowered by having to depend on the very women that a patriarchal culture designates as inferior to them. The dissonance between the cultural expectations of gender power relations on the one hand, and the reality of powerlessness on the other, sets off a vicious cycle of low self-esteem, resentment, anger and abuse of the very source of your support - the woman, mother, sister, wife, lover." (*Ibid*: 160). As apartheid ate away at the African man's ability to fulfill his role of 'provider', resentment would grow towards those for whom he was meant to be 'providing'. In many homes, domestic violence arose when 'the man of the house' was unable to provide for the needs of 'his home', either by having too little money and/or losing his job, and/or having too little time to spend with his family. At other times, it might be the fact that a woman's 'caregiver' role was coming under question as she began to work or earn an income.

Neoliberal policies reinforce gender inequalities

As the apartheid economy in the 1980s would be forced to respond to changes in the global economy, neoliberal policies would begin to be introduced. While the African National Congress (ANC) would assume electoral power on the promise of a broadly redistributive programme (the Reconstruction and Development Programme - RDP), it would tie itself to a logic of export-oriented growth in the form of the Growth, Employment and Redistribution Strategy (GEAR), adopted in 1996 by government, and underpinned by a number of neoliberal macro-economic principles. In the years following the adoption of GEAR, the gendered structure of the labour market would face a number of pressures and changes. Trade liberalisation would result in job losses in traditionally male sectors of the economy, such as mining, and female industries, such as footwear and textile, and flexible forms of labour, in the form of part-time, casualised, and seasonal forms of work into which women tended to move as forms of cheap labour, would be introduced (Kenny & Webster, 1999; Mosoetsa, 2001).

These changes with regard to labour have been accompanied by rising costs of living, with the introduction of the logic of cost recovery and corporatisation in the delivery of basic services, health, and education being a major contributory factor. In the experience of participants, life for working class men and women has become more difficult. In Orange Farm, it would seem as though very few people have full time jobs. Men and women 'are sitting at home'. The only form of work available is contract jobs, which both men and women have access to. In this context the roles of 'provider' and 'caregiver' continue to shape the ways in which men and women are expected to earn respect and acceptance in the family, community, and society, but the ability for men and women to live up to them is increasingly constrained. Domestic violence, and general instability in the home and community manifest along gendered lines.

Gendered socialisation

In the experience of this group, the roles into which men and women are socialised also determine how people respond to change and crises in their lives. In Orange Farm, it is the experience that many men, when they lose a job or source of income, become depressed and despondent, often turning on women and children, and becoming violent. Many men turn to alcohol and drugs, and become angry about not being able to be 'providers'. While there are also women who respond in similar ways, it was the experience of participants that more women than men in Orange Farm have been able to start informal activities and projects in order to sustain themselves and their families. Participants felt that this was probably due to the fact that women are socialised to be 'caregivers', ensuring that the most basic needs of the family are met at all times. Also that women often see men's well-being as coming before their own, and being dependent on women. Men are more likely to continue looking for formal employment than women who make up more of the informal economy and are more likely to take up positions as volunteers rather than full-time workers, these differences themselves produced by our acceptance of and socialisation into our different roles as men and women as those of 'provider' and 'caregiver' respectively, as well as the gendered nature of the labour market. For participants, there was no innately purer moral substance to woman than man that makes her a better 'caregiver'. Unfortunately, many current interventions that seek to alleviate poverty are based on the notion that women are morally better than men (more responsible and trustworthy), and that support of a poor woman thus allows an entire family to be supported. What such approaches miss is the fact that the lives of men and women are closely intertwined, and that the ways in which men and women relate today are based on the ways in which we are socialised to become 'providers' and 'caregivers' in society. The targeting of women alone serves only to allow for the most minimal interventions to be made, and often makes worse the divisions and tensions that already exist between men and women in homes and communities.

Participants also felt that it was often due to men's own perceived failure to live up to the role of 'provider', and not necessarily due to any expectations of women, that men became despondent, frustrated, angry, and violent. As one of the group said, "Even if a man doesn't work, he always moans, sits alone or becomes aggressive and violent because he is not working. And he thinks that the wife doesn't give him any respect and yet it's not so. Women do respect their husbands even if they don't work. But the men are too aggressive and violent. That is why women are always being harassed in the house and there is a lot of domestic violence." Participants went on to speak about how it is important to be accepted and respected in and by society, and how the gendered norms of society often prescribe to men (and women) the achievements by which to measure one's success in the world. Failure to reach these steps leads to feelings of resentment and anger that manifest in our relations with those closest to us, those who are also part of how people see themselves and their success in the world.

Participants also spoke about the changing roles and responsibilities into which men and women are being socialised today, under the sway of neoliberal policies. As women are being targeted for 'capacity building', 'skills development', 'entrepreneurship', and 'empowerment', traditional roles and responsibilities defined for women as those of 'caregivers' are being challenged as is the ability for men to live up to their traditional roles and responsibilities related to being 'providers'. Participants felt that targeting women for assistance with improving their socio-economic positions without addressing the problems of rising unemployment and flexibilisation of labour experienced by men, often leads to feelings of resentment and anger amongst men as a result of perceptions that their traditional roles are being undermined.

The group also came to interrogate issues related to socialisation, in particular culture and the stereotypes associated with living in Orange Farm, through a story that spoke of an experience different to the norm or the expected. While many women came to Orange Farm to escape poor domestic relationships, the group also shared the story of someone who had come to Orange Farm 'out of love'. For this woman from a well known middle-class family in Johannesburg, Orange Farm had meant the opportunity of continuing a love relationship that was forbidden by her family, through which she had had a son at the age of eighteen while still at school. It also meant a change in her class position and style of life as both she and her partner were unemployed. Being a committed activist in the anti-apartheid struggle, experiencing arrests and torture, her partner made many sacrifices that would compromise his ability to live up to the role of 'provider' that was expected by both their families. While the couple lived apart during apartheid, with their son being cared for largely by her extended family, as apartheid ended, the couple attempted to make a life for themselves as a family in Orange Farm. While they took up house together without being married, gaining respectability in the eyes of their families would become increasingly important. This would mean trying to secure the necessary money for her partner to pay 'lobola'. With his first cheque, earned through a contract job in the construction industry, this goal was achieved and the families gave the couple a wedding ceremony. For the group, this story is important as it demonstrates women's choice in matters of life, in spite of expectations and norms almost never reflected in the discourse of 'the feminisation of poverty'. It also shows how culture and the economy work together to reinforce gender inequalities and oppression.

Escaping problems in male-headed households

For many single women (mainly mothers) living in Orange Farm, the ability to purchase one's own site and erect a shack meant the possibility of freedom from unhappiness, and the tension, stress, and violence being experienced in male-headed households. With the emphasis of the discourse of 'the feminisation of poverty' falling on women without any real interrogation of the reasons behind the phenomenon characterising it (rising female-headed-households), what is erased is the involvement of men in women's increasing vulnerability, and the fact that the structure and production of poverty is deeply gendered. Using the term 'feminised' only describes the fact that more women are poor or that women are poorer than men. It does not describe the fact that men and women's oppression and exploitation are enmeshed. Before women leave violent relationships, what are their lives like within male-headed households? The 'feminisation' discourse neglects to explore the nature of life for women in poor male-headed households.

In the group, discussions revealed that divorce and separation bring tremendous problems and instability in the lives of children. Even when the cause of separation is not linked to tensions arising due to economic pressures (e.g. an extra-marital affair or a new love interest), women still tend to suffer economically. Their lives usually being completely dependent on their husband's, separation means a loss of income, a home, and the means to care for one's children (who usually accompany the mother).

The group shared the story of a young girl whose life was seriously disrupted by the divorce of her parents. Kicked out of the family home with her mother and brothers, she went from a life of relative comfort to one of complete vulnerability, first living in a shack and then moving into a hostel for Zulu migrant workers after the shack was burnt by residents accusing the family of being Inkatha supporters - they were Zulu-speakers. Her mother and brothers unemployed, she began selling sweets at school and clothes in the community, going door to door on weekends. She assumed the role of 'provider' for most of her school-life and beyond, yet continued to be disrespected by her brothers. She also bore the cruelty of other children at school, who questioned her about staying at the hostel, and taunted her for 'being Zulu'. In Std 9, she was raped by a brother's friend, and received no support in her crisis except the emotional support of her mother. The stress and emotional pressure became unbearable, and she dropped out of school. She worked extremely hard, selling goods, and was eventually able to purchase a site in Orange Farm, where she moved her mother and brothers into a two-roomed shack. In Orange Farm, she came to know about a local NGO through which she has received counselling and become part of a group committed to changing the lives of women with similar problems. Her mother has recently passed away, and she has subsequently broken contact with her brothers. However, she has been able to face these adversities through the support she has received from the NGO. Today, she is in a long-term relationship with a partner with whom she has a baby, is a volunteer in the local NGO that assisted her and so assists other young women with problems, such as rape, and continues to make a living by selling clothes and sweets. While she wishes that she had a better job or the ability to study further, she is content with life at present. Participants commended her for her resilience and strength in the face of opposition from her brothers and society in general.

The sharing of this story led to a discussion about the ways in which women often take control in situations of crises in households, and how it is often the absence of men in households that allows for the positive development of women. In many cases, it was felt that, female-headed-households have presented women with the space and opportunities to develop their own potential, unconstrained by the needs and demands of male partners.

In using the rising number of female-headed-households as an indicator of 'the feminisation of poverty', a negative development, proponents of this discourse deny the potential that female-headed-households do indeed present greater household economic stability and individual social and economic well-being as compared with male-headed-households, in which individual female and child well-being may be compromised for various reasons, some of which have been mentioned above (e.g. domestic violence). Recognition of this potential should lead to the strengthening of support for female-headed-households, and not its withholding. However, it should not allow for the problems faced within male-headed-households to go unaddressed.

With household income being the sole determinant for comparisons made between the poverty of male- and female-headed-households, little weight is given to the intra-household factors that might prejudice the individual well-being of women and children. With the targeting of female-headed-households, the problems experienced by women in male-headed-households go unexamined, and thus unsolved. While it might be important to target female-headed-households with certain socio-economic interventions, it is equally important to try to understand the problems being experienced by women in male-headed-households and to develop interventions to address them too.

While female-headed-households represent an important response from women against the abuse they face in male-headed-households, addressing their needs cannot define the sum total of the interventions necessary to eradicate poverty and the unequal position of women in society. Rather, such interventions need also to address the position of women in their situations of need.

Teenage pregnancies as a cause of female poverty

Participants also put forward the high incidence of teenage pregnancies as a possible reason for rising female poverty and female-headed-households. In trying to understand this phenomenon, participants spoke about the fact that poor young girls have very few choices in their lives with regard to higher education or jobs. Often, even school life is difficult, and many young girls are forced to drop out of high school in order to work or conduct informal economic activities e.g. selling sweets or clothes. And the aspirations that young girls are encouraged to hold are far from their reach. The group happened to hold its first discussion on 'Take a Girl-Child to Work' day. When one of the members asked what this day was all about and received clarification about it, all participants were extremely dismissive of the day, asking where the jobs were that young girls could be taken to. In the context where young girls are being encouraged to pursue consumerist lifestyles, the temptation for poor young girls to enter into relationships with richer and older men is common. The phenomenon of 'sugar daddies' and entire families becoming dependent on the relationship of a young girl with a richer man are common stories today. With the lack of proper sex education at school level, many young girls fall pregnant in this context.

There was also the feeling in the group that the existence of the child support grant (CSG) was a reason that poor young girls fell pregnant. Some participants disagreed. While participants accepted that there is a study that government has conducted that shows that the CSG is not 'a perverse incentive' for young girls (Department of Social Welfare, 2007), it was argued that many people still believe that the grant does encourage teenage pregnancies. In a focus group being conducted for another project, also held in Orange Farm, with a group of men who had been retrenched in the late 1990s by Premier Milling Company in whose full-time employ they had been, deep-seated anger was expressed at the CSG (Naidoo, forthcoming, 2010). An old man accused government of 'fathering' the children of teenage mothers, arguing that it was government's provision of the CSG that encouraged such pregnancies. A middle-aged man grew extremely angry, stating that government, through the CSG, had turned its back on the men who had slaved for so many years in jobs for their families, and was now supporting 'little girls who have never worked in their lives'.

Interestingly, this focus group discussion spoke clearly to the fact that men who were suffering the effects of post-apartheid neoliberal reorganisation of the labour market and economy felt that their ability to 'provide' had come under threat. A man who had not found full-time work in the last twelve years since his retrenchment, described how he had gone from supporting five families to 'being alone in the house'. Many of the men spoke about their failure to 'be fathers' and provide for the needs of their wives and children. The majority feeling in the small group, and these experiences in the focus group, speak to the fact that changes in the economy that have resulted in changes in the ways in which work is organised and in the sphere of reproduction have been deeply gendered, provoking responses that are deeply gendered. Targeted interventions, such as the CSG, in this context, even though they may not aim to be gender-specific (with the CSG, caregivers of children are not defined as needing to be mothers in order to receive the grant), end up having effects on gender relations as they do not address the underlying causes of problems and so reproduce and entrench gender inequalities.

Teenage pregnancies are, then, both a result of poverty and a reason for its continued existence. As such, holistic interventions need to be developed to address the context of poverty and inequality in which young girls fall pregnant today. This means changing how society views the respective roles and responsibilities of men and women in relationships, particularly with regard to birth control and protection during sexual intercourse; child-care; household duties; occupational roles; and family responsibilities.

AIDS, women and poverty

All participants spoke about the inescapable reality of the many effects of the HIV-AIDS pandemic on their lives and the lives of the majority of Orange Farm residents. Discussions focused on the difficulties presented by conditions of poverty for those living with HIV-AIDS and those caring for the sick (usually women, and increasingly older women, pensioners). In the experience of one participant, living with HIV-AIDS, watching her partner die from the virus, being unemployed and without access to anti-retroviral treatment, has made life often unbearable. However, she persists for the sake of her children, trying to keep healthy and 'occupied'. In this case, groups like the OWCC have provided women, and residents generally, with the spaces in which to find support in and from others with similar problems. All participants were involved in projects at community level in which support for members and their families with regard to the experience of HIV-AIDS was a priority. All participants spoke of the increase in the number of funerals as a result of HIV-AIDS, and the ways in which the community came together around these occasions. Participants felt that any discussion about poverty and its gendered nature today needs to include some reflection on HIV-AIDS, and the gendered nature of the context in which it has become a pandemic and the relations through which it is spread and addressed.

Reflections on experience

In trying to understand the commonalities and similarities in experiences and stories shared, the group agreed that growing up, attaining self-hood, and being accepted by a community of people are closely related to becoming men and women in society. And, being good men and women had come to be defined through culture, religion, education, the media, and so on. In the collective experience of the group, these roles had come to be defined as those of 'provider' (man) and 'caregiver' (woman). It was in the perceived failure of men and women to live up to these roles that many of the problems that participants had experienced in their lives had their roots.

Understanding apartheid society as a capitalist patriarchal one, the group also spoke of the fact that women's 'caregiver' role allowed (and continues to allow) particular reproductive forms of work (traditionally provided by women) to go unpaid in society, facilitating the paying of lower wages and the provision of less welfare and fewer social protections to workers. The unpaid labour of women has, in other words, always 'subsidised' the greater exploitation of men. The position of women in the household has also allowed families to weather poverty, and women have always been the poorest in society. The term 'feminisation' suggests a point in time at which poverty suddenly becomes characterised by women's greater vulnerability than men, without any real data to substantiate this claim. Most literature today states that 70 per cent of the word's poor are women. However, there is little gender disaggregation of poverty statistics to back this up (Chant, 2003; 2006). The group could understand that as poverty increased, women would suffer more than men as the nature of society was such that women occupied the lowest positions in the economy and the household, and the roles that would serve to provide the care and additional unpaid labour necessary to withstand increased poverty. But, it could not understand why there would necessarily be an increase in the proportion of women to men who are poor, necessitating the term 'feminisation'. Instead, the group began to ask when and why the term had become popular.

The feminisation of poverty'?

The term 'the feminisation of poverty' can be traced back to discussions in the United States in the 1970s related to single mothers and welfare (BRIDGE, 2001: 1). It has, however, gained popularity, particularly in the development sector, in the 1990s, continuing to be used today. In the words of Sylvia Chant, 'the 'feminisation of poverty' made its major breakthrough into the development lexicon in the 1990s. A critical catalyst was the fourth United Nations Conference on Women at which it was asserted that 70 per cent of the world's poor were female, and eradicating the 'persistent and increasing burden of poverty on women' was adopted as one of the twelve critical areas of the Beijing Platform For Action. Disregarding the fact that the 70 per cent level was supposed to be rising, and that ten years on there is still no change to the original estimate, this categorical claim, with its alarming(ist) predictions of 'worse to come', seems to have accorded "women, if not gender, unprecedented visibility in international fora on poverty reduction." (Chant, 2006: 202). This has been accompanied by an increase in the number of interventions aimed at alleviating or eradicating poverty that target women. Most major donor agencies include a focus on poor women, with several programmes targeting women specifically. As neoliberal policies have increased the vulnerability of the working and lower middle classes, women have come to be 'the shock-absorbers' of the system. But this does not mean that women survive without men. Using the term 'the feminisation of poverty' describes only one aspect of the gendered nature of poverty, allowing for easy interventions to be made that can be proclaimed as having answered to the needs of 'the poorest of the poor' without addressing the root causes of poverty, which are gendered, involving both men and women.

Presented with 'the feminisation of poverty' as a topic for research towards this conference article, discussions in the group tended towards trying to understand whether the discourse as presented above holds any value with regard to the experiences of women in Orange Farm.

In the experience of most in the group, such targeted approaches of donors had had positive effects in their lives. All participants belong to women's community projects that have at some point received funding from donor programmes targeting poor women. But their survival through these interventions has been difficult nevertheless. Participants shared their experiences of working in community projects, including a sewing income generation initiative; a recycling, crèche, and gardening income generation project; a project providing counselling and advice to young women, in particular survivors of rape and domestic violence; and a group campaigning for free access to basic services and better living conditions for Orange Farm residents. In all these experiences, problems had, however, emerged with regard to expectations and understandings of different members of the projects. In particular, many of the women who worked in the projects were expected to take home a salary, showing something material for their time spent away from home. However, most projects have often been unable to ensure that members receive stable incomes. Where projects have received donor or state funding, these funds have come with the stipulation that they not be spent on stipends or salaries. Often, not enough income has been generated to pay stipends. When this has happened in the past, some project members have experienced anger from their husbands or male partners, often unemployed and therefore also relying on the expected income from the project. While participants stressed that attempts are always made to address such problems, the existence of such expectations and the gender dynamics within households often result in project members leaving for more stable employment as soon as it becomes available. In cases where members are only able to find casual or contract jobs, they often return to the project only to leave again when better work becomes available. In this way, the projects have often become the spaces to which women turn only in desperation. At the same time, however, they have also offered many women the opportunity to build lives for themselves outside of quickly declining formal wage labour, and the possibility to imagine a different way of living for themselves as collectives.

These opportunities have, however, been determined by the interests of donors, with the targeting of women featuring as one of the focus areas for spending. In these targeted interventions, the development of women's entrepreneurial capabilities have been prioritised, and the building of capacity and skills amongst women to sustain themselves and their own projects, have become priorities. 'Sustainable livelihoods' has become a euphemism for the provision of the very basic and most minimal resources deemed necessary for survival to those considered to be unable to provide for themselves, and women have received attention as the most 'cost-effective' and 'reliable' vehicles through which to dispense these resources. In most cases, women's labour is once again not given value, and women are once again expected to be the 'shock absorbers' of the ills of our economy.

Participants spoke of the fact that, while donors might prefer to fund women's organisations, they have chosen not to prevent men from joining them. While women continue to be the majority in projects and continue to lead them, there are also men who work in some of the projects, accepting their positions as equals in the work and in decision-making related to the project. Participants argued that it was the fact that projects could not guarantee a stable salary or stipend that prevented more men from joining them.

In the view of participants, targeting women in poverty alleviation interventions, while undoubtedly bound to have some positive effects in contexts of extreme disadvantage, also entrenches certain gendered roles and divisions in society that do not benefit the lives of poor men and women in the long run. The role of woman as 'caregiver' continues to be played on in the ways in which it is presumed that the targeting of women will benefit more people than the support of a man, and in the provision of minimal interventions based on the belief that women provide certain tasks unpaid and driven by levels of sacrifice and voluntarism due to their 'caregiver' 'nature'. It also carries the danger with it that existing gendered divisions, inequalities, and stereotypes will be reinforced as people's lived circumstances change without their means of interpreting and making meaning of them changing.

Conclusion

As the group returned to discuss the main statements and assertions made by those using the term 'the feminisation of poverty', participants realised that none of the richness and detail of their stories and those of so many other women that they knew were reflected in these mainstream documents claiming to speak in the interests of 'the poorest of the poor' - women. In most of these documents, women's voices and agency were absent, erased, as poverty was described as an over-powering experience to which women are constantly on the receiving end, responding to effects of changing macro-economic policies. Participants did not dispute the fact that the circumstances in which the majority of women today find themselves are those of growing poverty and vulnerability. However, they argued that poor women fight and survive against this system, and choose to live in different ways in spite of the system. The system itself is allowed to change based on the resilience and creativity of women. And how changes are introduced are shaped by resistance and struggle undertaken by women.

While 'the feminisation of poverty' might serve as a useful descriptive term when speaking about poverty, the experiences shared in this group's discussions suggest that the discourse inaugurated by increased use of the term has neglected some of the detail necessary in understanding how poverty is produced in gendered ways in society, ways that involve men and women in relationships of inequality. Rather than developing interventions that speak to this gendered nature of poverty, the discourse of 'the feminisation of poverty' has resulted in the targeting of women and female-headed-households for intervention to the neglect of men and male-headed-households. Recognising the central role that gender plays in the ways in which people come to relate to each other and to the world, it is important that discourses of poverty pay attention to the ways in which the unequal position of women in society relates directly to the position of men and the power relationships between men and women, relationships also determined by intersections of class and race.

References

BRIDGE., 2001. *Briefing Paper on the Feminisation of Poverty*. Prepared for SIDA. Sussex: Institute of Development Studies.

Chant, S., 2006. Re-thinking the 'Feminisation of Poverty' in Relation to Aggregate Gender Indices. *Journal of Human Development*, 7(2), pp. 201-220.

Chant, S., 2003. Female Household Headship and the Feminisation of Poverty: Facts, Fictions and Forward Strategies. *London School of Economics Gender Institute New Working Papers Series*, Issue 9, 1-68.

Coalition Against Water Privatisation, Anti-Privatisation Forum and Orange Farm Water Crisis Committee. 2003. *Nothing For Mahala: The Forced Installation of Prepaid Water Meters in Stretford, Extension 4, Orange Farm*, research report.

Community Agency For Social Enquiry (CASE). 2004. *Voices of the Poor: Case Studies of Urban Poverty in the City of Johannesburg*.

Hassim, S., 2005. *Gender, Welfare and the Developmental State in South Africa*, draft working paper for UNRISD.

Kenny, B. and Webster, E., 1999. Eroding the Core: Flexibility and the Re-segmentation of the South African Labour Market. *Critical Sociology* 24(3), pp.216–43.

Khanya College/Kganya Women's Consortium. 2001. *The Status of Women in Orange Farm*, research report.

Mosoetsa, S., 2001. The Manchester Road: Women and the Informalisation of Work in South Africa's Footwear Industry. *Labour, Capital and Society*, 34(2).

Naidoo, P., 2007. Struggles Around the Commodification of Daily Life in South Africa. *Review of African Political Economy*, 34(111), pp. 57-66.

Naidoo, P., (forthcoming, 2010). *The Making of 'The Poor' in Post-Apartheid South Africa: A Case Study of Orange Farm and the City of Johannesburg*, unpublished Ph.D. thesis.

Parnell, S. and Mosdell, T., 2003. Recognising, Explaining and Measuring Chronic Urban Poverty in South Africa. Paper presented at 'Staying Poor: Chronic Poverty and Development Policy', Manchester: University of Manchester, 7-9 April 2003.

Parnell. S., 1992. Slums, Segregation and the Poor Whites in Johannesburg, 1920-1934. In R. Morrell, ed. *White but Poor*. Pretoria: University of South Africa Press, pp.115-129.

Ramphele, M., 2003. *Steering by the Stars: Being Young in South Africa*. Tafelberg: Cape Town.

UNDP International Poverty Centre. 2004. *In Focus: The Challenge of Poverty*. Brazil: UNDP International Poverty Centre.

UNIFEM. 2005. *Progress of the World's Women 2005: Women, Work & Poverty*. New York: UNIFEM.

8.
Wage labour, citizenship and social discipline
Franco Barchiesi

Introduction

This chapter is an investigation of the social policy discourse of South Africa's post-apartheid state, with specific regard to its conceptualisation of the relationships between wage labour and social inclusion within interventions aimed at addressing poverty and social inequality. The underlying assumption is that discourse and ideology are constitutive aspects of the state's normativity in relation to social actors and conflicts. The epistemological and ideational authoritativeness of governmental policy discourse depends on its ability to assert ethical and moral constructs aimed at disciplining social agency and expectations. At the same time, social agency is autonomously capable to appropriate categories of rights and entitlements underpinning state policies in order to strengthen popular claims to citizenship rights and social provisions.

In South Africa, the post-1994 ANC-led government has tried to combine institutional interventions aimed at overcoming racialised social inequality with a fundamental acceptance of the need to make the economy competitive within the scenarios of neoliberal globalisation. The resulting social policy discourse placed a priority emphasis on waged employment and labour market participation, to the detriment of universal, non-work related redistributive programmes. The concept of 'developmental social welfare' has combined a positive appreciation of individual self-activation with the stigmatisation of 'dependency' on state assistance.

The state's promotion of a form of social disciplining centred on wage labour has, however, clashed with a material reality in which waged employment faces an enduring crisis evident in both spiralling unemployment and the proliferation of precarious and unprotected occupations. The policy discourse's growing inability to reflect material realities of poverty in relation to the crisis of waged employment raises important questions concerning the capacity of the new institutional dispensation to govern South Africa's long transition.

Wage labour-citizenship nexus as object of contested signification

In his 2007 'State of the Nation' address, South African president Thabo Mbeki announced the forthcoming introduction of important changes in the country's social security system. He proposed, in particular, a new social insurance and retirement programme funded with payroll taxes, intended to cover all employed people, and a wage subsidy for low-wage employees, especially young first entrants (Mbeki, 2007). Such measures responded to suggestions contained in the 2002 report of the Taylor Committee of Inquiry into Comprehensive Social Security, according to which the existing system of private, contributory and earning-related social insurance schemes fails to cover many workers, especially in casual and informal occupations. The Taylor Committee report, however, also argued for an additional social provision to alleviate the impact of unemployment and working poverty: A modest basic income grant to be allocated to all South African citizens on an individual, non-contributory basis. The income grant would be universal and, in principle, decommodified, meaning that it would be provided to everyone regardless to individual employment status (Esping-Andersen, 1990). Mbeki's government has always been adamantly opposed to the basic income grant idea, regarding it as a state 'handout' that would act as a disincentive to jobseeking. Three days after his promise of sweeping social security changes, Mbeki restated the point by arguing that with a basic income grant, "the government would be effectively 'abandoning' its citizens" (Da Costa, 2007).

Mbeki's rebuttal of the basic income grant quashed the expectations of many, including government members like Minister of Social Development, Zola Skweyiya. Their hopes were that, following three years of uninterrupted growth, the government could be more daring in its move away from the tight budget constraints enforced under neoliberal adjustment during the first decade of post-Apartheid democracy. They therefore expected the government to finally opt for a genuinely redistributive, fiscally funded programme that does not subordinate access to social provisions to the recipient's position in the labour market. Mbeki's opinion was, however, ultimately consistent with a long-standing discourse, which, having accompanied the government of the African National Congress (ANC) since the first democratic elections in 1994, has seen waged employment and individual self-activation on the labour market as the main avenues to social inclusion and social citizenship. It also responded to a growing alarm, expressed by various academics as well as by the powerful Treasury Minister, Trevor Manuel. They warned that one quarter of the South African population, almost 12 million people, are now covered by non-contributory social assistance, mainly state old-age pensions and child support grants, despite the fact that such programmes are means tested, addressed to the very poor, and intended to target specific vulnerable groups outside the labour market.

Child support grants, disability grants and state old age pensions often represent the main source of income for unemployed or underemployed household members. This situation, deemed 'untenable' by the government (Daniels, 2006), is on the other hand a further reflection of the levels of social marginality in a country where 18 million people, or 45 per cent of the population, live below the poverty line. Mbeki's proposed wage subsidy and basic social insurance for low-wage jobs would, therefore, contribute to make such occupations preferable to receiving social grants, which, while well below the poverty line, are currently more generous than most entry-level low-skill occupations.

The centrality of wage labour in the government's responses to poverty was confirmed, on the other hand, by prominent functionaries. Shortly before Mbeki's announcement, Minister Skweyiya himself declared that social grants 'could promote dependency instead of boosting self-reliance', unless they are accompanied by policies designed to put welfare recipients to work (SAPA, 2007). His department was, on the other hand, committed to providing, on a 'case management approach' basis, grant recipients with 'half jobs' and training to encourage them to 'migrate from welfare benefits' (Gallagher and Russouw, 2007). More inventive, Minister of Labour, Membathisi Mdladlana, suggested a programme of militarisation of the unemployed, arguing for conscription in the army as an alternative to joblessness and a way to 'inculcate discipline' in unruly unemployed youth, who could in this way "understand better the importance of defending our hard-earned liberation" (SAPA, 2007).

A public discourse that so starkly prefers wage labour to decommodified social provisions, and asserts the centrality of labour market participation on such strong disciplinary and moral grounds raises many questions in the context of post-Apartheid South Africa. The country is in fact witnessing persistently high unemployment, with 26 per cent of the economically active population (EAP) out of jobs – a figure that rises to almost 40 per cent if discouraged jobseekers are counted – and with one third employed in casual or informal occupations, without benefits, job security or wages above poverty levels. In the mid-2000s, 65.8 per cent of the unemployed aged 25 to 34 and 37.9 per cent aged 35 to 44 had never worked in their lives (Bhorat and Oosthuizen, 2005).

Low-wage, temporary occupations provide a large share of the jobs that have been created in the wake of economic growth, especially between 2004 and 2006. South Africa's employment problem cannot in fact be confined to high unemployment rates, as government officials, policy-orientated academics and pro-business pundits recurrently do, but it crucially encompasses the expansion of working class poverty within wage labour itself. Altman (2006) observes that by defining the 'working poor' as employed persons earning less than R 2,500 per month (approximately the bottom individual threshold for income tax exemption), then 65 per cent of South Africa's waged population can be defined as 'poor', with half of them earning less than R1,000 per month. It should be incidentally noticed, however, that, in this study, workers with incomes between R1,000 and 2,500 (which include more stable, unionised employees) are, paradoxically, the ones who most frequently report chronic food shortages and the inability of their wages to provide for basic family needs. In fact, income levels below R 1,000 more likely benefit from paltry, means-tested state grants, which provide a form of household income integration from which higher incomes are excluded.

Altman (2006) concludes that, given the predominance of low skills in the South African labour market, policies that facilitate job creation in labour intensive activities will most likely expand low-wage occupations. As a result, a pattern of rising inequalities and declining earnings in low-skill activities – especially for women – which has accompanied the first ten years of post-apartheid democracy (Woolard and Woolard, 2006), would in all likelihood be confirmed. Persistently high unemployment has also proven to be, on the other hand, quite impervious to upswings in the economic cycle. At the end of 2006, even Deputy President Mlambo-Ngcuka had to admit that even if official growth targets are met, by 2015 the country will still fall two million jobs short of the government's target of a 15 per cent unemployment rate (Hamlyn, 2006).

Concomitantly, the informalisation and casualisation of South Africa's economy is driven not so much by the entrepreneurialism of the poor, but by technological innovations, outsourcing and work reorganisation as part of the restructuring of formal enterprises, which produce flexible employment contracts that expand the scope of exploitation within the wage relation (Cheadle and Clarke, 2001; Theron, 2004). According to Devey, Skinner and Valodia (2006), if 'informal' work is defined not in terms of the nature of the employer (registered or unregistered) but according to the nature of the work performed (in terms of the enforcement of legal provisions, statutory benefits, and protections), formality and informality tend increasingly to overlap. In fact, 44 percent of 'informal' workers (80 percent of which have no written employment contract) are in permanent relations with their employers, while 16 percent of 'formal' workers are not. Apart from casuals, more and more 'informal' workers are hired as subcontractors by 'formal' enterprises, even in manufacturing sectors where the externalisation of functions was once limited. While almost 90 percent of informal workers have no company-based retirement coverage (and in South Africa there is no national state-subsidised retirement system), this also applies to one third of formal employees. Finally, while 44 percent of formal workers are members of trade unions, only 8.4 percent of informal ones are. Posel (2003) observes that the remarkable resilience of domestic long-distance and commuting migration – well after the end of apartheid's system of coerced migrant labour – is linked not only to historic patterns of rural-urban inequality, but also to the movement of African women into low-wage, informal jobs that replace the income lost by laid off or casualised male household members.

This chapter investigates the persistence of a wage labour-centred social policy discourse throughout South Africa's post-Apartheid democratisation, contrasting it with wage labour's widespread decline as a form of dignified social existence. It argues that the seeming contradiction between wage labour centrality in the new democracy's policy discourse and the frail, problematic realities that characterise waged employment as a social reality reveal, at a closer look, peculiar features of post-Apartheid's governance project. Rather than envisaging universalistic citizenship frameworks, wage labour has reproduced a stratified, hierarchical social space. Whereas current social hierarchies are profoundly different from apartheid-era ones, reflecting the deracialisation of the political order, labour markets continue to play a decisive role in structuring social disparities. In this scenario, universalistic citizenship discourse operates mainly in the promotion of a national work ethic and the intimation to hard work and minimisation of welfare 'dependency'. At a practical level, however, the responsibility for social inclusion is shifted towards the individual, relieving the state of redistributive functions undermined by budget constraints and macroeconomic adjustment. The contradiction between a universalising state morality based on work, and the material inequalities shaped by waged employment reproduces for the democratic state the dilemma, already experienced by the Apartheid regime, of using wage labour as a form of social discipline, while remaining unable to place it as the foundation of meaningful social citizenship.

In the tradition of the modern democratic nation-state, policy discourse embodies forms of ideas and knowledge aimed to structure social actors' fields of action (Hall, 1989). Following Michel Foucault, and Zukin and Di Maggio's notion of 'cognitive embeddedness', Somers and Block (2005) argue that, in particular, discourses of welfare and social rights have operated as 'ideational causal mechanisms', where public narratives must, in order to gain the power of 'making themselves true' and influence policy outcomes, gain an 'epistemic privilege' based on the power of their internal claims to veracity and their imperviousness to empirical challenges. Such is the case, for them, of the late twentieth century neoliberal rollback of Keynesian welfarism.

In industrialised capitalist countries, the idea of 'welfare reform' enjoyed a substantial epistemic privilege due to its combination of seemingly unassailable economic logic (the unsustainability of 'big government' in a context of growing diversification of social claims), moral proscriptions (the stigmatisation of 'dependency' on state handouts), and positive incentives (the reevaluation of individual responsibility and work ethics). The empirical evidence suggesting a decline in the living standards of many former welfare recipients that were pushed into low-wage employment under coercive 'workfare' schemes (DeParle, 2004; Schram, 2005), therefore, did not disrupt the cognitive embeddedness of welfare reform. The fact that the removal of social programmes deepened existing racial and gender income inequalities did not act, likewise, as a deterrent.

The ideational turn of welfare reform, on the other hand, served to displace a previous public narrative, which, in a context of growing working class organisation, had also celebrated wage labour as the main avenue to social citizenship, but in different ways. T.H. Marshall's welfarist ideas were, in fact, based on the assumption that productivity and social peace could make full employment the basis of universal, state-funded social provisions (Mezzadra, 2002). In both cases, which reflected seemingly diverging policy trajectories, the social field of action of the individual as citizen of the nation-state was structured around the idea of wage labour as a morally superior and economically sounder form of membership of the body politic.

The policy discourse that has linked social citizenship to wage labour in the trajectory of industrialised capitalism can be understood as an example of what Jacques Lacan (1977) conceptualised as chains of signification through which subjectivity is constituted. Social citizenship's institutional discourse defines rights that are inseparable from the conceptualisation of wage labour as a subject in relation to other – the unemployed, the poor, the disabled and so on – which, lacking access to a stable wage, become specific problem areas and targets of social policy. The assumption, on the other hand, that waged employment is the normal condition of social existence, acts as a 'signifier' (*langue*, in Lacanian terms) that to build a signification requires a signified, or a 'non-overlapping set of the concretely pronounced discourse' in the form of the desired effect of policy interventions. As a signifier, the idea of wage labour implies a prescriptive ethical horizon, as in the praise of waged employment as a condition of independence, probity and respectability. At a 'signified' level, conversely, wage labour represents the enunciation of a disciplinary discourse aimed at shaping behaviours, proclivities and attitudes.

Signification for Lacan (1977: 137) does not refer to a 'real' thing. Similarly, the 'epistemic privilege' of wage labour does not necessarily need empirical validation of its actual functioning as a form of social inclusion, or even as a generalised condition characterised by decent jobs with benefits. The Keynesian welfare state collapsed under the weight of mass unemployment and the struggles and claims of a range of workers, including young casuals and women employed in unpaid household reproduction (Fortunati, 1996). For them, the view that productivity and employment lead to social provisions did not apply. Indeed, many of them rejected the Marshallian idea of citizenship as the imposition of despotic factory discipline (De Angelis, 2000). Neoliberalism responded to this early crisis of wage labour ideology with a further, aggressive reassertion of waged employment at the centre of the policy discourse, this time in the guise of cutbacks of social provisions for beneficiaries reluctant to seek employment (Peck, 2001; Jessop, 2002).

In both cases, despite being materially invalidated as a condition of generalised social uplift, wage labour emerges as an ordering principle through which disorderly, diversified living experiences and desires are regulated by state institutions. Despite their divergent outcomes, both Keynesianism and neoliberalism share the goal of enforcing a work-centred universalistic discourse (social citizenship rights in the former case, the responsibility of a disembodied individual in the latter) to contain, channel, and discipline a multiplicity of social existence perceived by the state as unruly and threatening (Ranciere, 2003; Hardt and Negri, 2000; Virno, 2004). The fact that social disciplining operated in the former case as 'modern' enforcement of social homogeneity (full-employment policies), and in the latter as 'postmodern' regulation of social difference (Hong, 2005) in the case management of welfare-to-work programmes, is more a matter of procedural diversity than of substantial divergence in principles.

At the same time, the policy linkage between wage labour and ideas of social rights is a slippery slope for the state and capital, and it is not entirely controllable by the rationality of the institutions. Such links, in fact, enable claims and expectations from below, which act as 'symptoms' of underlying grassroots social worldviews, alternative rationalities, and what Zizek (2000) calls 'leftovers' of unspecified desires outside the labour market. The existence of life forms that are unassimilable to the logic of capital (Chakrabarty, 2000), and whose claims are unintentionally triggered by the discursive and policy connections between wage labour and social rights, is particularly relevant to the transition from colonialism to postcoloniality, in Africa as elsewhere (Chatterjee, 2004).

Wage labour in Africa has never represented a generalised social condition, much less the foundation of a discourse of citizenship. The despotic forms of labour exploitation introduced by colonialism have not only limited wage labour numerically and confined it geographically to the urban and mining areas. They have also placed it in a privileged position within a discourse of colonial modernity that was overly hierarchical and unequalising (Ferguson, 1999; Quijano, 2000). Initially feared by the colonial state as a threatening organised proletariat, African urban waged workers came to be regarded under late colonialism as partners in the state's project of 'development' (Escobar, 1994), where they admittedly embodied wage labour's 'civilisational' qualities. Late colonial welfarism used universalistic European discourses of citizenship and rights to elicit the collaboration of urban waged social layers (Cooper, 1996; Lewis, 2000).

Here too, however, the universalism of citizenship ideologies belied the material unevenness and inequality that wage labour presided upon. But in this case as well, however, the linkage between wage labour and ideas of citizenship unintentionally encouraged African workers' social claims and demands for meaningful family allowances, retirement benefits, and unemployment insurance. These underpinned the struggles of the 'urban subaltern' (Bayat, 1997), despite the fact that only few of them were full-time waged workers, and many indeed preferred casual, informal jobs as alternatives to capitalist work discipline (Cooper, 1987; Scarnecchia, 2000). Colonial administrations eventually left postcolonial African nation-states with the task of addressing their citizens' claims. Continued dependency on Western markets, and later the imposition of neoliberal structural adjustment, allowed on the other hand the perpetuation of Western hegemony in new, globalised and deterritorialised forms.

A further legacy of the wage labour-citizenship linkages transmitted from colonialism to the postcolonial state, and then to the World Bank ideological templates, was the idea that those excluded from formal waged employment had to rely for the satisfaction of their claims not on public spending but on 'community development' and self-help. The fact that these groups were now fully-fledged citizens of African nation-states did not interfere with such inequalities of treatment. Actually, the idea of citizenship provided a powerful weapon to limit state obligations to the poor and the unemployed, for whom citizenship status was supposed to facilitate the acceptance of sacrifices and renunciations needed for the purpose of an orderly, united nation-building (Chatterjee, 1994). Traditionalist themes (the allegedly solidaristic, egalitarian basis of the African community) and new ethical imperatives (pride in one's hard work as opposed to depending on state transfers) were mobilised to provide a cultural foundation to the social discipline enabled by the postcolonial citizenship discourse (Eckert, 2004). More recently, such themes have powerfully resurfaced in World Bank-inspired literature on the self-regulated resourcefulness, safety nets and social capital of the African poor (Bahre, 2007; Ferguson, 2006).

To summarise, a main terrain of continuity between colonialism and postcoloniality has operated through a chain of signification that, by linking wage labour to citizenship, reproduced the seeming contradiction between the promise of rights that citizenship implies, and the material hierarchies and inequalities structured through wage labour. Two main outcomes emerged: Public policies cannot ultimately interfere with objective social hierarchies determined by the functioning of the labour market; and public policies' claims to veracity and their imperviousness to counter-evidence are enabled by the state's ability to prescribe virtuous behaviours for its citizens. The following section will look at South Africa's post-apartheid transition as a particular case of passage to postcoloniality, revealing important commonalities with the scenario here outlined. It will in particular focus on the ways in which the links between wage labour and social citizenship have been conceptualised in the policy discourse of the post-1994 democratic dispensation.

South Africa's racial state and the emerging wage labour pedagogy

The formative processes of a black industrial proletariat in South Africa present obvious, vast differences from the rest of the continent. The nature of social inequalities and legal hierarchies made particularly evident in this case a reality where, as Trapido (1971: 313) put it, "South Africa has not incorporated the major part of its working class into its social and political institutions."

Not only does the country possess an economic structure that is far more diversified than in the rest of the continent, but it also presents a unique level of industrialisation, and a waged working class numerically more developed (Mamdani, 1996: 218-284). The specific political regime that has presided over South Africa's capitalist industrialisation, and the peculiar dynamics and timing of its own demise and of the democratic transition, defined the interactions between wage labour and citizenship in rather exceptional ways. Institutionalised racial segregation and coercive labour control, in a context of lack of citizenship rights for the black majority, have shaped state policies of reproduction and stabilisation of the black working class well after the wave of decolonisation that started sweeping the continent in the 1960s. While gradually accepting, and trying to control, African working class urbanisation, Apartheid's labour and spatial policies defined social engineering interventions that deferred the establishment of a formally 'free' wage labour system.

Moreover, the post-1948 Apartheid state diverged from most African colonial governments, which were at that time privileging policies of stabilisation and social reforms to accommodate and co-opt urban strata of the African labour force. Instead, Apartheid's project chose to structure the legal status of the African workers as temporary urban residents, subject to coercive controls of movements and residence, and reproduced in the circuits of forced migration and short-term contract employment (Posel, 1991). Only at a much later stage, in the reform period of the late 1970s, triggered by renewed African working class insurgency, deepening economic crisis, and shortage of qualified black labour, did the racist regime adopt a policy of urban stabilisation and formalisation of rights for a section of African waged workers. In this late context, therefore, Apartheid started to experiment in earnest with a project of inclusion based on wage labour and market-determined, not only racial, differences (Ashforth, 1990). The project ultimately failed due to the regime's lack of legitimacy, its violently repressive nature, and the enduring absence of political democracy.

The links between wage labour and social citizenship, however, were not only shaped by institutionally enforced racial divides. In fact, even for the politically enfranchised white minority the segregationist state put in place a welfare model that eschewed decommodified social provisions, non-contributory schemes, and universal public programmes. The protection and benefits white workers enjoyed relied instead on their privileged labour market positions, which included better opportunities for education and training, state-sponsored job creation, and job reservations in qualified occupations (Seekings and Nattrass, 2005). The South African racial state, therefore, was not only a 'racialised welfare' state (Posel, 2004), in the sense that it enforced differential social provisions for blacks and whites. It was also, quite importantly, a heavily commodified society where wage labour and employment status, much more than public spending as such (Terreblanche, 2002), underpinned and structured, for blacks and whites alike, social provisions or the lack thereof.

On the other hand, the racist state has been traditionally reluctant in enforcing decommodified, non-contributory, or fiscally funded programmes, even for its white working class constituency. According to Martin Chanock (2001: 407), highly regulated forms of unfree black labour based on racial occupational segregation "made politically possible the continued dominance of market ideology in other sectors," which included the overall limitation of the state's responsibilities in the provision of social services. Only in 1928 did the state first introduce means tested old-age pensions for whites (Meth and Piper, 1984), while private provision of healthcare, mainly in the form of company-based schemes, was always preferred to publicly funded universal health coverage (Pillay, 1995). The rise of Apartheid, finally, meant the defeat of proposals, which gained momentum in sections of the white establishment during World War II, to expand non-contributory social security programmes, including old age pensions, which could have covered limited African strata (Nattrass and Seekings, 2000; Meth and Piper, 1984).

The idea of wage labour as a moral and civilisational force addressed to the African population was best expressed, in stark contradiction with the oppressive and exploitative conditions in which it was experienced, by the 1932 Native Economic (Holloway) Commission. Its words were particularly keen on underlining the pedagogical impact of wage labour as a signifier of social existence:

> When the raw Native has enough for his wants he stops working and enjoys his leisure (...). *He must learn to school his body to hard work*, which is not only a condition for his advance in civilisation, but of his final survival in a civilized environment (cit. in Ashforth, 1990: 84-85. Emphasis added).

Sure enough, however, Apartheid's social security and welfare policies *were* aimed primarily at reinforcing racial hierarchies. Therefore, the state's discourse of social insertion based on work ethic and commodification defined a set of social provisions that for most of the twentieth century privileged specifically the white population. Such objectives were most evident in policies aimed, during the 1920s and 1930s, to uplift urban 'poor whites' to standards deemed 'civilized', which could moreover defuse dangers of interracial solidarity among the poor (Giliomee, 1992; Grundlingh, 1999). The workplace, however, remained the core institution on which a modern civilisation based on wage labour ultimately rested. In this sense, the moral and pedagogical overtones with which work ethics was propagated among the white working class were not substantially different from the 'schooling bodies to hard work' approach that the Holloway Commission used with regard to African workers. In the context of Afrikaner nationalism's rise to power, the idea that government-funded non-contributory social programmes are a perverse incentive to work avoidance and an encouragement to welfare dependence became the norm. Quite significantly, this discourse was advanced across the racial spectrum, as in the words of J.G. Strijdom:

> Is it not a fact that natives only work to supply their immediate wants, and if you grant them old age benefits and other benefits you would only make them lazy? (...) They only work when starvation stares them in the face (...). *There are a large number of Europeans to whom that applies as well* (cit. in Meth and Piper, 1984: 9. Emphasis added).

The centrality of wage labour in South Africa's policy discourse was strengthened throughout the Apartheid age. The movement of white workers into managerial and supervisory positions, and their greater access to private benefit schemes, encouraged a further withdrawal of state interventions in the realm of social security. For example, between 1949 and 1981, the share of state contributions to the Unemployment Insurance Fund (UIF), created in the late 1930s and from which Africans were largely excluded from 1948 to the mid-1970s, was reduced from 50 per cent to 7 per cent (Meth and Piper, 1984: 27).

The struggles of the black working class, powerfully resumed in the wake of the 1973 'Durban strikes', placed the links between wage labour and social citizenship, and the role of decommodified provisions within them, once again at the centre of social contestation. The strikes were motivated by a deepening collapse of the living conditions of the urban black working class. Their wage demands responded to the needs of expanded social reproduction, which generally included migrant workers' families in the rural areas. Within this context, the government-appointed Riekert Commission identified widespread refusal of work by African township residents as a major impediment to capital's profitability (RSA, 1979). The late-1970s reports of the Riekert and Wiehahn commissions promoted, respectively, limited urban stabilisation and trade union rights for Africans, which were reminiscent of late colonial social reforms in the rest of the continent. Wiehahn's and Riekert's purported aim was to redefine waged employment, private corporations and the labour market as institutions of social cohesion, citizenship, and 'legitimate' socioeconomic inequalities, rather than ambits of mere racial despotism and discrimination (Ashforth, 1990: 205). Black trade unions generally rejected the government's reforms agenda, and used newly gained state recognitions to escalate their demands during the 1980s.

The struggle of the African working class came then to encompass not only workplace issues, but revolved around black people's living conditions, social security pensions, resistance to township residents' evictions, and demands for social rights and political democracy (Friedman, 1987; Ruiters, 1995). The unions' participation in social movement politics and community struggles underpinned a new discourse of citizenship (Seidman, 1994), for which wage labour was at the same time an enabling condition and a constraint to be transcended via broader social claims.

Restoring the dignity of wage labour?

The failure to make wage labour the foundation of a new discourse of citizenship, this time partially deracialised, was one of the main factors in the collapse of late Apartheid reforms, and expressed the capacity of South Africa's subalterns to turn that discourse into an opportunity for subversive social claims and desires. The task of managing such claims and desires was therefore inherited by the post-1994 ANC government as a decisive challenge. On one hand, democracy, political citizenship, and a newly found juridically 'free labour' regime restored the moral credibility of wage labour as an icon of state governance and policy discourse. As 'reconstruction', 'development' and 'nation-building' replaced 'resistance', 'ungovernability' and 'people's power' in public discourse and intellectual narratives, 'job creation' became the main demand for the labour movement – especially the 2-million strong, ANC-allied Congress of South Africa Trade Unions (COSATU) – as well as for vast sections of the civil society. Massive unemployment, poverty and social inequalities, on the other hand, conferred to this demand a particularly dramatic urgency.

Recognising the importance of working class organisation and expectations, the new democratic dispensation established corporatist-style organs of tripartite bargaining over labour and social policy, like the National Economic Development and Labour Council (NEDLAC), which included representatives from the government, business and trade unions (Adler and Webster, 2000). At the same time, however, the negotiated nature of the transition and its underlying compromises underpinned the ANC government's choice to privilege the terrain of global competitiveness, private investor confidence, and economic liberalisation as avenues to economic recovery (Hirsch, 2005). The institutionalisation of the labour movement within corporatist organs, therefore, was corralled by a programme of structural adjustment, the Growth, Employment and Redistribution Strategy (GEAR) – adopted by the government in 1996, unilaterally and despite COSATU's opposition – which reproduced the basic tenets of macroeconomic orthodoxy (Bond, 2005; Gumede, 2005). Particularly evident were the constraints imposed on public expenditures and budget deficits, while the state's fiscal capacities were concomitantly undermined by rapid reductions in corporate taxation and the government's advocacy of corporatisation of municipal services.

A programme of macroeconomic liberalisation and fiscal discipline contrasted therefore the expectations derived from political liberation, which included the survival needs of a largely poor, unemployed population. The contrast was conducive to the resumption by the ANC government of a social policy discourse that once again placed wage labour, once discredited and reviled by Apartheid-age black worker insurgency, in the position of master signifier of social existence, main response to poverty, and central form of social inclusion.

In its frequent warnings and admonitions to its COSATU allies, the ANC was well aware of the imperative of taming and controlling labour radicalism. In an important 1996 discussion document on *The State and Social Transformation* the party strikingly recalled post-independence African governments' calls to national unity and consent. It emphasised,

> the centrality of the continuing and special role of the progressive trade union movement and its leadership to the mobilisation of black workers to understand and adhere to the broader objectives of the process of democratic transformation, in their own interest. The instinct towards 'economism' on the part of the ordinary workers has to be confronted through the positioning of the legitimate material demands and expectations of these workers within the wider context of the defence of the democratic gains as represented by the establishment of the democratic state (ANC, 1996: 6.10).

As in Africa's late colonial and postcolonial state-building, the ANC government has maintained that an objective social hierarchy exists, and can be scientifically observed, based on individual citizens' positions in relation to waged employment. The government has adopted a view of the South African society as constituted by the asymmetrical coexistence of 'two economies'. In recent policy documents, South Africa's 'first economy' is defined as 'an advanced, sophisticated economy, based on skilled labour, which is becoming more globally competitive' (RSA, 2003: 97). The first economy, in short, involves a minority with access to stable wage labour, registered enterprises, and recognised participation in productive employment. In 'intersubjective' contrast to the 'second economy', it also defines an ideal status of social inclusion and active citizenry. In fact, the government defines the second economy in socially pathologising terms as, a mainly informal, marginalised, unskilled economy, populated by the unemployed and those unemployable in the formal sector . . [which] with the enormity of the challenges arising from the social transition . . risks falling further behind, if there is no decisive government intervention (RSA, 2003: 97).

The trajectory of post-Apartheid social policymaking, on the other hand, has made clear that 'decisive government intervention' is not intended to question the idea that no *real* social citizenship can be conceived of that does not depend on the insertion of the able-bodied within wage labour relations. In continuity, again, with state ideologies of African late colonial and postcolonial modernity, wage labour operates here as an ethical-pedagogical construct that gains an epistemic prominence over the material attributes, rights, and benefits that define actual employment conditions. As Mbeki summarised:

A society in which large sections depend on social welfare cannot sustain its development. Our comprehensive programme to grow the economy, including the interventions in both the First and Second Economies, improving sustainable livelihoods and create work is meant precisely to ensure that, over time, a smaller proportion of society, in particular the most vulnerable, subsists solely on social grants (Mbeki 2004).

The fact that, as noted at the beginning of this chapter, regular waged employment is a reality for only a shrinking minority of the black population, and work is currently created mostly in the form of unstable, precarious, low-wage occupations does not function here as a countervailing empirical evidence. Low-wage jobs are indeed regarded by the government as short term alternatives to, rather than part of, social exclusion. The principle of *letsema*, intended as volunteerism and mobilisation for development, in the government's *Vukuzenzele* ('arise and act') programme celebrates a work ethic made of self-sacrifice, responsibility, and renunciation of financial rewards (Twala, 2004). Before the 2004 elections the government launched an 'expanded public works programme' presented by President Mbeki as an incentive to 'productive employment' for millions that could concomitantly be 'moved off social grants' (McCord, 2004). For other government officials, the plan would 'eradicate poverty' and lift members of the second economy to the level of the first. McCord (2004: 8-9), however, estimated the impact of the programme in the creation of a meagre 200,000 temporary occupations, with the households of 90 percent of recipients remaining below the poverty line even in the optimistic scenario that new jobs would pay minimum wages.

The combination in post-Apartheid policy discourse of the absolute centrality of wage labour as a universal imperative of citizenship on one hand, and the material inequalities reproduced by wage labour on the other, shows many continuities with the colonial discourse of citizenship, which point at the permanence of unresolved legacies of Apartheid. The government's 1997 *White Paper on Social Welfare* (RSA, 1997) argued that, as workers in fulltime wage employment already enjoy pension and healthcare benefits through company-based private schemes, government social assistance and social security had to remain residual and focused on specific groups with 'special needs', namely children, disabled, and the elderly. The document phrased such commitments in terms of focusing on the needs of the 'poor' and the 'vulnerable'. With regard to the able-bodied, long-term unemployed, however, it recommended 'active labour market policies', 'more stringent and appropriate means testing and eligibility requirements', and welfare-to-work training to 'divert people from the welfare system' (RSA, 1997: 6.22).

Similarly to African colonial welfare discourse, as inherited by post-independence developmentalism and structural adjustment, the reassertion of the centrality of wage labour opposes here the extension of redistributive programmes on a universal basis. In South Africa as well, therefore, the state appropriated a discourse of 'authenticity' of local traditions to praise notions of 'community development' and 'self-help' as alternatives to state-based provisions (Sevenhuijsen et al., 2003). The government official that most directly influenced the White Paper's intellectual orientation, Welfare Department's director general Leila Patel proposed 'family centred and community-based programmes' to replace state expenditures and encourage the spirit of initiative of 'disadvantaged groups' (Patel, 2001). As in the language of colonial administrators in previous generations, Patel's rejection of universalism and public delivery of social services was phrased in terms of "self-reliance, dignity and respect of tradition" (Patel, 1991: 105). A selective welfare model where working age unemployed would have to fend for themselves was presented as "authentic development which has grown out of the real conditions and traditions of life in South Africa" (Patel, 1991: 124).

The 2002 report of the Taylor Committee, and in particular its proposal for a basic income grant as a genuinely universal, redistributive and decommodified provision, represented to a significant extent a departure from the framework of the 1997 Social Welfare White Paper. As I have argued elsewhere (Barchiesi, 2006), the Taylor Report responded positively to the concerns expressed both by labour organisations and large sectors of the civil society, concerns that by early 2000 were publicly uttered by the competent government official, Minister Skweyiya. According to them, too many vulnerable sections of the able-bodied population were not covered by basic social provisions, either because unemployed, or because in casual jobs with no benefits, or because they did not fall under the age and income requirements to access existing means-tested grants. Such perceptions were clearly reflected in the Taylor Committee's remarks that, "poverty and inequality in South Africa are rooted in the labour market" (RSA, 2002: 25), where "the wage-income relationship is breaking down" (RSA, 2002: 32). As indicated in the introduction of this chapter, however, the government's reception of the Taylor report has been highly selective. While new expansions of work-related social insurance schemes are foreseen, the government's opposition to the basic income grant remains unaltered, despite the extremely reduced monetary amount suggested for the grant, R100 (US$ 15) per month. Throughout its pronouncements rejecting this idea, prominent representatives of the cabinet and of the ruling party have revealed a persistent ideological vehemence, mindful that the task of social policy remains for them to 'school bodies to hard work', rather than running the risk of creating disincentives to jobseeking. The ideological crescendo is, on the other hand, evident in successive statements. Initial opposition to the basic income grant focused on its economic implications, and Minister of Finance, Trevor Manuel lambasted the basic income grant as an 'unsustainable' and 'populist' option (Makino, 2003: 19). Subsequently, ANC ideologue Joel Netshitenzhe refused the proposal arguing that the "opportunity, the dignity and the rewards of work" (Coleman, 2003: 122) remained the government's preferred alternative to decommodified social services. Eventually, minister of Trade and Industry, Alec Erwin, admitted that for the government, "the problem with the [basic income grant] is not the money but the idea" (Hart, 2006: 26).

The idea that social citizenship can rely, in other words, on interventions, no matter how limited, that reduce individual compulsion to work by virtue of universal redistributive provisions continues to be perceived as a threat by the South African government. Under such conditions, the 'epistemic privilege' enjoyed by wage labour as the cornerstone of post-Apartheid policy discourse can be reproduced indefinitely. In a context where the new democracy's episteme increasingly departs from a reality of deepening waged employment crisis, questions will remain concerning the continuing ability of the current policy discourse to normatively regulate social subjectivities and desires.

Conclusion

In interrogating the role of wage labour under Apartheid and post-Apartheid social policy discourse, this chapter has emphasised the problematic interactions between waged employment and social citizenship in South Africa as a case of transition from African colonialism to postcoloniality. It has also raised questions concerning the position of the subjectivity of the subaltern in countries that witnessed a transition to capitalism presided over by colonial and minority rule. The choice, apparent in the policies of South Africa's post-apartheid government, to keep wage labour at the centre of policies of social inclusion does not resolve or problematises the role wage labour has played in structuring social hierarchies, inequalities, and exploitation in the African continent.

The fact that, contrary to the experience of welfarist class compromise in Western industrialised capitalism, wage labour could provide in Africa only an extremely weak, highly selective foundation to a discourse of citizenship, turned such a discourse mainly into a set of ethical prescriptions and coercive pedagogical interventions aimed at, as the 1932 Holloway Commission put it, 'schooling the native body to hard work'. The overbearing normativity of post-Apartheid South Africa's policy discourse disguises the constant deterioration wage labour has suffered under the new democracy, after a brief period during Apartheid's final years in which black workers' struggles seemed to restore the possibility of a socially emancipatory discourse revolving around wage labour.

At the same time, maintaining a moral imperative for hard work, regardless to what hard work practically means in the daily lives of most black South Africans, is a reminder that the celebration by the postcolonial nation-state of the industriousness and probity of the poor actually endorses a form of subaltern citizenship that can only be premised on a fundamentally mutilated social subjectivity. South Africa's labour movement has found it increasingly difficult to square its representing such a mutilated social subjectivity with grand ideas of a future society where work for all underpins effective social citizenship. On the cracks and fissures of organised labour's identities and discourse, new struggles and conflicts have emerged over the past ten years. Some of them are structured by social movements openly critical of the ANC; most protests, however, take the shape of 'service delivery riots' with only a partial and uneven political articulation. Recent upsurges in strike levels and workers' wage radicalism – in the private and public sector alike – as well as working class support for Jacob Zuma as a populist alternative to Thabo Mbeki also revealed a growing discomfort with wage labour's failed promise of social emancipation. But the failure of Zuma's government to take advantage of this explicit support, and build further alliances with informal workers, was evident in the broken promise to outlaw labour broking in 2009-10.

Wage labour and its contradictions, therefore, and the unresolved legacies of South Africa's past in this realm, seem to remain at the centre not only of social conflict but of contestation over alternative ways of schooling the body of the citizen.

References

Adler, G. and Webster, E., 2000. *Trade unions and democratisation in South Africa, 1985-1997.* Johannesburg, South Africa: Witwatersrand University Press.

Altman, M., 2006. Low Wage Work in South Africa. Paper presented to the IZA/World Bank Conference on Employment and Development, Berlin, May 25-27.

ANC, African National Congress. 1996. *The State and Social Transformation. A Discussion Document.* Johannesburg: African National Congress.

Ashforth, A., 1990. *The Politics of Official Discourse in Twentieth-Century South Africa.* Oxford: Clarendon Press.

Bahre, E., 2007. Reluctant Solidarity. Death, Urban Poverty and Neighbourly Assistance in South Africa. *Ethnography,* 8 (1), pp.33-59.

Barchiesi, F., 2006. Social Citizenship and the Transformations of Wage Labour in the Making of Post-Apartheid South Africa, 1994-2001. PhD dissertation, Department of Sociology, University of the Witwatersrand, Johannesburg.

Bayat, A., 1997. *Street Politics. Poor People's Movements in Iran.* New York: Columbia University Press.

Bhorat, H. and Oosthuizen, M., 2005. The Post-Apartheid South African Labour Market. Working Paper 05/93, Cape Town: University of Cape Town, Development Policy Research Unit.

Bond, P., 2005. *Elite Transition. From Apartheid to Neoliberalism in South Africa.* 2nd ed. Pietermaritzburg: University of KwaZulu-Natal Press.

Chakrabarty, D., 2000. *Provincialising Europe. Postcolonial Thought and Historical Difference.* Princeton, NJ: Princeton University Press.

Chanock, M., 2001. *The Making of South African Legal Culture, 1902-1936. Fear, Favour and Prejudice.* Cambridge: Cambridge University Press.

Chatterjee, P., 1994. *The Nation and Its Fragments. Colonial and Postcolonial Histories.* Princeton, NJ: Princeton University Press.

———. 2004. *The Politics of the Governed.* New York: Columbia University Press.

Cheadle, H. and Clarke, M., 2001. *International Labour Office National Studies on Workers' Protection. Country Study: South Africa.* Geneva: International Labour Office.

Coleman, N., 2003. Current Debates around BIG: The Political and Socio-economic Context. In *A Basic Income Grant for South Africa,* edited by G. Standing and M. Samson. Cape Town: University of Cape Town Press.

Cooper, F., 1987. *On the African Waterfront. Urban Disorder and the Transformation of Work in Colonial Mombasa.* New Haven, CT: Yale University Press.

————. 1996. *Decolonisation and African Society. The Labour Question in French and British Africa.* Cambridge: Cambridge University Press.

Da Costa, W. J., 2007. Blanket Grant for Poor Not Envisaged. *The Star*, February 12, 1.

Daniels, L., 2006. Social Grant System 'Can't be Sustained'. *The Mercury*, August 21, 1.

De Angelis, M., 2000. *Keynesianism, Social Conflict and Political Economy.* London: Palgrave.

DeParle, J., 2004. *American Dream. Three Women, Ten Kids, and a Nation's Drive to End Welfare.* New York: Viking.

Devey, R. Skinner, C. and Valodia, I., 2006. Definitions, Data and the Informal Economy in South Africa: A Critical Analysis. In V. Padayachee, ed. *The Development Decade? Economic and Social Change in South Africa, 1994-2004.* Pretoria: HSRC Press.

Eckert, A., 2004. Regulating the Social: Social Security, Social Welfare and the State in Late Colonial Tanzania. *Journal of African History,* 45 (3), pp.467-489.

Escobar, A., 1994. *Encountering Development. The Making and Unmaking of the Third World.* Princeton, NJ: Princeton University Press.

Esping-Andersen, G., 1990. *The Three Worlds of Welfare Capitalism.* Cambridge: Polity Press.

Ferguson, J., 1999. *Expectations of Modernity. Myths and Meanings of Urban Life on the Zambian Copperbelt.* Berkeley, CA: University of California Press.

————. 2006. *Global Shadows. Africa in the Neoliberal World Order.* Durham, NC: Duke University Press.

Fortunati, L., 1996. *The Arcane of Reproduction. Housework, Prostitution, Labour and Capital.* New York: Autonomedia.

Friedman, S., 1987. *Building Tomorrow Today: African workers in trade unions, 1970-1984.* Johannesburg: Ravan Press.

Gallagher, C. and Russouw, S., 2007. Social Grants Given Dependency Shake-up. *The Star*, January 27, 6.

Giliomee, H., 1992. 'Wretched Folk, Ready for Any Mischief': The South African State's Battle to Incorporate Poor Whites and Militant Workers, 1890-1939. *Historia,* 47 (2), pp.601-653.

Grundlingh, L., 1999. Another Side to Warfare: Caring for White Destitutes During the Anglo-Boer War (October 1899-May 1900). *New Contree* (45), pp.137-163.

Gumede, W.M., 2005. *Thabo Mbeki and the Battle for the Soul of the ANC.* Cape Town: Zebra.

Hall, P. ed., 1989. Introduction. In *The Political Power of Economic Ideas. Keynesianism across Nations.* Princeton, NJ: Princeton University Press.

Hamlyn, M., 2006. SA Will Fall Short by 2m in 2015 Job Creation Push. *Business Report*, November 7, 3.

Hardt, M. and Negri, A., 2000. *Empire.* Cambridge, MA: Harvard University Press.

Hart, G., 2006. Post-Apartheid Developments in Historical and Comparative Perspective. In V. Padayachee, ed. *The Development Decade? Economic and Social Change in South Africa, 1994-2004.* Pretoria: HSRC Press.

Hirsch, A., 2005. *Season of Hope. Economic Reform under Mandela and Mbeki.* Pietermaritzburg: University of KwaZulu-Natal Press.

Hong, Y-S., 2005. Neither Singular Nor Alternative: Narratives of Modernity and Welfare in Germany, 1870-1945. *Social History* 30 (2), pp.133-153.

Jessop, B., 2002. *The Future of the Capitalist State.* Cambridge: Polity Press.

Lacan, J., 1977. The Freudian Thing, or the Meaning of the Return to Freud in Psychoanalysis. In *Ecrits. A Selection.* New York: Tavistock.

Lewis, J., 2000. *Empire State-Building. War & Welfare in Kenya 1925-1952.* Oxford: James Currey.

Makino, K., 2003. Social Security Reform in Post-Apartheid South Africa. A Focus on the Basic Income Grant. Paper presented at the *19th World Congress of the International Political Sciences Association*. Durban, June 29-July 5.

Mamdani, M., 1996. *Citizen and subject: contemporary Africa and the legacy of late colonialism.* Princeton, N.J.: Princeton University Press.

Mbeki, T., 2004. *Address of the President of South Africa, Thabo Mbeki, to the First Joint Sitting of the Third Democratic Parliament.* Cape Town, May 21.

———. *State of the Union Address, February 9,* 2007 [cited March 15, 2007]. Available at: http://www.anc.org.za/ancdocs/history/mbeki/2007/tm0209.html.

McCord, A., 2004. *Public Works and Overcoming Under-Development in South Africa.* Paper presented at the UNDP-HSRC-DBSA conference on 'Overcoming Under-Development in South Africa's Second Economy', Cape Town, October 29.

Meth, C. and Solveig, P., 1984. Social Security in Historical Perspective. In *Second Carnegie Inquiry into Poverty and Development in Southern Africa,* Conference Paper 250. Cape Town: University of Cape Town.

Mezzadra, S., 2002. Citizenship and Social Class di Tom Marshall cinquant'anni dopo. In Marshall, T.H., *Cittadinanza e classe sociale,* edited by S. Mezzadra. Bari: Laterza.

Nattrass, N. and Seekings, J., 2000. Apartheid Revisited: Analysing Apartheid as a Distributional Regime. Paper presented at the African Studies Seminar Series. Cape Town: University of Cape Town, October 11.

Patel, L., 1991. Social Welfare Options for South Africa, Vol.1. PhD dissertation, Department of Social Work, University of the Witwatersrand, Johannesburg.

———. 2001. *Redesigning Social Welfare Services: A South African Case Study.* Unpublished mimeo.

Peck, J., 2001. *Workfare States.* New York: Guildford.

Pillay, Y. G., 1995. The Politics of Exclusion: Health Policy in South Africa, 1910-1990. PhD dissertation, School of Hygiene and Public Health, Johns Hopkins University, Baltimore, MD.

Posel, D., 1991. *The Making of Apartheid, 1948-1961. Conflict and Compromise.* Oxford: Clarendon Press.

———. 2004. The Regulation of the Urban African Family in South Africa in the 1930s and 1940s: The Case for a Racialised Welfare State. Seminar Paper No.23, Johannesburg: Randse Afrikaanse Universiteit, Department of Sociology.

Posel, Dorrit., 2003. Have Migration Patterns in Post-Apartheid South Africa Changed? Paper presented to the Conference on African Migration in Comparative Perspective, Johannesburg, June 4-7.

Quijano, A., 2000. Coloniality of Power, Eurocentrism, and Latin America. *Nepantla. Views from South,* 1 (3), pp.533-580.

Ranciere, J., 2003. *Disagreements.* Minneapolis: University of Minnesota Press.

RSA, Republic of South Africa. 1979. *Report of the Commission of Inquiry into Legislation Affecting the Utilisation of Manpower, R.P. 32/1979 (Riekert Commission).* Pretoria: Government Printer.

———. 1997. *White Paper for Social Welfare. Principles, Guidelines, Proposed Policies and Programmes for Developmental Social Welfare in South Africa.* Pretoria: Government Printer.

———. 2002. *Transforming the Present – Protecting the Future. Report of the Committee of Inquiry into a Comprehensive System of Social Security for South Africa (Taylor Committee).* Pretoria: Government Printer.

———. 2003. *Towards a Ten Year Review. Synthesis Report on Implementation of Government Programmes.* Pretoria: Government Printer.

Ruiters, G., 1995. South African Liberation Politics: A Case Study of Collective Action and Leadership in Katorus, 1980-1989. MA dissertation, Department of Politics, University of the Witwatersrand, Johannesburg.

SAPA. 2007. ANCYL Calls for Military Service [cited February 20, 2007]. Available at: www.iol.co.za.

———. 2007. Grants 'Must Link with Development' to Work. *Business Day*, January 31, 3.

Scarnecchia, T., 2000. The Mapping of Respectability and the Transformation of African Residential Space. In B. Raftopoulos and T. Yoshikuni, eds. *Sites of Struggle. Essays in Zimbabwe's Urban History*. Harare: Weaver Press.

Schram, S., 2005. *Welfare Discipline. Discourse, Governance, and Globalisation.* Philadelphia: Temple University Press.

Seekings, J. and Nattrass, N., 2005. *Class, Race, and Inequality in South Africa*. New Haven, CT: Yale University Press.

Seidman, G., 1994. *Manufacturing Militance. Workers' Movements in Brazil and South Africa, 1970-1985*. Berkeley, CA: University of California Press.

Sevenhuijsen, S. Bozalek, V. Gouws, A. and Minnaar-McDonald, M., 2003. South African Social Welfare Policy: An Analysis Using the Ethics of Care. *Critical Social Policy,* 23(3), pp.299-321.

Somers, M. and Block, F., 2005. From Poverty to Perversity: Ideas, Markets, and Institutions over 200 Years of Welfare Debate. *American Sociological Review*, 70 (2), pp.260-87.

Terreblanche, S., 2002. *A History of Inequality in South Africa, 1652-2000*. Pietermaritzburg: University of Natal Press.

Theron, J., 2004. Employment Is Not What it Used To Be: The Nature and Impact of the Restructuring of Work in South Africa. In E.Webster and K. Von Holdt, eds. *Beyond the Apartheid Workplace. Studies in Transition*. Pietermaritzburg: University of KwaZulu-Natal Press.

Trapido, S., 1971. South Africa in a Comparative Study of Industrialisation. *Journal of Development Studies,* 7 (3), pp.309-320.

Twala, C., 2004. The 'Letsema/Ilima' Campaign: A Smokescreen or an Essential Strategy to Deal with the Unemployment Crisis in South Africa? *Journal for Contemporary History/Joernaal vir Eietydse Geskiedenis,* 29 (1), pp.184-98.

Virno, P., 2004. *A Grammar of the Multitude. For an Analysis of Contemporary Forms of Life*. New York: Autonomedia.

Woolard, I. and Woolard, C., 2006. *Earnings Inequality in South Africa 1995-2003*. Pretoria: HSRC Press.

Zizek, S., 2000. *The Ticklish Subject. The Absent Centre of Political Ontology*. London: Verso.

9.
Black poverty and white property in rural SA
Fred Hendricks and Lungisile Ntsebeza

Introduction

The main problem facing South Africa today is the problem of black poverty. Identifying the problem is easy enough. Understanding its generative mechanisms and suggesting feasible ways in which it might be addressed are much more difficult. We trace the contours of black poverty in South Africa in relation to land inequality, recognising that there are many other indicators of social differentiation, but insisting that land remains at the heart of the struggle for both livelihoods as well as citizenship. Our argument revolves around the colonial division of land in the country and how it should be overcome to create possibilities for the resolution of the problem of black poverty and dispossession.

There is urgency in the argument. The South African constitution currently provides a legal sanction for colonial land dispossession, yet the overwhelming majority of the population questions the legitimacy of the extent of white ownership of land. This racialised division of land fractures the nation into opposing camps of white owners and the black dispossessed. The identities of economic exclusion on the one hand and privilege on the other produce schisms which have proven to be incredibly durable after 1994. While formal apartheid is clearly dead, its legacy lives on in the deeply racialised social stratification of the society. Even today, you are far more likely to be poor if you are black.

It is in this context that the enduring colonial division of land acts as a spatial barricade against any effort at developing a unitary imagination of the South African nation. Resolving the land question is therefore not simply about creating livelihoods, but also very much about what it means to be a citizen in South Africa. In many ways, the very concept of a dispossessed citizenry is a contradiction. Poverty hollows out the notion of citizenship, especially since the constitutional franchise presumes a level of equality in rights that does not exist in reality and the fact that blackness and poverty still coincide to such a great degree raises critical questions about the legitimacy of the democratic state.

The chapter claims that linking land reform to agriculture only is far too restrictive in the South African context. While it is clear that there is an urgent necessity to change the structure of land ownership in South Africa's rural areas, we suggest that the land question also has relevance in urban areas, where the demand for a place to live is a potent force for resistance, mobilisation and the illegal occupation of municipal land.

There is an unfortunate conceptual linkage between the land question and agriculture that bifurcates rural and urban struggles. In its stead, we argue for a more nuanced conception of the land question which incorporates the quest for land in both urban and rural areas and considers the vital interconnections of race and class around land ownership in the making of South African citizenship.

The central argument of the chapter is that there are structural constraints in the current land reform programme in South Africa that make it impossible to make a substantial dent in levels of poverty. Analyses of the failures of the land reform programme have followed a very familiar and well-worn path. The narratives invariably start by mentioning the promises of the democratic government to redistribute 30 per cent of agricultural land within the first five years of democracy and they proceed to demonstrate just how inordinately slow the implementation of this programme has been against the backdrop of rising levels of poverty. The story is an important one, but it has reached an impasse. We need to move beyond the complaints of government failure in delivering on its election promises. This paper seeks to understand this failure within a broader context of the various debates around the land and agrarian questions in Southern Africa, the enduring realities of colonialism and civil society responses to the ongoing crises of landlessness and poverty.

The chapter has four sections. It commences by insisting that the colonial context remains a vital backdrop to any analysis of the land question in South Africa. The second section provides a critique of recent analyses of the agrarian question with a specific focus of the debate in Zimbabwe. We have included this discussion on Zimbabwe as an important lesson in what could happen if the question of land inequality is not addressed timeously and democratically. In the third section, the chapter highlights the constitutional constraints to land reform by examining the compromises of the negotiated settlement and the limits that they place on possibilities for land reform. The fourth section provides an overview of the lack of agency around the demand for land through a critical perspective on the role of NGOs. Finally we conclude the chapter with a discussion on the manner in which racialised land inequality impinges on the possibilities for imagining a unitary South African nation.

Colonial contexts

In very many ways South Africa is an exception on the continent. If we were to consider a continuum between the extent to which colonialism either disturbed or left untouched the pre-existing social structures and relations, then the country definitely resides closer to the former. Chege (1997) provides some insight into other extremes, "...long after independence there were regions in Africa, like Northern Chad and interior Mozambique, where it was news that the colonists had departed. The people had never heard of their arrival." With more than 90 per cent of the land surface actively alienated from indigenous belonging, there was little chance of this happening in South Africa. For the majority, there was no escape from the all-encompassing embrace of colonialism and later apartheid. Everybody felt it. The fact of this crushing dispossession poses serious problems for the formulation of the land and agrarian questions. In this respect, the land question cannot be reduced to a question of livelihoods only because it concerns fundamental claims of legitimacy over ownership and control of the country at large.

The various struggles for national independence in Africa were almost invariably premised on the idea of local control and the emancipation of the people from the shackles of colonialism. Nationalism was supposed to be the very antithesis of colonialism. However, across Africa there has been a profound dissatisfaction with the fruits of independence. Nationalism, in the guise of post-colonial regimes has turned out to be an imitation of colonialism rather than its antithesis and the process of decolonisation has not brought about a level of social citizenship capable of releasing the full potential of its denizens. Instead, the vast majority of the population remains impoverished even under a new set of indigenous rulers. There is a never-ending paradox on the role of colonialism. It was supposed to usher in modernity, yet it has to do that by undermining, oppressing and destroying the local culture, social structure and economy. The underlying racist assumption is that since Africans are incapable of their own modernity, it has to be brought home to them and thrust upon them by others from outside the continent.

It is important at this point to mention that we do not follow Jean Paul Sartre's depiction of colonialism as genocide, outlined so forcefully in his Preface to Frantz Fanon's (1961) *The Wretched of the Earth*. Clearly genocidal massacres were part and parcel of colonialism, but it was defined by conquest rather than by mass murder. If the current South African constitution legitimises the racialised division of land inherited from its colonial past, then it raises a whole host of questions about the nature of the transition to democracy and about the discourse of the national movement for liberation.

One of the more compelling questions in this regard is whether this brand of nationalism can be construed as the antithesis of colonialism. Across Africa, nationalist historiography was supposedly informed by the anti-colonial struggle. Yet, as Mamdani (1996) mentions, virtually all nationalist movements did not have an "...agenda for democratising customary power" and the struggle to overcome the legacies of colonialism are still with us today. Without exception, all African colonies were ruled by undemocratic regimes. Colonialism was intrinsically undemoctaric because it meant rule by outsiders over a subject population.

In South Africa, centuries of colonial exclusion have been replaced by an inclusive democratic government. It now faces the enormous task of correcting the injustices and inequalities inherited from the past. Virtually all analyses of the land question in South Africa point to how dismally slow the land reform programme of the new government has been. We will not go down that route. Instead we will try to show why the sanctity of private property premised on the notion of an atomised individual is singularly inappropriate under conditions of colonial expropriation of land. While countless individuals lost their access to land as a result of colonial dispossession, they did not lose their land as individuals but as members of a collective indigenous community of people. In this sense, the only viable corrective action has to be collectively-based rather than individually-ascertained like the current South African land reform policy.

Twentieth century Africa was indelibly marked by colonisation. Of course there are wide variety of ways in which colonialism affected agricultural production and rural social relations in Africa. Broadly, there is an inverse correlation between the extent of white settler expropriation of land and the survival of indigenous agricultural production, but there was no uniform way in which rural producers responded to the colonial encounter. Colonisation of Southern Africa by white settlers followed a particular trajectory. With few exceptions, the land seized by whites was held under freehold title, but Africans held land under various versions of communal tenure. There are varieties of overlapping rights of clans, lineages and households in relation to land and its fruits in Africa that defy neat categorisation as property. The fact that these rights are usually associated with affiliation by kinship has profound implications for the manner in which claims for land may be structured, including the attempt by chiefs and other traditional authorities to ensure that they monopolise the ownership of the community's land under their individual title deeds. An understanding of the peculiarities of these social relations of production, reproduction and domination is vital for any discussion on the land and agrarian questions in Africa. The white-claimed land became their private property as colonialism ushered in an entirely different conception of property - one of exclusive domain. In order to protect the newly-acquired private property of the settlers from the natives, they excluded them from access and prosecuted them when they trespassed on the land. This conception obviously contradicted the pre-existing customary forms of land tenure where the very concept of ownership over land as property did not exist.

While there were few possibilities for Africans to own land by individual title deed, the overwhelming reality for them was one of confinement to a distorted type of communal tenure in reserves with restricted agricultural potential. This form of land holding also contributed to the decline of the rural production in the designated reserves. Most land in the reserves was (and continues to be) legally owned by the state. However, unlike on commercial farms, residents had access to small allotments of land where they could build their houses and cultivate small gardens. Squeezed between the freehold tenure under white control and the customary tenure in the reserves were a number of quitrent tenurial arrangements which allowed some Africans access to considerable plots of land which they used for agricultural purposes.

Ntsebeza's (2006) research in the former Xhalanga district shows that descendants of a targeted group of progressive African farmers in this district continued with the legacy of their parents and grandparents under quitrent tenure well into the 1960s. Preliminary findings of current research conducted by Iiyama (2007) in the same district also demonstrates that cultivation still contributes a substantial part of the livelihoods of the people. Confirming the continued significance of agriculture in social reproduction in the rural areas, Ncapayi (2006) has shown that these households tend to be dominated by the elderly and would have begun their working careers as migrant workers, only turning to land based activities later on in their lives. The persistence of agricultural activity by indigenous people has been seen in the context of the overwhelming dispossession of the majority. It has happened despite the enormous obstacles placed in their way and because of their ongoing crisis of livelihoods.

The allocation and administration of land in the reserves was the responsibility of a complex mix of traditional authorities and colonial officials. Some land-based activities survived, but the major trend was towards a massive decline in agricultural production which further deepened the problems of reproducing families. While colonialism led to the modernisation and commercialisation of agriculture of white settlers who benefited from state assistance through tax rebates, transport concessions, marketing subsidies, low interest credit and so on, African farmers were denied the wherewithal to undertake proper farming. Their efforts to respond to the opportunities of producing for the market were stifled by the colonial demand for labour. Africans were not to be independent producers nor were they to be capitalising farmers, they were to be workers on white claimed farms, in white mines and later in white factories. The boundaries between settlers and natives were palpable and they remain the main factor in social stratification in South Africa today as the legacies of colonialism and apartheid are etched on the political and social landscape.

One of the main dividends of colonialism is the grossly unequal access to, control over, and ownership of land between whites and blacks. It is a situation of extraordinary inequality that requires an extraordinary response. However, when one views the fast-track land reform in Zimbabwe, there can be little doubt that it has fundamentally altered the nature of land ownership in that country. In this sense, it is important to provide a critical review of the Zimbabwean debate as a backdrop to the land question in South Africa.

The Zimbabwe debate

The fast-track land resettlement programme in Zimbabwe commencing in earnest in 2000 has stimulated a heated debate. On the one hand, Moyo and Yeros (2005: 165) assert that the land occupations in Zimbabwe represent the "...most notable of rural movements in the world today" and that it is "...the most important challenge to the neocolonial state in Africa." They conclude that these occupations are, "fundamentally progressive" (Moyo and Yeros, 2005: 188) and that, "...rural movements today constitute the core nucleus of opposition to neoliberalism and the most important source of democratic transformation in national and international politics" (Moyo and Yeros, 2005: 6).

Moyo (2007: 71) is at pains to demonstrate the inadequacy in civil society advocacy around land reform, a position confirmed by Kirk Helliker (2006) in a recent doctoral dissertation on NGOs in Zimbabwe. They are also impatient with the vacillation of the Zimbabwean government's policy in respect of redistributing land. It was to be expected, as far as they are concerned, that the war veterans would step into this leadership vacuum. Their argument is solidly enmeshed in a nationalist discourse with a major focus on the land question as the clarion call in the anti-colonial struggle. For them, the national democratic revolution and proper decolonisation can only happen with a fundamental return of the land to blacks. We agree.

However, Moyo and Yeros (2005) are so entirely committed to the notion of a radical redistribution of land in the former settler societies that they do not seem to notice that there are other processes at work as well. In the fervour of their support for the fast-track land resettlement programme, they do not appear to appreciate the level of authoritarianism in the making of the contemporary Zimbabwe state. They provide a crude class analysis with seemingly very little understanding of the methodological and conceptual problems in empirically demarcating classes and they rush to claim the agency of a movement in the occupation of land.

Kirk Helliker (2006) has summarised the views of the various critics of Moyo and Yeros in the following manner, as 'patriotic agrarianists' or 'authoritarian populist anti-imperialists' (Moore, 2004), or 'left nationalists' following a path of 'exhausted nationalism' (Bond and Manyanya, 2003). In contrast to their positive response to the land occupations since 2000, Hammer and Raftopoulos, (2003) characterise the regime as one of 'exclusionary nationalism' and Raftopoulos and Phimister (2004) call it a 'domestic tyranny'.

Hammar and Raftopoulos (2003: 21) provide a detailed account of the discursive and practical complexities involved in the political landscape of Zimbabwe and they conclude that, "such a dense and dynamic social fabric and the multiplicity of land and natural resource conflicts which it generates, can hardly be explained only in terms of the legacy of colonial conquest and land appropriation, no matter how profound their imprints on agrarian structures and relations." But while everything obviously can't be explained in these terms, abandoning the colonial legacy is also problematic precisely because of the deep imprints it has left in post-colonial former settler societies. Indeed, very little can be explained outside of the colonial context. It is precisely the colonial inheritance of structural inequality, especially in access, ownership and control over land that makes it possible for a tyrant like Robert Mugabe to masquerade as a legitimate liberator. In this respect, Mafeje's (2003: 28) claim is apt, "The African tragedy is that the state itself has become the single biggest development problem." Hammer and Raftopoulos (2003: 13-14) share this view, but they apparently de-link it from the enduring racialised inequalities of colonialism. The overwhelming thrust of their introductory chapter concentrates on the negative effects of the recent seizures of land in Zimbabwe. The occupation of large-scale commercial farms, increased rate of inflation, the fall of the currency, the fall in GDP, rise in unemployment, debt, loss of foreign investment, the loss of judicial independence, severe restriction on freedom of the press and so on, all paint a very accurate picture of economic collapse and political crisis.

In response, they propose to "expose and interrupt such rigid polarities and the essentialisms that underpin them" and "to open out the space in which the crisis can be told or read so as to facilitate greater transparency and nurture critical intellectual and political debate."

(Hammer and Raftopoulos, 2003: 17). Yet, in as much as Moyo and Yeros concentrate on the imperative of economic redistribution, Hammer and Raftopoulos focus on democratic rights, and in our view they contribute to rather than transcend this 'devastating rupture' (Hammer and Raftopoulos, 2003: 218). In the same way that Moyo and Yeros do not appear to see anything beyond the necessity for land reform, Hammer and Raftopoulos appear to see nothing beyond the need for a restoration of democratic and human rights in the context of an accountable government.

It is a schism that is related in complex ways to the intractable problem of political equality alongside economic inequality. This, after all is one of the abiding paradoxes of all democracies. They all uphold political equality through the franchise and a host of other rights and liberties. Simultaneously, they all maintain material inequality, essentially through the protection of private property. What is peculiar about Southern Africa is the extreme nature of this inequality and the fact that the division between rich and poor still coincides largely with the distinction between black and white. To put it bluntly, it is a problem of race and class. In Zimbabwe, there can be little doubt that the official view of land reform being crucial to maintaining the sovereignty of the state, is contested by the very manner in which the concept is employed. It is left up to Jocelyn Alexander (2006: 180) to attempt to accommodate both strands in her analysis when she asserts,

> Zimbabwe seemed to be entering the world described by the political scientists of Africa elsewhere – the 'politics of disorder', the 'politics of the belly'. But Zimbabwe did not easily fit these models. Violence, corruption and economic collapse were accompanied by a massive redistribution of land; nationalist history – and specifically race and colonialism – played a central role in political discourse. The state did not 'collapse' or 'fail': instead, a closely orchestrated process of remaking the state took place in which land took centre stage.

In countering Sam Moyo's point that land has always been a political issue in Zimbabwe, Alexander asserts that in both officialdom and in the public domain, the discourse around land has gone through major shifts. She periodises these shifts from the dominance of the concept of reconciliation during the 1980s to the increasing use of race in the rhetoric of the 1990s to the authoritarian role of the state in the recent fast-track land redistribution, with contested claims over land amongst its various beneficiaries – the war veterans, the urban poor, farm workers, rural residents in the communal areas (Alexander, 2006: 192).

Sachikonye (2005: 32) is in agreement with this view, "In the 1990's there was a discernable shift in how the land question was interpreted." Alexander (2003:104) takes an unambiguous position against the untenable and illegitimate distribution of land in Zimbabwe between white farmers and the black majority,

> Others, myself included, have felt ambivalent about criticising the occupations, and thereby seeming to belittle the real desire and need for land that motivated popular participation in them. Mugabe's political genius was to place the clearly unjust and unresolved question of land redistribution at the heart of his campaign. However, to focus narrowly on the occupations alone misses the point that what they marked was not just an unprecedented assault on the unequal distribution of land but also an extraordinary transformation of the state and political sphere.

Robin Palmer (2003) agrees, but his emphasis is different,

> While Mugabe has certainly become a brutal, self-serving tyrant, this does not negate the fact that the issues he is raising require much more imaginative responses than they have received to date. For example, I believe that he is right:
> - in categorising the colonial expropriation of land as unjust and oppressive - and needing radical solution;
> - in castigating colonial powers for encouraging and legalising it;
> - in appealing in the language of historical injustice which – because the fundamental issues have not been adequately addressed - has enormous popular appeal among the poor right across Southern Africa and so - to the chagrin of European governments - make it very difficult for neighbouring Presidents, especially Thabo Mbeki, to criticise him in public.

It is well known that Robert Mugabe is an undemocratic oppressor. Yet, there is enormous support on the continent for Zimbabwe's fast track land reform programme. Consider the statement by the President of Tanzania at the SADC meeting in Luanda in 2002: "the land question in Zimbabwe," says Benjamin Mkapa (2002), the current SADC Chairperson,

> ...needs to be put in its proper historical context. Above all, everyone must respect and uphold the independence and

sovereignty of Zimbabwe. We are convinced that the ongoing land reform in that country is aimed at the rational, fair and equitable distribution of land to be used for the benefit of the people of Zimbabwe. Such reforms also respond to the justified need to correct injustices of the past. For that reason, we in SADC remain united in appreciating the need for and supporting land reform in Zimbabwe.

There was little interrogation of the concept of sovereignty as implying consent by the citizens and accountability and responsibility by the government. Notwithstanding the overwhelming evidence of the violence and repression of the Zimbabwe government, at its meeting in Tanzania in 2003, the SADC reiterated these supportive statements. For its part, at its inaugural conference in Johannesburg in 2001, the Landless Peoples Movement resolved to "support the gallant actions of Zimbabwean President Robert Mugabe to return stolen land to the people of Africa."

The official opposition in Zimbabwe, the MDC, has not made any promises to reverse the recent fast track land reform programme. Whatever may be said about the land reform process in Zimbabwe, it has fundamentally altered the terms of the debate around the land question in that country and a great deal of this has spilled over into South Africa. In the midst of all the ideological and conceptual disagreements, there is one point of commonality - all scholars agree that the results of the 2000 constitutional referendum represented a turning point in Zimbabwean history.

Besides the corruption, the cronyism, the human rights violations, the violence and authoritarianism, the other main problem with the Zimbabwean experience of land redistribution is that it was not located within the production relations on commercial farms. In other words, tens of thousands of farm workers, those who have been directly involved in labour on commercial farms, often for many decades, have either been evicted from the farms or remain there with slim prospects of securing livelihoods. The evidence in this respect is varied, while Moyo claims 70 000, Alexander argues that 200 000 farm workers have been forcibly displaced from their places of residence and work. Sachinkonye (2005: 33) concurs with the latter. He goes on to explain the tensions between the farmworkers and the occupiers of the land in the following terms,

Farm workers were viewed as standing between the aspirant farmers and their goals, which was seizing ownership from the white commercial farmers...The occupiers had a vested interest in disrupting production on farms so that white commercial farmers would leave or share their farms with them through subdivision.

The economic collapse of Zimbabwe over the last five years is caused by various deep-rooted problems, but provides a potent lesson of what may happen if the question of land redistribution is not dealt with timeously and comprehensively. It has ruined the prospects of developing a non-racial democracy for many years and it has made it extremely difficult to build a non-racial Zimbabwean nation. When Robert Mugabe (2002) says, "If there are white farmers who want to continue working on the land, they must seek permission from us because the land is ours," he effectively denationalises white Zimbabweans, stripping them of their citizenship and imposing a racialised claim over the land.

This is what is at stake for us in South Africa as well. Land reform should and must happen in South Africa, but there are profound disagreements on the methods, the timing and the extent of redistribution. Now we have to ask a very awkward historical and sociological question. We believe that we must confront this question if we are to avoid the chaos of Zimbabwe: can land redistribution in pursuit of equality, a process of transferring ownership of and access to land from one group to another, ever be a pleasant thing?

Constitutional constraints

In South Africa, the democratic transition after 1994 produced a flurry of policy changes to deal with the palpable inequalities in land and to reorganise the institutional frameworks so that it may reflect the values of the new order. But policies don't easily translate into practice, especially when there are so many obstacles placed in their way, and when the policy itself encapsulates the broader contradictions between formal political equality and economic inequality. To all intents and purposes, land reform has been a dismal failure as White privilege, borne out of colonial land theft, has become firmly entrenched and redistributing land to the poor under these conditions is necessarily a fraught process.

In the debates leading up to the adoption of the constitution, Judge Didcott, one of the leading legal figures in South Africa, appeared to appreciate the contradiction,

> What a Bill of Rights cannot afford to do here ... is to protect private property with such zeal that it entrenches privilege. A major problem which any future South African government is

bound to face will be the problem of poverty, of its alleviation and of the need for the country's wealth to be shared more equitably ...

Should a bill of rights obstruct the government of the day when that direction is taken, should it make the urgent task of social or economic reform impossible or difficult to undertake, we shall have on our hands a crisis of the first order, endangering the bill of rights as a whole and the survival of constitutional government itself (quoted in Chalskalson 1993: 73-4).

> The central question we need to address is whether our constitution provides the necessary mechanisms for dealing with poverty or whether it merely offers a legal sanction for colonial land alienation.

The new constitution ushered in a system of formal legal, civil and political equality. It also committed the state to some second-generation rights and policies designed to offset the worst effects of apartheid on the formerly disenfranchised majority. There can be little doubt that the institutional mechanics of democracy are firmly in place in post-apartheid South Africa. However, the very constitution that guarantees formal equality before the law, also entrenches material inequality especially in the distribution of land ownership. Clause 25 of the Bill of Rights in the Constitution establishes property rights under which nobody may be arbitrarily deprived of their property. Expropriation of property is permitted for public purposes only and subject to agreement in the payment of fair compensation. It is our view that land reform should be regarded as an imperative public purpose. While blacks are now allowed to own and dispose of property freely in the country as a whole, that right is significantly circumscribed by the truncated possibilities for its realisation. People are simply too poor to buy land without the assistance of the state.

In his annual State of the Nation Address in 2007, Thabo Mbeki acknowledged that very little progress had been made in respect of land redistribution and he promised to investigate the factors preventing the implementation of the programme. While there is widespread agreement across that the country that the South African land reform programme is inordinately slow, there is very little concurrence on the reasons for this lack of progress or on the mechanism for speeding up the process. Some argue that the policy itself is coherent but the means for implementing it are woefully inadequate. Others suggest instead that there are structural and policy problems inhibiting the objectives of land reform. Our key argument is that both the policies as well as the mechanisms for its implementation require revision. In particular, the entrenchment of the property clause in the constitution, coupled with weak civil society organisations addressing the land question, are the major obstacles in the achievement of even the limited objective of the land reform programme in South Africa. Our paper revolves around these two factors.

The relevant section (28) in the Interim Constitution reads as follows:

> 1. Every person shall have the right to acquire and hold rights in property and, to the extent that the nature of the rights permits, to dispose of such rights.
> 2. No deprivation of any rights in property shall be permitted otherwise than in accordance with a law.
> 3. Where any rights in property are expropriated pursuant to a law of referred to in subsection (2), such expropriation shall be permissible for public purposes only and shall be subject to the payment of agreed compensation or, failing agreement, to the payment of such compensation and within such period as may be determined by a court of law as just and equitable, taking into account all relevant factors, including, in the case of the determination of compensation, the use to which the property is being put, the history of its acquisition, its market value, the value of the investment in it by those affected and the interests of those affected.

It is widely accepted that section 28 represented a compromise between the ANC and National Party positions. The major question was how the new state would accommodate both the need to protect the property rights of those with property and at the same time ensure that the historical injustices of land dispossession would be addressed. It is impossible to equally satisfy both the need to protect property rights and to ensure a policy of redistribution to a level that would approach a more equitable distribution of land in South Africa. The compromise reached at the negotiating table clearly favoured the existing property holders and consequently compromised any hope of genuine land reform that could fundamentally alter the pattern of land inequality. The constitution made the possibility of expropriation of land an extraordinarily litigious process, effectively giving the property holders (mostly whites, of course) a veto over the extent and pace of land redistribution. This is an untenable position because it undermines the vitally important object of land redistribution in correcting the injustices of apartheid.

Rights take precedence over policies. Hence, the right of protection of property has trumped the policy of land reform. The effect of this lack of delivery has meant that the colonial and apartheid division of land has remained more or less intact since the demise of apartheid. This remains an abiding grievance for the mass of the population because their dispossession has been sanctioned by the new constitution. The very recognition of existing property rights expunges the possibility for redistribution on a scale broad enough to ensure legitimacy. It also makes the task of the government in delivering land for redistribution impossible, because the courts in the country have already decided that the existing division of land is legitimate and legal. Any attempt to change the current colonially inherited division of land will have to contend with the force of freehold and the rights of title deeds to property. Under these circumstances, land redistribution is necessarily a dead letter. Since it is impossible to expect genuine land reform from the government in the current context, we need to understand the limits and the possibilities of pressures from below.

A critique of NGOs

Debates and discussions around land policy since 1994 have involved NGOs, with barely any direct participation of rural people. Often, NGOs have presented (or misrepresented) themselves as the voice of rural communities. As Davids (2003: 49) points out, there was a lack of rural community participation in the drafting of key documents on rural development such as the Integrated and Sustainable Rural Development Strategy (ISRDS), despite the fact that a Rural Development Initiative (RDI) had been established with the explicit purpose of mobilising rural communities. As a result, very few rural people are aware of the ISRDS and this makes nonsense of the constitutional obligation requiring the participation of communities in policy and implementation processes, particularly with regard to local government.

The marginalisation of rural communities in these discussions must be viewed against the back-drop of the active role rural residents played in the struggles against 'Betterment' between the 1940s and early 1960s. There is overwhelming evidence that these struggles were led by the rural residents themselves, who were directly affected by the policies they were challenging. The liberation movements in South Africa, including the ANC, were largely pre-occupied with urban struggles. When resistance against apartheid re-emerged following the Soweto uprisings of 1976 and shifted to the countryside in the 1980s, the struggles of rural residents were, with few exceptions, led by NGOs.

How then do we explain the apparent invisibility of rural communities in struggles since the early 1970s, particularly considering wide-spread rural resistance against the colonial and apartheid regimes in the period up to the late 1950s and early 1960s? At a very basic level, this can be traced to the brutal and mass dispossession of land of the indigenous people in South Africa, which forced large numbers of rural people to gradually depend more and more on wages and less and less on agricultural production for their survival. This, coupled with the ruthless suppression of the rural revolts in the early 1960s, followed by the consolidation of the Bantustan strategy hastened the decline of agriculture in these areas, thus contributing to greater levels of urbanisation, despite the many repressive pieces of legislation designed to keep Africans out of the towns. The nature and form of organisation and struggle against apartheid was invariably affected by this reality. Resistance took an urban character and the land question and rural struggles assumed secondary significance especially in liberation movements. As the work of Ntsebeza (2006) in Xhalanga shows, organised struggles that took place in the rural areas of the former Bantustans from the late 1980s were largely directed by migrant workers and students, particularly from tertiary institutions, when they returned home for their holidays.

This however should not be interpreted to mean that there is no land question in South Africa. There may be no coherent and overt organisation around the demand for land in the country but there are many covert, disorganised expressions of the manner in which the majority of the population consider the widespread occupation of land by whites as illegitimate. The unequal division of land between whites and blacks is in itself a major question around land that needs urgent resolution. The land question and its role in the livelihoods of South Africans cannot be adequately understood in isolation of the broader political economy of the country.

Inasmuch as there is a clear link between the decline of rural production amongst Africans and the role of migrant labour, there is also an urgent necessity for social movements to involve the active participation of rural people. There is no escaping the fact that there are still people residing in the rural areas of the former Bantustans, regarding these as home without any intention of permanently settling in the urban areas. Once again, the research of Ncapayi referred to above makes this point. In these circumstances, the building of urban-rural alliances, rather than substitutionism remains firmly on the political agenda.

Another explanation for the lack of active involvement of rural residents in struggles since the early 1960s can be attributed to the emergence of NGOs, particularly in the 1980s. This coincided with the decline of organised resistance in the countryside noted above. It seems clear that the invisibility of rural communities contributed to the emergence of NGOs, mostly urban based and led by whites, in the 1980s as the main representatives of rural communities.

Since a resolution to the land question is elusive in the current constitutional context, we provide a critical appraisal of the role of NGOs as a mobilising force in the post-1994 period. As noted, the organised voice from below in the land sector at the advent of democracy in 1994 was led by NGOs, specifically a group of land based NGOs that established a network referred to as the National Land Committee (NLC). These organisations had emerged during the apartheid period, mainly in the 1980s, in response to the forced removal of millions of black Africans from white designated areas. Thus, land and agrarian movements were led by NGOs who acted on behalf of black victims of segregation and apartheid in South Africa. In contrast to these NGOs, the pre-existing rural movements of the 1940's, 1950's and early 1960's were led by those directly affected by land dispossession. In the majority of cases, there was no direct involvement of political organisations and NGOs hardly existed (Matoti and Ntsebeza, 2005).

When resistance re-emerged in the late 1960's after the massive clampdown in the wake of the Sharpeville massacre the focus was, as already indicated, on urban areas, particularly around trade unions. This culminated in the 1973 Durban Strikes and the subsequent formation of the independent trade union movement. The urban struggle intensified after the student uprising of 1976 and the establishment of the United Democratic Front (UDF) in 1983. It is in this context that NGOs like NLC which were urban based but with a focus on rural issues emerged. In the 1980s, most of the affiliates of the NLC supported the broad liberation movement under the auspices of the UDF. In the early 1990s, during the political negotiations, the NLC became part of the land lobby identifying with the ANC. Although some affiliates were not happy with the adoption of the property clause in the constitution, they nonetheless remained loyal to the ANC.

A question that arises is how land activists and their organisations have responded to post-1994 developments around questions of land. It is also necessary to examine how deeply they were involved in the shaping of government policy? Despite the fact that the ANC has adopted a market-led approach to land reform, there seems to have been a sense amongst many that the ANC government was seriously committed to redressing historical injustices and that this would somehow be done within the limits of neoliberal capitalism. The new South African constitution clearly stipulates the three main pillars of the land reform programme - land redistribution, land tenure reform and land restitution. The government followed a World Bank recommendation that 30 per cent of white-claimed agricultural land be transferred during the first five years of democracy. This target has been altered a few times since then, but it remains a fiction.

Some organisations, including the National Land Committee (NLC), and a number of individuals supported the ANC-led government in its efforts to formulate a programme and implement a plan for land reform. Some members went as far as resigning from their organisations and joining the Department of Land Affairs as government officials. The presumption was that the ANC-led government was a people's government seriously committed to accomplishing the objectives of the constitution. The endorsement of the protection of existing property rights, the unilateral decision by the ANC leadership to adopt the extremely conservative set of macro-economic policies under the acronym of GEAR in 1996, as well as the entrenchment of the market-based 'willing buyer, willing seller' principle as the basis for land reform, did not discourage land activists in the NLC and its affiliates from pushing ahead with their strategy of working within the structures of government. This was despite clear signs that policy decisions between 1996 and 1997 represented a key moment of closure in efforts by the NLC and its affiliates to push land reform policy in a more progressive direction from within the structures of government.

By 1999, when Thabo Mbeki came to power, the NLC affiliates found themselves in an increasingly difficult position. On the one hand they were drawn into implementing the limited, technocratic, and hopelessly under-funded land reform programme. In addition, NGOs were under pressure from their donors to collaborate with the government. Some of these funding agencies began to channel their funding through government departments and expected NGOs to do commissioned work for the government. These factors contributed to the weakening of NGOs and, more importantly, to an almost total neglect of rural mobilisation, on both farms and the former Bantustans. This was particularly the case in the first few years of South Africa's democracy.

On the other hand, NGOs were confronted with growing pressure from below in different regions. Most significant was the escalating anger of black tenants over ongoing abuse on white-owned farms, despite the Extension of Security of Tenure Act which simply instructed white farmers on how to go about evicting tenants. The continued inequality in land, the limitations of the land reform programme, the ongoing repression on white-claimed farms, as well as the 'hidden struggles' around land issues on farms and urban areas, combined to create conditions for mobilisation around the issue of landlessness.

The formation of the Landless People's Movement (LPM) was by far the most significant event in the resurgence of resistance in the land sector in South Africa at the start of the 21st century. Its significance in the context of our discussion about the invisibility of rural communities above, lies in the fact that this initiative had the potential of not only involving the landless, but also of pushing forward a movement that is led by the landless themselves, along the lines of the Brazilian movement, the Movimento dos Trabalhadores Rurais sem Terra – MST. The LPM was launched in Johannesburg in 2001. Events in neighbouring Zimbabwe in 2000 clearly had an impact on the fledgling organisation as President Mugabe of Zimbabwe received warm praise for his role in the Fast Track Land Reform Programme.

For their part, COSATU, the giant South African trade union federation, was critical of Mugabe's undemocratic methods of implementing 'fast track' land reform in Zimbabwe. Apart from developments in Zimbabwe, the formation of the LPM was preceded by land occupation on a farm in Bredell, outside Johannesburg where the Pan Africanist Congress, parliamentary political party 'sold' land to squatters. The new movement noted the extent of dispossession in the country and the lack of progress in the official land reform practice, and hence proposed that the government should urgently hold a land summit. It moreover committed itself to a programme of mass mobilisation around the demand for land.

There were two other major events which helped promote the LPM: the United Nations World Conference on Racism and the World Summit on Sustainable Development. In the run up to the United Nations World Conference on Racism which was held in Durban in August 2001, the LPM together with the NLC, the South African Non-Governmental Organisation Coalition (SANGOCO), the Rural Development Services Network, the Trust for Community Outreach and Education embarked on a Landlessness = Racism campaign just in time to highlight the plight of the landless in South Africa and elsewhere under the banner of the Durban Social Forum.

A year later, at the World Summit on Sustainable Development also held in Johannesburg, the LPM was one of the prominent organisations behind the 'Week of the Landless'. This time these organisations came under the umbrella of the Social Movement Indaba (SMI). Towards the end of the Summit, the organisations led a huge march to Sandton, the venue of the Summit, demonstrating against the negative effects of neoliberalism in South Africa in the form of privatisation of essential services and landlessness. Apart from these two major events, the LPM in Gauteng in particular also joined forces with movements protesting water and electricity cut-offs and rent evictions.

There is little doubt that the formation of the LPM marked a major shift in the form of organisation of the land and agrarian movement in South Africa and the methods used in the demand for land in the post-1994 scenario. Additionally, this was the first time since the 1950s and early 1960s that a movement having the potential of a mass base, led by those directly affected was emerging. As already noted, rural resistance from the 1980s was led by urban-based NGOs, with left-wing white activists, lawyers and researchers playing prominent roles. The LPM, at least in theory, was a social movement with membership drawn from the 'grassroots' of landless people themselves. In this regard, the LPM followed the tradition of the powerful land and agrarian movements in Latin America and Asia. Above all, the formation of the LPM clearly showed that the land question is not only about rural areas and about agriculture, but is as important for those in urban areas. It also highlighted the importance of urban-rural alliances in the struggle for land in South Africa.

Despite its potential, there were by 2003 clear signs that the LPM was in disarray. Part of the explanation for this decline were tensions within the NLC and its affiliates. The NLC, or more precisely, prominent activists such as Andile Mngxitama, played a prominent role in the establishment of the LPM. Tensions within the NLC revolved primarily around the critical issue of how civil society organisations should relate with the democratic state, on the one hand, and social movements on the other. The formation of the Landless People's Movement in 2001 deepened these tensions. Yet, there was no unanimity within the NLC on the involvement of the organisation in the struggles of the LPM. Some affiliates of the NLC were against the involvement of the NLC in the struggles of the LPM which were increasingly confrontational. These affiliates argued that support of the LPM would harm relations with the state. Tensions within the NLC reached a peak in the period following the World Summit on Sustainable Development. The organisation never recovered from these tensions and ended up disbanding as a network, with affiliates pursuing their own independent existence.

In the midst of all this, yet another actor emerged on the land scene: the South African Communist Party (SACP). In 2004, the SACP launched its Red October campaign with a focus on the land question. In a bid to win mass based support among rural people, the SACP established an ambiguous relationship with the LPM. Both organisations supported the need for a land summit. It appears as if the SACP in particular used its influence as a member of the Tripartite Alliance to persuade the then Department of Land Affairs to hold a Land Summit in July 2005. The

SACP played a prominent role in the summit. The role of the LPM, however, was not as prominent. Part of the reason is that by this time, the LPM was almost moribund. Furthermore, its relationship with the SACP would have been jeopardised by the 'no land, no vote' stand it took in the 2004 election. More research needs to be done on these processes.

While the NLC and LPM were riddled with tensions and in disarray, a new actor, the Trust for Community Outreach and Education (TCOE) entered into the land struggle debate. There is little doubt that the entry of TCOE would have strengthened the land and agrarian movement had these tensions not existed. The TCOE, like the NLC, represented a network of six affiliates in the Western Cape, the Eastern Cape and Limpopo. Its roots lay in the Black Consciousness movement after the death of Steve Biko, and in Liberation Theology. At a time when the NLC and LPM were garnering most of the publicity and attention, TCOE and its affiliates were quietly involved in low profile rural organisation. Their initial programmes were in response to the education crisis following the students' protests and boycotts against 'gutter education' in the 1970s and early 1980s.

In the transition to democracy, TCOE resolved to move away from its 'welfarist' moorings which characterised the 1980s to a more 'developmental' approach to working with communities. The TCOE adopted a strategy with origins in Bangladesh called People's Participatory Planning (PPP), which emphasises the need to involve poor communities in all aspects of their development, including planning. TCOE has over the years built locally based Community Development Committee (CDCs) in its areas of operation. There is a strong focus on the 'poorest of the poor', in particular building capacity and local leadership with a stress on community ownership of development initiatives. Since 2000, the focus of TCOE has been on issues of land, local government and basic needs. To mark its 20th anniversary in December 2003, TCOE organised a People's Tribunal on Landlessness in Port Elizabeth, Eastern Cape.[1]

The announcement by the then Department of Land Affairs of a Land Summit that would be held in Johannesburg in July 2005 galvanised activism among various organisations that had an interest in land issues. At the time, there was no nationally organised movement that would mobile resources and people and plan for the Summit. The NLC was no longer effective, the LPM was weakened by the demise of the NLC, and

---

1. Very little research has been done on this organisation. However the organisation writes annual reports and has been evaluated externally on a few occasions. There are also detailed recordings and reports of its People's Tribunal which give one a good sense of the organisation, its origins and activities.

the TCOE a relatively young actor. Given this organisational vaccum, there appeared on the scene a new organisation named the Alliance of Land and Agrarian Reform Movements (ALARM). This was a consortium of movements, including TCOE, LPM and some affiliates of the former NLC. ALARM's stated mission is "for a people centred rural transformation rooted in a rapid and fundamental transfer of land to the poor and the promotion of security for those living and working on the land." At the July Summit, ALARM became the voice of the landless and their supporters. Far reaching resolutions were taken at the Summit. The principle of willing buyer/willing seller came under major attack from several different quarters – and, for the first time, ANC government officials appeared to be backing away from it. In his State of the Nation address to Parliament in February 2006, President Mbeki referred to the Summit resolution that the willing buyer/willing seller condition should be revisited.

However, despite all the rhetoric, the impasse in respect of land policy and practice remains. It must be said that land based organisations in South Africa remain very weak and unorganised. The demise of the NLC and the reported divisions within the LPM are some of the examples. Furthermore, hopes that ALARM would fill an organisational gap were dashed when debates arose about the future of the initiative after the Land Summit. Former affiliates of the NLC such as the Surplus Peoples Project (SPP) argued that ALARM was a short term response to the crisis that faced NGOs when the Land Summit was announced. Something had to be done. After the Summit, the SPP argument was that there was no room for ALARM.[2] Others, mainly in the TCOE and the Transkei Land Service Organisation (TRALSO), which was an affiliate of the NLC, argued for the continued existence of ALARM in order to, inter alia, take forward the resolutions of the Land Summit. These debates continued for the rest of 2005 and most of 2006. In the final analysis, the debates petered out and ALARM, as with the LPM, faded away. Most of the existing organisations in the land sector on the whole continue to operate in isolation, although now and again they work together, as the annual reports of the SPP and TCOE suggest.

In summary, the key issue around tensions amongst the NGOs in the land sector seems to be how these movements should relate to the democratic state. Indeed, this is a challenge that has confronted most organisations in post-colonial/independence Africa. It is an issue, it seems, which has yet to be resolved. We have seen how in the case of

---

2 These discussions and debates are based on interviews and conversations Lungisile Ntsebeza had with some members of the SPP, Nkuzi Development organisation in Limpopo, TCOE and CALUSA, an affiliate of TCOE.

South Africa, organisations such as the NLC have moved backwards and forwards between collaborating with the state (the period roughly between 1994 and 1999) and adopting a more confrontational approach at times (during the Mbeki Presidency). These are of course broad generalisations as some organisations continued their collaborative role with the state, while others were in favour of a much more confrontational approach where the mobilisation of the landless themselves would be a key strategy.

Another issue which the formation of the LPM brought to the fore is the relationship between NGOs and 'grassroots' social movements. Here, some of the key questions and issues revolve around how to build an autonomous people-centred organisation that can contest powerful forces which support global capital; who should build this organisation; what is the relationship of the poor to those who support them; who should determine the agenda and so on. It is also a question about the sustainability of rural based organisations in the era of globalisation, particularly in situations where they operate on their own without positively seeking alliances with urban based organisations which are committed to social change and geared towards not only political liberation but socio-economic emancipation too.

Conclusion

The Reconstruction and Development Programme initially promised to transfer 30 per cent of white agricultural land to previously dispossessed blacks within the first five years of democratic rule. After 15 years, less than 3 per cent has been redistributed. This single fact, together with the recent history of land seizures and farm occupations in Zimbabwe has forced the land question into the public mind in South Africa.

A question on many people's minds is: Will the kind of fast track land redistribution in Zimbabwe which transferred virtually all white owned land into black hands in the space of merely three years, happen in South Africa? There are many differences between Zimbabwe and South Africa - the level of proletarianisation and urbanisation is much higher in South Africa, the fact that the struggle for liberation was largely an urban affair in South Africa, as opposed to a rural guerilla war in Zimbabwe, the low level of industrialisation, settler alienation of land accounted for about 50 per cent of the land surface of Zimbabwe and about 90 per cent in South Africa. Yet there are also some telling similarities between the two countries in respect of their colonial histories.

One of the more striking anomalies between Zimbabwe and South Africa is the number of people who have died in rural violence. In

Zimbabwe, the evidence is contradictory, but the highest figure presented is that 12 white farmers were murdered in the turmoil during the process of land redistribution. In South Africa, with no apparent turmoil in sight, about 1 500 white farmers and farm workers have been killed since 1994. This is a staggering number of murders. The South African Human Rights Commission (2003) published its report into farm violence in 2003. Its main finding was that these murders were criminally and not politically inspired. Jonny Steinberg (2002) tells an entirely different story in his gripping investigative account of the murder of a farmer's son in the Midlands of KwaZulu-Natal. It is a story of communal collusion in murder, premised on perceptions of the illegitimacy of white ownership of land in the heart of KwaZulu-Natal.

Claims over land, and beliefs about how it should be returned to African ownership, are as widespread in South Africa as anywhere else in southern Africa, including Zimbabwe. It is impossible to extinguish these claims because they concern the perception of a birthright and not only the possibility of using land to create livelihoods or for residence. The market-based willing-buyer/willing-seller model of land reform adopted in South Africa can never hope to reverse the horrors of colonial and apartheid dispossession which have prompted these claims in the first instance. The violence on farms, the illegal occupation of municipal land, the problem of unfarmability, of stock theft, cutting of fences, theft of electric wires and land invasions in rural areas all relate in complex ways to the grossly imbalanced distribution of land ownership between blacks and whites.

An organised campaign around land issues, with clear objectives and strategy and involving those who are directly affected is a *sine qua non* for successful land redistribution. Such a structure becomes all the more necessary given the organised nature of commercial farmers and the alliances they enjoy with other formations of capital in South Africa.

There are two inter-linked issues. In the first place, we reject the tendency to define the land question as a rural phenomenon with an exclusively agricultural focus. This is a very narrow and limited way of thinking about the land question. Not only does it exclude urban struggles around the land question, including housing and the possibility of urban agriculture, but the mining industry is also erased. This takes us to the second issue which has to do with the nature of land and agrarian movements and questions of strategy. Defining the land question as rural and concerned with agriculture shapes the nature and strategy of land and agrarian movements in particular ways, which pose challenges for the possibility of forging alliances with urban based movements which are also involved in land struggles.

Besides the clear necessity for a greater degree of urgency around the demand for land by organisations of civil society, it is also important that the state be held accountable on its own terms and by its own targets for land reform. In order to ensure the survival of democracy, there will have to be a way in which the state navigates between the legitimate claims for land by the dispossessed and the claims over land by those who currently hold it. Up to now, the government has not taken this issue seriously at all. The budgets are woeful, there is no political will to see to it that delivery takes place, and the market as well as the constitutional and legislative frameworks favour the existing property holders. There is a huge gap between popular expectations of land reform delivery and the actual possibilities for transferring land ownership to the majority under the current constitutional arrangement, and the stated objectives of safeguarding existing property holders in their landownership on the one hand, and redistributing land to the previously dispossessed on the other, are manifestly contradictory. It was always going to be difficult to simultaneously redistribute land to the rural poor and maintain the rule of law in the context of the extreme racial distortions left by apartheid and in an environment of political compromise. The current government has opted to protect the rule of law against any opposition, including the homeless seeking a place to live.

While the current division of land is safeguarded by the constitution, this is no guarantee of its legitimacy. The unequal division of land, premised on conquest, is a constant reminder to the majority, that they remain excluded from the ownership of their country. Seen in this way, the claims about land are directly linked to the meaning of citizenship after 1994. The political legitimacy of the state through the franchise, and other civil and political rights enshrined in the constitution must be seen in the context of continued and extreme inequality, and land is merely one of the indices of this inequality.

One of the most compelling questions in South Africa is whether the construction of a unitary democratic nation is viable in South Africa as long as the colonial division of land remains more or less intact. A recent survey conducted by James Gibson (2004) reveals the extent of racial polarisation in attitudes to land. Using a sample of 3 700 people, one of the statements he put to his respondents in face-to-face interviews was "(M)ost land in South Africa was taken unfairly by white settlers, and they therefore have no right to the land today." He found that "an astonishing 85 per cent of the black respondents agreed with the statement while only 8 per cent of the whites held the same view." In so far as this polarisation threatens nation- building, it also threatens democracy. Since the identities are formed out of the intersection between a racial and class experience, the level of inequality in our society remains our most urgent social problem.

We thus have to ask how we are going to reverse the accumulated privilege of being white in South Africa in favour of dispossessed blacks as long as the context remains an unequal colonial division of land. The democratic government has been very keen to uphold the rule of law, not least to allay the fears of potential foreign investors that their property will be protected by the state. The real challenge is whether redistribution will happen to an extent which will lend popular legitimacy to the state and encourage economic growth within the framework of the current constitutional recognition of property rights. The vital question in this regard is a temporal one. What is the pace of change and is redistribution of land happening quickly enough?

Our main concern is how the continued inequalities in land ownership translate into racialised identities, with negative consequences for the project of nation-building and with very real threats to the long term sustainability of democracy. Reconciliation was supposed to be the glue which holds our society together, but if land is not redistributed rapidly and drastically, there is a real possibility that continuing exclusion from ownership will turn into revenge rather than reconciliation.

It is commonplace that identities are complex, that there are contradictions in all of us that we may assume different subjectivities in different contexts, but this should not prevent us from attempting to deconstruct their meanings. What is clear though is that we have to avoid essentialising identities. Land is obviously not the only factor in the manner in which identities are formed in South Africa. People are clearly not one-dimensional zombies following a pre-determined path on the basis of the racial imbalance in the distribution of land. It is unquestionable that identities are forged by a multiplicity of sources, factors and variables, and that people may take on various identities in different situations, but there can be little doubt about the very powerful role of land as a metaphor of dispossession and as a continuing reality of poverty.

References

Alexander, J., 2003. 'Squatters', Veterans and the State in Zimbabwe. In A. Hammar, B. Raftopoulos and S. Jensen, eds. *Zimbabwe's Unfinished Business*, Harare: Weaver Press

Alexander, J., 2006. *The Unsettled land. State making and the Politics of land in Zimbabwe 1893-2003*. Oxford: James Currey.

Bond, P. & Manyanya, M., 2003. *Zimbabwe's Plunge: Exhausted Nationalism, Neoliberalism and the Search for Social Justice*. Harare: Weaver Press.

Chaskalson, M., 1993. Should there be a property clause: Implications of the constitutional protection of property in the United States and the Commonwealth. In Venter, Minnie and Anderson, eds. *Land, Property Rights and the New Constitution*, University of the Western Cape.

Chege, M., 1997. Review of M. Mamdani, Citizen and Subject: Contemporary Africa and the Legacy of Late Colonialism. *In African Studies Quarterly. The Online Journal of African Studies*, 1. Available at: http://web.africa.ufl.edu/asq.

Davids, I., 2003. Developmental local government: the rural context and challenges. In *Development Update*, 4(1), pp. 31-53.

Delius, P., 1996. *A Lion amongst the Cattle: reconstruction and resistance in the Northern Transvaal*. Johannesburg: Ravan Press.

Fanon, F., 1961. *The Wretched of the Earth*. London: Penguin Books.

Gibson, J.L., 2004. *Overcoming Apartheid: Can Truth Reconcile a Divided Nation?* Pretoria: HSRC Press.

Government of South Africa. 1993. Interim Constitution of the Republic of South Africa. Pretoria: Government Printer.

Hammar, A. & Raftopolous, B., 2003. Zimbabwe's unfinished business: rethinking land, state and nation'. In A. Hammar, B. Raftopoulos, and S. Jensen, eds. *Zimbabwe's Unfinished Business – Rethinking Land, State and Nation in the Context of Crisis* Harare: Weaver Press

Helliker, K.D., 2006. A Sociological Analysis of Intermediary Non-Governmental Organisations and Land Reform in Contemporary Zimbabwe. D.Phil Thesis, Rhodes University (unpublished).

Iiyama, M., 2007. Livelihood Diversification, De-agrarianisation and Social Differentiation: case studies on rural livelihoods from South Africa and Kenya. Unpublished PhD thesis, Department of Economics, University of Tokyo.

Lal, V., 2001. Subaltern Studies and its Critics: Debates over Indian History. *History and Theory*, 40.

Landless People's Movement. 2001. Statement on the Land Occupations in Zimbabwe, Pretoria.

Mafeje, A., 2003. The Agrarian Question, Access to land and Peasant Responses in sub-Saharan Africa, *Civil Society and Social Movements Programme*, Paper No.6 UNRISD, Geneva.

Mamdani, M., 1996. *Citizen and Subject: Contemporary Africa and the Legacy of Late Colonialism*. Cape Town: David Phillip Publishers.

Matoti, S. & Ntsebeza, L., 2004. Rural resistance in Mpondoland and Thembuland, 1960-1963, in SADET: *The road to Democracy in South Africa, Vol 1 (1960-1970)*. Cape Town: ZEBRA and Struik Publishers, pp. 755- 782.

Mbeki, T., 2007. President of South Africa's State of the Nation Address, Capetown.

Mkapa, B., 2002. Press Statement after SADC Heads of State Meeting in Daresalaam, Tanzania.

Moore, D., 2004. Zimbabwe's triple crisis: primitive accumulation, nation-state formation and democratisation in the age of neoliberal globalisation. *African Studies Quarterly* 7(2 & 3).

Moyo, S., 2007. Land Policy, Poverty Reduction and Public Action in Zimbabwe. *ISS/UNDP Land, Poverty and Public Action, Policy Paper No.11.*

Moyo, S. & Yeros, P. eds., 2005. *Reclaiming the Land: The Resurgence of Rural Movements in Africa, Asia and Latin America*. London: ZED Books.

Mugabe, R., 2002. President's Speech at Heroes Day, *Herald*, 13 August 2002.

Ncapayi, F., 2006. Land Demand and Rural Struggles in Xhalanga, Eastern Cape: who wants land and for what? Unpublished Masters mini-thesis, Faculty of Economic and Management Sciences, University of the Western Cape.

Ntsebeza, L., 2006. *Democracy Compromised: Chiefs and the Politics of Land in South Africa.* Cape Town: HSRC Press.

Ntsebeza, L., 2007. Land Redistribution in South Africa: the property clause revisited. In L. Ntsebeza and R. Hall. *The Land Question in South Africa: The challenge of transformation and redistribution.* Cape Town: HSRC Press.

Palmer, R., 2003. Struggling to secure and defend land rights of the poor in Africa.*Austrian   Journal   of   Development   Studies,* XIX.http://www.oxfam.org.uk/landights/

Raftopoulos B. & Phimister I., 2004. Zimbabwe now: the political economy of crisis and coercion. *Historical Materialism,* 12(4).

Sachikonye, L., 2005. The Land is the Economy: Revisiting the Land Question. *African Security Review,* 14(3).

South Africa Human Rights Commission. 2003. Inquiry into the Human Rights Violations in   Farming   Communities-Final   Report.   Available   at: www.sahrc.org.za/sahrc_cms/downloads/farminginquiry)

Steinberg, J., 2002. *Midlands.* Johannesburg: Jonathan Ball Publishers.

Trust for Community Outreach and Education (TCOE). 2003. Full transcript, including translations from Xhosa and Afrikaans, of the Peoples' Tribunal on Landlessness, held at the Port Elizabeth Technikon on 6 and 7 December.

10.
Transforming education and training, or reconstituting power and privilege?
Enver Motala, Salim Vally and Carol Anne Spreen

Introduction

In South Africa, as indeed in many other countries, there is considerable interest in developments relating to the public (and to a lesser extent, the private) education systems. Its importance in South Africa is not simply fortuitous since it is both a consequence of the struggles against the apartheid state, in which the need to overturn a cynical and calculated education *and* training system was an important pillar of the broader demands for democratic change, and a struggle for the ascendancy of particular approaches to the reform of the education and training system, post-apartheid. At the end of apartheid there was a real expectation that the death of the racist, fragmented, incoherent yet planned education and training system together with its policies and practices - the manufactured bureaucracies spawned to give effect to the intentions of apartheid ideologues and political leaders and its deleterious outcomes would be terminated once and for all. Everywhere the talk was about 'transformation' and no vision seemed too implausible or difficult to grasp.

Soon however, the intractabilities of reform confronted the state and all those who were intent on securing a 'transformed' education and training system for the 'benefit of all'. It was clear that the meaning, purposes and content of what was implied by the idea of 'transformation' was by no means uniformly understood and that in fact it was the subject of conflicting interpretations, contesting perspectives and ideologies contesting the domain of education and training reform.

Nzimande (who is presently the Minister for Higher Education and Training in the South African Cabinet under President Zuma) and Mathieson (2004) (Nzimande and Mathieson, 2004), writing about the role of the ANC's Education Study Group in Parliament during the period 1994 to 1999, characterise the idea of a transformed education and training system by explicit reference to its political and democratic content. They aver that its policy,

> (w)as based on the premise that the inherited education system would need to be fundamentally transformed if it was to overcome the legacy of the past, while at the same time becoming responsive to a new set of challenges. The transformed

education and training system was to be a unified system based on the principles of equity, quality, non-racialism and non-sexism, and that was more appropriate to the socio-economic needs of the emerging democratic society. These goals were to be met by moving towards the provision of lifelong learning, so that workers, adult learners and others who had been denied access in the past would gain access to education and training opportunities. It was asserted that the state would have to play a leading role in overcoming the inherited fragmentation and achieving these policy goals. (Nzimande and Mathieson, 2003: 3)

This approach to the transformation of education and training suggested that the ANC was intent on thoroughgoing reforms based on a number of fundamentals such as equity and quality, entrenching the principle of lifelong learning for adult learners and working class constituencies, affirming the directive role of the state and arguing that the state itself had to be "sufficiently empowered to carry out the most thorough transformation of the inherited education and training system." (Nzimande and Mathieson, 2003: 5)

Outside the ANC, academic researchers and analysts, public commentators, institutional representatives, members of social movements and trade unionists have adopted approaches that are less overt in their political predispositions. These extensive analyses and commentaries range over a variety of issues affecting education and training at all levels and reflects a comprehensive list of learning contexts both formal and non/in formal, from early childhood to adult basic and pre-school to tertiary. They refer to issues relating to urban and rural contexts, nearly all the sub-disciplines in education, epistemological concerns, subject areas and pedagogical strategies, learning environments, the management and organisation of learning, quality and assessment, the management of research and its outputs, the development of research capability and other topical areas.[1] Moreover, these writings reflect the perspectives of legislators and bureaucrats, the demands of the labour market and the economy, institutional planning and reform, ideas emanating from systemic reviews and reports,

---

1. The intersections between aspects of these systems (education *and* training) derive from an overarching qualification framework which seeks not only to provide a canvas for the acquisition of education and training related qualifications, but also attempts to 'integrate' these into a 'coherent' national system of education *and* training. The creation of a new higher education Ministry which specifically includes training issues and bears the responsibility for the variety of related training institutions is an expression of this intent - to produce coherence between education on the one hand, and training on the other.

academic scholarship and media coverage. There is little doubt that the perspectives that are represented in these interests differ widely in their orientations, focuses, analysis and critique and exemplify contradictory and conflicting political, economic and social interests.

Extant explanations

In these writings and commentaries, a wide range of causalities is used to explain the persistent failures of the education and training system. They refer to specific symptomatic characteristics as explanations of the system. In regard to schooling for instance, its failure is attributable to poor school and curriculum management, inadequate teacher knowledge and competence, low teacher and pupil discipline, the unavailability of good teaching and learning text, poor school infrastructure, lack of support from officialdom at the various levels of government, conflicting labour relations, poor language policy and the lack of community participation in encouraging greater levels of school accountability, undemocratic decision-making processes at all levels of the system and other related issues. For most commentators these systemic failures find expression in the recurrent phenomenon of low matric pass and high school drop-out rates, low scores in international benchmarking, poor performance in areas relating to the mathematics and science, and the phenomenon of unemployment that faces most learners passing through the schooling system. In higher education these would refer, *inter alia*, to the weaknesses of teaching and learning and the absence of meaningful support for students and faculty, the problems of institutional differentiation, poor student accommodation, the persistence of racist practices, the general lack of funding, the challenges of revitalisation of academic profession, and the dispiriting quality of leadership in the institutions of higher education.

Several other explanations have also been offered by academic and other commentators about the causes of failure in the education and training system. Most of these are based on the premise that while there is a high degree of well developed policy in this area, the problems lie in the domain of policy implementation. It is suggested that in the area of policy making the government has provided both a framework and the legislative authority for qualitative changes in education and training and that very little, if anything, has to be done to augment these polices. In reality, the complaint sometimes is that the overabundance of policies constitutes a heavy load for those charged with its implementation, since in practice this is foreboding for those unaccustomed to the complexities of law and regulation leading often to contradictory and inconclusive interpretations of the public mandate.

Explanations about state failure on account of its lack of 'capacity' are unrelenting and persistent. The concept of 'capacity' is invoked widely and refers *inter alia* to the lack of knowledge and competence of bureaucrats regarding their mandates and the legislative injunctions by which they must operate, their poor work ethic, lack of commitment to the underlying values espoused in the Constitution and laws, the absence of certain 'critical skills', poor management and leadership, the prevalence of corruption and other such difficulties. This lack of 'capacity' is also attributed to legislators themselves. It is suggested that they simply do not have a sufficient grasp of the complexities of their role, are unwilling or unable to submit to public account, have no understanding of the public perceptions of their weaknesses or are indifferent to these, and, are themselves implicated in corrupt and other deplorable practices.

These criticisms are often associated with suggestions about how such 'capacity' can be augmented including by a re-evaluation of the affirmative action policies of government whose effect, it is alleged, is to exclude whites who are endowed with the very skills which are in short supply, the need to open the doors to the importation of such skills from abroad, intensifying the training of public servants, stronger oversight in respect of public mandates and greater judicial sanction against corrupt practices and the like. All these criticisms moreover are made in the context of the repeated attempts by government to deal with them through a variety of strategies, such as public hearings and lekgotla, the commissioning of research and consultancy reports, the appointment of advisors on strategic issues and even permanent positions for the purpose, the convening of commissions of enquiry and review panels on various issues, and the writing and rewriting of position papers, plans and strategies.

In the light of these criticisms and the state's responses to them, how are we to understand the paralysis in education and training better? There is no question that many of the criticisms directed at the actions of bureaucrats and politicians resonate with commonsensical experience and are in fact supported by a considerable body of evidence. Yet the question remains about why, in the light of these criticisms and the public dissension about many of these issues, the government remains unable to mitigate the criticisms against it. What is the explanation for the persistence of its failures and its inability to climb out of the morass? Why, despite the radicalising perspectives first adopted by the ideologues of the leading party of state (such as that of Nzimande above) has the promise not materialised? Or is the answer simply, as some commentators critical of government suggest, the absence of 'political will' and 'weak states' an issue we return to later.

Although there is some agreement about the causal explanations above amongst educationalists and other commentators (policy-makers, researchers, analysts, public commentators and the media), there is little to suggest that the present impasse is likely to be resolved soon. This begs the question about why, despite the many pointers to the failures of the education and training system, do those who are responsible for it remain unable to resolve these difficulties? Why, despite the unabated criticisms of the systems failures, do those who are responsible for it remain paralysed? What meaningful explanation can there be why despite the seeming 'self-evidence' of the 'solutions' to the crisis, nothing seems to work? Why, despite all the 'consultations', conferences, reviews and special committees, does the education and training system seem transfixed? And why, despite the agreement between analysts and policy makers, the many new initiatives, plans, strategies, lekgotla, and roadmaps, the widely recognised characteristics of the 'crisis' and 'dysfuntionality' of the education system[2], does the crisis persist while Ministers and their departments remain incapable of effecting the changes that are necessary even while governments have changed, leaderships have mutated and bureaucrats fired?

In our analysis we hope to show that although extant explanations of the causes of failure are instructive, they remain *partial* since they speak only to the 'endogenous' characteristics of the education system and have little or no orientation to *the exogenous and relational* issues that frame the education and training system, its policies and practices. Despite the important insights these causal explanations might provide, such explanations (mono and multi-causal) are inadequate and, inevitably, tautologous and circular. More fundamental insights are required which go beyond these causalities to provide a stronger critique and a theorisation of the crises. Such a theorisation is necessarily historical and contextual and seeks to explore the relational issues affecting the sovereignty of the state in developing countries like South Africa, and understanding the 'limits and possibilities' shaping the process of reform and change post 1994. Such analysis does not exist in

---

2. In fact both the present and previous Minister of Education (now Basic Education) have pronounced on the 'dysfunctionality' and 'crisis' of the education system and the gravity of the challenges of constructing a quality public education system. Even as recently as 12 May 2010, Parliament debated a plan intended to address such *basic issues* as the question of literacy, numeracy and quality of education and even now a long term strategy – *Schooling 2025* - is being finalised to deal with these issues. Despite the repetitive monotony of affirmations about the need to 'transform' education and training, it has become ever more apparent that the possibilities for its achievement are no more than whimsical impulse and unrealisable hope.

extant writings about the education and training system in South Africa despite the large body of texts about it.

Explaining the impasse

For us, the most important factor explaining the impasse is the failure of the post-apartheid state to take up the challenge of *fundamental and socially transformative change* in education and training. This failure is in turn explicable by reference to the limits imposed on the possibilities for change by a combination of local and global factors, whose impact on the process of post-apartheid reform has not been properly understood or subjected to critical analysis. We deal with this latter issue further in the paper since we should firstly clarify our conception of fundamental and transformative change, an approach which refers to several conditions.

The *first condition* emphasises definitive alterations in the nature of the *pre-existing relations of power* exemplified by the racial, gendered, class, geographic and other discriminatory practices of the apartheid state. This conception of social change would refute any approach which simply reconstitutes forms of social power and privilege along new class and gendered lines and especially seeking to reconstitute new forms of power through the creation of black elites. These relations of power are central to any understanding of the possibilities for social reform since they constitute the most intractable barrier to change. Secondly, in our approach transformation is a complex and multi-faceted process affected by history and context. It refers to a wide range of systemic, structural and ideological (value-based) interventions through state policy, regulation and practice. It seeks to affect the behaviour of individuals, institutions and whole societies. It requires change in the behaviour of both the public and private sectors, and protects the sovereignty of its policies against the incursions of corporate globalisation and its negative consequences. Thirdly, the purposes of such change must produce, at a minimum, freedom and social justice, equity and fairness, accountable systems based on democratic mandates and public review, and ensure that the power of public systems is meaningfully directed towards the achievement of the 'public good', especially in serving the interests of the most marginalised and vulnerable citizens.

Assessed on the basis of these criteria, very little has changed in the lives of working urban and rural poor and the unemployed who constitute the majority of the population of this country. This, despite the constant refrains about South Africa being a democratic society, a 'rainbow nation' in a state of 'transition'; and despite the references to the 'best Constitution in the world', the 'many lessons to be learnt from South Africa' and other such appellations. Poverty and inequality are rampant in South Africa affecting women more severely than men, rural dwellers more than those in urban areas and unsurprisingly blacks more than whites. In fact inequality has grown consistently over the last eight years and unemployment has increased even in the last year even while there are programmes intended to address it. In education the situation can be characterised as follows:

> Just over a year ago we came together as concerned South Africans, committed to public education, to issue a call for public participation in education. Yet as the year passed we saw little progress in overcoming the challenges facing our education system. Poor South Africans have placed their hope in education, since the social system, as it exists, seems to be a dead-end for most people. It remains a fact, though, that our system of education is in a crisis and is failing our children. If left unaddressed this will not only undermine any potential for economic and social development, but also the vibrancy of our democracy.
>
> Despite initiatives, policies and good intentions, we continue to propagate a two-tiered educational system – one for the children of the rich, and another for the children of the urban and rural poor. Too many of our children attend schools that are under-resourced, bleak and fearful places. Too many of our children still do not have access to education in their mother tongue, and, shamefully, too many of our children are forced to learn on an empty stomach. Our scores in literacy, numeracy and our critical thinking skills show how much the education system continues to reproduce the characteristics of apartheid education.[3]

A great deal more has been written about the increasing level of social differentiation in South Africa, regarded as one of the most unequal societies in the world; the failure to provide basic services as evidenced by the widespread upheavals in a number of South African townships, the inability of government at the local level to understand that the 'service delivery' protests are no less than a demand for democratic expression and the right to proper consultation and the inclusion of local communities. The state continues to be incapable of engaging such communities in the selection of the choices and priorities in the use of local resources; is unable to deal decisively with the high levels of

---

3. See SEKOLO, Public Participation in Education Network (PPEN) website http://www.ppen.org.za for its *Call to Action 2010*.

corruption evinced by public representatives, and permits these practices which frame the terms of governance in ways that reproduce the economic system where market relations trump the public purposes of democratic rule. South Africa scores poorly in a number of the usual indicators used for the purposes of establishing the country's human development indices.

In the light of these realities we do not accept arguments about the 'weak' state or about the absence of 'political will', nor are the claims about the lack of 'capacity' sufficient as explanations for the parlous state of education. Here we draw on the explanation offered by Shalini Randeria, who argues that criticisms relating to the lack of 'political will' or a 'weak state' are not useful since the state has not had much difficulty in supporting policies which, despite their unpopularity, resonate with its sometimes unpopular choices and priorities. This she argues, is prevalent in situations where, "the new architecture of global governance characterised by legal plurality and overlapping sovereignties has facilitated a game of 'passing the blame' among these four actors" - referring to international finance and trade organisations, multinational corporations, governments and NGOs (Randeria, 2007). Contrary to the view that the nation state can no longer be relied upon for the range of functions it must discharge, Randeria argues that,

> the state is both an agent and an object of globalisation. The capacity of subordinate states in the international system to make and enforce rules as well as to set and achieve policy agendas is being limited from without and contested from within. Although inadequate the state remains indispensable, as its laws and policies play a key role in transposing neoliberal agendas to the national and local levels (Randeria, 2007: 2).

According to her, globalisation uses the violence of law in place of political violence to establish its ascendancy in sovereign states. Since law now transcends sovereign boundaries it is no longer "coterminous with the state and its sovereignty over a well-defined territory and a population to be governed" (Randeria, 2007: 2). The new forms of global governance have in her view led to "the erosion of entitlements and of the rights of citizens marginalised by processes of economic restructuring" (Randeria, 2007: 2).

The implication of this approach to sovereignty is that analyses which are limited to an evaluation of the behaviour of national states are truncated and partial since they are unable to reckon with the power of global regimes, the overlapping claims of local and international rule, reconfiguring the relationship between states and the law. In this connection Randeria fashions the notion of a 'cunning state' and repudiates the notion of the 'strong' and 'weak state'. She argues that although these states are hamstrung by the lending institutions such as the World Bank and the International Monetary Fund and have little freedom in designing their own policies, it would be a mistake to accept their 'self-representations' as to their weaknesses since they seek to

> (r)edistribute their responsibilities. Whereas weak states lack the capacity to protect their citizenry from external incursions, 'cunning states' show strength or weakness, depending on the domestic interests at stake. "Cunning" is a weapon of weak states ... It does not describe a characteristic of state structure or capacities but the changing nature of the relationship of national elites (very often in concert with international institutions) to citizens. The notion of a cunning state is therefore a useful way to delineate a range of tactics deployed at various sites of negotiation where a shift in responsibilities and sovereignties occurs (Randeria, 2007: 3).

Following upon this characterisation of the behaviour of national states, she examines various case studies to explore how globalisation "as a transnational apparatus, discourse and as a social reality is (re)produced (Randeria, 2007: 3). This approach to the impact of globalisation on the performance of national states is instructive for our purposes since it reveals to us the causal basis of the equivocal behaviour of the national state, the nature of the interests which it subordinates and those which it advances purposively. Graphically illustrative of this is the South African government's support for hosting the football World Cup. Here there was no shortage of will or 'cunning' in proclaiming the ostensible benefits that would accrue to the country in spite of the fact that no tangible evidence can be adduced about its long term positive effects, if any. In fact, careful analysis (which we are unable to provide here) is likely to reveal that the real beneficiaries of the showpiece phenomenon are the self-same elites and large corporations and that there is not likely to be any consequential benefits for the working class and the poor. Yet there is little 'will' to support the basic requirements of the citizenry as we have argued above.

An associated reason for the intransigence of the state is that policy makers, (and even researchers and mass-based organisations) are hostages to the *conceptual conservatism* of the ideas that are dominant in education and in other related social arenas. The fact that there may be a few 'progressive' voices amongst educationists does not provide an adequate counter-weight to the dominance of this ideological conservatism which is pervasive in the influential discourses about education and training. Its effects are profound and not to be underestimated since it bears the imprint of powerful international 'advice' and the ever present spectre of its sanction. This conservatism has shaped the *policy and practice* terrain despite the best intentions of the law and public policy and it is essentially *ideological,* despite the fact that it is never explicitly so, nor candid about the underlying assumptions framing its prescriptions. Moreover, its approach to the public education and training system threatens to paralyse researchers and policy makers alike who have yet to mount a proper, sustained, defensible, alternative approach to its hegemonic propositions. The effects of this ideological position are manifest in:

- How and what *questions* are examined for the purposes of policy making and practice.
- The ascendancy of *technical solutions* uninformed and deliberately obfuscatory of contextual and historical analysis.
- The reliance on so called *experts* who provide such technical advice to the exclusion of other expertise, especially since the criteria by which they are chosen is rarely defined or agreed by those who are directly affected by the nature of their advice as such experts.
- The *socially divisive and privileging effects* of the 'solutions' that are provided by such advice and its deleterious consequences for socially and economically disadvantaged social classes.

The skills discourse

A brief examination of the contemporary skill discourse in South Africa is illustrative of the ascendancy of these approaches in the domain of 'skills, competencies, and knowledge'. As the constant refrain in South Africa goes, *"If we want to become a strong economy again, the best thing we can do is have an educated workforce."* The pre-emptive implication of these refrains is that the only permissible approach to the skills discourse is that which bears the imprimatur of big business and those officials in government who support its approach.

Even a casual reading of the media or a listen-in to the many 'chat' shows on it, will show how unrestrained the power of a particular way of thinking about skills and knowledge has become. The nation, and regrettably it seems even organisations of the working class, are hostage to a particular way of thinking and are largely paralysed by it. In this thinking the main proposition is the idea that there is a great shortage of skills in our society and that in particular areas of skills these are so critical as to make any possibilities for economic advancement in particular sectors of the economy unimaginable; that the education and training system is hopelessly out of sync with the demands of the economy, that the lack of skills is one of the (if not *the*) greatest obstacles to achieving high levels of economic growth, that the lack of skills is the primary cause for low levels of productivity, and that the country cannot compete internationally given this poverty of skills and will therefore fall further behind relative to the developed and other developing economies of the world.

We know that knowledge, skills and competencies are important for all societies, critically important even – for the well-being of nations. Reducing the discussion about knowledge and skills to its use for employment in market dominated economic systems is a serious limitation on how the question of skills can and must be understood. This is because in the first place no capitalist economy in the world or in any period of its history, outside the periods of worldwide war, has been able to provide full employment in the economy. In fact, the reality for most developing countries is high levels of unemployment *as a structural condition* of the economy – as an inevitable and crucial condition necessary to its reproduction.

Capitalist profitability has and will always be dependent on the availability of 'surplus labour'. In South Africa that level of 'surplus' has hovered around 28-30 per cent even in the period after apartheid, and if those who are numbered amongst the so called 'discouraged work-seekers' - much higher. Indeed if the figure is disaggregated to some parts of the country or for gender, that figure is egregious. Discussions about the skills needs of society rarely transgress the bounds of these economic-determinist approaches, despite the strong and seemingly instructive legislative injunctions about the broader humanising and citizenship related role of education and training systems. This, despite the occasional genuflections by political leaders and the leaders of education institutions to the idea that knowledge is essential to the development of a citizenry, for the fullest expression of civic rights and responsibilities, for such elementary rights as numeracy and literacy, accessing public goods, making choices, understanding the complexities of the market and importantly for ensuring greater levels of democratic accountability of public representatives and organisations.

There is sometimes a recognition too that the role of education *and* training involves understanding the many cultures, values and belief systems in society, rebutting race, gender, ethnic and other stereotypes; the ability to evaluate ideas and systems critically, for tolerance and independent thinking, the ability to communicate socially and to work for oneself *and* for society. Despite the occasional realisation that in developing countries in particular there are a wide range of socially useful activities which members of society can be engaged in, such as in the case of health and the general welfare of working class and poor communities, and that a wide range of activities are possible to support the lives of working class families from child care and the processes of early childhood development to care for the aged, frail and disabled.

Furthermore, that communities can and must be supported in these endeavours since they have limited resources to do so themselves and that there are a wide range of community projects which can be supported relating to areas like primary health, the local economy, housing development, service infrastructure, land usage, recreation and cultural activities and support for schools. Indeed, there are examples of communities who support the unemployed through finding useful activities such as child care, community and school meals services, and school renovation, maintenance of public spaces, etc. And these activities are undertaken collectively often leading, as in the case of the Argentinean factory occupations, to co-operative forms of production and distribution. We know too that much more has to be done to exemplify the potential for co-operative forms of production and distribution and to understand the educational requirements of such forms of production, as here too there is a valuable history of worker co-operatives which provide the evidence and the potential for humanising and creative approaches to the formation of skills and competencies in developing societies.

Limiting the discussion to skills for the 'economy' is also problematic because its effect is to place the blame for the lack of skills and knowledge on the poor themselves or on the government alone, the poor being answerable for their predicament since they have 'no one to blame but themselves'. The ideologues of this ascendant discourse about skills have managed steadfastly to persuade policy makers about the inefficacy of discussing the combination of social and economic circumstances which make the acquisition of knowledge and skills difficult for the poor, not the least of which are questions of access and costs, the pedagogical barriers confronting learners who have no educational resources, the absence of locally based educational infrastructure for workers and the poor, and the social circumstances impacting on the possibilities for education that face them daily.

Blaming government alone too is disingenuous - since business itself was hugely complicit throughout the past decades for erecting the structural barriers to high quality education for the working class and the poor. Corporate capital's culpability on acquiescing to the idea that black people were only good as 'hewers of wood and drawers of water' remains unacknowledged and hidden from view purposefully - since any acceptance of such culpability can only be meaningful if it is accompanied by structural atonement – changes to the regime of capital itself which is hardly likely to be contemplated by it. Similarly, the expectation that government will resolve the skills crisis re-enforces the false idea *that supply side interventions* are adequate in and of themselves. This idea hides from view, once again, the culpability of capitalists in regard to the low levels of employment creation and the inadequacy of its investment in jobs in the first place. And despite the occasional protestation about the 'tardiness' of business about plans to mitigate job losses no tangible benefits for the unemployed are likely to follow.[4]

Several other factors attributable to the behaviour and choices made by the leaders and ideologues of corporate capital too affect the level of jobs in the labour market, including its ability to relocate to centres of cheaper labour in the world, the unthinking replacement of workers by technologies, the low levels of training investment in occupational skills following sea-changes in technological innovation and the absence of a protective and supportive environment for workers. In addition, in some approaches to the issue of skills and knowledge especially in relation to labour markets, so much of the analysis is no more than an extension of neoclassical economics and to mathematical modelling that factors that do not lend themselves to mathematical models are ignored.[5]

All these *demand side factors* are largely ignored in the propagandistic approaches adopted by those who insist that the poor supply of skills is the only cause of the knowledge and skills crisis in South Africa. The reality is that low paid and insecure jobs, low levels of investment in skills acquisition, unsatisfactory conditions of work, and the spectre of unemployment are an inherent part of capitalist systems

---

4. The Congress of South African Trade Unions (Cosatu), 23 August 2009, lauded President Jacob Zuma 's government after its first three months in office, but singled out business, saying its tardiness in implementing the plan to mitigate job losses was "deeply disappointing."

5. In this regard, the wisdom of the eminent physicist John Ziman [(1991) *Reliable Knowledge,* Cambridge: Cambridge University Press] is appropriate. Writing about the use of mathematical models as 'permissible' in the physical sciences because its approximations are 'applied only to carefully chosen subject matter under highly contrived conditions' (1991: 160) he warns against the unwarranted use of mathematical models in the social sciences. In his view, "For such intellectual feats to succeed, however, the formal properties of the mathematical symbols must be isomorphous with the empirical relations of the categories they purport to represent in the real world. The language of theory must correctly mirror reality. In physics, of course, this isomorphism is imposed by convention; it is taken for granted that nature is inherently 'mathematical', and the subject matter for research is selected accordingly." [1991: 163]

of production and blaming the government and the poor themselves is obfuscatory and disingenuous.

Another important issue to free the discussion about education and skills from its current bondage concerns the idea that for members of the working class and their families only technical knowledge, knowledge useful in the workplace, is possible. This is the old 'head and hand' issue resurfacing itself. Regrettably it has a pervasive grip even amongst some progressive academics. In their view, worker's knowledge and experience is inadequate for grasping the requirements of 'higher learning'. This conceit is fostered despite the fact that many academics themselves have working class backgrounds and yet accept this view uncritically. Yet the history of human civilisation over tens of thousands of years reinforces the idea of collective knowledge, is dependent on and has been built upon the knowledge of ordinary human beings going about their daily lives and fashioning new ways of doing things, of thinking, of observation and experience, of trial and error and practical application, intelligently solving many of the vexing issues that faced humanity over the millennia. Without these contributions to human knowledge there would be no civilisation as we know it.

Knowledge and skills are indispensable human attributes and not the preserve of special castes or classes in society; they are what makes us human and are derived from the mutually reinforcing socialisation that makes possible the progress of society. They are utterly reliant on the idea of sharing, collective learning and caring in the community of all nations. They are as cumulative over time as they are interdependent. This is despite the searing tribulations suffered in some moments of extreme inhumanity such as the periods of slavery, colonialism and Nazism in Europe, the recent episodes of genocide in many places, or indeed, Apartheid here. The fact that some individuals have made outstanding contributions to the stock of civilisation knowledge is entirely due to its collective social origins; they were able to rely on the pre-existing body of knowledge bequeathed to humanity by previous generations wherever they may have been located. These great leaps in human understanding that occur at some times in human history are entirely reliant on the slow and steady accumulations of generations of knowledge produced by humanity over time. This humanity is no other than the vast multitudes of those who toil to produce the socially useful labours in all societies throughout the world.

Schooling and higher education

The ideological assault on the prerogatives of an ostensibly sovereign state can also be illustrated by reference to the power of the conservative discourses about schooling. Here the normative prescriptions about school reform seek to elide all reference to the underlying social construction of the school and classroom.

Elsewhere (Motala and Vally, 2010), we have shown that while educational analyses about South African education have great merit, they have largely ignored any direct reference or analysis of the social pathologies and structures created by racial capitalism in South Africa and have consequently not provided any theoretical (or practical) basis for understanding the continuing and pervasive phenomenon of class and its analysis of school reform in South Africa. This absence leads to a debilitating failure in our understanding of the deeper characteristics of society. Motala and Vally (2010argued) that where social class applies,

> this is done tangentially, mostly to recognise the social location of students as 'poor', or 'disadvantaged', to provide descriptions of the conditions under which children (and even communities) are found, to evoke characterisations of the conditions prevalent in 'poor' and 'disadvantaged' communities, and to provide testimony for the rigours of school life, the intractability of the problems of access, the grinding incapacities and effects on the lives and potential opportunities for the children of the 'poor'. These descriptions have meaning because they evoke for policy-makers, administrators, the general public and even academic commentators, a sense of urgency about the challenges of achieving educational equity, fairness and social justice in and through education. They make graphically evident the educational symptoms that typify the conditions under which 'poor' communities learn since they deal not only with issues of infrastructure or the lack of it, the lack of teachers in critical subjects, poor or non-existent learning materials, indefensible approaches to teaching and learning, but also provide rich evidentiary material about the social cleavages predetermining the life chances and opportunities available to the children of the 'poor' and the intractability of these conditions.

The implication of this is that the schooling system is treated as homogenous and subject to the same template of policy and practice which ignore all references to the actual existing class, racial, geographic and gendered forms of differentiation that exist in the system, the implications of home language in working class and poor rural schools, subjected to the anarchic choices of school text, the continued struggles over schooling costs and the idiosyncratic, fragmentary and

uncoordinated agenda of reform which is unable to make deliberate
choices in favour of the most disadvantaged members of society. This
failure allows conservative forces to regain ascendancy in their nostalgic
calls for apartheid era authoritarianism characterised by its
differentiated opportunities for learners (including the fundamental
pedagogics of didactic and choral recitation, 'talk-and-chalk' instruction,
rote learning and corporal punishment) and blaming teachers and
learners (and not structural inequality) for educational shortcomings.

Similarly in higher education, this ideological conservatism lies in
the emphasis on the responsiveness of universities to business to the
virtual exclusion of all else. This means that a closer relationship
between universities and industry is regarded as an unmitigated good
despite its danger for relinquishing the broader mandate of 'public good'
as ameliorative of the needs of the poor and the use of public resources
for private profit; the conversion of research into private consultancy;
undermining the integrity of public institutions through the
commodification of their outputs, the marketisation of their core
activities in teaching and research enforced by the concomitant
pressures on university managements to become 'managers' instead of
intellectual and social leaders. There is an abiding failure, until now, to
examine a substantive approach to what is the 'community' that
universities are meant to serve and an abdication to the idea that 'third
stream income' generation is a prior and more pressing mandate for
higher education.

The ideological struggle to assert a broader conception of education
and training reflective of a humanising discourse exemplifies the
contradictory nature and the contestation over how the role of education
and training is to be interpreted and what social outcomes, for whom,
and at what cost these are to be achieved. The intentions of the
Constitution and its subsidiary legislation cannot ameliorate the
structural realities which provide an impenetrable bulwark against the
possibilities for genuine social transformation. The implication of this is
that authoritative references to the power of the Constitution and the
law remain unhelpful since they can only have meaning in the context of
the struggle over the form and content of the 'negotiated settlement'
itself and by recognising that such a settlement was fashioned on the
basis of a 'substantial consensus', which deferred the fundamental
structural characteristics of apartheid capitalism for resolution 'on
another day'. Recognising this conditionality on the 'freedom' of the
post-apartheid government and its entrapment within a global regime of
capitalist accumulation provides a sounder basis for understanding its
possibilities and the constraints of the reform process. It is equally
instructive in interpreting the seminal legislative incursions by the new

state into such matters as human rights and education or other social legislation given the inseparability of the concerns of the law and its conjunctural nature.

This also means that despite the strong injunctions in the Constitution about the entrenched right to education, it remains erroneous to assign to the law attributes that it cannot have outside the contestation over historically evolving social and political relations. Any conception of rights must pay attention to these larger framing conditionalities (local and global) bequeathed to social systems by the force of global context since the rights discourses too are limited by it. Examining the precepts of the law for their efficacy is only a part of the analytical framework for understanding what goes on in the world of workers and the poor, since meaningful analysis must rely on a wider range of factors and circumstances which themselves play a critical role in defining the limits of legalism and its muted role.[6]

Finally we have no doubt that democratic political agency is essential to advance the progressive agenda of change – i.e. the necessity of particular forms of social and political agency beyond and in addition to the formal legislative structures of representation. This agency is indispensable for advancing the interests of the poor and working classes and fundamental to the realisation of the transformative social, political, economic and cultural aspirations of the majority of the population. Agency is vital to the ability of communities and individuals representative of the interests of the working classes and the urban and rural poor to engage in autonomously generated activities to change the material conditions in which such communities find themselves – even though they might not do so with complete freedom. Hence, critical to all social policy and its implementation is the question of who participates in it, who is privileged by its processes and who ignored, since questions of social power are deeply connected to issues of social mobilisation, advocacy and agency[7].

Regrettably, government and even political organisations have become increasingly reliant on so-called experts to the exclusion of social processes, public engagement and democratic debate. This is perhaps the most pernicious of the mechanisms of ideological conservatism. It privileges those who are business oriented in their

---

6. This is not to deny for instance that in some cases 'explanations' based on the efficacy of policies or the desultoriness of bureaucracies in implementing policies are inappropriate. But these explanations are from 'inside' the framework of policy. They cannot explain why even where no such policy or implementation barriers exist, human rights infractions continue to be pervasive.

7. See Dreze and Sen (2002) for an extensive argument about the critical importance of participation to democracy.

approach to education and training, endows huge contracts to consultancy firms, abandons educational research to accountants at hugely profitable rates for them and removes education policy and practice from history, context and critique. The idea of participation needs to be defined politically to avoid its treatment "in a normative manner as purely a positive phenomenon. We can begin to treat the problem of participation analytically and ask on what basis people participate, around what goals and to what ends" (Putzel, 2004: 3). This in turn deals with the question of how and where 'ordinary and poor' people are organised, the critical role of the state in guaranteeing 'associational space', and the forms of support for civil society associations engaged in strategies for 'poverty reduction' and other rights based strategies.

Conclusion

Our approach points to the need for a more complex analysis - extant in South African historiography. Especially in relation to apartheid capitalism such analysis evinces a complex set of causalities based on the complexities of its contradictory history; including the wide ranging factors shaping its political economy and the struggles against it. Such analysis must seek to transcend the simplistic economism characteristic of some of the writing about the period, since the concept of 'political economy' can encompass a wider range of political, social and cultural relations and perspectives affecting 'race' and gender, class and geographic and other forms of social differentiation and the structural conditions which reproduce them.

Associated with such a critique of the apartheid state was an analysis of the role of the state in securing the hegemony of mining and agricultural capitalism in the early years of its development and of the military industrial complex in its latter years. The apartheid state represented a form of capitalism which attempted to perfect an avalanche of draconian and racist forms of control over the working classes and the poor in establishing the pre-eminence and rights to capitalist accumulation and control. This form of accumulation is evidenced by some of the most concentrated forms of wealth anywhere giving rise to massive differentials in the wealth, incomes and capabilities between the apartheid ruling elite (and its backers) and the population as a whole.

Towards the end of the apartheid regime for instance, shares in the stock exchange represented graphically this concentration of wealth and its concomitant expression in power. One conglomerate corporation alone - the Anglo American Corporation - owned 44.2 per cent of all the shares quoted on the country's stock exchange while the leading four conglomerates together owned no less than 80 per cent of those shares. It is this pervasive and unmitigated aspect of the potent mix between capitalism and the apartheid regime which in our view continues to cast the widest shadow on any possibilities for fundamental social change in South Africa and nullifies the effects of any alternative to the concentration of wealth and capitalist interests. Indeed it is possible to show that its effects, together with the unmitigated power of corporate globalisation, have deepened the forms of social differentiation so evident now. It is this which belies any suggestion that there can be fundamental changes to the organisation of power in society outside the reorganisation of the proprietary relations guaranteed by the Constitution.

Discussions today about this or that model as appropriate to the idea of a South African 'developmental state' remain truncated in the absence of such critical analysis and an exploration of the process of capital accumulation, state formation and the restructuring of class and other social relations of power as new forms of the global hegemony of market relations and indeed the sub-imperialism of the South African state. In our view, any attempt at understanding the underlying possibilities for changing social relations remains obtuse without such analysis. The possibilities that face the post-apartheid state and its ostensibly unifying constitution and the quest for social cohesion across the divides that presently exist remain no more than capricious hope for as long as the conditions for the real democratisation of the state are not understood. Without such an understanding, the expectation that state formation post-apartheid will be unaffected by its past, is misplaced.

References

Dreze, J. and Sen, A., 2002. *Development and Participation*, Delhi: Oxford University Press.
Motala, E. and Vally, S., 2010. 'Race', Class and Education in Post-Apartheid South Africa. In D. Kelsh, D. Hill and S. Macrine, eds. *Class in Education: Knowledge, pedagogy, subjectivity,* London: Routledge.
Nzimande, B. and Mathieson, S., 2004. Transforming South African Education. Occasional Paper No. 3, Centre for Education Policy Development: Johannesburg.
Putzel, J., 2004. The Politics of Participation: Civil society, the State and Development Assistance. Development Research Centre, LSE, UK.
Randeria S., 2007. The State of Globalisation, Legal Plurality, overlapping sovereignties and ambiguous alliances between civil society and the cunning state in India. *Theory Culture and Society*, 24 (1), pp.1-33.

11.
Golf's caddies and cronies
Jacklyn Cock

Introduction

As a way of illustrating several aspects of class, race, inequality and environmental abuse, this chapter will show that the apparently harmless scene of the golf course is embedded in two processes - social polarisation and ecological degradation - which are increasing both globally and in contemporary South Africa. It illustrates the shift from race to class-based exclusion that has characterised South Africa since 1994, and the increasing conspicuous consumption that shift has involved. The chapter argues that golf is contributing to two apparently contradictory processes - the exclusion of the majority of South Africans from crucial resources, at the same time that it promotes inclusion into a new power elite that is marked by the co-existence of political and economic power.

There are over 500 golf courses in South Africa (almost 100 in Gauteng), and they are sharply stratified in ways that reflect the social mobility of some of the new players. For example, keen golfer Cyril Ramaphosa learned to play golf on the Parkview course which only costs R6,000 to join but now belongs to the exclusive River Club which has an entry fee of R200,000 and an annual fee of R25,000. The top end of the market, the recent and growing phenomenon of golf estates illustrates the dynamics of exclusion most dramatically. There are now some 81 golf estates (defined as areas with a golf course with residential stands) in South Africa[1].

Six features of the contemporary golf course

Golf estates have the following features:

(i) Social and spatial enclavisation: These estates are fortified enclaves of wealth. To cite some examples, recently a house at Zimbali Golf estate, north of Durban which describes itself as 'one part golf, two part paradise', sold for R19 million. A new development there will include six beachfront villas which will be priced from R30m each.[2]

---

1. 'In recent years, the demand for exclusive residential conglomerations built around luxurious golf courses has far outstripped supply' and 'provides concrete evidence of the strong appeal of the high-security, green lifestyle offered by such enclosed residential estates'. (Murray, 2004: 149)
2. *Business Day*, 30 March 2007

Property prices at Mount Edgecombe Golf Estate "range from R2.2 million to over R20million."[3] The cheapest house available at Pecanwood Golf Estate, near Hartebeespoort Dam is R2.5 million but earlier this year a house sold there for R15 million. A house currently on show at Pezula Golf Estate, balancing on the clifftops of the Knysna Heads overlooking the ocean, is advertised for R10,6 million.[4] Pezula describes itself as "the best luxury development in the world."[5] The Pinnacle Point Beach and Golf resort was voted by *Golf and Leisure* magazine as one of the ten best new golf courses in the world.[6]

The first golf estate in South Africa, Selbourne Hotel, Spa and Golf Estate, established in 1983 south of Durban, "offers a unique opportunity to experience a gracious style of hospitality in a cocoon of utter exclusivity and privacy." This 'cocoon' exists in a sea of the desperate rural poverty. But golf estates (along with gated communities more generally) involve a retreat from any substantial engagement with such social issues. Selbourne and other golf estates illustrate what Steven Gill has called "a new politics of inequality" in the contemporary world. He writes,

> This is a global phenomenon, where the affluent are increasingly not only economically, but also socially, spatially and politically segregated from the rest of society and especially from the poor of the world's population (unless of course the poor are their domestic servants (Gill, 2003: 201).

He calls this process of social enclavisation, "a new medievalism that separates and segregates rich and poor communities" (Gill, 2003: 201). In this process the poor are often rendered invisible. As Starns expresses it, in golfing resorts "The white-collar masters of postmodern corporate capitalism are welcomed into a fantasy island of 'comfort', 'amenities' and 'luxury' and the real world of poverty, inconvenience and social division is fenced out into invisibility." (Starn, 2006: 460).

(ii) Fortification: These are fortified enclaves based on a new kind of class-based segregation. Golf estates are marked by an emphasis on security in all their promotional literature. For example, Zimbali is a secure gated estate with vehicular access controlled via two security entrance points manned 24 hours a day. The entire perimeter fence is

---

3. *Saturday Star*, 23 June 2007
4. *Saturday Star*, 5 August 2006
5. *Sunday Times*, 24 September 2006
6. *Sunday Independent*, 24 June 2007

patrolled on foot and a security control centre monitors pedestrian and vehicular access points via CCTV cameras.

(iii) Social homogeneity: This involves what Thorsten Veblen stressed the 'social confirmation', which "nothing but a considerable body of like-minded people can give" (Veblen, 1899; 2005: 63). It means the exclusion of people perceived as different or threatening. "The golf estate lifestyle has captured the interest of South Africans who seek the freedom of living in a secure, rural setting, AMONG PEOPLE OF SIMILAR PERSUASION. (My emphasis) These are the driving forces behind what some are calling a phenomenon, with demand for golf estate property seemingly insatiable." (Lloyd Nicholson cited in *The Star*, 2 June 2006). As one resident of Pecanwood Golf estate, said, 'The people here are all PLMs' ('people like me'). Here, as in other golf estates, there are a small minority of black residents.

The class exclusivity of golf estates is illustrated by the strict controls to which 'the other' is subject. Generally no workers are allowed to live on site. At the golf estate of Blair Atholl, access involves 'biometric fingerprint technology'. At the planned Chintsa Golf Estate, "domestic workers will be picked up at the entrance and transported to residents homes by an internal shuttle service." At Cove Rock near East London, the few domestic workers and gardeners employed are issued with permits and special aprons for identification.

(iv)This homogeneity involves a kind of social closure. In golf estates the trend is towards creating self-contained residential environments. For example, the Dainfern Golf Estate includes a preparatory and secondary school and shopping centre and describes itself as a "self contained residential community ideally suited to families." (Van Eyk, 2007: 4).

(v) The fifth feature of golf estates are extravagant claims about contributing to development and creating employment. For example, empowerment millionaires Saki Macozoma, Bulelani Ngcuka and Dali Mpofu "have launched a campaign 'Plough your millions back home' to encourage other tycoons from the Eastern Cape to invest in it. Leading by example Macozoma has taken a 25 per cent stake in the company which is developing a R2 billion golf estate in Chintsa."[7] A Pam Golding agent refers to substantial benefits for "our local community."[8]

Some employment is provided for local people but it is very limited and largely casualised labour, lacking security, regulation, a living wage or benefits. Furthermore, the establishment of golf estates often involves dispossession and a loss of employment. The establishment of the 600ha

---

7. *Sunday Times*, 28 January 2007
8. *Business Day*, 16 February 2007

Blair Atholl golf estate north of Johannesburg on former farmland involved the removal of a number of families to create the "country sanctuary... offering an exceptional lifestyle emphasising nature, privacy and security" for those who can afford the R2 – R4.5m stands.[9]

Golf estates are lucrative investments and there are other examples of direct links between the new black elite and golf courses and estates. For instance, Lazarus Zim is a member of a consortium that has bought a 26 per cent stake in property developer Pinnacle Point Holdings, which is committed to the multi-billion-rand Pinnacle Point Beach and Golf Resort on the cliffs near Mossel Bay. The company is also constructing golf resorts in Port Elizabeth and Clarens.[10] Cyril Ramaphosa is a key actor in the development of Huddle Park golf estate.

(vi) Lastly, these golf estates involve appeals to nature, while destroying it. For example, Zimbali claims to be 'inspired by nature' and the Zimbali ethos is 'living in harmony with nature'. The marketisation of nature is very clear in their advertisement which reads:

> Start living your dreams. Imagine waking up every morning to a view over the Indian Ocean with schools of dolphins surfing among the breakers. Imagine having two championship golf courses to choose from, any time you feel like playing a round. Imagine living among indigenous coastal forest, with natural lakes, bushbuck and blue duiker, set against pristine golden beaches.[11]

Promotional material for Blythedale estate promises, "Home to a pair of Crowned Eagles nesting in a Marula tree, Blythdale Coastal Resort offers a rich heritage of natural flora and fauna."

In similar terms Chintsa River Golfing Estate offers, "A world of quiet pleasures and glorious sunsets." Arabella offers visitors an "African Rainforest experience" and frequently appeals to nature in its advertising, such as citing a quote from Cezanne, "Art is in harmony, parallel with nature."[12] According to the promotional literature, "The splendour of Pecanwood Estate wraps you in nature, embracing the good life and encompassing a lifestyle rich in relaxation, giving you a time to pause, enjoy and take in the stylish comforts this illustrious development has to offer." A new golfing estate in the Drakensberg, Nondela is described as "nature undiluted."

---

9. *Business Day,* 16 May 2008
10. *Sunday Times,* 22 October 2006
11. *Sawubona,* July 2006
12. *The Sunday Times,* 11 June 2006

These appeals are characteristic of golf courses more generally. According to one landscape architect, "A golf course is man interacting successfully with nature."[13] This is a preposterous claim given the ecological damage involved in golf courses and estates in relation to the amount of chemical pesticides and fertilizers used for maintenance, the destruction of wetlands and indigenous vegetation during construction and particularly the amount of water they use. Not only golf estates, but golf courses more generally, involve a process of exclusion of various kinds.

Forms of exclusion

Consider seven forms of eco-social exclusion associated with the golf course.

(i) Exclusion from arable and grazing land:
Recently the minister for agriculture and land affairs raised concerns about the use of prime agricultural land for golf estates.[14] The concern is that this converts land to non-productive use while depopulating the areas and reducing employment. A spokesperson from AgriSA, the commercial farming association agreed that this involved the conversion of good agricultural land and the intensive use of water.This is especially worrying given declining production of major staples of the poor such as maize and wheat.

The size of an average 18 hole course is between 50 - 60 hectare and golf estates about 400ha, although some are much larger, for example Zimbali covers 700 ha.Using the last figure, the total amount of land devoted to golf is thus in the region of 57,400 ha.

The exclusion involved is illustrated by the case of Bushman Sands golf estate established in 2003 in the desperately poor village of Alicedale where most of the 4,500 residents survive on social grants. Locals are bitter that this multimillion-rand golf estate housing development included 60ha of municipal commonage land, traditionally used to graze their cattle. "The developers gave the stock owners another piece of land as compensation but this is a rocky mountain with no river. You can't plant anything."[15]

A golf course is contested as part of the land claim of the Umgungundlovu clan who were removed from a fertile coastal strip of

---

13. Sabine Baring-Gould, cited in the *Mail and Guardian,* 30 October 2006
14. *Business Report,* 10 November 2008.
15. Interview with Peter Skara, manager of the ANC constituency office. Alicedale, 12 Jan 2007.

land in 1980 to make way for the luxury resort that became the Wild Coast Sun. Young clan members are threatening to plough up the golf course.

The Blythedale golf estate on the KwaZulu-Natal North Coast is presently the subject of a bitter land battle between the developers and the Dube community who lodged a claim in 1998 with the Land Claims Commission, arguing that they had been forcibly removed from their ancestral land, a claim which was declared valid by the Land Claims Commission. A R20 million offer to the community was rejected as "peanuts compared with what the developers would gain out of the project."[16] A similar struggle is underway near Dullstroom in Mpumulanga where a multimillion rand golf estate, designed by Ernie Els involves the eviction of local farm workers. "We want to plant maize and green beans and potatoes, but this new land they're offering is not good," said Solomon Mahlangu.[17]

Associated with dispossession from land are other problems such as the displacement of farm workers who do not necessarily find employment on the golf estates, and inflated land prices. A Western Cape Department of Environmental Affairs and Planning (DEADP) report points out that the inflated prices that are paid for agricultural land with a view to development prevents farmers from expanding their operations. They cite the case of the "average price paid per hectare for agricultural land of 50ha or less in 2004 in the George area has been R42,751. In one instance in excess of R293,000 ha was paid for land apparently with the view to golf estate type development." (DEADP, 2004: 36). A golf estate is planned at Woody Cape, adjoining the Addo National Elephant Park. This was prime agricultural land used for dairy farming. The farmer was paid R38 million for his 400 hectare farm which is 10 times the going rate for agricultural land[18].

Overseas investors are involved in several golf estates, for example, the portfolio of IFA Hotels and Resorts Kuwait includes Zimbali, Boschendale in the Western Cape and a planned development in the Waterberg. (Enslin-Payne, 2007). The Australian company Medallist is to develop a R5bn 'lifestyle community, the Eye of Africa', including a golf course near Johannesburg.[19] A high proportion of residences on golf estates are owned by overseas investors at Zimbali, for instance (Robertson, 2007). The relatively cheap price of land in South Africa for this social category is contributing to inflated land prices.

---

16. *Sunday Times,* 17 June 2007
17. *Sunday Times,* 20 July 2008
18. Interview with local farmer, 12 Jan 2007
19. *Business Day,* 25 January 2006

(ii) The second form of exclusion is from scarce water resources

South Africa is a water scarce country. As Western Cape Environmental Minister Tasneem Essop said when she introduced ground-breaking guidelines in December 2005 for future development of golf courses, golf estates and polo fields, "Our water resources are under threat."[20] One of the difficulties is that such governmental guidelines and regulations are often ignored.[21]

Golf courses use on average 1.2 - 3 million litres of water a day. (Endangered Wildlife, 2006: 44). This is equivalent to the water consumption of a town of 20,000 people. Using the RDP calculation of 25 litres a day, this is equivalent to the basic amount 30 million people - 75 per cent of South Africans - should receive daily.[22] The River Club Golf course obtains its water from the Jukskei River to maintain its manicured greens and emerald fairways, even during the Highveld winter, and on both my site visits, sprinklers were operating in the mid-day sun.

While Pecanwood golf course uses over 1 million litres of water a day from the Hartebeestpoort dam, many of their workers lack access to water and electricity. The Pecanwood workers who live in an informal settlement known as 'Jan's place' have to walk 5 km to buy water at R3 for 20 litres. This illustrates what Marx called 'savage capitalism'. Labour is 'only a naked commodity', any sense of responsibility of the employer towards employees is dissolved.

Golf courses are also environmentally damaging in that they involve the destruction of indigenous vegetation, a reliance on exotic grass types and the harmful use of fertilisers, pesticides and herbicides. The destruction of indigenous vegetation in the course of these developments also means a significant loss of biodiversity. For example, a golf course being planned at Kathu, on the edge of the Kalahari desert will destroy a camelthorn forest, which is one of only two in Southern Africa.

(iii) Exclusion from traditional access to fishing and recreational sites:

For example Pecanwood denies access to traditional fishing sites on Hartebeestpoort Dam, the Fish River Sun Golf course blocks access to the

---

20. *Mail and Guardian,* 24 February 2006
21. For example, the developer of the Ebotse Golf Estate, Benoni ignored prescribed bufferzones. (*The Star,* 15 Aug 2008). The legislation provides for Environmental Impact Assessments but these are often biased, marked by inadequate public participation and a 'lack of investigation of key issues (particularly social impacts and water use impacts)' (DEADP, 2004: 66).
22. *Mail and Guardian,* 24 February 2006

beach as do the Blythedale and Prince's Grant golf courses in Kwa-Zulu Natal.

(iv) Exclusion from heritage sites:

A few miles west of East London there is a rocky cliff at the end of a wide, sandy beach. Known as 'Gombo Rock' it is a place of great spiritual power and has great significance for Xhosa traditionalists. It is "a scene of indescribable pathos to contemplate" (Mostert, 1992: 483). Thousands of Xhosa converged here in 1819 after their defeat at the battle of Grahamstown, and their leader, Makana, declared that he would summon the Xhosa ancestors to rise from the sea and come ashore to help drive the white man from the land.

Today the mainly white inhabitants of the gated Cove Rock Golf Estate have erected an electrified fence which makes access to the beach impossible. As one informant told me, "the beach is ours. If we find a stranger there we chase them."[23]

One of the world's most important early human habitation sites, with artifacts dating back to the Middle Stone Age, is being damaged by water seeping on to it from the irrigation of the 9th and 18th holes of the Pinnacle Point Golf Estate. [24] Pinnacle Point is a luxury estate with house prices varying from R3 to R22m.[25]

(v) Exclusion from decision making:

As Peter Skara said of Bushman Sands, "Locals were not consulted about the loss of their communal grazing land."[26] Of course this is true more broadly as many EIA procedures allow for very shallow public participation.

(vi) Exclusion from decent work:

Some local employment is provided for maintenance workers, caddies, gardeners, domestic workers and security guards but it is largely casualised labour lacking security, regulation, decent wages and benefits. In this sense golf estates illustrate both exploitation AND exclusion. For example, the Fish River Sun only employs 2 security guards who are paid R80 a day. The general pattern is for golf estates to use outsourced private security companies. These "often employ illegal

---

23. Interview with resident, Cove Rock. 28 Dec 2006. The golf estate of Dainfern generated considerable controversy as it was built on a traditional burial site.The South African Heritage Resource Agency has 'noted their concern that large-scale developments such as golf estates in agricultural or rural settings are incongruent.' (DEADP, 2004: 40).

24. *Sunday Independent*, 15 July 2007

25. *Business Day*, 6 June 2008

26. Interview Alicedale, 12 Jan 2007

immigrants and security staff from outside the local area on the grounds that they will not be part of any local criminal networks."[27]

Employment is largely outsourced at Pecanwood Golf Estate. While some 400 workers are employed, it is entirely casualised labour lacking benefits or protection, thereby effectively operating outside the labour legislation which was one of the most important achievements of the transition. For example some 100 people are employed by 'Golf Data', the firm which manages the golf course (and most of South Africa's top golf courses and estates). One informant whose job is 'to look after the golf carts' works 9 hours a day for R2,400 a month.

There were thirty young African men pressed against the wire fence of the Royal Port Alfred Golf Club hoping for employment as caddies, earning R60 for 18 holes on the day I visited. On that day only 3 were successful According to the 'caddiemaster: "Most people take a golf cart at R150 a round. These people are very cruel. People say they don't like caddies because they steal, but they must steal. They have nothing. If I was hungry I would also steal."[28] The exclusive River Club only provides employment as caddies "twice or three times a week" to some forty African men (mostly from nearby Alexandra township), at R150 a round.

At Bushman Sands in Alicedale there were no caddies on site when I visited. However, according to the Golf Director, it is possible "to find a caddie from the township but most people use golf carts." While caddies are paid R70, a golf cart is hired at R180 for a round of golf[29]. Some 400 people were employed during the construction of Bushman Sands and a total of 125 are now employed by the complex as waitresses (earning R1,100 a month), maintenance workers and security guards.

According to Peter Skara, Bushman Sands has brought some employment but they are low level jobs. At the time the R20 million project was launched, Premier Stofile called the project 'a new dawn', which would transform life for the people of Alicedale. The Chairperson of the Alicedale Management Committee said, "Poverty is going to disappear."[30]

> The developers made many promises....There were high expectations. But now even the people who work there are not happy, the money is not good. No one earns more than R1,300. Bushman Sands promised to train people to become managers,

---

27. Interview with key informant Roger Roman, of Land for Peace, 29 May 2007
28. Interview, 17 Jan 2007
29. Interview Grey Thomas, Alicedale. 12 Jan 2007
30. *Daily Dispatch*, 12 July 2003

but this is not happening. Good jobs are reserved for outside
people. [31]

Caddies do not only carry golf bags but provide advice on how to play.
But they are employed on a casual basis and are excluded from the core
economy and the rights conferred on core workers by post-apartheid
labour legislation. The overall trend is that motorised golf carts are
preferred to caddies. At Zimbali, the hire of golf carts is compulsory at
R160 a cart. At the same time golf estates are often surrounded by
desperately poor communities. Whenever I have visited Cove Rock the
entrance was crowded with men from the informal settlement of Fort
Grey waiting in the hope of obtaining work as day labourers or
gardeners.

An indication of the desperation for employment is that,

> poor communities (either mobilised by developers or self
> mobilised) are putting the most pressure to have these
> developments approved, organising marches, petitions and so.
> This is counter-weighed by environmental groupings
> (unfortunately still predominantly white and perceived to be
> privileged) who also mobilise...this furthers the polarisation of
> our communities and its race and class dynamic.[32]

In the same way that it was only as 'nannies' that black women were
allowed onto whites-only beaches during apartheid, it was only as
caddies that Africans were allowed onto the golf course. The
humiliations and indignities caddies were subjected to is illustrated by
Joseph Leyleveld who never explored the social dynamics of golf though
the title of his book, *Move Your shadow. South Africa: black and white,*
taken from a golfer's phrase book.

'Moving your shadow' could be an example of what Thorsten Veblen
called a 'Tactic of subservience'. He wrote, it is 'imperative' that
subordinates "should show an acquired facility in the tactics of
subservience - a trained conformity to the canons of effectual and
conspicuous (in this case invisible) subservience" (Veblen, 1899; 2005:
38).

(vii) Finally, golf courses involve the exclusion of subordinate social
classes and (historically) social categories such as Jews and women:

Playing golf is a means of asserting class privilege; a vehicle of
identity. In South Africa, as Starn has written of the USA, "embracing a

---

31. Peter Skara interview, Alicedale. 12 Jan 2007
32. Personal communication from MEC Tasneem Essop, 23 June 2007.

game with pricey equipment, elaborate etiquette and exclusive clubs allowed America's elites both to mark a special identity and to isolate themselves from their social inferiors" (Starn, 2006: 451). A common feature of most golf courses, whether parts of golf estates or not, is a social, class-based exclusivity. This is illustrated by the expensive nature of the game (for example, at Fancourt, membership fees are R13,350 and R550 for 18 holes) and elaborate etiquette and dress codes are strictly imposed. For example, at Elements Private Golf Reserve north of Pretoria, "Strictly collared shirts with tailored trousers or shorts are allowed and socks must be worn at all times." At Eagle Canyon in Honeydew, only white or light beige socks are allowed.

These class exclusions of cost and style are replacing the race-based exclusions of the past when golf courses were for whites only. This generated some controversy, for example in the case of Papwa Sewgolum, a self taught golfer who achieved international fame and managed to secure entry into whites-only local golf tournaments during the 1960s. He won the Natal Open championship at the Durban Country Club (beating Gary Player). In terms of the Group Areas Act he was not allowed in the club house and was given his trophy outside during a rainstorm.

One of the most dramatic changes in South Africa since 1994 is the rise of a black middle class among whom golf is a popular sport, perhaps as a marker of social mobility and choice. According to one source, "the number of registered golfers in this country has doubled in the last 3 years." (Dirk Els, cited by Ray, 2006: 19)

Golf "is no longer the sole preserve of the white-skinned, the wealthy and the politically warned." (Winter, 2007: 23). The SABC show, 'The golf bag' appeals to these new black players. For example, on 'The golf bag' shown on 24 March 2007 hosted by Thabiso Tema, the 'personality of the week' was Bafana football coach Khabo Zondo. We are told that, golf 'teaches us to manage your situation', 'control your anger', 'discipline', 'respect', 'high level of concentration', 'create friends' and 'meet people who come from a different environment'. However, blacks remain a minority, for example only 15 out of the 230 members of the exclusive River Club[33] and only 3 out of 64 participants in a recent tournament. Patricia De Lille, who plays golf once a week, told the BBC that golf "was never accessible to us as blacks so there is an inquisitiveness about it."[34]

---

33. Interview with club official, 5 September 2007.
34. *Sunday Times,* 10 Dec 2006; It is significant that De Lille chose to specify her racial identity. Women have traditionally been excluded from golf which is partly why the British suffragettes poured acid or inscribed 'Votes for Women' on golf greens. Access to this masculine sport happened very slowly, and women are still excluded from

While the apartheid exclusion of blacks and the patriarchal exclusion of women means that the social composition of the 300,00 golfers in South Africa is changing, it remains a predominantly white male game and is linked to assertions of class and masculinist power.

While the situation of caddies is at the centre of the dynamics of exclusion, this chapter uses 'cronies' as the peg for the paradoxical process of inclusion.

Dynamics of inclusion

In South Africa the golf course is one site where the new power elite is coalescing. Here golf involves the inclusion of a small number into a tiny black elite and a growing black middle class. "The golf course is emerging as one terrain on which the relationship between the emergent sections of the black bourgeoise and the state is being cemented."[35]

For Nzimande this is a problematic relationship because the black bourgeoise is parasitic and compradorist; (in the sense of being driven by self interest) rather than patriotic. It is "not only tiny, but is highly dependent and parasitic on the white capitalist class ('the single biggest beneficiary from the current growth path') and the state" (Nzimande, 2007). He noted that in the 2003-4 annual report of the National Prosecuting Authority to parliament, "one item that appears on the budget is the Penuell Maduna Golf Classic." Nzimande asks, "What a golf classic tournament is doing in a national prosecuting authority is baffling."[36]

But corporate sponsorship of such 'Golf Days' is a major activity and brings together the small but growing black bourgeoisie and various factions of the new power elite. Among the most popular are the Presidents Cup, and the SAA Open Golf Tournament. A total of 2,738 golfers and over 50 companies participated in Sentech's World's Biggest Company Golf Day held on 24 May 2005 on golf courses throughout South Africa. The popular Nelson Mandela Invitational charity golf tournament was cancelled after a campaign led by Desmond Tutu calling for Mandela to distance himself from the organiser Gary Player on the grounds of his involvement in a golf course design in Myanmar that

---

membership at the Augusta Golf club, the site of the US Masters (this club admitted its first black members in 1990), and from the famous Royal and Ancient Golf Club in Scotland.

35. Blade Nzimande, *Sunday Times*, 4 Dec 2005
36. *Sunday Times*, 4 Dec 2006

involved forced labour and dispossession[37]. As George Monbiot wrote at the time in Burma, "golf is a powerful symbol of oppression."[38]

The cost of such golf days "is relatively small at about R750 per person (R250 green fees for one of the finer courses, R100 caddie fee, R200 for drinks and R200 for a shirt). That equates to just more than a meal per person at a fancy restaurant."[39] It should be noted that caddies earn half the amount spent on drinks.

The social interactions between business and politics that occurs in these golf days has worried a number of different commentators. For example, Richard Calland has called the "overlapping of business with politics," the "congealing embrace." (Calland, 2006: 5). Jeremy Cronin believes that a major point of concern is the collapse of boundaries between business and public office. "The key boundary that has been crossed is the business/political boundary," he said.[40] A 2006 SACP discussion paper referred to the entanglement of two groups: a new political elite (state managers and technologically inclined ministers) and (often overlapping with them) a new generation of black private sector BEE managers/capitalists. [41]

However a recent advertisement states, 'Business and Politics should never mix: but what happens when you're invited to play with the Premier?' ABSA Premiers Invitational. By personal Invitation Only.[42] On the initiative of keen golfer, Premier Sam Shilowa, ABSA began in 2007 to organise these events in all nine provinces with a final to be played at Fancourt in October 2007. Their aim is explicitly to "improve our relations with government."[43] 'A typical field involves about 120 players about 50/50 black and white; three-quarters of the field is by invitation from ABSA targeting our key customers, wealthy and corporate clients. The other quarter is made up of government officials selected by the premier of the relevant province... We give away R250,000 to a charity of the Premier's choice." [44]

What is significant here is the integration of both black and white and of men from both business and politics. At the Absa Premiers Invitational played at Centurion Golf Estate in August 2007, this formula of integration was very deliberately followed in the construction of each

37. *Star,* 8 Nov 2007
38. *Mail and Guardian,* 5 Oct 2007
39. Harold Jones, in a letter to *Realbusiness,* 2005
40. *The Star,* 1 Dec 2006
41. *Bua Komanis,* vol 5, no 1, May 2006
42. *The Weekender,* 24 April 2007
43. Interview with ABSA organiser Matt Ellenbogen, Johannesburg 2 July 2007
44. *Ibid*

4 ball. Also "at least one Absa person is included"[45] One corporate player commented, "In todays business environment government and municipal accounts are key. Events like this means you can create or loose a government account."[46] Premier Shilowa was clearly the kingpin in the drinking and socialising after the event. He feels it is a very valuable occasion. In his view, 'golf is not necessarily an elitist sport. It's only that here in South Africa because there are no public courses'. He "invites players who do business with the provincial government as well as friends."[47]

Another source of evidence of this mixing is this account:

> President Thabo Mbeki has friends too. But while Jacob Zuma's supporters are calling for machine guns, Mbeki's are reaching for their golf clubs. Hosted by the ANC-linked Network Lounge, Mbeki's friends will be teeing off in the second Friends of the President Golf Day at the Pretoria Country Club this weekend. But it is only when all the clubs are stored away that the real action will take place. Prominent South Africans - 'captains of industry', sporting celebrities and ministers - will join the president for cocktails and dinner.[48]

Pursuing its commitment to facilitating a collaborative relationship between big business and the ANC, the Network Lounge has hosted three such days. "Every 4 ball is hosted by a minister, a celebrity, a Director General or an ambassador." Nicholas Wolpe maintains that "these occasions are valuable networking opportunity for people. They can engage in dialogue in a relaxed, warm and friendly atmosphere." Wolpe promotes golf because "all the ANC leadership are playing; relationships are established, a lot of business is done on the golf course, deals are finalised and secured. The golf course is an enabling environment." The most recent golf day held at the Pretoria Country Club involved 120 golfers and 250 guests at the final dinner. A minimum payment of R50,000 allows sponsors to invite two people to cocktails (involving bottles of Johnny Walker Blue Label at R3,000 a bottle) and dinner. This is cheap compared to the R159,000 corporations are required to pay for a stall at the Network Lounge tent at ANC policy conferences which gives them "three days of unfettered access to the ANC leadership."[49] This amount was increased to R140,000 each for

---

45. *Ibid*
46. Anonymous informant, Centurion 8 Aug 2007
47. Shilowa Interview, Centurion 8 Aug 2007
48. *Mail and Guardian*, 12 Oct 2006
49. Interview with Nicholas Wolpe, Johannesburg, 2 Oct 2007

companies to occupy the stalls Wolpe terms 'bonding sites' in a 'luxury networking marquee' at the ANC national conference in Polokwane.[50]

President Mbeki made an effusive speech when he opened the 2003 Presidents Cup hosted by Dr Hasso Plattner, the billionaire owner of Fancourt Golf Estate. This event cost R8 million or R27,000 a head at a time when the per capita income of all South Africans was R14,000. On the menu for the 30 guests were salmon trout that had been specially grown for the party so that they would all be the same size. The opening party was attended by Nelson Mandela former President FW de Klerk, Patrice Motsepe and Tokyo Sexwale.

Capitalism is grounded in the hubs and networks of power and influence that are forged at these events and that promote a mix of economic and political elites. These are people with real power - these events include corporate leaders, politicians and state officials who are keen golfers, such as Trevor Manuel, Paris Mashile (chairman of Icasa), Jacob Maroga, chief executive of Eskom, Johannes Magwaza, described in the *Sunday Times* of 14 Jan 2000 as 'the father of BEE' executive chairman of Nkunzi Investment Holdings, Khaya Ngqula CEO of SAA, and the ex CEO of the IDC. (SAA sponsors the SAA Open, and the popular Golf Directory, with a comprehensive list of all golf venues), Khutso Mampeule, CEO of the Post Office, ex-Gauteng Premier Sam Shilowa, ex-Western Cape Premier Ebrahaim Rasool, Dali Mpofu, CEO of the SABC, Peter Mageza, CEO of Absa and Buhle Mthethwa who succeeded Patrice Motsepe, as president of the National African Federated Chamber of Commerce, Minister of Corectional Services, Ngconde Balfour, Moses Ngoasheng of Nail and a member of the R25,000 a year River Club, Jabu Mabuza chair of the Tsongo Sun Group, journalist Xolela Mangcu, Gauteng's director general Majopodi Mokoena, Kingley Makhubedu, Zanosi Kunene, chair of Coca-Cola Fortune and the chair of the Government Employees Pension Fund Martin Kuscus.

Former president Thabo Mbeki is a keen golfer, as are former Public Enterprises Minister Alec Erwin, Irvin Khoza of the World Cup 2010 local organising committee ,Thobile Mhlahlo who was Eastern Cape Safety and Transport MEC, and other important political and business personalities of the last decade such as Bulelani Ngcuka, Snuki Zikalala, Penuell Maduna, Patricia De Lille, Nondumiso Maphazi (executive mayor of Nelson Mandela Bay), Murphy Morobe, Bantu Holomisa, United Democratic Movement leader, Johannesburg mayor Amos Masondo, Cyril Ramaphosa, Don Ncube, Peter Vundla, Khehla Mthembu, Kaizer Motaung (chairman and managing director of the Kaizer Chiefs),

---

50. *Sunday Times,* 9 Dec 2007

columnist Xolela Mangcu as well as Tony Yengeni, who has joined several of Cape Town's exclusive golf clubs.

Golf is one space where these members of the new black elite interact with keen golfers who are members of the established white elite such as Brian Joffe, Derek Cooper of Standard Bank, Steve Booysen of ABSA, Whitey Basson of Shoprite, Ian Kirk of Sanlam, and John Gnodde, executive director of Brait. In this sense, golf is a lubricant of the new power elite.

Their interactions could be significant. According to Nzimande, the black bourgeoise is "preoccupied with deal making and other shenanigans" and points to many deals involving prominent ANC politicians and vast amounts of money. A number of informants stressed that the golf course is a popular site for this 'deal making'.

> Golf is part of the 'comfort factor' which facilitates informal networking. There are a lot of deals done on the course. Business is discussed. Many people learn the game specifically to make deals and to entertain business colleagues. Black and white mix and play together. [51]

Another informant explained "there was pressure on the established white elite to find BEE partners. The golf course was where social contacts could be made and relations established." The empowerment charters added to the pressure to establish partnerships with black business interests by establishing targets to be attained such as black representation at board level, at executive level and of procurement expenditure.

This 'deal making' is anchored in establishing the personal relations of trust on which business depends, for "companionship flourishes on a golf course, as it does in few other climes" (Talamini, 1973: 407). The golf course promotes team building and 'networking' and "for those who successfully use their old school ties and inner circle business contacts to generate growth and profit, effective networking is their most important marketing tool."[52] "Furthermore the unique thing about golf is you can be sure of undivided time spent with your clients and colleagues, and good relationships can be forged. Golf is also recognised as a very good test of people's temperament and personal integrity."[53] "Businessmen like to play golf. Relationships get built on the golf course."[54]

---

51. Golf Director, Parkview Golf Club interview, 18 May 2007
52. Trevor Nel in a letter to *Realbusiness,* 21 May 2005
53. Letter from Cyril Lincoln to *Real Business,* 2005
54. Interview with ABSA Premiers Invitational organiser, Matt Ellenbogen, 2 Jul 2007

According to Lerato Motsoeneng, "in business there is no better place to be with your client than on a golf course."[55] According to Ramotena Mabote,

> the golf course has become the extension of the boardroom, the Internet or even the business-class seat aboard an aircraft. It is often on the golf course that business deals are initiated or even concluded....attitude and temperament throughout the day helps fellow players determine whether or not you are a suitable business partner for the future... [56]

Published monthly in *Business Day*, *The Golfer* advertises itself as "tailor-made for executives."

The golf course is one terrain where the carriers of economic and political power are coalescing, a space which promotes the integration of the new black elite and the established white elite into a new formation. By 'power elite' is meant the concentration of political and economic power in a small interlocking and cohesive group or node who maintain dominant class interests. The social construction of this new power elite raises interesting sociological questions. Writing of the power elite in the USA, C. Wright Mills talked about them as "a homogeneous group," marked by a "similarity of *origin* (my emphasis) and outlook," and "social and personal intermingling." (Mills, 1956: 292).

The new power elite in South Africa lacked this 'similarity of origin and outlook' that is generated by going to the same schools and universities and even intermarrying like the British and US elites. There are no 'old school ties' to promote bonding, no tradition of family interactions or intermarriage. On the contrary, relations were historically marked by social distance, completely different life worlds and often deep ideological antagonisms. So the sites of 'social intermingling' and social cohesion that comes from 'easy intermingling' have to be manufactured to connect the various fractions of the new power elite - the established white elite and the new black elite.

The golf course is one such site. As Nicholas Wolpe expressed it, "Golf helps to promote the assimilation of black and white capital. Capital doesn't see colour, it only sees green. The cementing of new capital with the old has happened through the golf course."[57] In this sense golf is a lubricant of a degree of social cohesion in the new power elite, marked

---

55. *Mail and Guardian*, 21 Dec 2007
56. *Sunday Times*, 29 Jan 2006
57. Interview, Johannesburg, 2 Oct 2007

by the co-existence of black and white, old and new, and the co-existence of political and economic power.

This is not unique to South Africa. Golf seems to play a part in the new more 'diverse' power elite that Zweigenhaft and Domhoff (2006) have described in the US. They quote an ambitious woman manager who lamented the fact that her men colleagues played golf with a broad range of people in business and government including corporate executives. She said, "I wish I played golf. I think golf is the key. If you want to make it, you have to play golf."[58]

What this chapter is claiming is that golf is connected to capitalism and its excesses of wealth and social display. In South Africa it has long been part of the lifestyle of conspicuous consumption of the old white elite, and now seems to be becoming part of the lifestyle of conspicuous consumption that marks the small new black elite, some of whom have used their political power for self enrichment.

This process of elite formation involves some unlikely connections and alliances. For example there are reports that ex SADF and ex-MK players are frequent golfing partners at the Pretoria Golf Club. In April 2007, Tasneem Essop stopped a huge R1 billion golf estate development planned on the Garden Route in which former Scorpions boss Bulelani Ngkcuka is a major shareholder, in partnership with an apartheid-era SA Defence Force officer in the controversial Recces forces.[59] These examples illustrate the "curious interlocking elite interests that have formed since 1994" (Calland, 2006: 27).

However perhaps the most 'curious' connection is the golf partnershp between Jackie Selebi, the National Police Commissioner who used to play golf with Glen Agliotti, now named as 'the Landlord' in an international narcotics syndicate and arrested for Brett Kebble's murder last November.[60] Selebi insists that Agliotti "was my friend, finish and klaar."[61]

Does this golf friendship point to a corrupt relationship that is part of an emerging 'crony capitalism'? Calland has pointed to a new network of influence comprised of those who wield political and economic power. To him this represents "a congealing of elites with a defiant crony-capitalist agenda" (Calland, 2006: 46). But it could be argued that 'crony

---

58. Cited by Zweigenhaft and Domhoff, 2006: 56. Writing of how women and minorities have been incorporated into the power elite in the US, Zweingenhaft and Domhoff conclude that 'the power elite now shows considerable diversity... but its core group continues to consist of wealthy, white, Christian males, most of whom are still from the upper third of the social ladder' (Zweingenhaft and Domhoff, 2006: 7).
59. *Cape Argus,* 5 April 2007
60. *Sunday Times,* 12 Nov 2006
61. Cited in *Mail and Guardian,* 11 May 2007

capitalism' is an incoherent notion, and rests on a false dualism between 'crony capitalism' and 'normal capitalism'. The notion of 'normal capitalism' implies that it operates on a Weberian basis of impersonal rationality with strict boundaries between corporations and government. In reality, corporate capitalism depends on networked power; it involves highly personalised networks and connections which blur the distinctions between politics and business. As Harvey points out, the global trend is that "the boundary between the state and corporate power has become more and more porous" (Harvey, 2007: 78). Furthermore, capitalism always involves what Ndebele has called undermining "corruptive conditions."[62]

There is much cronyism, 'connectivity' and a reliance on 'clubby networks' in South African business life. This is evident in South Africa's extensive interlocking directorships. For example, keen golfer SAA Ceo Khaya Ngqula holds 38 directorships.[63] Crotty and Bonorchis report that the boards of the 50 companies they surveyed are predominantly comprised of white men and the 'cosy' relationship between CEOs, boards and remuneration committees suggest a system of highly personalised networks which could help to explain excessive executive salaries.

The game of golf promotes these 'connectivities', and is often associated with corruption.[64] For example, "Former Western Cape Premier Peter Marais was accused of bribery and corruption at the Roodefontein (golf) estate." David Molatsi, Wesern Cape Minister of Environmental Affairs was sentenced to 5 years imprisonment for accepting a bribe to approve a Plettenberg Bay golfing estate. Questions have been raised about whether Western Cape Premier Ebrahim Rasool used his influence to drive through the controversial Arabella Golf Club and Country Estate situated in an environmentally sensitive area, the Kogelberg Biosphere Reserve. It has been reported that top Land Bank

---

62. Cited in *The Sunday Times,* 22 Oct 2006
63. *Business Day,* 16 March 2007
64. In 1981 Sol Kerzner used golf as the vehicle to promote his new gambling resort at Sun City and break the international boycott of apartheid. In the USA there was the Abramoff scandal which exposed golf as 'not only a cherished pastime but increasingly... a critical cog in the wheels of campaign financing and lobbying' (Anne Kornblut cited in *The Sunday Times,* 29 Jan 2006). In South Korea 'public servants are sometimes banned from playing the game which is associated not only with wealth but also neglect of duty and corrupt business links.' (*Mail and Guardian* online 30 Oct 2006). This link between golf and the neglect of duty goes back to it origins when an Act of Parliament of 1457 banned golf because its 'popularity strongly interfered with archery practice, importance for the defence of the realm' (Pinner, 1988: 8).

officials siphoned off more than R2 billion, meant for farmers to fund their close friends' ventures, including luxury golf estates. [65]

The central issue of public debate is the nexus between politics and business. There are several references to golf in these debates. To cite only three: firstly, the Young Communist League has claimed that there is a need to defend the ANC from "outsourcing of key decisions by the movement to the Golf courses, Native Club and Working groups etc."[66] Ben Turok (2006) has warned of "emerging partnerships, reflecting golf-course activity, whereby an elite is encouraged, out of sync with the values of the ruling party." A very different source has referred to golf in his critique of BEE as blacks simply buying shares in companies run by white people. He asks,

> What insights into business does a black man who becomes rich through the efforts of white people share with his children around the dinner table?... As things stand today, most BEE players have nothing more than golf course tips to share with their children (Sikhakhane, 2006).

Globally, golf is a multibillion dollar industry. There are approximately 32,000 courses and some 56m golfers - nearly half of them in the USA - involved in an industry worth about R150 billion (Blitz, 2007: 38). Some emphasise that the growth of golf in South Africa is a positive development which may contribute to economic growth, job creation, attract tourists and benefit surrounding communities. According to Didi Moyle of South African Tourism, foreign tourists contributed R222 billion to SA's economy between 2003 and 2006.[67] But these 'benefits' must be questioned. For example, Vietnam is planning to build 123 more golf courses because "golf courses create employment, bring more money to local people, develop services and attract high-end foreign tourists," according to an official. But 76 of the courses are taking up more than 23 800ha of which 15 400 is farmland and it is claimed that these plans "are posing a hazard to the nation's rice crop and threatening food security" (Thomas and Van Nguyen, 2008). Golf courses also deepen social polarisation, and

> deplete water resources, consume agricultural land, spoil landscapes and heritage resources, impact on biodiversity, impact on scenic landscapes , routes and heritage resources,

---

65. *Sunday Times,* 11 Nov 2007
66. YCL message on the occasion of the 62nd anniversary of the ANC youth league
67. The Tourist, *Business Day,* February 2008

displace and divide especially rural communities, and impact on access to resources such as the coast (Department of Environmental Affairs and Development Planning, 2005)

Fortunately some political leaders are acting on the negative social and environmental consequences of the game, and civil society is beginning to speak out.[68] In 1993 the Global Anti-Golf Movement was launched to draw attention to the "toxicity of golf courses" and document how golf course development is associated with "the displacement of farmers and fishermen, water supplies, the eco-system and the promotion of a consumerist lifestyle" (Cole, 2002: 1). Golf courses have been criticised by the Endangered Wildlife Trust and the Wildlife and Environmental Society of Southern Africa, the Southern Cape Land Committee, the Guardians of the Garden Route and Land for Peace.

Conclusion

To conclude, some of the golfers who are the focus of this chapter are cronies in the sense that they are enmeshed in the personalised networks on which capitalism is structured, with an overlay of struggle networks in the case of the small black elite faction. Golf is ultimately about class power. It is tied into capitalism and its excesses of wealth and social display. This is why it was banned in communist China and why Castro shut down Cuba's golf courses after seizing power in 1959.[69]

Caddies and 'cronies' are highly gendered and racialised social categories. Their structural locations illustrate "the gangrenous inequalities that lie untreated in an untransformed South Africa" (Saul, 2005: 227). Millions of South Africans live on less than R300 a month which is the cost of a game of golf at many courses. At the same time many of the white men who constitute the majority of golfers earn enormous salaries. They are part of what John Saul has called "a dominant, transnational capitalist class" which is surrounded by "vast

---

68. According to Tasneem Essop, the government view is that golf, polo and other luxury housing estates perpetuate apartheid style segregation. (*Finweek* off course 24 March 2006). Essop's department has rejected an application for the development of a second golf estate in the Kogeberg Biosphere Reserve by Arabella. The first phase of the estate consumes about 4 million litres of water a day - two million on the golf course and 2 million in the luxury resort. *Mail and Guardian*, 24 Feb 2006.

69. However the social meanings of golf are changing. For example, while banned by Chinese Communist Party chairman Mao Zedong as decadent and elitist, day 'golf has become the latest fashion among wealthy Chinese - a way to exercise and, more importantly, a way to affirm one's status' (Fan, 2007: 11).

outer circles of less privileged people, in both North and South" (Saul, 2006: 22).

Saul takes these "present inequalities within the world-wide economy as the ... central fact of the current global reality." He also takes the struggle to overcome such inequalities as the absolutely central challenge that confronts humankind in the new century (Saul, 2006: 6).

References

Blitz, R., 2007. Cash Courses. The Business of Golf. *Financial Times,* 20 July 2007.

Calland, R., 2006. *Anatomy of South Africa. Who holds the Power.* Cape Town: Zebra Press.

Cole, C.L., 2002 Golf Wars. *Consumption.* American Sociological Association, 4(1), December 2002.

Department of Environmental Affairs and Development Planning, Western Cape, 2004. *Rapid Review of Golf Course and Polo Field Developments.*

2005. *Guidelines for Golf Courses, Golf estates, polo fields and polo estates in the Western Cape.*

Enslin-Payne, S., 2007. Investors pour R3b into new estate for Waterberg. *Business Report,* 5 September 2007.

Fan, M., 2007. For new elite, a once-banned pastime is now par for the course. *Washington Post or Sunday Independent,* 13 May 2007.

Gill, S., 2003. Social reproduction of affluence and human in/security. In I. Bakker and S. Gill, eds. *Power, Production and Social Reproduction.* New York: Palgrave Macmillan, pp.191 - 207.

Hyslop. J., 2005. Political Corruption: Before and After Apartheid. *Journal of Southern African Studies,* 32(4), pp. 773 - 789.

Lelyveld, J., 1986. *Move your shadow.* London: Michael Joseph.

MacDonald, M., 2006. *Why Race matters in South Africa.* Scottsville: UKZN Press

Murray, M., 2004. The spatial dynamics of postmodern urbanism: social polarisation and fragmentation in Sao Paulo and Johannesburg. *Journal of Contemporary African Studies,* 22, May, pp.139 -164.

Nzimande, B., 2007. BEE helps white capital more than black majority. *Sunday Times,* 21 January 2007.

Pinner, J., 1988. *The History of Golf.* London: Quintet.

Ray, C., 2006. Investing in Golf Estates. *Living on course,* Issue no 1, pp.13 -27.

Robertson, D., 2007. Golf estates still flying high. *Sunday Times,* 9 September 2007.

Saul, J., 2006. *Development after Globalisation,* Scottsville: UKZN Press

Sikhakhane, J., 2006. Current BEE state of mind is a mockery of Mandela's dream. *The Star,* 10 October 2006,

Smith, A., 2007. A golfer's paradise. *Business Day,* 22 June 2007.

South African Communist Party. 2007. The motive forces of the National Democratic Revolution, Umsebenzi online, vol 6, no 4.

Southall, R., 2007. The ANC state, more dsyfunctional than developmental. In S. Buhlungu et al., *State of the Nation. South Africa 2007.* Pretoria: HSRC.

Southall, R., 2006. South Africa's emerging black middle class. *HSRC review,* 2(3).

Starn, O., 2006. Caddying for the Dalai Lama: Golf, Heritage Tourism and the Pinehurst Resort. *The South Atlantic Quarterly,* 195(2), pp.447 - 463.

Thomas B. and Nguyen V., 2008. Vietnam weights pros and cons of adding golf courses to its tourist attractions. *Sunday Independent,* 14 September 2008.

Turok, B., 2006. The dilemma of accumulation. *Mail and Guardian,* 18 August 2006.

Veblen, T., 1899, 2005. *The Theory of the Leisure Class*. Extract published as *Conspicuous Consumption*. Harmondsworth: Penguin.

Winter, G., 2007. SA's emerging black talent simply amazing. *The Sunday Independent*, 27 May 2007.

Wright Mills, C., 1956. *The Power Elite*. New York: Oxford University Press.

Zweigenhaft, R. and Domhoff, G., 2006. *Diversity in the Power Elite*. Lanham, Maryland: Rowman and Littlefield Publishers.

12.
AIDS and inequality
Hein Marais

Introduction

An AIDS epidemic as severe as the one ploughing through South Africa will change society, but in ways that are not yet fully understood.[1] Literature on the impact of serious AIDS epidemics anticipates severe outcomes, and places special emphasis on the epidemic's likely effects on productive and governance capacities. Foreseen is a chain of effects in hard-hit settings that culminates in stunted economic growth, dysfunctional state institutions, possibly even 'derailed development' and state failure.

This approach expresses dominant ideological trends of our time, not least the overriding obsession with productive processes and growth potential, governance and security. The well-being of humans is refracted through these cognitive screens. What emerges is a fuzzy picture of a calamity that flattens everything in its path with a sort of 'democratic' disregard. Emptied of its unsightly injustices and inequalities, society becomes a fiction. In this fanciful world, we're all bobbing in the 'same boat', if not exactly equal then at least equally-at-peril. Consequently, AIDS is seen to induce a kind of levelling panic.

Neglected in such narratives is the powerful interplay between the epidemic and those factors that determine the distribution of power, resources and entitlements in society. Plagues zero in on the dispossessed, on those forced to build their lives in the path of danger. AIDS is no different in South Africa, where more than five million people are living with HIV. Here the epidemic is entangled in the circuitries that determine the distribution of power and privilege.

Epidemiological overview

South Africa's AIDS epidemic exhibits two striking features. It evolved with astonishing speed (HIV prevalence in women attending antenatal clinics was less than 1 per cent in 1990, but surpassed 22 per cent in 1999), and has become extraordinarily intense. At the turn of the century, when new HIV infections were probably peaking, more than 600 000 people were being infected with HIV each year (ASSA, 2003). A recent analysis estimated 571 000 HIV infections occurred in 2005 in

---

1. This essay substantially updates and further develops sections of Marais, 2006.

persons older than two years, and that incidence rate among adults (15-49 year-old) was very high, at 2.4 per cent (Rehle et al., 2007). Some 5.5m [4.9 million - 6.1 million] people, including 240 000 [93,000-500,000] children younger than 15 years, were living with HIV in 2005 (UNAIDS, 2006). Approximately one in five adults (19 per cent) is infected with HIV.

As in the rest of sub-Saharan Africa, the epidemic in South Africa disproportionately affects women: young women (15-24 years) are four times more likely to be HIV-infected than are young men: 17 per cent compared with 4.4 per cent (Shisana et al., 2005). HIV incidence rates among women in their prime child-bearing ages (20-29 years) were more than 6 times higher than among men in the same age bracket in 2005, 5.6 per cent compared with 0.9 per cent (Rehle et al., 2007). In the 2005 national household HIV survey, 17 per cent of young women (aged 15-24 years) tested HIV-positive, as did 4.4 per cent of young men (Shisana et al., 2005). Although the data are not directly comparable, those infection levels were very similar to those found in the 2003 national survey of 15-24 year-olds: 15.5 per cent among young women, and 4.8 per cent among young men (Pettifor et al., 2004). One in three women aged 30-34 years were living with HIV in 2005, as were one in four men aged 30-39 years, according to a 2005 national HIV household survey (Shisana et al., 2005).

South Africa's epidemic has matured to the stage where a large and growing number of AIDS deaths are now occurring. Despite the expanded roll-out of antiretroviral treatment, the AIDS death toll is likely to keep increasing until well into the next decade. The latest official mortality data show South Africans are dying in unprecedented numbers, at exceptional rates and at unusually young ages. Total deaths (from all causes) in South Africa increased by 87 per cent from 1997 to 2005 (from 316 505 to 591 213) (Statistics SA, 2005, 2006, 2007). Death rates for women aged 20-39 years more than tripled and for males aged 30-44 they more than doubled over that period. A large part of these trends in death rates is attributable to the AIDS epidemic (Anderson and Phillips, 2006; Actuarial Society of South Africa, 2005; Medical Research Council, 2005; Bradshaw et al., 2004; Dorrington et al., 2001). The increasing death toll has driven average life expectancy below 50 years in four provinces (Eastern Cape, Free State, KwaZulu-Natal, Mpumalanga) (Actuarial Society of South Africa, 2005).

Epidemiological imprints of inequality

William Budd's assessment of cholera in 19th century England – that "the disease not seldom attacks the rich, but it thrives most among the poor

(Budd, 1849)"—would seem to apply to AIDS, too, in South Africa.[2] Certainly, wealth and privilege does not provide a shield against HIV infection. But in South Africa, privilege seems to be associated with a swirl of contextual factors that deflects at least some of the risk.

Typically, such analysis does not aid attempts to rattle the complacency of the privileged. Which is why Budd went on to sermonise that "he that was never yet connected with his poorer neighbour, by deeds of charity or love, may one day find, when it is too late, that he is connected with him by a bond which may bring them both, at once, to a common grave" (Budd, 1849). Subsequently, others have sought to establish an empirical basis for such prompting. Richard Wilkinson, for example, argues that high levels of inequality aggravate health problems among the poor, but also cause overall health standards to deteriorate (Wilkinson, 2002) An injury to some becomes, in one way or another, an injury to all.

AIDS, though, seems to be cutting a much more discriminatory path through our society. The effects of an epidemic as sustained and intense as South Africa's ultimately will penetrate the breadth of society, but in various ways and to varying extents. Those effects are likely to be inordinately concentrated in and around the lives of the disadvantaged.

Poverty, inequality and HIV in South Africa

HIV infections are not distributed evenly in South Africa; infection levels differ significantly according to gender, age and population group.[3] HIV prevalence is considerably higher among black South Africans than among any other population group. A national HIV household survey in 2005 found HIV prevalence of 19.9 per cent among black African adults, 3.2 per cent among Coloureds, 1.0 per cent among Indians and 0.5 per cent among whites (Shisana et al., 2005).[4] Geographically, distribution also varies. Adult HIV prevalence in 2005 ranged from 26 per cent in KwaZulu-Natal, to 20-22 per cent in the Gauteng, Free State, Mpumalanga and North West provinces, and 8-12 per cent in Limpopo, Northern Cape and Western Cape (Shisana et al., 2005).

---

2. Regarded as virtually axiomatic in some circles, the association between poverty and HIV has been questioned in recent research in Africa. The debate is discussed below.

3. Women are significantly more likely to be HIV-infected than men: 20.2 per cent of adult women were living with HIV in 2005, compared with 11.7 per cent of men (Shisana et al., 2005).

4. The very small samples of Indians and whites mean it is possible that the prevalence figures are underestimations (Shisana et al., 2005). Subsequent analysis suggests that HIV incidence among black Africans older than two years was nine times higher in 2005 than among other South Africans: 1.8 per cent compared with 0.2 per cent (Rehle et al., 2007).

As in the rest of sub-Saharan Africa, infection levels in South Africa tend to be higher in urban and peri-urban areas compared with rural areas. The distribution of HIV in South Africa seems also to mirror the spatial order established under apartheid. HIV prevalence is by far the highest among persons living in urban and rural 'informal' areas, where it was 25.8 per cent and 17.3 per cent, respectively, in 2005 (Shisana et al., 2005). Needless to say, these are areas typified by high levels of livelihood insecurity, and poor infrastructure and services (Shisana et al., 2005).

The contours of privilege and deprivation in South Africa express deeply-lodged class, racial and spatial patterns of accumulation and dispossession. These are not static patterns. Since the mid-1980s especially, they have been modulated to varying degrees, but they retain distinct and familiar features. The vast majority of South Africans living in poverty are black Africans, among whom slightly more than half (55 per cent) were earning less than R400 per month in 2004. A full 16 per cent of Africans earned less than R100 a month in 2004, while, at the other end of the scale, a mere 3.2 per cent earned more than R5000 per month (Meth, 2006).

Even if HIV infections were distributed evenly among all income quintiles, as many as half of South Africans living with HIV would be persons surviving below the poverty line. According to UNDP (2003), 48.5 per cent of the population was living below that income threshold in 2003.

The potential interaction between various forms of deprivation and insecurity (poverty among them) and HIV risk is complex, and remains inadequately understood. In addition, there is some evidence that the interaction can be counterintuitive.[5] As of yet, there is no national population-based study that correlates income to HIV prevalence in South Africa. Nevertheless, research does indicate that poverty-related factors or 'stressors' are associated with higher HIV risk in South Africa. Kalichman et al., (2006), for example, conducted surveys in three residential settings – an overall impoverished African township, an economically impoverished but fairly well-serviced and racially integrated township, and a relatively wealthy urban neighborhood. The findings showed that HIV risks were closely related to poor education, unemployment, discrimination, violence and crime. (Alcohol and

---

5. See, for example, Mishra, V., 2006. Understanding the positive association between household wealth status and HIV prevalence in sub-Saharan Africa. Paper presented to the International AIDS Economic Network. Toronto, 11-12 August. A copy of the presentation is available at:
http://www.ukzn.ac.za/heard/whatsnew/AIDS2006pres/Presentations11aug/Vinod%20Mishra%20HIVWealth.ppt.

substance abuse did not moderate the effect of poverty stressors on HIV risk (Kalichman et al., 2006).[6] Several workplace and sectoral studies also provide evidence that HIV infections are disproportionately concentrated among poorer and lower-skilled South Africans, the majority of whom are black.

A national study among educators has found HIV prevalence was highest among those with lower socio-economic status: among those earning R132 000 (US$ 19,000) or more a year, HIV prevalence was 5.4 per cent, while among those earning less than R60 000 (US$ 8,000) a year, prevalence was 17.5 per cent (Shisana et al., 2005). An HIV prevalence survey among employees of the Buffalo City Municipality in 2004 found higher prevalence among temporary than permanent staff, with infection levels highest in the lowest skills levels (Thomas et al., 2005). Among health workers surveyed at private and public health facilities in four provinces, HIV prevalence was just under 14 per cent among professionals but exceeded 20 per cent among non-professional staff (Shisana et al., 2003). Among South African workers participating in a three-country seroprevalence survey of 34 major companies in 2000-2001, HIV prevalence was 15 per cent for unskilled workers, 18 per cent for their semi-skilled counterparts and 20 per cent for contract employees—but 7 per cent among skilled workers and 4 per cent among management staff (Evian et al., 2004). A recent analysis of the epidemiology of HIV in 22 public and private sector organisations in all nine provinces of South Africa, found that HIV prevalence among workers on average was more than twice as high as among managers (12.4 per cent compared with 5.3 per cent) (Colvin et al., 2006).

This does *not* mean that HIV infections are distributed in a neat, linear pattern that corresponds to income, with prevalence highest among the very poorest South Africans and then tapering off as incomes rise. Workplace studies illustrate patterns of infection among employed persons, who generally tend *not* to fall in the bottom income quintile. It is likely that, if charted, the correlation between HIV prevalence and income quintiles in South Africa would describe a distorted bell curve – with prevalence highest in the second and third quintiles, and considerably lower in the fourth and lowest in the fifth quintile.

Towards a political economy of AIDS

In the 1940s, the social epidemiologist Sidney Kark linked syphilis outbreaks to the migrant labour regimes servicing mining corporations

---

6. It is possible, too, that income poverty might also be a proxy for other risk factors that could include sociocultural and psychosocial factors.

in South Africa. Kark observed that "the problem of syphilis in South Africa is so closely related to the development of the country that a study of the social factors responsible for its spread is likely to assist in its control" (Kark, 1949).[7] South Africa's AIDS epidemic similarly iterates particular configurations of social, cultural and economic systems.

Many of the factors that appear to drive South Africa's AIDS epidemic are entangled in the social engineering and economic accumulation strategies that have moulded the society over the past 120 years. Large-scale circular migration and accelerated urbanisation (encompassing ever-greater numbers of women since the 1980s) are salient features against a background of rising unemployment levels. Systematic dispossession and dislocation, the destabilisation of social systems, the undermining of social cohesion (particularly in the urban peripheries) and the entrenching of highly unequal social relations helped create a social and ideological terrain that strongly favours the spread of sexually transmitted infections such as HIV (Walker et al., 2004). Taking shape in the slip-stream of such social engineering – and the chronic humiliation and disempowerment it entailed – were aggressive constructions of masculinity and the valorisation of sexual risk-taking, which spawned a kind hyper-machismo. These are partly reflected in South Africa's high rates of violence against women. High unemployment and the profound marginalisation of African women in the labour market have likely also encouraged resort to sexual liaison as a survival tactic or as a lever for fulfilling various aspirations (Hunter, 2007; Dunkle et al., 2004; LeClerc-Madlala, 2003).

In his examination of the changing political-economy of sex in South Africa, Hunter (2007) highlights the significant increase in female entrants into the labour market (which rose by two million in 1995-1999) while median wages for women fell sharply (Casale, 2004) – against a backdrop of collapsing agrarian and wage livelihoods generally. According to Hunter (2006: 19), South Africa's epidemic surged in a context where "the sexual economy overlapped with the informal economy in ways that involved a much larger number of people and reflected dramatic shifts in economic circumstances and household composition." He emphasises (2006: 21) that such ostensibly 'transactional' sexual networks "are not simply instrumental," but have complex affective, emotional and cultural dimensions, and are sometimes used also to foster kinship ties. Ultimately, it was "the coming together of very poor single women and economic hardship" that helped

---

7. Kark (1949) reprinted in *International Journal of Epidemiology*, 2003, 32(2): pp.181-186, and Myer, L. Morroni, C. & Susser E, S., 2003. Commentary: The social pathology of the HIV/AIDS pandemics. *International Journal of Epidemiology*, 32(2), pp.189-192.

cause the HIV epidemic to explode in South Africa (Hunter, 2006: 23). The AIDS epidemic is interlaced, in other words, with the circuits and terms on which power, opportunity and entitlements are distributed and desires and needs are pursued. In the case of South Africa, these remain highly unequal (Marais, 2005; Walker et al., 2004). The effects of AIDS morbidity and mortality are likely to reinforce those inequalities.[8]

Moreover, access to medical aid and other forms of health insurance is comparatively rare. Only 15 per cent of South Africans have any form of medical aid, according to Statistics SA (SSA, 2005). Among low-income earners (individuals in households earning less than R6,000 or US$ 850 a month) only 7 per cent have some form of medical scheme coverage (Broomberg, 2006). The racial disparities are striking: three out of four whites belong to medical schemes, compared with one out of fourteen black Africans (Ijumba and Ntuli, 2004). (Steps are underway to create a new class of medical scheme aimed at persons with an income of R2,000-R6,000 or US$ 280-850.) According to one survey, only one quarter of workers in the private sector have access to subsidised medical care (Torres et al., 2001). Community-based burial insurance and 'stokvels' are widespread: as many as 4 in 5 households in parts of the country belong to such schemes. But they provide meagre protection (De Swardt, 2003).

Savings levels are very low and debt levels are high. More than 90 per cent of poor households are paying off debt each month, according to one recent study, and one quarter of them are 'highly-indebted' (Saldru, 2005). In another study, between three quarters and nine-tenths of surveyed households had no savings whatsoever (de Swardt, 2003), while 85 per cent of urban and 89 per cent of rural respondents in a recent survey said it was 'difficult' or 'very difficult' to save (Everatt et al., 2006).[9] The baseline reality for a large proportion of South Africans, the majority of them African, is distressed and insecure with little padding to cushion the impact of shocks such as AIDS.

The unequal impact of AIDS

Two powerful dynamics are interlacing: on one hand, the deeply-embedded social and economic inequalities that define South African society and, on the other hand, a burden of disease – principally the

---

8. See, for example, Salinas, G. & Haacker, M., 2006. HIV/AIDS: The impact on poverty and inequality. IMF Working Paper WP/06/126. May. Washington: International Monetary Fund.

9. De Swardt C., 2003. Unravelling chronic poverty in South Africa: Some food for thought. Paper presented at the conference 'Staying poor: Chronic poverty and development policy', University of Manchester, 7-9 April.

overlapping AIDS and TB epidemics – which are disproportionately severe among the more vulnerable and disadvantaged sections of society.

AIDS piles hardship upon adversity. There is ample evidence that households affected by chronic illness tend to be poorer than other households—and in some cases by a wide margin. Those battling serious illness in a rural part of Zambia's Kafue district were found to have annual incomes 46 per cent lower than other households in the late 1990s (Topouzis, 2000) and a similar discrepancy was seen in a Cote D'Ivoire study around the same time (Bechu, 1998). This was partly due to the fact that the costs of health care are regressive—i.e. they impose a bigger burden on poor households, compared with their better-off counterparts. On average, poor households spend less on health-care, but those expenditures constitute a bigger share of their overall income than for wealthier households (Russel, 2003). It also expresses the fact that health outcomes tend to mirror other inequalities, and that health prospects are, to a significant extent, a function of the distribution of resources and power in society (Wilkinson, 2002; 1986).

AIDS corrodes household viability in many other ways, too. The reigning understanding is that AIDS robs households of income earners and carers, distorts expenditures patterns, depletes savings and assets, and erodes livelihoods. In sum, it further impoverishes the poor and threatens to dump even the relatively secure into poverty (Barnett & Whiteside, 2002; UNDP, 2001). According to Aliber, by 2010 AIDS could be expected to push between one quarter and one third more households into chronic impoverishment than would have been the case in the absence of the epidemic. This would mean that 24-30 per cent of households would be chronically poor (Aliber, 2003).[10]

The research evidence supports such forecasts. A longitudinal study in urban and rural parts of the Free State province has found that AIDS-affected households' income and expenditure were 10-20 per cent lower than unaffected households and that they spent 20-30 per cent less on food.[11] Income levels appeared to drop significantly after an AIDS death—due mainly, it seemed, to high funeral expenses (Booysen & Bachmann, 2002).[12] Note, though, that affected households also tended to be poorer than unaffected ones; the discrepancy in food expenditure could therefore also have preceded illness or death.

---

10. Aliber notes that these estimates do not take account of the indirect effects of AIDS on households and communities.

11. These findings were based on observations six months into the study.

12. According to a study in four South African provinces (Steinberg et al., 2002), households experiencing a death spent an average of one third of their annual incomes on funerals.

According to another study, conducted in four provinces, AIDS care-related expenses on average absorbed one third of their monthly household income (Steinberg et al., 2002). [13] Mills' (2004) research in KTC, Cape Town, made similar findings: AIDS-affected households were found to be rationing food and relying on donations of fruit and vegetables. Again, it's the underlying, pervasive poverty that catches the eye: almost 50 per cent of the households surveyed in the four-province study were already experiencing food shortages before AIDS struck (Steinberg et al., 2002).

But the uniform category of 'affected households' tends to obscure the variety and contingency of experiences and responses, and veils the unequal distribution of authority, duties and resources within households. This is especially obvious in the ways that gender relations distribute the effects of AIDS.

Gender, households and AIDS

The epidemic's impact at household level is complex and varying. Neither the effects nor the responses necessarily conform to a predictable pattern, but are shaped by a range of other factors that can fluctuate over time and according to circumstances. This has an important bearing on the kinds of policies and interventions that are most likely to cushion the epidemic's impact.

Many households, for example, regularly add and shed members—not only in response to their own predicaments and aspirations but also to those of others. When Hosegood et al., (2003) examined data gathered from some 10,000 households in Umkhanyakude district in rural northern KwaZulu-Natal, they found that households with an adult death tended to dispatch one or more of the surviving members elsewhere—probably to supplement income and reduce the strain on the household. Some households, however, seemed to dissolve after an adult death; those which had lost an adult to AIDS were three times more likely to dissolve than any other households. (Note that the rate of household dissolution might be overestimated in many studies, possibly because not enough effort is made to trace households that moved; see Mather et al., 2004.)[14] Similar patterns have been observed elsewhere in southern and in East Africa. But they by no means fully describe household shifts, the realities of which tend to be more obtuse.

---

13. A total of 771 households were surveyed in parts of Free State, Gauteng, KwaZulu-Natal and Mpumalanga.

14. According to Mather et al., (2004: 31), "panel surveys in Kenya, Malawi, and Rwanda show that while household dissolution does occur as a result of adult mortality, the rate of dissolution due to mortality is not as high as that found in some of the literature."

Household adjustments are not discreet events that occur linearly in a simple, cause-effect-cause-effect chain. In the KwaZulu-Natal study, for example, about half the households that took in unemployed members fell deeper into poverty, which is to be expected—but a similar proportion saw their income *rise* after adding unemployed members. Why? It appears that households that increase their overall income often also attract new members who are unemployed (causing per capita income to fall again). Or, after welcoming a new member, they despatch someone into the job market (whose remittances can send per capita income higher again). Whereas impact narratives tend to picture households reacting more or less mechanistically to misfortune, with AIDS the main variable, these (re)configurations remind that responses to AIDS illness or death are entangled with other, 'routine' adjustments. People try to remain agents of their destinies—but within limits that extinguish many, sometimes most, options.

The hidden toll of home- and community-based care

In all countries, women and girls perform the lion's share of social reproduction work—raising and nurturing children, schooling them in norms and values, managing their introduction into wider society, performing domestic labour and tending the ill, and much more. Most of this labour is not remunerated. In societies defined by extensive labour migration systems—including those hardest hit by the AIDS epidemic in Southern Africa—women also head a large share of households. Almost three quarters of 'AIDS-affected' households in South Africa are female-headed, a significant proportion of whom are also battling AIDS-related illnesses themselves, according to one study (Steinberg et al., 2002).[15] The epidemic's impact therefore pivots especially on the ways in which women are being affected: "[Their] burdens are greater, their time limited, and their lives shortened. Can social reproduction be secured when half of all adult women die before they are forty?" (De Waal, 2003a: 17).

Home- and community-based care are generally seen as a vital parts of the AIDS response. Elsewhere in Africa, the AIDS epidemic has underscored the fiscal frailty of the state and highlighted the public health system's apparent inability to meet care needs. Home- and community-based care came to be regarded with reverence since the

---

15. In 17 per cent of the cases, households heads were suffering from AIDS-related illnesses, and in a further 14 per cent of cases, household heads were described as chronically ill (a possible indicator of unrecognised HIV infection). See Steinberg et al., (2002: 12).

sheer volume of care needs in high-prevalence countries would swamp hospital and clinic systems. Limited public resources required that community organisations, NGOs and households step into the breach.

In South Africa's case, such an approach jibes well with the post-1994 overhaul of its health-care system, in which great emphasis is placed on ensuring that 'care in the community' becomes 'care by the community'.[16] In theory, this entails marshalling the respective strengths of households, of the communities they constitute and the organisations they spawn, and of the state—and create 'continuum of care' that boosts the quality, scale and sustainability of care (African National Congress, 2001). Home- and community-based care in particular would involve "the provision of health services by formal and informal caregivers in the home, in order to promote, restore and maintain a person's maximum level of comfort, function and health, including care toward a dignified death" (Department of Health, 2001a). In the Department of Health's view, the advantage of home-based care is that it is a cost-effective, cheap and flexible way of providing basic palliative and symptomatic care (Department of Health, 2001b).

In theory, all this seems admirable. By slotting home- and community-based care into a 'continuum of care' which links together the various levels and zones of the public health-care system and other role-players, the aim is to boost the quality, scale and sustainability of the care effort. In such a context, home-based care in South Africa is seen as a more humane and dignified form of care,[17] while community-based care is seen as a way of drawing on and enhancing communal solidarity and mutual assistance.[18] Supported in various ways by the public sector and NGOs, care-givers at the home and community levels would, to the extent possible, tend to the daily needs of patients, provide emotional support and help patients draw on 'formal' health-care and other services (for example, accessing grants, etc.). This would occur against a backdrop of 'integrated services' that addressed the basic needs of

---

16. Like most public health strategies of this era, the shift also consummated the centuries-long transformation of hospitals away from their previous functions as poor houses, orphanages and refuges for the mentally ill, and into secularised, medicalised and exclusive institutions.

17. The definition in the National Guideline on Home-based Care and Community-based Care makes that much clear. It defines home-based care as 'the provision of health services by formal and informal care-givers in the home in order to promote, restore and maintain a person's maximum level of comfort, function and health including care towards a dignified death' (African National Congress, 2001, cited in Mills, 2004: 3).

18. Thus the National Guideline defines it as care which "the consumer can access nearest to home, which encourages participation by people, responds to the needs of people, encourages traditional community life and creates responsibilities" (African National Congress, 2001, cited in Mills, 2004: 4).

people infected with or affected by AIDS to food, shelter, education, health care and more.

The reality is more profane. Home- and community-based care might reduce the cost of care to the health system (and state), but it does so in the main by displacing costs onto care-givers, patients and the neighbourhoods they live and work in—with women bearing the brunt (Mills, 2004). As Hunter (2006) reminds, imbedded in home- and community-based care are stout assumptions about the respective roles of the state, the family and women within in it.

The burdens are shifted mainly in two ways. Firstly, patients (and care-givers trying to tend to their health and other needs) bear the cost of not receiving the levels of care and support they require—the consequences of which spill across households and families. Secondly, patients and care-givers themselves often subsidise care provision (investing their time, borrowing and lending money, paying for transport, consultancy fees, food and more). Thus the poor subsidise the poor. These appear to be widespread features of home-based care, not just in South Africa but elsewhere in the sub-region too.

Such outcomes fit squarely within neoliberal frameworks of social governance and resource allocation. In Hunter's summary (2006: 4), they involve:

new frameworks for the allocation of resources for individual and social welfare ... between the state, the family, the market, and the voluntary and informal sectors ... social citizenship therefore appears to be giving way to market citizenship, where citizens now become responsible for helping themselves.

The fetish of 'coping'

A curious paradox emerges. Reams of studies have appeared examining the impact of AIDS. The literature and the programmes aimed at cushioning that impact tend to share a deep faith in the presumed pluck, grit and altruism of the poor. Households are described in sweeping, generalising terms—ignoring the many inequalities and other dynamics, internal and external, that shape them and the communities they constitute. The hobbling circumstances of households are acknowledged in cursory manner (they are 'poor'), but the systemic reproduction of those realities usually escapes mention. A similar blind-spot occurs in poverty research and analysis generally, as John Harriss (2007) has reminded.

Ritually talked up are interventions that can 'empower' households, strengthen kinship and community safety nets, and support the 'coping strategies' households deploy. All this seems beyond reproach. The resilience, resourcefulness and endurance people deploy in the throes of adversity can be a marvel. But this does not remove the unsightly, sometimes cynical, assumptions that lurk in an unquestioning admiration for 'coping' capacities.

To 'cope' is to 'deal successfully' with hardship or misfortune; it's to see off adversity. Thus a 'coping strategy' is generally understood to be a coherent set of actions aimed at managing the costs of an event or a process that threatens the welfare of a household. At the very least it involves returning to the *status quo ante*, at the very best it enables one to achieve a better state of affairs than had pertained. To be sure, some studies have indicated that a partial recovery in consumption levels can eventually occur, suggesting that the households have overcome the shock and are again 'coping'. But to describe as 'coping' the activities of households sunk in impoverishment is to unmoor the discussion from ethics. By any humane definition of the word, such households are not 'coping'; a 'successful coping strategy' becomes an oxymoron. Regaining a precarious and chronically insecure form of household 'viability' cannot reasonably be declared a success.

Tapping into networks of mutual assistance and other forms of social support are vital aspects of poor persons' survival strategies. But these social connections tend to lack a transcendent thrust powerful enough to propel the poor out of poverty. "Social networks and relations at best seem to stabilise incomes, but provide little in the way of longer-term accumulation or economic advance," is the conclusion of Adato, Carter and May (2006: 245) after reviewing South African poverty and trends for 1993-1998 and 1998-2001.

Indeed, as Davies (1993) has pointed out in the context of famine studies, coping strategies actually are not about success—they're about failure. They can enable one to survive, but not to transcend the circumstances that trapped one in the path of mishaps in the first place. Implicit in the discourse of 'coping' is an acceptance, an endorsement even, of the way things are, a patronising gloss on a reality of privation and marginality.

It's instructive to track the lineage of 'coping' strategy-speak, which acquired theoreticised footing during the African famines of the 1980s as part of efforts to explain—and anticipate—households' responses to disasters. Researchers sought to answer three important questions: what strategies did households use to survive, could coping strategies be used as a kind of 'early warning system' for impending famines, and what kinds of support could buttress those strategies? (Goudge & Govender, 2000). From this emerged a relatively standard schema that described a sequence of responses that contained a 'tipping point' beyond which households would 'plunge' or 'tip over' into destitution and, quite possibly, dissolution.[19] This notion of famine as a unique, singular shock would later be adopted in the AIDS impact literature, even after a more refined understanding had found favour in famine studies. (By the early 1990s, studies were placing famine-related shocks in the wider context of long-term and structural vulnerability; the shocks, in other words, formed part of an agglomeration of chronic adversities.)[20] The concept of 'coping strategies' entered AIDS discourse in the late 1990s[21] amid a spate of research into the effects of the epidemic on households (and their likely capacities to mount and/or participate in home- and community-based care programmes) (Rugalema, 2000; Ogden & Esim, 2003).

But 'coping' strategy orthodoxy emerged also against the backdrop of ascendant neoliberalism (Bailies, 2002), with states shorn of their capacities to fulfill key societal duties and were recast as little more than interlocutors between the market and individuals. In subsequent years, notions of community resilience and coping strategy gathered enthusiastic support among multilateral agencies, some of them active promoters of structural adjustment programmes in the South. After years of scorched-earth social policy directives, 'the community' found itself cast in an almost redemptive role as a repository of unfathomed vigour, invention and grit. Coping dogma schematised those qualities.

Home- and community-based care and 'coping' dogma orbit around similar principles and assumptions, central among them the consigning of care to the sphere of the home. This veritable 'privatisation' has coincided with the increasingly implacable subordination of social life to the rules of the market. As more dimensions of life and work are ceded to the rule of the market, the responsibility for providence and calamity, for life and death is lodged with ever-smaller units of society (and is ultimately, in the neoliberal ideal, ceded to the individual). Hence the loud iteration of household and community 'resilience', and its centrality in policy and strategy.

In practice, in a society like South Africa, the model rests on and underwrites a *status quo* of unconscionable inequality. Neoliberal discourse, of course, tries to skip around such contradictions. It

---

19. See, for example, Walker, P., 1989. *Famine early warning systems: Victims and destitution.* London: Earthscan Publication.

20. See, for example, De Waal, A., 1989. *Famine that kills: Darfur, Sudan, 1984-1985.* Oxford: Clarendon Press; Keen, D., 1994. *The benefits of famine: A political economy of famine and relief in southwestern Sudan, 1983-1989.* New Jersey: Princeton University Press.

21. See, for example, UNAIDS 1999. A review of household and community responses to the HIV/AIDS epidemic in the rural areas of sub-Saharan Africa. Geneva: UNAIDS Best Practice Collection.

proposes, for example, that households' and communities' close knowledge of their circumstances and environment enables them to act as rational agents within a market-governed context. In theory, the market, by rewarding and penalising various courses of action over time, not only confers a good deal of this accumulated 'knowledge' but also imbues households' and communities' actions with rationality (Rugalema, 2000). When ambushed by adversity, households juggle alternatives and take decisions which, however apparently unpalatable, ultimately yield rational and provident outcomes. Such assumptions, although rendered in slightly more fragrant manner, circulate also in many multilateral agencies' thinking. Hence the widely-embraced tenet that what's required to make home- and community-based care 'work' is a secondary, reliable infusion of support from other sources, including the state. The fundamental, overriding narrative of amputated options and foreclosed alternatives is backhandedly endorsed as 'the way things are'.

Ubuntu and the market

South African history applies a further twist. On one hand, an ethos of communalism and mutual obligation survives and is encoded in social practices and arrangements. Since the mid-1990s, that ethos has been enlisted also in an avowedly Africanist project of ideological recuperation and self-identification that taps into indigenous popular practices, "the capacity for innovation, reinvention of traditions and resurgence of native skills" (Ela, 1998). As a result, it now also forms part of the 'language' or signifiers of identity and distinction that circulate in South Africa. In this sense, the ethos appears to be in fine fettle.

On the other hand, the fracturing impact of colonial and apartheid social engineering—and, in its wake, the ascendancy of values appropriate to the hyper-animated consumerism that governs increasingly large parts of social life—should not be underestimated. Alongside this ranged the government's attempts to restrain claims on state beneficence and social provisions, as part of 1996 Growth, Employment and Redistribution (GEAR) strategy. The promotion of self-empowerment and community responsibility meshed well with a policy framework that sought to restrict claims on the state (Barchiesi, 2005). Indeed, the system, as Shireen Hassim (2005: 3-4) has reminded, "remains constrained by narrow conceptions of the state and by distrust of rights-based demands on state resources."

All this while poverty, joblessness and disease saps the support that can be proffered. Powerful dynamics are shrinking the boundaries in which obligations and entitlements circulate, and the extent of support that is on offer.[22] It is within this material and ideological environment that home- and community-based care practices operate. An odd confluence occurs between two apparently contrary ideologies: *ubuntu* and neoliberalism.

The guiding principles of communitarianism, mutual assistance and the bonding sense of shared destinies that underpin *ubuntu* provide a bedrock for the anticipated community-level resilience and solidarity that is expected to animate and sustain home- and community-based care. The strategy of home-based care in particular rests on such assumptions. This is surprisingly compatible with a central thrust of neoliberalism – which is to absolve or at least excuse the state from its encompassing responsibility for social reproduction. On one hand, then, there is the aggrandised faith in 'coping' capacities at community and household levels; on the other, government strategies are marked with an overarching obeisance to the market and its organising principles. Around AIDS, these two, apparently contradictory, value patterns converge. This is not to disparage the associational flowering that *ubuntu* is meant to evoke and which home- and community-based care, in theory at least, could entail, but to underline the wretched inequality and exploitation this cloaks as 'normalcy'. Claude Ake's cautioning rejoinder to the celebration of "an explosion of associational life in rural Africa," seems better-aligned with reality:

> By all indications, this is a by-product of a general acceptance of the necessity of self-reliance ... Some have welcomed this development as a sign of a vibrant civil society in Africa. It may well be that. However, before we begin to idealise this phenomenon, it is well to remind ourselves that whatever else it is, it is first and foremost a child of necessity, of desperation even.[23]

To pretend that home- and community-based care express a reanimated social solidarity that can supplant the logic and the ethics of the market is to miss the plot entirely. While the well-being of the poor becomes

---

22. Mutangadura's (2000) research findings in urban and rural Manicaland, Zimbabwe, are instructive. Fully 95 per cent of respondents said it was difficult getting relatives and friends to help with loans or child fostering. Community support mainly involved food and clothing, and rarely extended to assistance in paying school or health-care fees or rent. This underscores the need to waive at least certain fees and to extend and deliver state grants more effectively.
23. Quoted by Bond, P., (2001). The African grassroots and the global movement. January. Znet. Available at:
http://www.zmag.org/CrisesCurEvts/Globalism/african_grassroots.htm. The quote is drawn from Ake, C., 2000. *The feasibility of democracy in Africa*. Dakar: Codesria.

ever more precarious, additional burdens are being shifted onto them. Celebrating this as an expression of hardiness and vim, an affirmation of *ubuntu*, seems morally base. In practice, home- and community-based care displaces much of the burden of care into the 'invisible' zones of the home and the neighbourhood—and especially onto women, most of them poor, many of them desperately so.

The model reinforces firmly-entrenched assumptions about women and domesticity, about their roles as bearers of children, nurses of the sick, nurturers of families. It rests on and further entrenches the assumption that 'care' is what 'comes naturally' to women, effectively locking women even more securely into the domestic sphere.[24] The esteem and worth women draw from this should not be belittled, circumscribed as it is. It is worth recalling that the ideology of motherhood and the realities of women's fortitude were enlisted very successfully as part of the idiom of the South African national liberation struggle, becoming "a defining trope in nationalist discourses on gender" (Hassim, 2005: 628). The burdens and responsibilities borne by women often are extraordinary, but generally the expectations they live up to are an utterly conventional iteration that women shall serve, literally, as 'mothers of a nation'. Home-based care today ratchets up the exploitation of women's labour, financial and emotional reserves—a form of value extraction that subsidises the economy at every level from the household outward; little wonder that such 'enforced', free care-giving has been likened to levying a tax on women (Glendinning and Millar, 1987).

State support for home- and community-based care is too threadbare, unpredictable and poorly-coordinated to reduce those burdens to any significant extent.[25] In sum, home- and community-based care is not 'cheap'. It only appears that way because the true costs are hidden, deflected back into the communities and domestic zones of the poor. Not only is this unjust, it also undermines the sustainability of care provision in the drawn-out crisis that AIDS presents. Expecting the poor to provide the backbone and lifeblood of care—with a minimum of structured support—is unreasonable and unrealistic.

---

24. When quizzed, care-givers complain, for example, that they are expected 'to be always around home' and have 'to do everything'; as reported in assessments of care-giving projects in Khayelitsha, Gugulethu and Delft (Cape Town), 2004; personal communication.

25. Hunter's analysis of the 2004/05 spending and allocation figures of the KwaZulu-Natal departments of health and social welfare showed that 0.2-0.3 per cent of total allocations went toward supporting home-based care in general (not only for AIDS-related care) (2006: 8). That, in the province with the largest number of persons living with HIV in South Africa.

South Africa's dual health-care system, of course, mirrors such disparity. One part of it is a profit-making venture, run by the private sector and fed with contributions to medical and other insurance schemes. Its clientele represent not only the wealthier but the healthier in society. Hence a good deal of its services are highly-niched and arcane. The other part is an overburdened public health sector. The danger, of course, was that the restructuring of the public health system—noble intent notwithstanding—would serve as a footnote to these much more robust and polarising trends that shape health care provision and the allocation of resources across society in general. As a percentage of gross domestic product, public health expenditure in 2000 was 3.7 per cent, while private health expenditure was 5.1 per cent, an exceptional ratio that is seen in fewer than two dozen countries around the world (UNDP, 2003b).[26] The private sector, which is accessible to less than one fifth of the population, consumes more than 60 per cent of health-spend and employs more than 70 per cent of healthcare specialists (Yach & Kitsnasamy, 2006). The principle of universalism lacks even a toehold in this arrangement. Government promises to expand access to medical insurance, and make it more affordable. However, the dualism (which is not of the government's making) will remain in place and will continue to define the quality of health-care provision and the terms on which it is provided. And it is expressed—and reinforced—in home- and community-based care.

Deflecting the economic costs

That South Africa's epidemic will affect economic activities seems beyond dispute—but it is much less obvious what the extent of that damage might be. Some estimates seem to trivialise the effect of AIDS by suggesting a negligible effect on national economic output, while others anticipate severe damage.[27] The disagreements stem from the fact that the estimates rest on different assessments of the epidemic's demographic impact, about the channels along which AIDS affects the economy, and about the nature of those effects themselves.

---

26. Only one of those countries (the United States of America) ranks in the top 60 of the UNDP's Human Development Index. Countries with similar ratios include Brazil, Cambodia, Cameroon, Dominican Republic, El Salvador, Georgia, India, Kenya, Lebanon, Morocco, the USA, Viet Nam and Yemen. See UNDP (2003b: 254-257).

27. AIDS: SA not facing doomsday scenario. *Mail and Guardian*, 13 July 2006. http://www.mg.co.za/articlePage.aspx?articleid=277346&area=/breaking_news/breaking_news_business/;

Arndt, C. & Lewis J., 2000. The macro implications of HIV/ AIDS in South Africa: A preliminary assessment. *South African Journal of Economics*, 68(5), pp.856-887.

The direct costs of AIDS to organisations and businesses tend to manifest in the form of higher health-care costs and more expensive workers' benefits, while the indirect costs take the form of reduced productivity, loss of skills, experience and institutional memory, as well as (re)training and recruitment time and expenses. Indirect costs are significantly higher for skilled workers, as are employee benefit costs (Whiteside and O' Grady, 2003). In a serious AIDS epidemic, such costs can add up to a hidden employment or payroll tax (De Waal, 2003).

South Africa has a very stratified labour pool, marked by shortages of highly-skilled workers and a surplus of low- and medium-skilled workers. Increased demand for an already-limited pool of skilled and highly skilled labour could push up wages and salaries at that end of the labour market. Some analysts expect the epidemic to also discourage private-sector investment in skills training and education, with companies more inclined to poach or lure top skills from elsewhere in the world, especially from other African countries (Vaas, 2003). One effect of this would be to widen income inequalities.

A handful of major companies have introduced high-profile ARV treatment programmes for some of their employees, and several more also emphasise HIV prevention. At least one major retailer has diversified its operations abroad and tightened credit control systems in a bid to limit the anticipated effect of the epidemic on its market share.[28] Most companies, though, especially medium-sized ones, seem to be taking AIDS in their stride. They have considerable leeway for deflecting the effects of the epidemic—and they are using it (Rosen and Simon, 2003).

In bids to achieve greater flexibility in production and employment, companies continue to shift the terms on which they use labour, a trend that predates AIDS but is having a huge effect on working South Africans' abilities to cushion themselves against the effects of the epidemic. AIDS is likely to intensify that trend (Nattrass, 2002). Companies have been intensifying the adoption of labour-saving work methods and technologies (spurred by a host of incentives) (Rosen et al, 2006), the outsourcing and casualisation of jobs (and the use of labour brokers for recruiting new workers), and cutting worker benefits (Rosen and Simon, 2003; Rosen et al., 2006; Vass, 2002). When surveyed in 2004, almost one quarter of mining companies and almost one fifth of manufacturing companies reported that they were investing in machinery and equipment in order to reduce their labour dependency because of AIDS (Bureau for Economic Research, 2004). Partly as a result of such

---

28. What next for retail? *Moneyweb*, 15 February 2002. Available at:
http://moneyweb.iac.iafrica.com/shares/boardroom_talk/366902.htm

changes, unemployment levels remain very high, and real wages for lower and medium-skilled workers have stagnated or declined (depending on the sector) in the past decade (Altman, 2005).

For the minority of employed workers with access to private health insurance (roughly one quarter in 2001), medical benefits are now often capped at levels far too low to cover the costs of serious ill health or injury, while companies have been slashing employer contributions and requiring that workers pay a larger share of the premiums for the same benefits. By 2000, on average more than one third of workers with access to medical schemes had withdrawn from them because they couldn't afford to pay their contributions.[29] According to one of South Africa's largest insurance companies, the burden of medical aid costs is being borne by employees.[30] Regulatory changes proposed by the South African Government in 2006 could improve some workers' access to medical insurance schemes, but 'casual' and 'piecemeal' workers are unlikely to benefit. In addition, a major shift has also occurred from defined-benefit retirement funds to defined-contribution funds (the latter offering meagre help to workers felled, for example, by disease in the prime of their lives) (Barchiesi, 2004; Van Den Heever, 1998). The net effect is a whittling of benefits for those South Africans with jobs—at a time when they and their families face increased risks of severe illness and premature death. Left to fend for themselves, meanwhile, are the masses of 'casual' workers, and the unemployed.

While such adjustments are enabling many companies (particularly larger ones) to sidestep much of the epidemic's impact, many thousands of small enterprises lack similar evasive abilities.

The faith in entrepreneurial activity as a route out of poverty is well-entrenched. But it's not at all clear to what extent demand exists to drive significant growth in small and micro enterprise development in poor communities (Aliber, 2003). The impoverishing effect of AIDS on poor households further underlines that question. As the epidemic shrinks household incomes, small businesses are likely to be badly-affected—especially those in the 'informal sector' of the economy which rely heavily on the custom of poor households, such as informal retailers, spaza shops and 'microenterprises', which typically are operated by vulnerable households themselves. Cohen's (2002) anticipation that reduced discretionary household spending due to AIDS would hamstring capacities to invest in informal sector activities, is plausible in South

---

29. Will your trustee fund survive AIDS? *Old Mutual Trustee Times,* February 2000.
30. Old Mutual (2003). *Old Mutual Healthcare Survey 2003.* Cape Town: Old Mutual. http://www2.oldmutual.com/CR/reports/ccr/2003/indicators/economic/customers/needs.htm

Africa, too. As well, reduced growth in demand for informal sector sector services and goods is equally likely. Give that the growth of the informal sector is partly a response to high unemployment, such outcomes would further sharpen the socio-economic insecurity of poor households.

In such ways, many of the costs of the epidemic are 'socialised'— trapped or deflected into the lives, homes and neighbourhoods of the poor. A massive, regressive redistribution of risk and responsibility is underway.

Conclusion

In a society with South Africa's characteristics, the AIDS epidemic feeds off and aggravates existing inequalities. A range of deflective factors and actions – some systemic, others more calculated – funnel the most grievous effects of the epidemic in and around the households of the poor. High unemployment, income precariousness, and employers' grab-back of workers' wages and benefits are some examples. Another is the current reality of home-based care, which expresses a basic assumption lodged in South African economic policy: that rationed social welfare spending will be subsidised by women's unpaid labour (Naidoo & Bozalek, 1997).

The epidemic and its effects are long-term, and these will remain severe for at least another generation – leaving in their wake deeper impoverishment, wider inequality and intensified polarisation. The ultimate extent and duration of these outcomes will depend partly on whether South Africans can improve and expand HIV prevention, treatment and care efforts, and at the same time temper the effects felt by the disadvantaged and distressed sections of society.

These basic components of an AIDS response – along with efforts to reduce HIV transmission from mothers to children, and develop effective microbicides and, hopefully, vaccines – form the backbone of South Africa's new AIDS Strategic Plan for 2007-2011 (Government of South Africa, 2007). The Plan, which has drawn widespread praise, also includes a set of objectives aimed at reducing "vulnerability to HIV infection and the impact of AIDS" by reducing gender inequality and gender-based violence, "accelerat[ing] poverty reduction strategies and strengthen[ing] safety nets" (Government of South Africa, 2007: 61-63). Chief among those interventions are:

- Scaling up access to government poverty alleviation programmes,

- Ensuring equitable provision of basic social services (especially in rural and urban informal settlements, where HIV prevalence tends to be highest),
- Introducing a sustainable income transfer system for poor families,
- Implementing all national policies and legislation aimed at improving the status of women,
- Increasing the proportion of vulnerable children accessing social grants,
- Recruiting and training 25,000 new community care givers by 2011 and paying each of them a stipend (Government of South Africa, 2007: 61-63, 95-96).

Implicit in those requirements is a recognition that stronger social protection is needed to mitigate the epidemic's impact. Some of the basic elements of such a package already feature in current Government commitments and policies. So, for example, social grants serve as a lifeline for millions of South Africans, while access to basic services continues to expand. Similarly, food security ranks among Government's many social development commitments. But current efforts to protect people against hunger are dwarfed by the scale of need and the trammeled capacity – and will – to meet that need. Indeed, various surveys indicate that between one quarter and one third of households cannot afford to meet the dietary requirements of children at any given time (Roberts, 2005).

The compounding and discriminatory nature of AIDS impact in South Africa demands a more far-reaching response that slots into an overarching programme of rights-realisation and redistribution that strongly favours the poor.

Leaving aside the need for deeper, structural changes in South Africa's development path, trends as severe as these underline the importance of social protection in any strategy aimed at shielding households against privation and precariousness. In the South African context, social grants are proving to be a powerful tool in that respect. More than a mere stopgap, they are potentially an integral *part* of a long-term social protection strategy.

The best evidence indicates that South Africa currently has no better poverty-alleviating tool than its social transfer system, especially the child support grant and old-age pension (Lund, 2007). Indeed, the single-biggest income poverty-reducing instrument currently is the child support grant (Meth, 2006; Everatt et al., 2006).[31] Whether measured by income or by a more expansive matrix, poverty levels have fallen since 2000-2001 (Everatt et al., 2006). According to Van der Berg et al., (2004), the poverty headcount fell by 3 million in 2001-2004.[32] However, Meth's careful examination of the data (2006)[33] calls into question van der Berg's suggestion that "improved job creation in recent years" possibly also lowered the poverty head count, and shifts the poverty head count decrease closer to 1.5 million.[34]

There is also ample evidence of the poverty-reducing and developmental functions of such transfers in the South African context (Aguero, Carter, Woolard, 2006; Barrientos, DeJong, 2006; ODI, 2006; EPRI, 2004; De Swardt, 2003; Taylor Committee, 2002). The observed effects include improved school enrolment, reduced stunting in children, and better nutrition levels. Aguero, Carter and Woolard (2006: 25) point out the long-term effects of improved child nutrition, including improved physical and mental development which is likely to affect school performance and, later, labour productivity. Case, Hosegood and Lund (2004) have found a positive association between receipt of the child support grant and school enrolment of young children.[35] Booysen & Van der Berg's (2005) research in the Free State province among AIDS-affected households echo such findings. Social grants, they found, reduce inequality and decrease the prevalence, depth and severity of poverty in those households. Disturbingly, however, they also found that uptake of available grants was weakest among the poorest households, probably an index of their social exclusion (Booysen and Van der Bert, 2005).

---

31. See van der Berg, S. Burger, R. Louw, M. and Yu, D., 2005. Trends in poverty and inequality since the political transition, Stellenbosch Economic Working Papers No: 1
32. A heartless irony is also at play, however. Several factors – central among them the AIDS epidemic – have pushed South Africa's population growth rate into decline. (Note that it is the growth rate that is declining, not the population size.) In 2004-2005, the growth rate was estimated at 0.92%, down from 1.1-1.2 per cent a decade earlier.
33. See page 9, in particular, for a trenchant example of the politicisation of data.
34. Meth claims to find no evidential basis for assuming that *disability* grants have reduced the poverty headcount, or for determining by how much they might do so. One reason for this is that it is not clear to what extent the grant in fact meets the special needs of the disabled.
35. There is no evidence to support claims that young women are deliberately having children in order to claim the child support grant. See, for example, Makiwane, M. & Udjo, E., 2007. Is the Child Support Grant associated with an increase in teenage fertility in South Africa? Evidence from national surveys and administrative data. Final Report. December. Pretoria: Human Sciences Research Council. Biyase's (2005) analysis of data also found no association between the child support grant and fertility rates; see Biyase, M., 2005. A simple analysis of the impact of the child support grant on the fertility rate in South Africa. Paper. Available at:
http://www.essa.org.za/download/2005Conference/Biyase2.pdf

Expanding social grants – for example, by increasing and extending the eligibility for child support grants (Lund, 2007) or by introducing a new instrument such as a basic income grant – would be one, essential cornerstone of a stronger social protection package. In the context of the overlapping AIDS and TB epidemics, such a package also has to include a drastic overhaul of the current home- and community-based care systems. Stronger financial and institutional support, more user-friendly administrative procedures, and a much sharper focus on using and developing existing skills in communities in order to boost access to social services should be one priority. That could include developing a para-professional cadre to improve community access to services such as early child development and education, and various forms of care provision (including, urgently, mental health care and support) (Altman 2005: 448).[36] Their value and importance are intuitively obvious, even if this does not reveal itself neatly in spreadsheet arithmetic: sharing and socialising the individualised burdens caregivers currently bear with respect to care-giving, reducing the mental health strain in stressed households and communities, providing a more solid and reliable basis for the development of human capital, strengthening social cohesion, and possibly even increasing gender equity in home and family. This could help reduce the extreme exploitation of women in the spheres of care provision and social reproduction.

Such a protection package would also include job creation strategies that benefit the masses of low-skilled jobless workers, a restructured system of social transfers, a more resolute strategy to ensure food security, a massive boost for community social services (including overhaul of the home- and community-based care system), and decommodification of essential services (to ensure that the poorest 30-40 per cent of households benefit manner from improvements in social wage provision). AIDS is hardly the only shock wrenching lives, homes and communities in South Africa apart. But it casts a horrifying light on the need for a comprehensive social protection strategy that forms part of an enveloping programme of rights-realisation.

References

Actuarial Society of South Africa. 2003. AIDS and demographic model. Cape Town: Actuarial Society of South Africa.

---

36. Some steps are being taken in that direction, such as the Early Childhood Development Programme and support for orphan care projects. The funding requirements, though, can be labyrinthine, partly because the purse strings are controlled at provincial level – which can lead to delays and frustrating application and reporting procedures.

Adato M. Carter, M.R. and May, J. 2006. Exploring poverty traps and social exclusion in South Africa using qualitative and quantitative data. *Journal of Development Studies*, 42(2), pp.226-247.

African National Congress. 2001. A national guideline on home-based care and community based care. Johannesburg: African National Congress.

Aguero, J.M. Carter, M.R. and Woolard, I., 2006. The impact of unconditional cash transfers on nutrition: The South African Child Support Grant. Paper. Available at: http://www.cgdev.org/doc/events/11.07.06/unconditional%20cash%20transfers. pdf;

Altman, M., 2005. The state of employment. In J. Daniel, R. Southall, J. Lutchman, eds. 2005. *State of the nation: South Africa 2004-2005*. Cape Town: HSRC Press.

Anderson, B.A., & Phillips, H.E., 2006. *Adult mortality (age 15-64) based on death notification data in South Africa: 1997-2004*. Report No. 03-09-05. Pretoria, Statistics South Africa: Actuarial Society of South Africa.

Barchiesi, F., 2004. Classes, multitudes and the politics of community movements in post-apartheid South Africa. Paper presented at the 'How class works' conference, 10-12 June. State University of New York, Stonybrook

Barchiesi, F., 2005. Social citizenship and the transformations of wage labour in the making of post-apartheid South Africa, 1994-2001. Ph.D. Dissertation, University of Witwatersrand, Johannesburg.

Barnett, T. & Whiteside, A., 2002. *AIDS in the 21st century: Disease and globalisation*. London: Palgrave MacMillan.

Booysen, F. & Van der Bert, S., 2005. The role of social grants in mitigating the socio-economic impact of HIV/AIDS in two Free State communities. *South African Journal of Economics*, 73(s1), pp. 531-640.

Broomberg, J., 2006. Consultative Investigation into Low Income Medical Schemes (LIMS). Available at:

http://www.medicalschemes.com/publications/ZipPublications/Low%20Income%20M edical%20Scheme%20Publications/LIMS%20Final%20Report%20Draft%2028-2-06.doc.

Budd, W., 1849. Malignant Cholera: Its Mode of Propagation and Its Prevention. London: John Churchill.

Bureau for Economic Research. 2004. The impact of HIV/AIDS on selected business sectors in South Africa, University of Stellenbosch.

Casale, D., 2004. What has the feminisation of the labour market bought women in South Africa? Trends in labour force participation, employment and earnings, 1995-2001. Development Policy Research Unit Working Paper, 04(84). Cape Town.

Cohen, D., 2002. Human capital and the HIV epidemic in sub-Saharan Africa. Working paper 2. International Labour Organisation. Geneva.

Colvin, M. Connolly, C. and Madurai, L., 2006. *The epidemiology of HIV in South African workplaces*. AIDS, in press.

De Swardt, C., 2003. Unravelling chronic poverty in South Africa: Some food for thought. Paper presented at the conference 'Staying poor: Chronic poverty and development policy', University of Manchester, 7-9 April.

De Waal, A., 2003. Why the HIV/AIDS pandemic is a structural threat to Africa's governance and economic development. *Fletcher Forum of World Affairs*, 27(2), pp.6-24.

Department of Health. 2001a. National guidelines on home-based care and community-based care. Available at:

http://doh.gov.za/docs/factsheets/guidelines/homecare/index.html

Department of Health. 2001b. An enhanced response to HIV/AIDS and tuberculosis in the public health sector – key components and funding requirements, 2002/03 – 2004/05. Available at: http://www.doh.gov.za/aids/docs/response.html

Economic impact of AIDS in South Africa: A dark cloud on the horizon. ING Barings 2000.

Ela, J., 1998. Looking to a new Africa. *Le Monde Diplomatique*. October. Paris, cited in Marais, H., 2001. Principle and expediency: South Africa and the African Renaissance. Conference paper. April. Dakar.

Everatt, D. Smith, M.J. Solanki, G., 2006. Baseline survey of the 21 ISRDP and URP nodes. Research study for the Department of Social Development. November. Johannesburg:Department of Social Development.

Evian, C. et al., 2004. Prevalence of HIV in workforces in southern Africa, 2000-2001. *South African Medical Journal*, 94(2), pp.125-130.

Glendinning, C. & Millar, J. eds., 1987. *Women and poverty in Britain*. Harvester Press, cited in A. Mills, 2004. citing African National Congress 1994. *A national health plan for South Africa*. African National Congress. Johannesburg.

Government of South Africa. 2007. *HIV & AIDS and STI Strategic Plan for South Africa, 2007-2011*. April. Pretoria: Government of South Africa.

Harriss, J., 2007. Bringing politics back in to poverty analysis: Why understanding of social relations matters more for policy on chronic poverty than measurement. Q-Squared Working Paper no.34. April. Toronto: Centre for International Studies.

Hassim, S., 2005. Turning Gender Rights into Entitlements: Women and Welfare Provision in Post-apartheid South Africa. *Social Research*, 72(3), pp.621-646.

Hassim, S., 2005. Gender, welfare and the developmental state in South Africa. Draft working document. Geneva: United Nations Research Institute for Social Development.

Hunter, M., 2006. Was the scale of the South African AIDS pandemic inevitable? Rethinking the political economy of sex in contemporary South Africa. Draft paper. Hanover: Dartmouth College.

Hunter, M., 2007. The changing political economy of sex in South Africa: The significance of unemployment and inequalities to the scale of the AIDS pandemic. *Social Science & Medicine*, 64(3), pp.689-700.

Hunter, N., 2006. Crises in social reproduction in a developmental state: Home-based care in KwaZulu-Natal. Working paper. School of Development Studies, University of KwaZulu-Natal, Durban.

Ijumba, P. Day, C. and Ntuli, A., 2004. South Africa health review 2003/2004. Health Systems Trust. Available at: http://www.hst.org.za/publications/423

Kalichman, S.C. et al., 2006. Associations of poverty, substance use, and HIV transmission risk behaviors in three South African communities. *Social Science and Medicine*, 62(7), pp.1641-1649.

Kark, S.L., 1949. The social pathology of syphilis in Africans. *South African Medical Journal*, 23, pp.77-84.

Lund, F., 2007. Changing social policy: The child support grant in South Africa. Cape Town: HSRC Press.

Marais, H., 2006. *Buckling: The impact of AIDS in South Africa*. Pretoria: Centre for the Study of AIDS, University of Pretoria.

Meth, C., 2006. *Income poverty in 2004: A second engagement with the recent van der Berg et al figures*. Working Paper 47. September. School of Development Studies. University of KwaZulu-Natal, Durban.

Mills, A., 2004. citing African National Congress 1994. *A national health plan for South Africa*. African National Congress. Johannesburg; and African National Congress 2001. *A national guideline on home-based care and community-based care*. Johannesburg: African National Congress.

Naidoo, M. & Bozalek, V., 1997. Maintenance grant parity: women pay the price. *Agenda*, (33) 30.

Nattrass, N., 2002. AIDS, growth and distribution of South Africa. Centre for Social Science Research, University of Cape Town, working paper No 7.Available at: http://www.cssr.uct.ac.za/papers/wp7.zip

Pettifor, A.E. et al., 2004. HIV and sexual behaviour among young South Africans: a national survey of 15-24 year-olds. April. Johannesburg: Reproductive Health Research Unit.

Rehle, T. et al., 2007. National HIV incidence measures – new insights into the South African epidemic. *South African Medical Journal*, 97(3), pp.194-199.

Rodgers, G.B., 1979. Income and inequality as determinants of mortality: An international cross-section analysis. *Population Studies*, 33, pp.343-351.

Rosen, S. et al., 2006. The private sector and HIV/AIDS in Africa: Taking stock of six years of applied research. Paper. May. Submitted for publication.

Rosen, S. and Simon, J., 2003. Shifting the burden: The private sector's response to the AID pandemic in Africa. *Bulletin of the World Health Organisation*, 81(2), pp.133-137.

Saldru. 2005. The financial diaries: Investigating the financial lives of the poor (Findings in brief). Cape Town: Centre for Social Science Research, University of Cape Town.

Topouzis., 2000, citing Mutangadura and Webb (1999).

Shisana, O. et al., 2003. The impact of HIV/AIDS on the health sector: National survey of health personnel, ambulatory and hospitalised patients and health facilities 2002. Cape Town: HSRC Press. Available at: http://www.hsrcpress.ac.za/index.asp?areaid=4

Shisana, O. et al., 2005. *South African National HIV Prevalence, HIV Incidence, Behaviour and Communication Survey*. Pretoria: Human Sciences Research Council. Available at: http://www.hsrc.ac.za/media/2005/11/20051130_1.html

Shisana, O. et al., 2005. The health of our educators: A focus on HIV/AIDS in South African public schools. Cape Town: HSRC Press.

Statistics South Africa. 2005. General Household Survey, July 2004. Available at: http://www.statssa.gov.za/publications/P0318/P0318July2004.pdf.

Statistics South Africa. 2005. Mortality and causes of death in South Africa, 1997–2003: Findings from death notification. Pretoria: Statistics South Africa. Available at: http://www.statssa.gov.za/publications/P03093/P03093.pdf;

Statistics South Africa. 2006. Mortality and causes of death in South Africa, 2003 and 2004: Findings from death notification. Pretoria: Statistics South Africa.

Steinberg, M. Johnson, S. Schierhout, S. & Ndegwa, D., 2002. *Hitting home: how households cope with the impact of the HIV/AIDS epidemic*. Cape Town: Henry J Kaiser Foundation & Health Systems Trust. October.

Thomas, E.P. et al., 2005. HIV prevalence study and costing analysis undertaken for the development of an HIV/AIDS workplace strategy for Buffalo City Municipality. Medical Research Council and South African Cities Network.

Torres, L. Drury, D. Eldring, L. Lewis, P. and Vass, J., 2001. Cape Town: Mesebetsi Labour Force Survey. Topline Report.

UN AIDS. 2006. Report on the global AIDS epidemic. Geneva: UNAIDS.

United Nations Development Programme (UNDP). 2001. *HIV/AIDS: Implications for poverty reduction*. Position paper. New York: UNDP.

United Nations Development Programme. 2003. The Challenge of Sustainable Development in South Africa: Unlocking People's Creativity. Johannesburg: UNDP.

Van den Heever, A., 1998. HIV/AIDS and employee benefits. *AIDS Analysis Africa*, 9, pp.3-4.

Vass, J., 2002. The relationship between labour market dynamics and HIV/AIDS prevalence: A literature review. Cape Town: School of Economics, University of Cape Town.

Vass, J., 2003. Impact of HIV/AIDS on the labour force: exploring vulnerabilities. *CODESRIA Bulletin*, special issue 2, 3 & 4..

Walker, R. Reid, G. and Cornell, M., 2004. *Waiting to happen: HIV/AIDS in South Africa.* Cape Town: Double Storey Books.

Whiteside, A. and O'Grady, M., 2003. AIDS and private sector: Lessons from Southern Africa. In A. Sisask, ed. 2003. *One step further: Responses to HIV/AIDS.* Stockholm: UNRISD.

Wilkinson, R. G., 1986. Unhealthy societies: The afflictions of inequality. London: Routledge.

Wilkinson, R, G., 2002. Commentary: Liberty, fraternity, equality. *International Journal of Epidemiology*, 31, pp. 538-543.

Yach, D. and Kistnasamy, B., 2006. Health care in a democratic South Africa. Paper presented to the 'After Apartheid Conference', August 11-12. University of Cape Town.

13.
Justice and the Treatment Action Campaign
Mark Heywood

Introduction

It is a terrible irony that the need for an effective and ongoing response to the AIDS epidemic will be one of the defining legacies left to the ANC by a President who tried to deny the existence of HIV. It is also ironic that the Treatment Action Campaign (TAC), an organisation that Mbeki once branded as 'flag carrier for pharmaceutical companies', is heralded as one of the few organisations that was able to force a complete overturn policy in an area defined and defended by himself, during his Presidency. However, rather than looking back, this chapter attempts to draw some lessons from TAC and the Mbeki era. It aims to inform how both government and civil society (hopefully together) approach AIDS, as well as health more broadly, during the Zuma government.

There is no question that, in the last decade, the health of millions of South Africans has deteriorated. Over 5.5 million people live with HIV. An estimated 2.5 million people have died of AIDS since the mid 1990s. Tuberculosis (TB) has exploded and multi-drug and extremely drug resistant TB have assumed epidemic proportions. There has been a growth in non-communicable disease among the poor. Malnutrition is rife. Infant and maternal mortality have risen (South African Health Review, 2008).

There is both a social and political explanation for the crisis in public health. In general, the importance of health promotion and disease prevention not just to the individual, but to national development was not understood by the ANC or the government. Symptomatic of this was the trusting of health to an incompetent Minister.

But this chapter argues that health is also about politics, and the health crisis grew in the places where post-apartheid democracy failed: in the patronage and protection of an inefficient Minister of Health, in the failures of internal democracy in the ANC and the inability to admit and overcome AIDS denialism, in the blurring of lines between the views of the party (or its President) and the duties of the state. But whilst the declining health of poor people, and particularly the scale of the AIDS epidemic, can be attributed to political negligence, it was not its only cause. As important has been the growth of socio-economic inequalities – and their impact on both health and development.

By the time of its 52nd National Conference in late 2007, the ANC had recognised the disastrous consequences of its political omissions on health. It adopted resolutions that promised that "education and health must be prioritised as the core elements of social transformation."[1] In 2008, this was carried into several ANC-led initiatives to develop new policy for health reform, a process which culminated with the adoption by the ANC of a 'road map for health reform', including the introduction of a system of National Health Insurance (NHI). The result is a health plan that foregrounds AIDS, TB and the resuscitation of health systems. However, what remains unclear is whether there is sufficient will to finance the reorganisation of health care. It is also unclear whether the ANC understands that arresting and reversing the health crisis also means tackling inequality. Both require massive social investment -- in a period when global and national economic forces will cause more pronounced inequality.

Civil society will once more have a major role to play in ensuring implementation of health policy. During its first decade, 1998 to 2008, TAC made a name as an organisation fighting for health. But its actual campaign has been less for health, than for health goods, particularly medicines, for the poor. The strategy of the TAC was shaped by the political context, largely made by President Mbeki, and defended acolytes such as Essop Pahad, Manto Tshabalala-Msimang, Smuts Ngonyama, Ngoako Ramathlodi and the late Peter Mokaba. TAC had no choice other than to mobilise people to challenge and overcome AIDS denialism and to reduce medicine prices. Both campaigns had demonstrable success. In early 2002 the price of first line anti-retroviral medicines fell dramatically, making them affordable in South Africa. AIDS denialism ended with the appointment of Barbara Hogan as Minister of Health in October 2008.

But with Mbeki gone, and access to ARV medicine guaranteed to the extent that the health system has the capacity to provide it and the government can afford it, the next decade will contain different challenges, for both government and civil society. A balance will have to be found between sustaining campaigns for access to ARV treatment and health care services, and robust political advocacy and action against inequality. Campaigns for health goods will be self-defeating if they ignore the link between social and economic inequality and poor health. In the words of Daniel Becker, a Brazilian health activist: "How much good does it do to treat people's illnesses, only to send them back to the conditions that made them sick?" (Becker, 2007). Similarly, Dr Paul Farmer asks whether it is possible to practice medicine effectively "without addressing social forces, including racism, pollution, poor

---

1. ANC, 52nd National Conference Resolutions, available at:
http://www.anc.org.za/ancdocs/history/conf/conference52/resolutions-f.html

housing, and poverty, that shape [the course of ill health] in both individuals and populations?" (Farmer, 2006).

This chapter considers the implications of the changing political and economic environment for continuing efforts by civil society to ensure the right of 'everyone' to have access to health care services, and for conditions that make for health.[2] It questions whether the government will have the will to take all measures that are available to it in law to advance health. The 'road to health' will require that TAC and its allies unite more effectively to directly challenge governmental policies which cause and reinforce inequality. It will also require that pro-poor organisations of civil society, including political parties, better understand and act on the relationship between health and development.

Finally, in the context of ongoing global economic pressure towards austerity, it will almost certainly necessitate compelling the government to use of the state's legal power and moral legitimacy to ensure it can carry out its positive constitutional duties to protect and promote health. This requires an intention to defend the Constitution and sustain community mobilisation in order to utilise the national state as an instrument of democracy that can deliver on poor people's needs.

What did TAC achieve?

The work and achievements of TAC have been extensively documented and analaysed, including by myself (Heywood, 2009). This chapter looks at TAC, and the struggle for AIDS treatment, in a broader political and social context. It frames TAC's achievements in gaining access to medicines in a longer term perspective of health and development. TAC was launched on 10 December 1998, the 50th anniversary of the Universal Declaration of Human Rights. The ideal was the realisation of the right to equality, specifically in relation to poor people's right of access to life-saving medicines for the treatment of HIV, and the belief that the South African constitution could advance this right.

In the late 1990s it seemed as if AIDS would follow the course of other diseases of the third world: treatable if you were rich and life-threatening and invariably fatal if you were poor. However, TAC and AIDS activists globally were able to change that course. By late 2008, it was estimated that 500,000 people were receiving ARV treatment in the

---

2. The Constitution of the Republic of South Africa states that: "Everyone has the right to have access to health care services, including reproductive health care" and that the "the state must take reasonable legislative and other measures, within its available resources, to achieve the progressive realisation of each of these rights" (s 27).

public sector in South Africa, and over three million world-wide (UNAIDS, 2008). In terms of absolute numbers South Africa has the largest ARV treatment programme in the world, achieving some of the best results in terms of drug-adherence. In late 2008 it was estimated by the Treasury that every month 20,000 additional people were being initiated onto treatment every month. But this is still only meeting less than 50 per cent of the existing need for treatment.

That so many people are on treatment has a great deal to do with TAC's social, political and legal mobilisation. For over a decade it was able to develop and sustain a cadre of activists, at its peak numbering over 20,000, who confronted both government policy and private health sector profiteering from medicines. TAC's volunteers were mostly marginalised young women and men from poor communities, many of them living with HIV and in need of treatment. They were assisted to organise and unleash their power as rights-bearing citizens of the democratic South Africa, through utilising constitutionally entrenched rights to demonstrate, organise, educate and have resort to the courts to promote and fulfill rights. In many ways TAC developed as a model of how human rights, law and mobilisation can be combined to further the interests of poor people.

TAC's achievements are real. The course it followed in overcoming the obstacles to access to treatment was unavoidable. Guaranteeing access to life-saving medicines was, after all, its primary mission. But TAC has grown into more than just a limited campaign for ARV treatment. Delegates at its fourth national congress in 2008 amended its constitution to reflect its aspirations to protect human rights more broadly and sustain access to treatment through transformation and improvement of the state health system. This therefore requires us to examine TAC in the broader context of the social and political factors, which (as I argued in the introduction to this chapter) determine health, including HIV.

In its first decade, TAC became very much a creature of the context of President Mbeki's AIDS denialism (Nattrass, 2007). The contest with AIDS denialism was the backdrop to the struggle for access to treatment. Every major breakthrough in the struggle for treatment access -- whether in relation to the prevention of mother-to-child HIV transmission (2002), a national treatment plan (2003), the implementation of the treatment plan (2004), access to treatment for prisoners (2006), an ambitious National Strategic Plan on HIV, AIDS and STIs (2007), and the battle against state-encouraged quackery (2008) – was also a victory over AIDS denialism. Against this constant, the question of profiteering from medicines by multi-national pharmaceutical companies was an issue taken on by TAC successfully, but only sporadically. Similarly, the critical issues of access to a quality health care system and HIV prevention, received scant attention. In fact, it could be argued that the malign shadow cast by AIDS denialism, and the relentless campaign that had to be waged to overcome it, largely eclipsed other factors that were driving the HIV epidemic, factors that suddenly loom large with the defeat of AIDS denialism.

The next challenges

Two issues can be postponed no longer:

- preventing new HIV infections and
- resuscitating South Africa's health system.

The sustainability of access to treatment for people with AIDS is dependent on both. Unless the tap of new infections is turned off, it will be impossible to meet the demand for treatment. Unless, the health system is sorted out, it will be impossible to supply the demand.

Successful HIV prevention on a large scale has thus far proved elusive and intractable. It cannot be undertaken without challenging the socio-economic drivers of HIV infections, drivers that have become more pronounced in the last decade. Similarly, unleashing the potential quality of South Africa's total[3] health system means challenging the inequalities within it, and the systems for its governance, particularly its financing. These issues necessitate a new approach to AIDS by civil society as a whole and TAC in particular. In this respect the end of AIDS denialism may not mean the end of conflicts with the ANC or the next government.

In late 2008 it was still estimated that over 1,500 people daily were being newly infected with HIV (Rehle et al., 2007). However, these 1,500 people are not random innocent bystanders who happened to be in the path of a virulent virus. They have at least one and sometimes a combination of the following characteristics: being black and poor, women, young, unemployed, living in rural areas and being without formal homes. In other words, they are people who live in a country where although 'all people are equal under the law',[4] millions of people

---

3. The South African health system is divided between a privately financed system, accessible to wealthy and employed people via medical aid schemes, and a tax-funded public system, used by the poor. Although poor people utilise the private system when they can afford it, rich people do not use the public system because of its disrepair. They two systems do not work together or share the same vision. In order to meet South Africa's health needs it will be necessary for the two to complement each other.
4. S9 (1) and (2) of the South African Constitution.

are less equal than others and do not have "the full and equal enjoyment of all rights and freedoms."

This requires an examination of inequality and its relationship to HIV and AIDS. It is a reasonable supposition that that it is inequality, rather than just 'extreme poverty' - as was claimed many times by Mbeki[5] - that has become the major driver of declining ill health generally and rising rates of HIV infection particularly. For example, research conducted in a number of developed countries has demonstrated that inequality, rather than just wealth, is a major social determinant of health. This is the case even when the inequality is between people who, comparable to developing country standards of living, are socially secure. Thus, Daniels et al., point out that: "the relationship between economic development and health is not fixed, and that the health achievement of nations is mediated by processes other than wealth" (Daniels et al., 2004: 67). Put simply, a country may simultaneously be gaining in wealth, and failing in health.

This would suggest that a social and economic strategy which promotes narrow economic growth (measured primarily by GDP, FDI etc), whilst at the same time using a parallel strategy to alleviate poverty primarily through selective cash transfers to a segment of the poor (child support grants, foster grants etc), will increase inequality even whilst it mitigates poverty. Such a policy was followed by the Mbeki government. But it is contrary to the method of government required by the South African constitution, which must progressively reduce inequality. It will also not assist HIV prevention. If HIV cannot be prevented it will be hard to improve public health generally or make progress against specific Millennium Development Goals (MDGs).

Put another way, economic policies that widen inequality, both between classes and within classes, fuel both disease and ill health. This makes public policy questions such as access to social security, sufficient food and fair labour practices integral to HIV prevention and treatment.

Inequality and HIV

There may be dispute about the depth and breadth of poverty, but there is no doubt that inequality has grown. Fewer people are classified as living in absolute poverty. But more very poor people live side-by-side with less poor people in urban formal and informal settlements all over

5. See Mbeki, T., Speech at the Opening Session of the Thirteenth International AIDS Conference, July 2000. Available at:
http://www.anc.org.za/show.php?doc=ancdocs/history/mbeki/2000/tm0709.hml "The world's biggest killer and the greatest cause of ill health and suffering across the globe, including South Africa, is extreme poverty."

the country. The growth in proximal inequality creates an immediate vulnerability to disease, however distant its political causes.

In the words of the report of the Commission on the Social Determinants of Health (CSDH):

> The poor health of the poor, the social gradient of health within countries, and the marked health inequities between countries are caused by the unequal distribution of power, income, good, and services .... This unequal distribution of health-damaging experiences is not in any sense a 'natural' phenomenon but is the result of a toxic combination of poor social policies and programmes, unfair economic arrangements, and bad politics (WHO, 2008).

What is meant by this in South Africa? The vast majority of people in South Africa are poor. But people's experience of poverty is not uniform. Poverty (like wealth) is layered, with sex and disability in particular being associated with deeper degrees of inequality.[6] In South Africa the fact that women and girls experience deeper social and economic disadvantage than men and boys, is thought to explain their earlier and higher rates of HIV infection and mortality. Girls and young women, who are the least equal of poor people, adopt survival strategies that are not necessary for boys and men.[7] For some, sex becomes a commodity they can exchange in return for a degree of social security (or greater equality) (Weiser et al., 2007). This is obtained from men who may be only slightly less poor (after all, they often live in the same community), but whose access to income is linked to their sex, limited access to the economy and often slightly older age.

In the past (before the emergence of HIV) the migrant labour system, and its enforcement by apartheid laws, penned millions of women into rural areas, and hundreds of thousands of men in soulless hosteels. This shaped a demographic of sexually transmitted disease, particularly syphilis (Jochelson, 2001).

Fifteen years after the end of apartheid, internal migrancy driven by economic rather than political factors, remains a major risk for disease (Lurie, 2000). According to some research, in the post apartheid years changes to the South African economy have created "a changing political economy of sex' and 'most African women today are no longer waiting in

---

6. The association between disability and poverty has not been properly studied or quantified in South Africa.

7. It is important to note that by 'survival' I do not mean solely ensuring access to food, but also access to other commodities and resources that define modern living, and which very poor people see all around them, but lack money to acquire. In the words of *King Lear*: "Allow not nature more than nature needs, man's life is cheap as beasts."

rural areas to be infected by their migrant partners" (Hunter, 2007). Women are as poor as they were under apartheid but more mobile, making them much more the active agents of their own vulnerability. But in this changed socio-economic context one particular area of state failure has been glaring and has added to the risks of HIV infection: that is the failure to invest in gender equality and to protect women and girls from sexual violence. This is an issue that TAC has also attempted to tackle, but one on which it has not been able to make the same social imprint with its ideas, as it has for example on access to ARV treatment. In a number of communities, particularly Khayelitsha, TAC showed that it is possible to mobilise against domestic violence and ensure that the legal system fulfills its responsibilities towards women. But these campaigns have remained localised.

The result of social insecurity and inequality is that if awareness of HIV is not accompanied by access to income, or a dependable justice system that can prosecute domestic violence and rape, or support services for women and girls, it will be insufficient to reduce risk behaviour. But although women have a particular vulnerability, poor men are also not immune to behaviours that are directly influenced by their marginalisation and inequality. Catherine Campbell has drawn attention to how:

Frequent and unprotected sex with multiple partners may often be one of the few ways in which men can act out their masculinity. This might be the case particularly in situations where men, at best, work in difficult conditions over which they have little control or, at worst, have little access to jobs and money (Campbell, 2003: 184).

This analysis helps us to understand how, during the Mbeki years, inequality, migration and sex coalesced into a risk vector to health and well-being. The theatre where this risk is acted out is poor residential communities where people live their 'private lives'. But the factors that influence people's behaviours (or choices) are being heavily influenced by the social, economic and political policies of government.

The vicious circle that fuels HIV infections can be summarised as follows. For people who are poor, vulnerability to HIV starts by being driven by external factors, particularly inherited disadvantage in access to education and employment. However, once greater risk has become actual HIV infection, then illness that is caused by HIV provides a further motor to the cycle of inequality. Unless people with HIV have access to health care services that provide treatment and care, illness deepens pre-existing deprivation: it incapacitates people, creates new needs and diverts household resources. HIV infection becomes not just the symptom, but an agent, of inequality.

For these reasons, if HIV prevention is to succeed it requires that organisations such as TAC campaign on two levels: *directly* through a social mobilisation to diagnose, prevent and treat HIV and *politically* through challenges to the policies that create, or fail to alleviate, inequality.

Health systems decline

Because of the lack of competition from the public sector and because good health is essential to life and well-being, health services have become a site of ruthless profiteering by private companies and of growing inequality in access to health care services. Tragically, in the post apartheid period two processes, until recently both largely unchecked, have made the national health system worse and more unequal.

On the one hand, the public health system has been gravely underfunded and subject to constantly growing demand. It has been placed under the tutelage of mostly incompetent and sometimes corrupt politicians. In the mid 2000s, despite the mounting evidence of the near collapse of this system in many districts, ANC politicians protected each others' backs and claimed that health systems were improving. Those who spoke out, most notably Nozizwe Madlala-Routledge, the Deputy Minister of Health from 2004 to 2007, were ganged up against. Routledge was eventually dismissed in August 2007.

As public health services deteriorated, the private health system became more necessary for access to health care both for those with money and those without – the diametric opposite of the intention of the ANC's 1994 National Health Plan and the 1997 White Paper on Health. For example, it is estimated by the Health Roadmap that nearly 50 per cent of poor people first seek primary care from private doctors when they are ill 'despite having access to free care', paying out of pocket, and accounting for nearly 20 per cent of total national health expenditure. Approximately 15 million people use private health services of one kind or another for out of hospital care. But, because of its expense, private hospital care can be afforded by only 7.5 million people.

Profits in the private health sector soared because firms were relatively free from legal regulation and oversight in most areas of operation (with the exception of medicine pricing and medical schemes[8]). Netcare, for example, made post tax profits of R1bn in 2007.[9] In this respect it is also important to note that TAC's focus on private profiteering from medicines, albeit necessary, obscured the fact that profiteering was also taking place in other parts of the health system as well, particularly by the large hospital groups.

When it came to the public sector, TAC initially concentrated its fire on public health sceptics who claimed that the public health system would 'collapse' if ARV treatment was introduced, overlooking the deeper processes that were taking place in health provision. As a result of TAC's campaign, health services for AIDS treatment were one of the only areas in the health system that experienced consistent investment and strengthening. Unfortunately, under less pressure and scrutiny, most other areas of health care suffered an unchecked decline.

In 2004, after TAC's pressure on the government finally secured a National Treatment Plan, the movement began campaigning for a People's Health Service, aiming to draw attention to the crisis of health systems. However, TAC's calls for investment in the public sector and regulation of the private sector were inconsistent. Pressure for health reform could not be sustained, not only because of the continual re-surfacing of AIDS denialism, but because the demand was much more complex than the call for AIDS treatment and needed a new alliance to be built.

TAC's campaign was eventually overtaken by a process launched by the ANC in mid-2008, following up on resolutions taken on health at the Polokwane Congress. This process, facilitated by the ANC's Health and Education committee, recognised both the crisis of disease and the crisis of health systems and made proposals to address both. In its early stages Manto Tshabalala-Msimang, the then Minister of Health, had almost nothing to do with it. But a new era began with the appointment of Barbara Hogan from October 2008 through May 2009, and Aaron Motsoaledi from May 2009. The report and its recommendations appear to have largely been adopted by both the government and the ANC, even if progress on the National Health Insurance component is not yet visible.[10]

The 'health road map' appears to be consistent with the constitutional duties of the state in relation to health, and has therefore been welcomed by activists. It recognises the importance of establishing health budgets based on needs assessment, on resolving the human

---

8. In its first term the ANC amended both the Medical Schemes Act and the Medicines and Related Substances Act, to try to control prices and improve affordability.
9. *Financial Mail*, A Sore Point, 9 May 2008.
10. A Roadmap for the Reform of the South African Health System, A Process Convened and Facilitated by the Development Bank of South Africa, 8 November 2000.

resources crisis, and and on prioritising the reduction of AIDS, TB and infant mortality. But the roadmap is silent on the crucial questions of cost, how it will be financed and how it will be implemented in the context of government's fiscal constraints. For example, in late 2008, reports began to surface of massive, uncontrolled over-expenditure on the health budget, and the running out of funds for the purchase of ARVs four months before the end of the financial year in several provinces.[11] In addition, the government must address powerful private sector resistance to fundamental reform and a depleted and demoralised health workforce.

The political will may be there, but the political how is uncertain. One thing we may be certain of: without the external pressure of civil society, the ANC's ambitious goals will not be implemented.

Duties of government and uses of the state

The final report of the CSDH points out that "the structural determinants and conditions of daily life constitute the social determinants of health." In keeping with this, the analysis I have offered in this chapter of how social inequality influences *state of health (including relative risk of HIV infection)*, as well as how inequality influences the *degree of access to health care services,* begs the question of what is likely happen to health and health services under South Africa's next government.

If the ANC's 2009 Election Manifesto is to be believed, it will: "aim to reduce inequalities in our health system, improve quality of care and public facilities, and boost our human resources and step up the fight against HIV and AIDS and other diseases. Health reforms will involve mobilisation of available resources in both private and public health sectors to ensure improved health outcomes for all South Africans." [12]

Should this aspirational statement be trusted? There is certainly a qualitative difference between Motsoaledi and Tshabalala-Msimang, and between the Mbeki and Zuma governments more generally. But at this stage it is not possible to say yet whether the left rhetoric emanating from the new ANC leadership is mere posturing and positioning in the quest for leadership or whether it will translate into a genuine concern

---

11. See: *Independent Newspapers,* 'Opposition Wants MECs Head', 14 November 2008, reporting a budget shortfall of R3.1bn in KwaZulu Natal ; 'No Money for New ARV patients in the Free State', Health Department, Health-E News, 14 November 2008, reporting that the Free State had stopped enlisting new ARV patients because it had run out of money.
12. ANC 2009 Election Manifesto, Together We Can Do More, available at: http://www.anc.org.za/show.php?doc=elections/2009/manifesto/manifesto.html&title=2009+Election+Manifesto.

for the poor. If it is the latter, it is also not clear whether the ANC will operate by means of populism or constitutionalism. But whatever happens, there is no doubt that in its first few years at least, the next government will find itself even more restricted than its predecessor. How will it deliver costly and necessary social reforms in a turbulent global economy drifting from deficit-spending to austerity? How will it calculate and apportion its 'available resources'? How will it justify decisions to invest in social services, such as health, to the financial markets which judge the value of SA state securities?

Regardless of the pressures, the health crisis will not pause while these questions are answered, or wait for a more expansive fiscal outlook. If the health crisis is not arrested in coming years the damage may end up being beyond repair. As a result, there is now a need for AIDS and health activism to become enmeshed with political activism and vice versa. But, this will require a mind shift.

Up to this point, health has been marginal in campaigns for equality and justice. In the words of a group of authors, including the former UN Special Rapporteur on the Right to Health, writing in the Lancet: "until recently, the right to health was only dimly understood and attracted little support from civil society or any other sector" (Backman et al., 2008).

There are many ways in which the right to health can be used to mobilise around other social ills, and improve other aspects of the lives of poor people, even if these are still largely overlooked.[13] Ill health seems to be regarded by many in social movements primarily as the *consequence* of poverty and inequality, rather than equally as a *contributor* to it. As a result, it is rare to find health advocacy at the centre of the campaigns and programmes of pro-poor and social justice organisations. Internationally, socialist parties, trade unions and social movements have rarely shown any sign that they appreciate how integral health is to dignity and development. Consequently very few have prioritised and aggressively implemented health programmes and platforms – and the duties of the state in this regard have been forgotten.

Compounding this problem is the way in which many activists and analysts seize too quickly on explanations for poor health that are nearest to hand and which offer grist to their mill about the 'inherent evils' of neoliberalism and globalisation. Of course, there have been good reasons to draw attention to the negative consequences for health of

---

13. In *Public Health, Ethics and Equity* (see footnote 8) Sen et al., provide evidence to show how re-distributive economic policies have a positive outcome on health. On the other side of the coin, however, successful campaigns for health can also bring about economic and social redistribution.

IMF-led structural adjustment programmes, debt repayment and World Trade Organisation (WTO) agreements, particularly the Agreement on Trade Related Aspects of Intellectual Property (TRIPS).

But globalisation and neoliberalism are an insufficient explanation for state failure on health, and when it is offered as the main explanation it is disarming. Decline in health indicators is not caused by globalisation alone, but by the *voluntary* retreat of governments from their social responsibilities – sometimes citing 'globalisation' as a feint for its own omissions.

South Africa is an example. Between 1994 and 2003, South Africa reduced its external debt as a per cent of GDP, and avoided taking loans from the IMF.[14] This changed in 2003 as the country's rising current account deficit required inflows of funds not covered by other financial capital. But although there were 14 World Bank loans, including hospital refurbishment, South Africa was not under the direct thumb of global finance the way many other African countries were. The debt burden did not impede increases in social spending. But despite this, between 1996 and 2000, under the Growth Employment and Redistribution Strategy (GEAR), the ANC government voluntarily imposed arbitrary limits on public spending on health with profound consequences for the capacity to meet health needs, and it was only in the mid-2000s that per capita state spending on healthcare began to rise (after inflation is discounted). In some ways, the subsequent increases were wasted, because by then, nursing colleges were closed, scare skills had migrated, and hospitals fell into disrepair.

The Health Roadmap suggests that to achieve staffing ratios similar to a decade ago and to take into account population growth and added disease would require an additional R12 billion to be spent per annum. Despite the health system's desperate need for funds, Tshabalala-Msimang refused to calculate the country's health needs and properly quantify its human resource or budgetary deficits. For example, in 2007 she belligerently asked the SA Human Rights Commission why "we need to get into an exercise, which will be very expensive and costly, of determining for all these areas and others the extent and the resource requirements of the backlogs, in order to determine needs based budget for the realisation of the rights in the Constitution?"[15]

Similarly, although Mbeki and the ANC occasionally engaged in fierce rhetoric against pharmaceutical company profiteering, his government

---

14. The Presidency, Republic of South Africa. 2007. Development Indicators Mid-Term Review, p 10.
15. See address by the Minister of Health to the SA Human Rights Commission, 30 May 2007.

did not take advantage of the flexibilities negotiated by developing countries at the WTO Ministerial meeting in Doha, in November 2001, under the TRIPS agreement (Loff and Heywood, 2002). These flexibilities permit developing countries to issue compulsory licenses on essential medicines under conditions that they consider constitutes a, "national emergency or other circumstances of extreme urgency" including HIV/AIDS, TB "and other epidemics." Hence the political determinants of the health crisis lie in large part with the refusal of developing country governments (particularly the so-called emerging economies that have available resources) to use state resources or legal authority to prioritise health in public policy. In the current context of a global financial turbulence and competing demands for huge social investment which will be deemed 'unaffordable' in the current economic climate, the health system may not receive the political attention or financial and other resources that it urgently requires. What can be done about this?

Stand up for your rights

One of TAC's most valuable contributions to post apartheid democracy has been its demonstration of the supremacy of South Africa's constitution, which encompasses both human rights and rules of government. This makes it possible to combine law with mobilisation in order to improve social conditions. TAC has given practical demonstration of the role that courts can play in protecting rights, ensuring democratic practice, political accountability and insisting on openness and ethics in government. Its legal challenge to government in the PMTCT has been described as "a new form of political trial" (Davis and le Roux, 2008).

Invoking and utilising the Constitution, and all the rights it gives people in relation to government, is going to become more rather than less necessary in the years ahead. In addition, the demand for constitutional government, policy making and the fulfillment of duties needs to be directed at more than just issues of AIDS or housing. Such an approach is also relevant to some of the most fundamental inequalities in South Africa, including access to food and education – both rights in the Constitution.

But here too there is a hurdle to be overcome. The legalisation of socio-economic rights by many countries, including South Africa, represents an important advance in the quest for social justice. However, many academic writers on health still appear to be in a quandary on this issue and activists are sceptical of the value of this development, largely because of a distrust of law and suspicion of 'liberal values' such as human rights. David Fidler, for example, worries whether human rights will become "a morally compelling but politically ignored mantra" (Fidler, 2004). Aginam says we should "de-emphasise justiciability and stress human dignity, indivisibility and the interdependence of all human rights" (Aginam, 2005: 36). From a different perspective, *The Economist* tried to pour cold water on a human rights approach to challenging inequality:

> Food, jobs and housing are certainly necessities. But no useful purpose is served by calling them 'rights'. When a government locks someone up without a fair trial, the victim, perpetrator and remedy are fairly clear. This clarity seldom applies to social and economic 'rights'. It is hard enough to determine whether such a right has been infringed, let alone who should provide a remedy or how.[16]

The Economist is not alone it its thinking, although some progressive academics come to the same conclusion through different arguments. In 2003, Patrick Bond questioned TAC's ability to use a rights-based campaign to compel the SA Government to introduce a national anti-retroviral treatment programme, something that happened later in the same year. In a mea culpa he nonetheless concludes:

> Such socio-economic human rights can be won, in my view, only through deglobalisation, namely the delinking of countries and regions of the world from the bureaucratic straightjackets designed in Washington and Geneva-structural adjustment, TRIPs, etc-on behalf of corporate interests. [17]

These writers are correct insofar as they think that the recognition of human rights in themselves will make a difference in the struggle against inequality. But they are mistaken insofar as they overlook the value that rights can play in social mobilisation that aims to compel governments to carry out their duties. They are also mistaken in underestimating how rights can be utilised to reshape public policy and resource allocations. In a December 2007 issue of *the Lancet*, dedicated to the right to health, various writers assert that, "an equitable health system is a core social institution, no less than a fair court system or democratic political system."[18] But they also point out,

---

16. *The Economist*, 24 March 2007.
17. *Z Net Daily Commentaries*, Can Victory on AIDS Medicines Catalyse Wider Change? 1 Dec 2003.
18. *Ibid*, Lancet 2082.

The right to the highest attainable standard of health encompasses medical care, access to safe drinking water, adequate sanitation, education, health-related information, and other underlying determinants of health.[19]

In the same issue Amartya Sen states that human rights are necessary as not as 'the children of law' but as the 'parents of law': that is, as aspirations that law must find means to advance and protect:

The right to health has similarly broad demands that go well beyond legislating good health care (important as that is). There are political, social, economic, scientific, and cultural actions that we can take for advancing the cause of good health for all (Sen, 2008: p.2010).

Thus the wheel comes full circle, and we are back at the confluence of health, inequality, the duties of government to fulfill the right to health and the necessity for sustained and organised pressure on government from civil society. In this context, let us look again at how law may assist the campaign for the right to health in South Africa and internationally. Today there is a growing body of domestic law on the right to health and state duties. More than 150 countries have become State parties to the International Covenant on Economic Social and Cultural Rights (IESCR) which recognises states' duties to take steps to achieve "the highest attainable standard of physical and mental health" for their populations. [20] Fully 83 have signed regional treaties which recognise the right to health. And, more than 100 countries have incorporated the right to health in their national Constitution (Hogerzeil et al., 2006).[21]

---

19. *Ibid*, Lancet 2048.
20. Articles 2, 11 and 12 of the International Covenant on Economic, Social and Cultural Rights (ICESCR) deal with duties of States to assist each other and the rights to 'adequate food' and the 'highest attainable standard of physical and mental heath.'
See: http://www.ohchr.org/english/law.index.htm
21. These cases were in Argentina, Bolivia, Brazil, Columbia, Costa Rica, Ecuador, India, Nigeria, Panama, San Salvador, South Africa and Venezuela.

The Economist and fellow rights-sceptics[22] would not dispute that a wrong is committed when people starve in a country that has a grain surplus (like India) or die of AIDS within proximity of under-utilised private health care facilities (as they do in South Africa). But they would argue that such a finding is essentially moral rather than legal, and therefore of little remedial value. There was a time when this was true. However, in the last few decades, human rights have become more than just 'pious wishes'. Since 1990, there have been 71 documented court cases concerning the right to medical treatment, 59 of them successful (Hogerzeil et al., 2006). Therefore the justiciability of the right to health no longer seems to be an issue. Rather, the problem revolves around how a court can meaningfully remedy its infringements and ensure the enforcement of its orders. It is also about how to persuade governments to take into account in all policy-making and resource allocations the positive duties that they have assented to. The international human rights Covenants, Treaties and Declarations such as the 2001 UNGASS Declaration of Commitment on HIV should all have bearing on what the state must do in relation to health. These are political issues as much as they are legal duties.

For those who are committed to social justice (including justice in health), the growing recognition (if not respect) for fundamental human rights in national and international law (Klug, 2000) provides an opportunity to mobilise poor people to compel their governments to fulfill the duties they have accepted on paper. But, it is also incumbent on civil society to better define the content and duties arising from crucial socio-economic rights. It is necessary to be able to state 'when a right has been infringed' and what a state must do to fulfill it. As the *Lancet* says: "the right to health is not just a slogan, it has a concise and constructive contribution to make to health policy and practice."

What are the duties that arise from the Constitution's recognition of the right of 'everyone' to 'sufficient food', 'appropriate social assistance'[23] and of children to 'basic nutrition' and 'basic education'?

---

22. See: Neier, A., *Social and Economic Rights: a Critique*:
http://www.wcl.american.edu/hrbrief/13/2neier.pdf. Neier claims that the socio-economic rights in the SA Constitution and Universal Declaration of Human rights 'get [us] into territory that is unmanageable through the judicial process and that intrudes fundamentally into an area where the democratic process ought to prevail'. But this claim entirely misses the dialectical relationship that should exist in a democracy between legal systems and politics. The two should be part of a continuum and a process for ensuring accountability.
23. In early 2009 a proposal for Chronic Illness Grant was developed under the auspices of the South African National AIDS Council (SANAC). It arises from the Constitutional duty to provide appropriate social assistance. Predictably it has major cost implications

How will government be monitored to ensure that it is under constant pressure to fulfill these rights? Linked to this, is the necessity for civil society to demand that legal systems are made more affordable and accessible to people to assist them to 'remedy' violations of human rights (Hassim and Heywood, 2009).

Looking at the years ahead, we can say that we have a policy framework rooted in the right to health, particularly the National Strategic Plan on HIV, AIDS and STIs and the Health Roadmap. Both documents create legal duties on government generally and the Minister of Health in particular. However, whether these duties are fulfilled will depend upon an active and effective civil society; the precise contours of the struggle for the realisation of the right to health will depend upon how the Ministry sets about implementation of policy.

Towards a politics of rights

In the same article in which it denounces the notion of socio-economic rights, *The Economist* states: "For people in the poor world, as for people everywhere, the most reliable method yet invented to ensure that governments provide people with social and economic necessities is called politics."[24]

The denial of health is political. Health (or the lack of it) has an impact on human capability, dignity, and the right to life, in a similar fashion to whether people have access to sufficient food or not. The denial of the right to health has been described by Paul Farmer as a form of 'structural violence' against the poor. That is, not just a violence of omission, but the predictable result of political neglect of poor people's socio-economic rights. Health is described as a socio-economic right, and a positive obligation that must be acted upon by the state. By contrast, protection against torture is described as a civil right, and a negative injunction. But the effect of a violation of either is the same: pain, indignity, incapacitation and often death. Both are preventable.

But whilst a growing acceptance of civil and political rights protects people in many countries of the world (although by no means all) from torture, the lack of respect for the right to health blights lives across the globe, but overwhelmingly the lives of the poor.[25] The outcry about the

---

and will be an early struggle to test whether constitutional duties trump fiscal restraint by the next government and how 'available resources' are determined.

24. *The Economist, Ibid.*

25. In 2006, Lawrence Gostin published an article arguing for the development of a UN Framework Convention on Global Health. See Gostin, L., 2007. Meeting the Survival Needs of the World's Least Health People, A Proposed Model for Global Health Governance, *JAMA*, 11 July 2007, Vol 289(2), pp.225-228.

AIDS epidemic has contributed to a new focus on health and justice, which has exposed the whittling away of public health systems to a point where there are few doctors, few medicines and, with the exception of South Africa, a huge dependency on donor aid. It is estimated that AIDS has caused the death of 25 million people since the 1980s. Most of these deaths are in Africa. But, despite the social and humanitarian crisis this has caused, according to Alex de Waal:

> HIV/AIDS has turned out to pose a political threat no greater than familiar pathologies such as hunger and homelessness. AIDS has been politically domesticated. Anti-retroviral treatment has become the central mechanism for managing AIDS (de Waal, 2006: 119).

What does de Waal mean? In many African countries, AIDS has led to the emergence of independent civil society organisations, such as the AIDS and Rights Alliance of Southern Africa (ARASA)[26]. These organisations have begun to examine and challenge governmental conduct, including resource allocations and commitment to health. They have exposed gaps between pledges and practice, such as the AU's 2002 Abuja commitment to spending 15 per cent of government expenditure on health.[27] In South Africa, AIDS spawned one of the most successful social mobilisations of the post apartheid era. AIDS was a political running sore of the Mbeki government and contributed to the readiness of the ANC to dismiss him as President.

De Waal's conclusion may ultimately prove correct, but it is premature. AIDS activism has won access to treatment for many people who, in the past, governments would quietly have let die, believing that nobody would notice their deaths. However, if AIDS activism does not extend beyond the campaign for ARVs, then it may well end up being 'politically domesticated'. AIDS has exposed the fault lines of inequality in society. Ultimately, it is these fault lines that must be attended to.

This chapter has tried to illustrate how health is heavily influenced by the political choices made by government. Promoting and demanding the fulfillment of human rights is a political response to health that measures these choices against nationally and internationally agreed standards. In South Africa TAC pioneered a political campaign for health that was founded in human rights. However TAC's method has a potential not only for health, but also for mobilisations to demand

---

26. http://www.arasa.info
27. African Union. Abuja Declaration on HIV/AIDS, Tuberculosis and Other Infection Diseases, April 2001.

delivery by government of housing, sufficient food, social security, education and employment – all ultimately determinants of health.

But what will it take to realise this potential? A cohesive civil society is essential. But unfortunately, it is arguable that in the drawn out politics of the succession battle for the ANC leadership, civil society, whilst not becoming more divided, has become more fragmented, and thus weakened. There are deep fissures that divide civil society over the approach adopted by the Alliance in its justifiable quest to unseat Mbeki, but its unprincipled quest to promote Jacob Zuma. The trade union movement in particular has encouraged the belief that a Zuma presidency, however tainted, will be the foundation for policies that are more sympathetic to the poor and to equitable and sustainable development. As was evident from the ANC's 2009 election manifesto, new policies have been thrown up, but much less thought seems to have been given to how to implement these plans.

It seems probable that the next ANC government, whilst more sympathetic to the poor in its outlook, will not find itself in a position to better deliver on basic rights (or needs). What George Orwell termed 'doublespeak' in *1984* will become the order of politics. Already, for example, the promise to create jobs is being redefined as a promise to protect jobs.

As important as civil society coherence, is its ability to work strategically, building on legal principles and institutions that exist to ensure social progress. In the health arena, for example, TAC's advocacy has led to the fleshing out and empowerment of institutions of co-governance between civil society and government departments, such as the South African National AIDS Council (SANAC).[28] With regard to health more broadly, civil society should recognise and act upon the opportunities that have been created by the National Health Act, which sanctions the creation of Hospital Boards, district health committees and national and provincial health consultative forums.[29]

However, both of these are ultimately dependent upon encouraging and building active citizenship, based upon knowledge of rights and the responsibilities of government. In the context of the complexity of markets, political and legal reform, there seems little value in resuscitating the hackneyed mantra of political 'alternatives' that have been superseded by modern history.

In this context, the South African Constitution - and how it obliges government to use its resources – could be the ally of a government that

---

28. http://www.sanac.org.za
29. AIDS Law Project, Siberink. The National Health Act 61 of 2003, A Guide. Available at http://www.alp.org.za

genuinely seeks social betterment. It could be used to justify policy choices that may not be considered 'wise' by international financial institutions, but which can be framed as reasonable and legally binding state duties. In the advent of precedents that spent trillions of dollars bailing out failed companies in order to restore market stability, there is a strong legal and moral case to be made that this recession should not take its normal toll on poor people. But taking advantage of the Constitution in the years ahead, means protecting the Constitution and its institutions now, something the ANC is flagrantly not doing. To protect its President, it must perforce cast aspersions on the rule of law and its institutions.

If South Africa's leading political party and liberation movement will not protect the totality of the Constitution that it gave birth to, then this will be one of the most immediate and pressing responsibilities of civil society. South Africa is deeply divided in its inequality. In many areas (not surprisingly after 300 years where the majority of the population was legally disadvantaged), government is weak. As has been evident from the tender-fest of the South African government at all levels, the opportunities for corruption and self-enrichment are great. Social reform and, in the context of this chapter, reform of health systems, depends upon active democracy, continual engagement in policy making, monitoring of implementation and the unrelenting external and independent pressure of the poor on the government that owes a legal duty to improve their lives.

References

Aginam, O., 2005. Global Health Governance International Law and Public Health in a Divided World. Toronto: University of Toronto Press.

Backman, G. et al., 2008. Health Systems and the Right to Health: an assessment of 194 Countries. *The Lancet*, 372, pp. 2047-2085. December 13.

Becker, D., 2007. Health, Equity and Social Determinants. Presentation to the University of Nijmegen. Centro de Promoção da Saúde (CEDAPS), 23 May.

Campbell, C., 2003. *Letting Them Die, How HIV/AIDS Prevention Programmes Often Fail*. London: The International African Institute.

Daniels, N. Kennedy, B. and Kawachi, I., 2004. Health and Inequality, or, Why Justice is Good for Our Health. In S. Anand, F. Peter, and A. Sen, eds. *Public Health, Ethics and Equity*. Oxford: Oxford University Press.

Davis, D. and le Roux, M., 2008. *Precedent and Possibility, The (Ab)use of Law in South Africa*. Cape Town: Double Storey Books.

de Waal, A., 2006. AIDS and Power – Why there is No Political Crisis Yet. London: Zed Books.

Farmer, P., 2006. Structural Violence and Clinical Medicine. *Plos Medicine*, 3.

Fidler, D., 2004. Constitutional Outlines of Public Health's 'New World Order.' 77 *Temple L. Rev*, 313.

Hassim, A. and Heywood, M., 2009. Remedying the Maladies of 'Lesser Men or Women':

The personal, political and Constitutional Imperatives for Improved access to Justice. *South African Journal on Human Rights,* 24, 2, pp.263-280.

Heywood, M., 2009. South Africa's Treatment Action Campaign: Combining Law and Social Mobilisation to Realise the Right to Health. *Journal of Human Rights Practice,* 1(1).

Hogerzeil, H. et al., 2006. Is Access to Essential Medicines as Part of the Right to Health Enforceable Through the Courts. *The Lancet,* 368, July 22. Available at: www.thelancet.com.

Hunter, M., 2007. The Changing Political Economy of Sex in South Africa: The Significance of Unemployment and Inequalities to the Scale of the AIDS pandemic. *Social Science and Medicine,* 64, pp.689-700.

Jochelson, K., 2001. The Color of Disease, Syphilis and Racism in South Africa, 1850-1950. London: Palgrave Macmillan.

Klug, H., 2000. Constituting Democracy, Law, Globalism and South Africa's Political Reconstruction. Cambridge: Cambridge University Press.

Loff, B. and Heywood, M., 2002. Patents on Drugs: Manufacturing Scarcity or Advancing Health? *The Journal of Law Medicine and Ethics,* 30(4), Winter.

Lurie, M., 2000. Migration and HIV/AIDS in Southern Africa: A Review. *South African Journal of Science,* 96.

Nattrass, N., 2007. Mortal Combat, AIDS Denialism and the Struggle for Antiretrovirals in South Africa. Pietermaritzburg: University of KwaZulu Natal Press.

Rehle, T. et al., 2007. National HIV Incidence Measures – New Insights into the South African Epidemic. *South African Medical Journal,* 97(3), pp.194-199.

Sen, A., 2008. Comment: Why and How is Health a Human Right? *The Lancet,* 272(9655), 13 December.

South African Health Review. 2008. Health and Related Indicators. Durban: Health Systems Trust.

Weiser, S.D. Leiter, K. Bangsberg, D.R., Butler, L.M., Percy-de Korte, F. et al., (2007). Food Insufficiency Is Associated with High-Risk Sexual Behavior among Women in Botswana and Swaziland. *PLoS Medicine,* 4(10).
e260 doi:10.1371/journal.pmed.0040260

World Health Organisation. 2008. Closing the Gap in a Generation, Health Equity Through Action on the Social Determinants of Health. Final Report of the Commission on Social Determinants of Health, Executive Summary.

UNAIDS. 2008. Report on the Global AIDS Epidemic. Available at: http://www.unaids.org/en/KnowledgeCentre/HIVData/GlobalReport/2008/2008_Global_report.

14.
Rural survival, development or advocacy?
Mary Galvin

Introduction

Lip service is paid to addressing poverty in rural areas, but little effort is made by either government officials or activists to understand what is really going on in these areas, which remain "terra incognita". Instead of unpacking the variety of organisational structures in rural areas, the tendency is to make assumptions about the "rural periphery" and to "see what you want to see". Aside from being highly insulting to the masses of people who live in these areas, essentially dismissing their realities and agency, these projections undermine prospects for anti-poverty programmes to succeed, as well as for social movement activists to promote more "revolutionary" responses to the structural causes of poverty.

To date practitioners and researchers have failed to engage adequately with one of the most difficult and important realities characterising civil society and its relationship with the South African government. The major study on the size and scope of the non-profit sector in South Africa concluded that the number of CBOs proliferated to 53 per cent of the total number of non-profit organisations (Swilling and Russell, 2003). The main non-governmental actors at the grassroots level are no longer NGOs, but CBOs, ranging from development committees to sewing and gardening clubs. If NGOs are praised internationally for being able to extend service delivery while contributing to the participatory nature of democracy, CBOs combine these advantages with a local and, because local people themselves rather than outsiders are driving the organisation, arguably a more legitimate base. Thus, at first glance, CBOs appear to be an ideal organisational form. But further questions require exploration.

What is the overall motivation or *reason d'etre* of CBOs? How do they relate to outside organisations? What potential do they exhibit for implementing development plans? Do CBOs operate as an independent component of civil society? What contribution do they make to a vibrant civil society? Do CBOs provide a basis for a burgeoning anti-neoliberal social movement?

Research concentrated on dynamics in rural areas, which are often ignored even though the need for development is dire. Based on key informant interviews, areas were selected based on evidence of variance in community dynamics and levels of organisation. The three areas in

KwaZulu Natal included Mvuzane, about 40 kilometres west of Eshowe; Nsukangihlale, about 30 kilometres west of Escourt in the Drakensburg mountains; and Mbazwana, next to Sodwana Bay. Mvenyane, Masakala, and Diaho are in close proximity to Matatiele, but fall in the Eastern Cape. These areas can all be described as rural but differed enough in location and history to produce findings that are both interesting and characteristic of a range of rural areas.

Contextualising rural CBOs

While there have been interesting analyses of NGOs and their changing role in South Africa (e.g. Habib and Taylor, 1999), the academic literature has yet to capture adequately the history of CBOs and the ways in which they arose from and interacted with the history of South Africa. This section begins by providing a simplified overview to help contextualise the rise of CBOs during this period.

In response to South Africa's apartheid history, South Africa has not only NGOs but also CBOs, whose differentiation and relationship is unique to the country. Local NGOs were formed in South Africa to challenge aspects of apartheid and to channel resources to black people. These organisations were typically run and staffed by whites. International NGOs worked through local NGOs, so they did not have a presence of their own. Local civics that arose in townships were the first equivalent of what are now termed CBOs. They were locally based and locally run organisations that responded to the daily concerns of people's lives and placed them in the larger context.

The South African National Civics Organisation (SANCO) organised civics to fight the apartheid system, became politicised, and represented civics nationally (Seekings, 2007). Although civics arose in some rural areas, they were more difficult to organise, one reason being that it was difficult to organise around specific grievances since the whole rural existence was often a result of apartheid policies. In addition, civics were frequently blocked by existing power structures, such as Traditional Authorities in KwaZulu Natal. Other precursors to CBOs included Zenzele Women's Groups, which focused on income generation and were survivalist in nature, as well as faith based organisations and black consciousness groups.

From 1990, and particularly from 1994, the number of CBOs multiplied, as freedom of organising and a chance at improving local circumstances widened. The RDP clearly raised people's hopes of government delivery. However, the RDP Office also sent the message that participation was a cornerstone of the RDP and that people would be expected to have structures to assist government with setting local priorities and helping to deliver its development promises. Although new RDP committees were formed, CBOs were considered attractive for the same reasons that NGOs are praised internationally: they are stereotyped as participatory and community sensitive. Moreover, South African CBOs have the added value of being closer to the people, being their own spokespersons, and avoiding the patriarchal approach of whites that is often part of the apartheid legacy.

The international development literature has produced classifications that include organisations whose nature is either 'grassroots-social change' or 'technical-private sector'. CBOs can be accommodated in existing classifications as grassroots organisations. The chart below outlines classifications of four authors. Friedman, in reference to Villegas' classification, distinguishes between popular organisations, politically progressive NGOs, professionally oriented NGOs, and parastatal NGOs (Freidmann, 1992). These relate well to the types of organisations referred to above.

Author	Grassroots-Social Change	Technical-Private sector or state
Villegas	Popular organisations, politically progressive NGOs	Professionally oriented NGOs, parastatal NGOs.
Clark	Advocacy groups and networks, grassroots development organisations, popular development agencies	Public service contractors, technical innovation organisations, and relief and welfare agencies
Korten	People's organisations, voluntary organisations	Public service contractors, governmental NGOs
Smillie	Community based voluntarism, institutionalisation	Professionalisation, welfare state

Similarly, Clark's typology (above) refers to Advocacy Groups and Networks, Grassroots Development Organisations, and Popular Development Agencies, which would all fall on the Grassroots Organisations-Social Change end of the continuum. His remaining organisations, public service contractors, technical innovation organisations and relief and welfare agencies, belong alongside the technical-private sector and state organisations end of the continuum (Clark, 1991). Korten's typology is straightforward, ranging from people's organisations to governmental NGO (Korten, 1987). Yet the requirement that voluntary organisations depend on voluntarism pushes many different NGOs into the public service contractor type by default. Finally, Smillie refers to stages through which organisations move back and forth (Smillie, 1995).

What is the basis for classifying organisations as 'grassroots-social change' or 'technical-private sector'? Classification depends largely on the attributes one deems to be important. Although the development literature treats ideology as a significant aspect of organisations, it has not been developed into an organisational classification. Yet an important basis of difference amongst NGOs is often ideology, or the dominant values, norms, or orientation within an organisation.[1] In terms of ideology, NGOs can be classified as social change or technical according to several characteristics:

Grassroots/ CBOs	Social Change	Technical outputs
Based in the community	People-centred or driven, bottom up Internal aim of democratic practice	Top down with participation Internal Hierarchy
Community need as end	End as social transformation Empowerment	Process as a means to achieve end, product as end Delivery
Relatively ad hoc	Learning organisation, shifting strategies	Blueprint
Politics of survival	Political, strong ideals (can include 'radical' causes that are not necessarily left wing)	Non-political
Local realities	Local realities	Linear, mainstream approach Modernisation

In contrast, as grassroots organisations, CBOs are placed alongside social change NGOs. In general, they may appear to exhibit a mixture of the characteristics listed above: they are based entirely in the community, pursue a community need as an end, and are less conscious of organisational approach and structure. The overriding factor is often

1. I refer to the 'dominant' ideology in recognition of the fact that there are ongoing power struggles within organisations over ideology, as discussed in organisational theory literature.

that, at some level, CBOs are simply about survival. In terms of their approaches, internal functioning, and the ends being pursued, CBOs differ from NGOs in that many CBOs are not driven by what many might recognise as an ideology per se, but by creating an immediate response to local realities. However survival itself can serve as an ideology, allowing these CBOs to "demand access to the resources it mobilises in a manner that refutes orthodox developmental logic" and to locate themselves as closer to social change NGOs or social movements (Bond, 1999).

Since organisations often embody a mixture of characteristics, they can be placed along a continuum. Grassroots organisations/ CBOs as well as social change and technical NGOs are presented above as ideal types. It is highly unlikely that any organisation will fit one of these descriptions entirely. Organisations are constantly in flux, interacting with their environment and with other organisations. Thus they can be placed along a continuum according to what is given priority and to what degree, depending on their embodiment of these characteristics. It is also useful to place this continuum within its wider environment, including what is often referred to as the first (state) and second (private) sector (Clayton et al., 1996: 20):

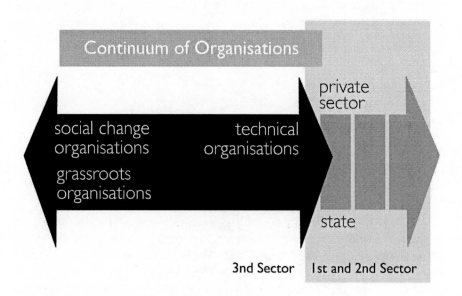

Conceptualising organisations along a continuum allows for their movement in response to financial pressures, new formative experiences, and ideological shifts. Analyses of NGOs and CBOs often focus on how CBOs are becoming more like NGOs and NGOs are becoming more like consultants. They assess why NGOs have tended to move toward the technical end of the spectrum and some CBOs have also moved toward becoming more professionalised.[2] However it is often implied that it is fruitless to study NGOs and CBOs since they are in flux. While acknowledging that CBOs move along this continuum, and that their characteristics may shift, this should not deter researchers from gaining a better understanding of CBOs within this organisational range. This is also important to monitor potential movement in the opposite direction, as CBOs respond to the impact of neoliberal policies.

CBOs' motivation may differ depending on their location along the continuum. Kotze ponders whether the motivation of CBOs is to help extend the reach of the state's service delivery, which she refers to as the "efficiency argument," or to "organise against the human fallout of neoliberal policies" (Kotze, 2004: 21-23). She seems to subscribe to a third option, which is that communities have formed CBOs to help them survive in response to desperate economic circumstances and the neglect of the state. The first two motivations reflect debates and divisions taking place within the NGO sector; the 'efficiency argument' seems to characterise a technical NGO and the organising argument seems to characterise a social change NGO. Analyses that consider CBOs as having either of these motivations are probably observing CBOs that have essentially become NGOs. As evident in the following section, the motivation Kotze proposes is far more consistent with characteristics of a typical CBO in rural areas.

A typology of CBOs

Most rural CBOs can be characterised as one of the following types: coping or survival; income generation; service delivery, governance, and advocacy; and culture, youth and sport. This typology offers a framework to assist in organising and examining the complex reality of rural CBOs, but does not claim to be definitive. A couple of issues arise immediately. First, there can be overlap between types. For example, a small block-making project not only generates income, but also offers its members a way of coping or survival. A dance project can be both cultural and income generating. The following profiles illustrate how the defining characteristics of CBOs were used to place organisations in a given type. Second, while types appear neatly defined, what happens in

---

2. Organisations' need to obtain funding explains much of their behaviour. Other pressures arise from being part of a wider network, when primary accountability can shift from local members to the network. Clearly there are competing demands that make the ideal of remaining accountable and attentive to the local level difficult to maintain.

rural areas does not lend itself to easy definition. This is because local people act on their own initiative to establish local structures that work for them or access other resources available through NGOs, other CBOs, or government and adapt them to their local needs. This section describes each type of CBO and discusses typical issues that they encounter.

Coping/ survival CBOs

As their name indicates, coping or survival CBOs help people deal with life realities such as food security, sickness, and death. These include CBOs such as burial societies, stokvels, and HIV/AIDS or other health care and awareness groups. It is likely that historians would date this type of CBOs to the mid-1800s when mutual aid organisations emerged with the rise of migrant labour.

Based on this history, two characteristics distinguish coping and survival CBOs. First, this type of CBOs depends almost exclusively on funds from within the community. Stokvels and burial societies most clearly take a local form, with people joining and providing funds. Many HIV/AIDS CBOs also use their own resources, although some work within a governmental framework.

Second, coping or survival CBOs tend to be both driven and comprised almost exclusively of women, on one hand seeming to confirm the gender stereotype of women as the caregivers but also showing once again that women are the backbone of rural households. They also play a central role in these CBOs because coping and survival CBOs are ironically not perceived as entailing levels of power and responsibility.[3]

Most burial societies operate as they do in Nsukangihlale. Here there are two burial societies to which members make a small monthly contribution of R20. Both burial societies pay around R800 to the family when a family member dies. One has 105 members and has buried 47 people since 1997 (interview AP6). In Mbazwana, there is one burial society that also operates in this manner. Another does not take contributions or provide funds; instead it helps the bereaved with food and support. There is no dedicated burial society in Mvuzane, but a CBO with another purpose has occasionally provided limited funds to families. Burial societies were not found to be as widespread in these

---

3. Kongolo and Bamgose (2002) assert that women are generally inactive participants in development initiatives, 'especially where they entail significant power and responsibility'. Although this can explain their predominant role in coping and survival CBOs, this research shows that class as well as gender explains women's involvement as women do play a role in other CBOs.

three areas of KwaZulu Natal as one might expect given the increase in deaths due to AIDS related illnesses.

Burial societies appear to be more widespread in the Eastern Cape. In Masakala, there are many burial societies offering different benefits that people can choose between when joining. In Diaho, the significance of burial societies is evident in the fact that they are registered by the Traditional Authority and given the power to operate. The umbrella CBO in the area encourages women to select and join a burial society and helps resolve any disagreements between the burial society and the claimants.

Stokvels have become a well-known component of rural livelihood strategies. They save and invest money through the monthly contributions of members and buy food in bulk on an annual basis for distribution to members. The number of members varies depending on the stokvel, typically between 10 and 30. The number of stokvels in an area is likely to vary according to geography and relations/ trust between neighbours, but there is an average of at least three stokvels per ward or induna area.

Two interesting variants of stokvels were noted in these areas. First, some stokvels have begun to operate a parallel savings structure to meet children's educational costs. This shows that people have experienced stokvels as useful enough to extend the model to other areas of their lives where they struggle. Second, stokvels in Mvuzane compelled members to borrow a certain amount of money each year so that the stokvel can make interest on the loan. If a member does not borrow money, he or she must make a payment to the stokvel for the equivalent interest. Others do not compel members to borrow, but charge members who do borrow more than twice the prime lending rate.

The HIV/AIDS CBOs that exist in an area depend on what local people have considered necessary. In a small area like Mvuzane, which has not fully felt the affect of AIDS (or has not acknowledged its impact), there are no HIV/AIDS related CBOs. In contrast, in Mbazwana, there is an awareness CBO, Inhlelenyo Youth HIV and AIDS Awareness Group, that does performances and drumming around preventing HIV and taking care of people who are ill. The local development committee was the catalyst for the formation of this CBO and has provided limited funds. The CBO has received no outside funding (interview B5). In Nsukangihlale there is a singing group called Peace Against Aids that holds singing competitions and uses the event to talk about AIDS. This CBO also made a video that provides counselling on HIV and AIDS (interview A7).

While younger men are involved in awareness activities related to HIV/AIDS, the direct care of people with general health problems or illnesses due to HIV are almost entirely conducted by women, particularly middle aged or older women. Nsukangihlale and the three communities in the Eastern Cape followed the suggestion of the Department of Health at the time of the RDP to acquire community health workers and, more recently, to organise home-based care for those with HIV/AIDS. Although a promise to provide funding seemed to accompany government's 'suggestion', this has not been forthcoming.[4] Perhaps due to the lack of outside funding, community members perceive these initiatives as community driven and identify home-based care, as well as community health workers and the health committee, as important CBOs. Home-based care CBOs assist sick people by caring for the sick and providing food. These CBOs are well structured: volunteers are organised per district and feed into a wider committee for the entire area. Community health workers, who work on a voluntary basis, conduct door-to-door visits for the ill and provide education and information about HIV/AIDS. The Health Committee monitors and encourages health workers to do their job properly.

Income-generating CBOs

Income generating CBOs produce a good that is sold and the profit is then shared among its members. Some of their activities include sewing, gardening, catering, poultry, block making, candle making, and crafts. Most income generating CBOs are comprised mainly of women, since men are often working as migrant labourers or are disinterested. There is a clear gender division in the composition of various income generating groups. Although the gender composition of CBOs varies per area, men tend to be engaged in agricultural CBOs, poultry, or block making and women tend to comprise gardening, sewing, catering, candle making, and craft CBOs. The differences can appear minimal to an outsider, for example between agriculture and gardening or between crafts using beads or crafts using wood. The division reflects accepted gender roles and the status of women within the community. Issues that typically arise within income generating CBOs include needing funds for training, as well as start up capital and inputs. In running projects, CBOs often face the problem of a market for their goods and experience conflict among members around the administration of the project.

---

4. These findings are based on the three areas in the Eastern Cape. Here it was reported that, most recently, the Department of Health asked that NGOs and CBOs together form committees to bring together their needs. It appears that funds have been provided for community health workers in KwaZulu-Natal.

Some income generating projects start with enthusiasm and then fall apart because they are not profitable. Many goods that they generate are trying to compete with cheaper goods, which are often produced and imported in bulk and sold cheaply.[5] For example, a woman in Mvuzane studied sewing, returned to the community, and started a sewing CBO with her sewing machine. She taught the members, who contributed funds to buy materials (interview M3). This would appear to be an impressive case of entrepreneurship and the transmission of skills. However the project made little profit and the CBO gradually stopped operating. Donors who provide funds for income generating projects often support these projects because they are considered a means of empowering the local population. In cases such as the one above, it is not clear whether the net effect is empowering or discouraging future efforts.

Most rural communities have some form of gardening CBOs working on communal gardens, typically initiated by either an NGO or by an extension officer from the Department of Agriculture. Gardening CBOs are particularly important if there is a shortage of land with access to water. Working together also helps increase women's motivation because they are not working in isolation and can share responsibility. After the women take their share of produce for home use, the remainder may be sold locally and any profit is put back into the garden or possibly shared among members. Often there is very little profit generated by community gardens.

Another drawback is that gardening projects are often beset by the free rider problem, that is women who contribute different amounts of labour all obtain the same end benefit, leading some members to contribute little labour or to 'free ride'. This dynamic engenders resentment and infighting between members. In Mvuzane, after functioning for nearly ten years, the women became discouraged and gradually abandoned the Zamimphilo gardening project. Tired of infighting amongst members and frustrated by the theft of vegetables, more and more members opted to garden small plots next to their homes for their own use. The CBO collapsed (interview M1). In Nsukangihlale, an agricultural project was started on the newly redistributed land but experienced the problems of free riding and low profits and stopped operating during its first year (interview A21).

One conclusion is that less 'generic' projects, or projects responding to specific local circumstances or opportunities, have a greater chance of success. For example, one can compare the likelihood of success of a

---

5. The price of goods CBOs produce is already subsidised because the cost of sewing machines and materials has already been covered.

block making project in Mvuzane with a craft project in Nsukangihlale. Although five people were trained in Mvuzane, there is no clear market for blocks. In contrast, community leaders in Nsukangihlale are working closely with the Natal Parks Board that manages the nearby Giants Castle Nature Reserve to ensure that the project meets the demand of tourists (interview A11).[6] Such an option clearly depends on the proximity of a community to a tourism site. For example, in both Nsukangihlale and Mbazwana, the Natal Parks Board has liaised with youth who have formed cultural dance groups to perform for tourists. Otherwise it is the element of uniqueness that is important. Perhaps the paper-making project being initiated in Mbazwana using fibres from pineapple, sugarcane, bananas, and grass offers the most potential (interview B1).

In two areas in the Eastern Cape, Masakala and Diaho, community members have established CBOs to coordinate income-generating activities. Their logic is that this allows greater economies of scale as well as avoiding duplication and creating the framework for groups to support one another. In Masakala, the Community-Based Tourism Organisation was established to ensure fair share benefits to the community from tourism. In Diaho, the George Moshesh CBO has poultry and garden projects for the benefit of the entire area. Most of its members are women whose husbands are migrant labourers; this allows them to do something themselves to provide food for their families. Both of these CBOs are discussed below in more detail as case studies.

Service delivery, governance and advocacy CBOs

Service Delivery CBOs help bring services to rural areas or help manage them. Services include water, sanitation, roads, schools, and land. The members of Service Delivery CBOs are typically elected by a show of hands at a community meeting called by the Traditional Authority.[7] Those elected tend to be local 'big men' or people who have significant standing in the community. These positions are considered powerful and are highly visible, so it is not surprising that both gender and class are central to the selection of CBO members. This means that their level of commitment or availability to contribute to the project is generally limited. The community response to problems arising in CBOs is either to ignore them or to elect new members to the committee. Although many Service Delivery CBOs are linked to a specific project, most are

---

6. Still one can point to many craft projects that produce more of the same types of crafts for an already glutted market.
7. This form of 'election' limits competition, but gives legitimacy to the process.

sub-committees of a wider development committee and are rarely dissolved when a project is completed.

Development committees and service delivery CBOs played a particularly prominent role during the country's transition to democracy in the early 1990's, when state structures and institutions were not yet in place. These CBOs were formed to fill a gap in governance and began to see the coordination and implementation of local development plans as their responsibility. With the introduction of local government in 1995/1996, their role has become increasingly complex and contentious (Galvin, 1999). This is particularly the case since service delivery CBOs are elected by the community and consider themselves best able to represent local concerns.

Perhaps the most typical CBO in rural areas is the water committee or water CBO. Often the water committee is considered a sub-committee of a wider development committee. Water committees are often formed because a community wants to embark on a water project and it is well-known that NGOs such as Mvula Trust as well as the Department of Water Affairs and Forestry require a water committee. Sanitation committees have developed along the same lines, particularly as a consequence of the cholera epidemic in KwaZulu Natal in 2000/2001 during which over 100,000 cases were reported. It is frequently noted by outsiders that, while women are usually responsible for collecting water, water committees are often comprised primarily of men.

Since water committees are often formed to meet an external requirement, this has sometimes raised the issue of how 'real' they are. In Mvuzane, the Zamimphilo water committee relies almost entirely on the individual who applied to Mvula Trust. Although there were clearly meetings, members of the committee say that they do not know much about the project. Even officers of the water committee referred basic questions to the individual who applied. In other areas, such as Nsukangihlale, this external requirement has acted as a useful catalyst for the formation of a committee and the experience implementing a project has helped to build the committee's capacity. The strength of a committee seems to relate closely to the existing capacity within a community.

One of the main problems that emerged was that water committees or CBOs were handed responsibility for a basic service like water without the necessary authority. Before water schemes were implemented, water committees had to agree to implement cost recovery plans formulated by outside agencies upon the completion of the schemes. Desperate for water and unaware of the potential pitfalls of cost recovery, water committees usually agreed to do so. In Mvuzane, neither of the two water projects funded by the Municipality is functional. Not surprisingly, water committees were unable to implement untenable cost recovery plans, damaging the confidence of members trained for this purpose (interview M5). This has a significant impact on the emerging leadership in the area and the perceptions of community members of their capabilities.

As a result of the Water Services Act [8], all water projects were transferred to local government municipalities, raising the issue of whether there is still a role for water committees. In Nsukangihlale the local government municipality took over the water project and the Masibambisane water committee stopped functioning. Now the water project, which worked well before, is no longer working and many community members feel that they have no power over the situation (interview A28). In contrast, in two of the three areas studied in the Eastern Cape, namely Masakala and Diaho, Maluti Water implemented schemes and communities formed project steering committees to work on the projects. These schemes have been transferred to local government, which appointed the project steering committees as Water Service Providers. While this was the type of institutional arrangement anticipated in the application of the Water Services Act, many local government municipalities perceive water committees or CBOs in their areas as lacking the capacity to play this role (Galvin and Habib, 2003). In cases where CBOs play a role as Water Service Providers, this is either a transitional arrangement such as in Ugu District Municipality or the municipality treats CBOs as small businesses such as in Chris Hani Municipality (Galvin, 2009).

Sanitation committees have operated in a similar manner as water committees. The main difference is that rural communities have generally sought water, but have not been interested in sanitation projects since the need for sanitation is not immediately evident. The cholera epidemic in 2000/2001 resulted in an influx of resources for sanitation. As specified by Mvula Trust and the Department of Water Affairs and Forestry, CBOs took on the role of 'creating demand' and supervising the building of toilets. Their ability to play this role was significant to implementing a sustainable response to cholera and other diseases. However it is clear that sanitation committees were formed due to external demand. In Nsukangihlale, the Emahlutshini Sanitation Project was described by one interviewee as, "formed by Thukela Municipality with Mvula Trust" (interview AP17).

School committees or governing bodies are typically formed because the Department of Education in terms of the School Act wants to involve parents in the education of their children. However, they sometimes take

---

8. Republic of South Africa, *Water Services Act*, no.108 (Pretoria, 1997).

an interest in improving infrastructure. In Mvuzane, the school committee is comprised of a group of parents who have been trying to get financial assistance to build another school. Many children walk seven kilometres through steep terrain to reach school. The Traditional Authority's response was that the committee should do something on its own and then government may provide assistance when some progress is evident (interview M5).

In Nsukangihlale, the Natal Schools Project, an NGO, has assisted with the building and renovating of classrooms. In the Eastern Cape, each of the three communities studied has a School Governing Body (SGB).[9] The SGBs managed the building of three classrooms for each school in the area [10] and, based on this experience, another funder is planning to provide funds directly to SGBs for the construction of additional classrooms. All CBOs make input into the SGB, allowing for the linkage of issues. For example, there are often discussions looking at school funds and agreements around what people can do if they are not working.

With a clear advocacy agenda, communities form land committees to claim land from which they were removed during apartheid. In Mbazwana, the land committee claimed state coastal forest. It received 20,000 hectares in Emandeni from government; however it is specified that this land will not be used for households but for business. For the amaHlubi Land Committee to receive 8,600 hectares of land, a condition of the Department of Land Affairs was that the committee becomes a Trust responsible for managing the land. Not only did this change the nature of the CBO, but it also affected its functioning since the Trust is now in conflict with the Traditional Authority over power.[11]

Culture, youth, and sport CBOs

Culture, Youth, and Sport CBOs are formed around members' shared interests. Cultural groups formed around dancing and singing are often considered income generating CBOs if that is their main aim. Not only do sports groups improve members' playing skills, but they also offer a way for a member to become known outside his local area. When playing other groups, members can be identified to pursue a professional career.

---

9. As Minister of Education, Kadar Asmal arranged for SGBs to be registered as section 21 companies. Essentially this allows for a local CBO to manage the education of its children.
10. Classrooms were built with funding from the Japanese Embassy through the Independent Development Trust.
11. This information was provided by researchers who live in these areas and, in the case of the amaHlubi, was confirmed in interviews for another project.

Youth groups have been formed in these areas, but have generally lacked an aim and failed to initiate anything. Arguably this has not only been due to 'lazy' or 'undirected' youth, but also to a lack of support from the community at large. In more 'traditional' areas of KwaZulu Natal like Mvuzane, the tendency has been for active members of the community, who are elders, to suspect attempts by youth to organise as being instigators of the ANC. This is clearly a danger in rural KwaZulu Natal where there has been ongoing violence between supporters of competing political parties. In most areas this has eroded community support for youth efforts and acted as a strong disincentive for youth themselves to get involved.

Sometimes the 'community' supports the youth nominally. In Nsukangihlale, the umbrella development committee formed a youth committee by holding an election at a community meeting. Although probably well-intentioned, it seems unlikely that the youth committee will have much success with this genesis or with its aim 'to develop life skills of the youth, education, health, and economy'. However youth do play an important role in some rural areas. Youth organising has been exceptional in Mbazwana, where the development committee as well as individual leaders have supported the initiatives of youth to form CBOs that play a role in lifesaving and local security.

CBO complexities

Treating CBOs as an 'unknown', this research used an open-ended approach to avoid the tendency of outsiders to 'see what you want to see'. Instead of asking whether rural CBOs might help with state delivery (the 'efficiency' agenda) or act as a basis for a social movement (the 'organising' agenda), it explored the genesis and characteristics of CBOs, and their relationships with NGOs and local government in six rural areas of KwaZulu Natal and the Eastern Cape. On this basis, it proposed a rough typology of CBOs that includes very different organisations: survival or coping; income generating; service delivery, governance and advocacy; and culture, youth, and sport CBOs. Although typologies force a complex empirical reality into a simplified theoretical one by their very nature, this exercise was valuable because it provides us with analytical purchase in understanding CBOs. Including a range of CBO types made apparent the diverse ways in which people respond to a challenging environment. If less 'developmental' organisations are not considered CBOs, we miss important local dynamics and expressions of people's agency that are potential bases for engaging and challenging the state (Chazan, 1994).

Applying this typology, one can see how the formation and composition of specific types of CBOs is a direct reflection of local power dynamics, often expressed in terms of gender and class. Survival and income generating CBOs are typically comprised of voluntary members. Members are predominantly women, most of whom are middle aged or older. In contrast, service delivery, governance and advocacy CBOs are mainly elected members who have significant economic or political standing; they are predominantly men. The former are related to survival or caring for the household, which tend to be considered by the community as low status, where the latter are engaged in visible, high profile activities that build their power in the community. In other words, local power dynamics and gender divisions are reflected in the composition of CBOs. This in turn affects the potential for rural CBOs to help deliver services or 'development' and/or to pursue a social change agenda.

Potential for CBOs to play a 'larger' role

The divide between these types of CBOs has important implications for both the efficiency and activist agenda. Overall it appears that local dynamics in which CBOs are engaged often limit the likelihood of their playing a 'larger role'. How might it be possible to overcome these limitations? Clearly CBO members themselves need to challenge and change these power dynamics. This typically requires a change agent from inside the community, probably in the form of empowered community members willing to challenge the status quo, or an internal change or crisis that creates an opening, such as the weakening or departure of a leader. Although outside organisations working in the area can help strengthen the voices of the less powerful and affect power dynamics, their efforts are only likely to succeed in a community with a pre-existing social foundation for change (Galvin, 2005).[12]

In terms of the 'efficiency' agenda, survival and income generating CBOs tend to operate on a small scale, but some may offer potential for expansion to help the state meet its objectives. With capacity building and limited project funding, it is possible that members of these CBOs, who are often committed individuals, could expand health services or contribute to limited economic objectives in rural areas. This is a benefit of the way the macro-structures operate in the research areas in the Eastern Cape - the committed volunteers from small CBOs end up

---

12. See summary in Galvin, M., (forthcoming 2010). *Unintended Consequences: Development interventions and socio-political change in rural South Africa.* In W. Freund and H. Witt, eds. *Development Dilemmas in Post-Apartheid South Africa.*

forming a much more powerful intermediary capable of engaging with larger initiatives. Of course problems can arise if the intermediary assumes a dominant role and acts as a gatekeeper. In general, service delivery CBOs are more likely to have the capacity to implement larger scale development projects, but their elected members may be too busy to play a consistent role in implementing projects.

In contrast, given their capacity, one might expect service delivery CBOs to be more effective in adopting an 'organising' or activist position vis-a-vis power structures, particularly the state. Certainly this has potential in areas where the local leadership is open and interested in challenging the state around social justice issues that affect their area. But members are typically distracted by local power struggles rather than engaging with broader issues that are often perceived as external. A key consideration is that members of these CBOs themselves tend to be part of or closely aligned to local power structures, making such advocacy highly unlikely.

In some cases, instead of seeing external support to other CBOs as something to build on, development committees feel threatened by other groups developing contacts and perhaps obtaining some resources and spend their energies trying to assert control over projects. Moreover, it is difficult for rural people to see the link between their survival-related issues and the broader issues of social movements. There is clearly a material and issue basis for organising in rural areas, but it seems that an external catalyst is needed to widen CBOs' vision of power and of what they can achieve.[13] Building an understanding of the broader context of survival issues in rural areas is a significant undertaking for activists.

The majority of CBOs were formed to address the basic survival needs of rural people, although the definition of 'survival' is wider than originally hypothesised. CBOs exist to play a direct role in responding to local people's needs. Without an external catalyst, they are generally not interested in either the 'efficiency' or 'organising' agendas.

Personalising structures

Typically CBOs are initiated by individuals with a concrete purpose in mind that meets immediate rural needs. In many cases the strength and capacity of individuals seem to contribute more to rural development

---

13. In the late 1990s the National Land Committee and the Rural Development Services Network were active in trying to build a Rural Social Movement. The issues are clearly ripe in rural areas, even if activism is difficult to motivate. Reference is often made to Colin Bundy's, *The Rise and Fall of the South African Peasantry*.

than CBOs as such. This tendency to personalise activity may be indicative of either the agrarian status of these areas or the 'pioneer' stage of an organisation in terms of organisational development. In the most positive cases, the individual is not simply acting in his or her own interest, but initiates a CBO as a vehicle for individuals to organise, gain wider participation, and obtain community acceptance for his or her aim. Of course, there are cases in which individuals are clearly acting in their own self- interest. For example, some CBOs are formed with all their members from a single family and then seek funding.[14] While an individual with capacity can play a positive role in generating activity in an area, s/he can also play a dominant and controlling role in CBOs, fostering the dependence of CBO members. By developing the capacity of weaker CBO members, not only would skills be spread, but the reliance of CBOs on individuals and their ability to dominate decisions would be checked.

When NGOs work in rural areas, it is usually around implementing a specific project. An interesting research finding was that CBOs establish relationships with NGO staff members as individuals, reinforcing the tendency to personalise relationships in rural areas. For example, interviewees gave the name and description of individuals who worked in the area from outside, but struggled to give the name of the NGO the individual represented. One CBO member had worked on an NGO project for five years and only knew the names of the individuals. This confirms that the tendency of CBO members is to focus on local dynamics and what is most immediately significant to their lives, not organisations that are distant geographically and in terms of development 'language', identity, and capacity. Most rural CBOs do not develop ongoing relationships with outside organisations or organisational linkages or networks, which is an important component in being part of a social movement or in creating transnational linkages (Keck and Sikkink, 1998).

Resource dynamics and structures

The need for resources has also driven communities to form certain structures. In a rural area, one often finds as many committees as there are government departments, NGOs, and other organisations working there. Another example is that the RDP Office demanded that small CBOs organise themselves. So communities in the Eastern Cape developed their 'mega-structures' in the hope of obtaining funding. Now these are

---

14. After a steep learning curve, most donors have established means to insure that this is not the case before providing funds.

the only structures they consider to be CBOs. Community members insist that small groups are not CBOs, while outsiders tend to think about almost any community structure dealing with community issues as a CBO.

CBOs often work through or report to a wider development committee, which in turn relates to either the inkosi or local government councillors. On one level, this simply means that CBOs are 'small fish' that must deal with various power structures. The real question is whether CBOs' decisions are unduly affected or their identities seriously constrained. In some areas CBOs are simply required to present their plans to the traditional authority and can then go about their work. This is often a matter of protocol in KwaZulu Natal; in the Eastern Cape, government line departments such as the Department of Agriculture or the Department of Welfare often bypass these structures and deal directly with CBOs. In contrast, other CBOs must discuss all plans with the traditional authority, which must approve all funding and decisions. Similarly, development committees liaising with local government councillors can support and strengthen local CBOs or they can block local efforts by imposing their blueprint for development and organisation.

CBO leaders may be frustrated to see well-funded NGOs implementing projects while they struggle to obtain funds. Yet, the difference in scope and capacity of NGOs and CBOs in rural areas has typically meant that the competition over resources between CBOs and NGOs is not a reality. Instead CBOs look to NGOs as a source of resources and support. In fact, CBO leaders often complain that few NGOs reach rural areas. Of course, the absence of natural competition changed with the funding environment. Funds became scarce with the 'funding drought' which began in the mid-1990s and all civil society organisations began to compete for the same funds.

CBO relationships with local government

In the mid-1990s Jay Naidoo, then Minister Without Portfolio heading the RDP Office, referred to local government as the "hands and the feet of the RDP." NGOs expected new local government structures to provide funding to NGOs and CBOs to implement projects. Many projects that NGOs would have implemented in the past became the responsibility of local government. One would expect that local government would work with both CBOs and NGOs toward the implementation of such projects. This relationship would be a form of resource dependency that NGOs have established with national and provincial government departments, but it is not evident between NGOs or CBOs and local government in rural areas.

Although local government may see legitimate weaknesses in the ability of specific NGOs to deliver, no organisation is ideal for delivery. In many cases, the added value of using NGOs has diminished since there is an overall shift of NGOs toward the technical side of the organisational spectrum; NGOs can be difficult to distinguish from consultants. However it also seems that the tendency of some local government officials and councillors to criticise NGOs is a product of their political interest. For example, local government councillors establish databases of NGOs and consultants and act as middlemen with the community. The motivations of local government councillors and civil servants are complex: to 'protect' the community and to establish a patron-client relationship in the process; to monitor development as part of their technical responsibility; and to maximise their visibility and gain political 'credit' for projects. In general, officials and councillors appear to perceive NGOs as competition or as blocking them in playing these roles.

The tendency of outside agencies is to treat rural areas as if they are a 'blank slate'. Perhaps they do this because there appears to be a power vacuum. This is clearly a fundamental mistake. As this research has illustrated, there are a range of local structures, and a wealth of experience, for any development initiative to be built upon. The specific history of the area and the dynamics between community members and leaders are a major factor, explaining the nature of relations between CBOs and local government as well as the development potential of various areas.

Unresolved issues around the role of local government in rural areas and a lack of clarity by community members and their leaders about the system undermine socio-political dynamics in rural areas overall. As a result, locally specific outcomes have emerged in areas, depending on the history of local leaders and other influential individuals. These have taken a range of forms. Sometimes local government councillors are in conflict with CBOs, caught up in what one might call a 'battle over turf' or a contentious relationship. This is based on the question of who can represent rural people's concerns. Although a councillor may be elected to do so, local people often feel that their own structure more legitimately represents them. Councillors often want to work on their own and may even feel that CBOs should dissolve. Alternatively, local government councillors are unknown in the area and the CBO gets on with its work, in other words it is 'business as usual'. Although local government councillors are supposed to represent a wide area, they typically attend to local issues or concerns only when they actually come from the area. This relationship is also contentious, although unexpressed. Finally, an extension of this scenario is that the CBO or community has its 'own man' in place. This is typically someone who will work with the Inkosi and existing structures. The CBO and community feel they are involved or even running the show. Although it rarely emerges neatly, this has the potential to be a synergistic relationship.

Conclusion

Can CBOs drive rural change? Although structural relationships between CBOs and local government are unresolved or problematic, there is scope for agency in how local dynamics affect these relationships. NGOs can play an important role in supporting CBOs to participate in development, to work with local government, and to advocate greater attention to rural concerns. NGOs and CBOs can formulate plans around what is really needed at the local level, not just materially, which is largely the government's responsibility, but in terms of empowerment, participation and capacity building. The old adage that NGOs play an important role in 'teaching people to fish' may appear simplistic in today's world. NGOs are needed to continue with their 'teach people to fish' approach, but must also teach people how to negotiate and manoeuvre within an increasingly politicised and complex environment.

It is tempting to assume that this requires social change with NGOs establishing long-term relationships with communities.[15] Their activities require significant funding on 'process' components, such as meetings and workshops for consultation, training, and capacity building. However, even assuming that NGOs are committed to this role, it has become increasingly difficult for NGOs to secure funding for these activities in the present funding environment. Instead NGOs are shifting toward becoming more technical in nature, making long-term relationships between CBOs and social change type NGOs even rarer. Yet research elsewhere has shown that rural areas are likely to experience socio-political change not because of an outside organisation, whatever the type, but because of their social foundation for change. With this foundation, even limited interactions between technical NGOs and CBOs may have a positive effect on the socio-political development of rural areas (Galvin, 2005). So the question becomes: as development practitioners and activists, are we linking to rural groups through our

---

15. This research considered the role of social change organisations including the National Land Committee affiliate in KwaZulu Natal, the Association for Rural Advancement, and the now folded Environment and Development Agency in the Eastern Cape. It also encountered the Insika Rural Development Trust working in northern Zululand in KwaZulu-Natal.

networks? Are we imposing our lens of understanding or assumptions about rural areas, or are we open and really listening to their complex histories and local dynamics? If the latter, there is scope for engagement and possibly social change.

This research has provided a start in deepening our understanding of CBOs. It has also uncovered a range of issues requiring further research in the form of in-depth qualitative studies. Some of these questions include: How have NGOs and CBOs worked with local government around specific projects and what can be learned from this experience? Have programmes to assist rural communities understand local government, helped to resolve the 'battle over turf' or contentious relationship between CBOs and local government? Under what conditions are CBOs able to operate independently, and when have rural CBOs played a role in advocacy? If we want to promote rural development and more systemic social change, it is crucial that researchers pursue a research agenda that recognises and incorporates CBOs as significant actors in their own right.

References

Bond, P., 1999. *Cities of Gold, Townships of Coal*. Trenton: Africa World Press.

Chazan, N., 1994. Engaging the State: associational life in sub-Saharan Africa. In Migdal, Kohli, and Shue, eds. *State Power and Social Forces. Cambridge:* Cambridge University Press.

Clark, J., 1991. *Democratising Development: The Role of Voluntary Organisations*. London: Earthscan.

Clayton, A. ed., 1996. *NGOs, Civil Society and the State: Building Democracy in Transitional Societies*. Oxford: INTRAC.

Friedmann, J., 1992. *Empowerment: The Politics of Alternative Development*. Oxford: Blackwell Publishers.

Galvin, M., 1999. Rural Local Government in South Africa. *Transformation,* 40.

Galvin, M., 2005. Community Politics and NGOs: The Dynamics of Development in Rural South Africa. Ph.D. dissertation, University of California, Berkeley.

Galvin, M., 2009. Straight talk to Strengthen Delivery in the Water Services Sector. Synthesis report for The Water Dialogues-South Africa.

Galvin, M., (forthcoming 2010). Unintended Consequences: Development interventions and socio-political change in rural South Africa. In W. Freund and H. Witt, eds. *Development Dilemmas in Post-Apartheid South Africa.*

Galvin, M. and Habib, A., 2003. The Politics of Decentralisation and Donor Funding in South Africa's Rural Water Sector. *Journal of Southern African Studies,* 29(4).

Habib, A. and R. Taylor 1999, 'South Africa: Anti-Apartheid NGOs in Transition'. *Voluntas: International Journal of Voluntary and Nonprofit Organisations* 10, 1.

Keck, M. and Sikkink, K., 1998. *Activists Beyond Borders. New York:* Ithaca.

Korten, D., 1987. Third Generation NGO Strategies: A Key to People-centred Development. *World Development,* 15, supplement, pp.145-159.

Kotze, H., 2004. Responding to the growing socio-economic crisis? A review of civil society in South Africa. *Development Update,* 4(4), pp.1-32.

Seekings, J., 1997. SANCO: Strategic dilemmas in a democratic South Africa. *Transformation,* 34.

Smillie, I., 1995. *The Alms Bazaar: Altruism Under Fire- non profit organisations and international development.* London: Intermediate Technology Publications.

Swilling, M. and Russell, B., 2003. *The Size and Scope of the Non-Profit Sector in South Africa.* Johannesburg: Graduate School of Public and Development Management and the Centre for Civil Society.

15.
Poverty and social movements
Leonard Gentle

Introduction

Notions of poverty have a peculiarly will-o'-the-wisp quality, occasionally popping in and out of the language of politicians almost shamefacedly the way one may privately acknowledge flatulence – everyone has occasions to be affected by this condition but its not something to be discussed in polite society. The reason for this capricious nature of the term, poverty, is that a double movement is happening here. On the one hand poverty is being taken out of the economic policy priority list for neoliberal regimes, and, on the other, as economics is being separated from issues of political power, so poverty can be depoliticised by being seen as a purely economic issue. Under neoliberalism fighting poverty is no longer an articulated economic goal of governments. 'Make Poverty History' may look good on T-shirts and G8 governments can sign up for photo-shoots under such a banner, but none of these governments articulate this commitment in their national economic policies.

This can be contrasted with the 1930s and 1960s in the US when politicians responded to poverty reports in the land of plenty with socio-economic programmes such as the New Deal and the War on Poverty. And in South Africa the 1948 Apartheid regime embarked on an economic programme of state employment and public services for whites to solve the 'poor white' problem. But these were in the heyday of the Keynesian consensus – when accumulation required state intervention to manage demand and when governments in the parliamentary democracies (even the whites-only aberration that was South Africa) had to be seen to be doing something which could prevent electoral losses and social unrest.

Charles Meth (2007), exploring mainstream economic literature on poverty and pro-poor growth, found that for a period over the last twenty years poverty had simply disappeared off the agenda, and that there were few mainstream economists who even wrote about poverty. Instead poverty had become an issue for sociologists writing about issues of 'social exclusion'. Economists themselves were concerned mainly with seeking out greater mathematical models to ensure macro-economic stability or new forms of and opportunities for market speculation.

Powerful regimes which have flourishing stock markets speak to issues of poverty only in so far as they are relevant to the behaviour of money markets. Such is the case with unemployment data. This data is highly regarded by rating agencies as they may influence the direction of inflation and possible interest rate adjustments and, thereby, affect the ebb and flow of opportunities for the money mandarins.

Obsessed with competitiveness and growth and seeking out new opportunities for commodification and private investment, shielded from disengaged electorates by what Bob Jessop (1998) has called the 'hollowing out' of the neoliberal state under globalisation and the convergence of political parties, governments no longer need to engage poverty reduction as an economic priority. In fact for any political party to even suggest that poverty reduction may be any component of economic policy would be to incur the charge of 'economic populism' and the immediate opprobrium of, and punishment by, the finance markets.

Politics of poverty

Being removed from the lexicon of economic priorities does not mean that poverty does not appear in the policy discourse of governments. When it does, however, its purpose is as a weapon or a device whose objective is something else. Three instances are pertinent here.

Firstly, poverty does appear in the lexicon of imperialist governments as part of instructions issued to Third World countries; as a kind of backhanded rationale for why they should undergo even more restructuring to make their countries more investor-friendly. Poverty alleviation by adopting more market-friendly reforms is a disciplinary measure for weaker states imposed and check-listed by powerful regimes.

Secondly, poverty is also used as a stick for beating back and dividing mass campaigns. This is when neoliberal governments (including the South African government) evoke targeted groups for means testing – using concepts such as the 'poorest of the poor', the 'indigent' etc as a counterweight to the moral legitimacy of other struggles of the working class and as a political weapon in contestation with the people over access to resources. Thus the notion of indigency and of 'means testing' is a device used by the South African government to deny poor people universal access to services and an attempt to divide sections of the poor against other poor activists struggling for such universal access. Or as a means of policing and control, as in shifting the responsibility for sections of the poor to fulfil the requirements for means-testing so that they are seen to be 'genuine' rather than bogus (a device also used in rich countries to fight refugees).

Thirdly, definitions of poverty and measures of poverty sometimes serve the important function of legitimising current governments and their state policies. So governments try to massage the figures and use definitions to suggest that their policies are working. The World Bank has for years championed the notion of a dollar a day as the measure of absolute poverty, while its alter ego, the IMF, imposes structural adjustment programmes on Third World countries so that the harsh measures imposed – which, in their terms, were supposed to marshal savings and provide the lure for foreign investment, and thereby ensure growth, which would then lead to the trickle down of development - could eventually be seen to be working over time. The role of measuring poverty in this way would both be a vindication of the policies imposed as well as a universal standard which could be used by all countries. With the ensuing failures to achieve even this contentious approach to poverty, the IMF simply responded to see failure not as the failure of its policies but as failure to implement these policies sufficiently or with the required firmness, whilst the World Bank shifted the analyses of failure to issues of democracy, good governance or lack of consultation – all issues of which both these institutions are themselves particularly guilty.

In South Africa, the ruling party – the African National Congress – won electoral power in 1994, after decades at the head of a radical mass movement, with a pro-poor election platform called the Reconstruction and Development Programme (RDP), and then abandoned this programme in 1996 replacing it with a programme called the Growth, Employment and Redistribution Strategy (GEAR) whose claimed rationale was touted variously by the ANC as 'economic growth' and, later, 'macro economic stability', and poverty fell off the political agenda.

In the first uncertain days after the negotiated political settlement, which ushered in a form of democracy within the shell of apartheid neoliberalism, there was some sensitivity to the question of poverty and its measurement. In the early RDP days the state set up an RDP Ministry and Presidential Lead projects aimed at providing basic services, like water and electricity, for select sections of what was then called 'the poorest of the poor'. These were talked up in the Government's 10-year review in 2004 even though the RDP and its ministry were ended along with the Presidential Lead projects.

The South African state has redefined what is to be measured so that it looks better. Hence the change in unemployment statistics taking out the effects of so-called 'discouraged' workers. South Africa's unemployment rate drops from 40 per cent to 28 per cent. With other definitions like potable water – where the government has focused on access to water and, therefore, by putting a public tap in an informal settlement where households are within 200 metres of the tap can suddenly claim that thousands of people have 'access' to potable water. These definitions and measures reveal more about the current power relations and the concerns of the government, and to whom it speaks, than people's livelihoods and living standards.

There is however a possibly more important sense in which a descriptive and definitional approach to poverty is used as a political device and this is in the sense that poverty comes to be seen as a lack of resources rather than an absence of entitlements, as an 'economic' rather than a political problem. This separation of politics and economics has a long history in bourgeois ideology and masks the degree to which what is referred as to the 'economic' is itself a social relation of power between people, rather than a physical relation between things.

In South Africa, we have seen attempts to depoliticise poverty by making it appear as if it is a neutral, technical question of implementing policies better, of getting the right mix between the state and the private sector, of prioritising increased opportunities for investment, of expertise and so on. The responsibilities for creating and intensifying poverty of current patterns of ownership, of government policies, of capital flows etc are taken out of the equation and poverty becomes an exercise best left to technical experts – which is why the government launched its much-vaunted Accelerated and Shared Growth Initiative for South Africa as a product of the finest development economists at Harvard.

Depoliticising poverty is in itself political. On the other hand, attempts to make the social/relational nature of poverty explicit are not acts of 'imposing politics' but worthy acts of clarification.

Poverty indices and social mobilisation

In response to this sleight of hand approach to poverty measures and definitions of poverty, committed development sociologists and others have striven to get a greater integrity to the measure of poverty. Concerns here have been about absolute versus relative poverty and notions of chronic poverty, of reflecting on issues of assets and of measures of living standards (infant mortality, access to potable water, different gendered access to primary education etc). It is also from this side that there have been pressures from progressive lobbyists to quantify progress – like trying to use the UN Millennium goals to exert pressure on governments.

This is, however, not an argument against having a definition of poverty or even a measure – it is possible that social mobilisation and class struggles against the state can be waged on the basis of contesting measurements (after all the fact that trade unions recognise the class bias in the notion of inflation etc has not prevented them from making wage demands using inflation as a measure) – but is an argument for noting the 'this-sided', temporary, provisional nature of these, and that measurements are at best indices of processes being contested and not absolute categories which can stand forever.

In fact, from a social mobilisation perspective, there can be, and are, struggles against poverty even when the indices show a 'lessening' of poverty. Poverty and struggles do not amount to the same thing and do not necessarily have some kind of one-to-one causal relationship. Important as it is to have a clear language on the characteristics and defining features of poverty, it is also important to recognise that descriptions and definitions of poverty involve political contestation, which has assumed greater importance under neoliberalism.

In this sense it may be imperative to develop concepts of poverty that incorporate within them an understanding of the causes of poverty. In the absence of such an approach to poverty, interventions will be targeted at symptoms of poverty rather than its drivers, and for that reason will have little effect. Concepts of relative or absolute poverty similarly may end up with appeals to change public policy but not necessarily with dealing with its underlying causes.

But whatever the differences between those who massage the figures to make their policies look good or those who are earnest reformers and campaigners for better government policies so that the poor may genuinely benefit, there is a shared perspective of agency - which is that those who have the power either already have all the good policies so that its all just about the need for greater technical capacity, or instituting reforms so that they can deliver better services to the poor. The poor, however defined, are in both these senses passive recipients of the largesse of others – whether vindictive or benevolent.

Notions of poverty and poverty reduction are rooted in issues of agency and power. The social surplus generated by society is appropriated by a minority because this minority has effective control over the repressive and ideological apparatuses which can ensure that this appropriation is maintained. At the same time this apportionment is constantly challenged by struggles on the part of those not having this control. The poor, in this perspective, makes its own decisions as to what constitutes poverty and acts through struggles to contest the terms of its impoverishment.

Discussions of poverty as a relation or a process (of impoverishment) emphasise the extent to which poverty is chronic because of the social relationships and structures within which particular groups of the poor are embedded. In this sense poverty should be understood as a socio-political relationship rather than a lack of assets. In such an understanding, processes of social mobilisation and social movements become central to any discussion of poverty because they are vehicles through which such relationships are argued over in society and potentially changed (Bebbington, 2006: i).

Starting from this observation social movements are key in addressing the vicissitudes of poverty and the measure and acceptability of what can be considered poverty. There are two domains in which movements might influence poverty.

Firstly, social movements change dominant meanings associated with poverty, make their own sense of what constitutes poverty and influence the ways in which the poor are thought of in society. Secondly, they challenge the institutions, social structures and political economy dynamics that underlie poverty. In this domain, movements can play potential roles in changing the conditions under which accumulation occurs and attacking relationships of adverse incorporation or social exclusion.

Social movements and perceptions of poverty

The conception of poverty as a social relation leads one to reflect on why poverty is not a mainstream priority of the dominant elite in the world. And why, in South Africa, poverty measures have been so easily manipulable, and the poverty-relief concerns of the RDP so easily trumped by the (so it is claimed by its architects) 'achieving of macro economic stability' concerns of GEAR. Poverty has become depoliticised and reduced to special groups – those qualifying for 'special grants' and 'poverty programmes', free basic water and electricity etc once they prove their 'indigency'. This is a South African variant of what policy-makers in the imperialist countries call the 'socially excluded'.

None of the political parties in South Africa express any sense of poverty being a priority. All agree that economic growth and having sound economic fundamentals are a priority. They differ in degree and how the terms are couched to different strata within the electorate – the ANC couching pro-growth neoliberalism in terms of black economic empowerment, the DA pro-growth with no concessions to a future black bourgeoisie, the smaller parties like the ID and the PAC etc wanting less corruption and patronage.

Where a poverty index – unemployment – is championed as a policy priority, it is as a rationale for further attacks on the poor – in the form of calling for greater labour market flexibilities and less state intervention in any form of welfare. The disappearance of poverty from the dominant concerns of the elites is not because inequality has been so reduced as to make any special claim for the poor to be highly exceptional. Rather it is that the poor, as a politically active voice challenging the dominant classes and forcing concessions from them, is, at present, incapable of making its mark – except as a vector of crime and disease – on those dominant strata.

On the one hand much of this is a story of the reconfiguration of social strata in South Africa after 1994. Sections of the black middle class have become detached and no longer occupy the same moral universe as their working class township counterparts, while others have sunk into increasing precariousness alongside informalised workers and evicted labour tenants. Poverty for many new middle class blacks, and for the suburban white middle classes in protected villas and townhouses, is no longer an issue except as a vector of crime. And it is their opinions which are reflected in, and courted by, the media and government.

But, on the other hand, inherent in the notion of poverty is a sense of passivity of the poor and their incapacity to move beyond being the study of sociologists and other poverty experts. The poor have become an object of study and not a subject of their history. In South Africa this relative weakness of the poor allowed the state to implement its neoliberal strategy of commodifying public services, cutting access to water and electricity and evicting homeless people from land they had occupied. Lacking a challenge from the poor, the government could get away with reducing its obligation to its past programme of social transformation, to providing social grants.

Social mobilisation has the capacity to change that – to re-insert poverty as a national and international priority and, to this end, social movements can change dominant meanings of what constitutes poverty and the issues associated with poverty – lack of basic services, homelessness, HIV/AIDS, unemployment etc.

We began to see this in the rise of new social movements after 1999, firstly in the way the Treatment Action Campaign (TAC) took HIV/AIDS and turned it from an issue of insurmountable, plague-like proportions to one that had a clear target and a demand – public provision of ARVs. From one associated with the passive poor dying 'out there, somewhere', to one where the poor were in the streets making demands on government and pharmaceutical companies. We have also seen this new re-insertion of issues of poverty starting with Anti-evictions Campaign (AEC) activists putting housing on the agenda, Soweto Electricity Crisis Committee (SECC) activists reconnecting water and electricity, and then the 2005 service delivery revolts that made these issues matters of general public concern and were forerunners to the kind of public support being given to the public sector strike of June and July 2007.

In important ways, social mobilisation filled in meaning at the level of the social construction of concepts such as property, rights, restitution etc. This has been significant in South Africa because the nature of South Africa's political settlement between 1990 and 1994 left a Constitution which articulated the balance of forces at the time - between a radical mass movement and an undefeated Apartheid regime and its beneficiaries. The Constitution contains a curate's egg of first and second generation human rights together with endorsing Apartheid property relations and committing South Africa to paying all external debts. Much of the human rights part of the Constitution was left to interpretation by judicial precedent and the Constitutional Court.

In the absence of social mobilisation the Constitutional Court gave a very narrow definition of the Bill of Rights clause on the right to health in the case of an indigent patient – Soobramaney – who fought for the right to dialysis treatment at public hospitals and lost a Constitutional Court decision which ruled that the right to health had to be within the budgetary restrictions of the fiscus. Soobramaney's death indicated a triumph of conservative meaning in law in the first years after Apartheid, when the case provided media discussion but no social mobilisation.

On the other hand the rise of social movements such as the TAC, the Anti Privatisation Forum (APF) and the AEC has seen cases taken up by these around issues of property clauses and patent rights receiving much more human-rights centred approaches by the courts even at the expense of the public opinion of middle class property owners.

Social movement challenges to the institutions of accumulation

Social movements rarely emerge around poverty *per se*, and social movements of the chronically poor, in a self-declared sense, are even rarer. Cleaver (2005) argues in large measure that the chronically poor are so asset-deprived that engaging in organisation, mobilisation or political action would demand time, social networks and material resources that they do not have, and incur risks they are unlikely to tolerate. Social movements do, however, emerge in response to social relationships and dynamics of capital accumulation that are implicated in the creation and reproduction of poverty.

Bebbington (2006: 2) notes that many of the classic types of social movement in Latin America are of this nature:

> Indigenous movements, women's movements, Afro-Latino movements, and landless people's movements were all motivated and sustained by aspirations that derive from shared identities, and are directed against social relationships and structures that have adverse consequences for these identity groups: in these examples, relationships of racism, ethnic prejudice, patriarchy and land ownership.
>
> Other movements are directed against forms of capital accumulation that are deemed adverse to human well-being: anti-globalisation movements, environmental movements protesting deforestation or oil and mineral extraction, fair trade movements and so on. Of course, social relationships are closely related to forms of accumulation (patterns of participation in ownership and regulation, for instance, affect the forms that economic growth takes and how its benefits are distributed). Likewise, identity based movements are generally also concerned that the social relationships that they are contesting are also implicated in the ways in which wealth is distributed and markets regulated – as for instance when Ecuadorian indigenous movements protest the signing of a Free Trade Treaty with the US. (Bebbington, 2006: 2)

Elsewhere Naila Kabeer (2005: 41) refers to the tasks facing those seeking to support poverty reduction in Bangladesh in the following way:

> the challenge for the future ... lies in the field of politics as much as in the domain of policy ... in creating the capacity of poorer and more vulnerable sections of society to influence those that make policies ... and hold them accountable.

Barbara Harriss-White (2005) advances a similar argument as she reflects on the possibilities that anything might be done to address destitution. For her, the workings of power – embodied in and exercised through distinct sets of social and political economic relationships – are central to the production of destitution. The destitute are exploited, denigrated, and ignored, deemed less than citizens by others – all acts of power that reproduce their destitution. In the face of this power, even if the destitute have agency of some sort, this is merely an agency that allows them to 'defy death' (Harris-White, 2005: 887) – it does not allow them to challenge the conditions of their existence or the powers that reproduce their destitution. These conditions will only change when poor people have political power to effect social change and when elites begin to feel their own well-being challenged by the existence of the destitute.

The challenge, then, is to understand the possible sources of such political change. There is no panacea in this regard. Social movements, political parties and groups, other civil society organisations (churches, sports clubs etc) may all have a role to play, but each comes with a health warning. Some of the potential pitfalls in any reliance on, or alliance with such actors, might include a systematic lack of interest in the very poorest except for reasons of patronage, institutional fragility, or tendencies towards self-serving behaviour – all calling into question any inherent pro-poor qualities of these actors. The more general point relevant for this discussion, is that political action and change are essential if poverty is to be addressed. This means not only linking civil society and political society but also linking social mobilisation and justice-based forms of agency with the state – and, more exactly, with processes of state power and transformation.

Few if any of these politically sensitive analytical interventions suggest that social movements are in and of themselves vehicles for addressing poverty. Instead, they suggest such movements can be vehicles for forms of political action that attack the social relationships underlying chronic poverty and that therefore increase the likelihood that poverty will be addressed, by the state or that the current state will be overthrown. That is, social movements are the progenitors of change in the form and culture of the state, and this is their main contribution to poverty reduction.

What does the emergence of new social movements say about the present conjuncture?

The emergence of revived mass struggles in Latin America in the 1990s, the post-Seattle global justice movement and, in South Africa the post-Apartheid struggles against evictions, cut-offs and poor service delivery etc have seen a plethora of explanations of what has been dubbed 'new social movements'. Attempts have been made to characterise them and their apparent newness by looking at them in terms of their forms (networks, loose, sometimes transnational), their content (identity, eschewing state power and electoralism), their methods (direct action) etc. Some like David Harvey have found support for distinguishing them from older social movements by delineating between contesting accumulation by exploitation (older movements, notably trade unions) and contesting accumulation by dispossession (new social movements) etc.

There has been considerable difficulty within social movement literature with tying down a definition which appears sustainable. Increasingly there is evidence of acceptance that new social movements are a recent form of a long historical tradition of struggles, and to each apparently unique feature there are, sometimes, centuries of precedent. In a recent South African study the editors had this to say: "Social movements are thus in our view, politically and/or socially directed collectives, often involving multiple organisations and networks, focused on changing one or more elements of the social, political and economic system within which they are located." (Ballard, Habib and Valodia, 2006: 3)

This, however, seems to me to be describing all instances of social mobilisation in South Africa over more than 100 years. Having said that, I do not want to add to the pursuit of some kind of quintessential social movement theory except to reflect on two things pertinent to the topic of this chapter, and in this way derive a perspective on social movements useful for this discussion.

Firstly, much of the talk of the newness of new social movements is a comment on other, older 'politically/socially directed collectives' who are either absent from the attempts to change 'one or more elements of the social, political and economic system' or are now part of that system. As such it is the defeat/decline/cooption of the old that gives some conceptual credibility to the apparent newness of the new, not so much the distinction between modes of accumulation, forms of struggle etc.

Secondly, the emergence of new social movements after the decline/co-option etc of the old movements indicates that we are recovering but from low water mark, i.e., the emergence of new collective actions comes after a period of serious and widespread defeat. As such, the fact that poverty has been for some time off the horizon of neoliberal governments and their international agencies such as the WTO, the IMF and the World Bank, speaks not so much to a decrease in human inequality but because the capacity of social mobilisation, of social movements, has been weakened since its height in the 1980s.

In this context as well, it is the notable absence of older social movements – particularly COSATU and its trade union affiliates in issues of contestation over the structures of power in the state and against workers' decreasing control over their own labour power – and the cooption of the ANC as a social movement into power in a neoliberal state – that has left the new social movements as the main social force contesting the terms of impoverishment.

I therefore favour the much more relational view of social movements of Nilsen and Cox (2005) – one which draws on the contestation between social forces over the surplus product and the institutions and relations which sustain the current modes of appropriation and distribution.

> To say this suggests a much broader view of social movements than that dominant in much mainstream sociology, where social movements are thought of as field-specific institutional formations - i.e. unconventional or informal political organisations and campaigns, but excluding (with a few honourable exceptions) such issues as revolutions, political parties, popular culture and consciousness, states and capital. What we propose is that the conflictual historical process of developing needs and capacities through the social organisation of human practice constitutes the kernel of Marxism as a theory of social movements. Rather than taking the status quo for granted and examining social movements as ripples on the smooth surface of society, this means seeing the *whole* of society as socially produced through collective agency – and hence open to contestation and transformation (Nilsen and Cox, 2005: 2).

Social movements, in this perspective, are not considered as ruptures on an otherwise passive or institutionalised political landscape. They are the ways in which human practices are socially articulated. And that what is regarded as the current conjuncture, and everything in it - including the state, political parties, notions of poverty and who are the poor etc – are the outcomes of past struggles of social movements and that are being, in the present, contested by current social movements.

Under neoliberalism, poverty has been intensified as social services get commodified and poor people's access to any public services individualised. Social movements are instances of collective action which challenge this impoverishment.

New social movements – particularly those fighting the service delivery struggles in South Africa - are partial struggles of a working class re-constituting its combativity in the 1990s and early 21st century, after a decade of defeats in which the ruling class successfully intensified the neoliberal order. The fact that poverty is still a discussion formulated and dominated by elites is a reflection of the state of South Africa's social movements today. They are present by invitation at the wedding but they are not the wedding planners and they are certainly not getting married.

South African social movements

In South Africa, new social movements have emerged after 1999, in the wake of the failure to take up social mobilisation on the part of COSATU and the cooption of the ANC, and in response to the new mode of accumulation today - a mode of accumulation that I have elsewhere styled as neoApartheid (see Gentle, 2006). Accumulation has been filtered through and sustained by social relations inherited from colonialism but reconfigured in the service of white monopoly capitalism after the country underwent its mining revolution at the turn of the 20th century. Apartheid is best understood as a form of racial capitalism in which capital accumulation took place based on a racially-divided working class, in which black labour power was cheapened through extra-economic state interventions in the wage relation. These measures included political exclusion, sampling of forced labour in the Reserves (and later Bantustans) using the contract labour system and policed labour segmentation in the urban areas. These schemas of cheapening were bolstered by the use of patriarchy to exploit forms of black female domestic and rural labour. The capitalist class at whose behest these arrangements were made was white and South African. This characterisation was based not so much on the electoral behaviour of individual capitalists (some of whom supported the all-white parliamentary opposition) but on their being the direct beneficiaries of the policies pursued.

From the 1970s the apartheid state began a series of reforms in response to increased concentration and centralisation of capital and a growing urbanised black proletariat. These reforms, however, precipitated a tide of radical working class militancy which began to challenge the legitimacy of existing social relations and the state which stood at it head. While these processes were underway in South Africa, neoliberalism and globalisation were underway internationally. With the legitimacy of the South African state in question and South African monopoly capital ready for its own shift towards international capital and commodity markets, the mode of accumulation began to change and an elite pact between the ANC and the reformed apartheid state ushered in a far-reaching new political order.

This change is from a Keynesian racial capitalism,[1] in which the state secured the conditions for accumulation of capital as a whole based on cheap black labour power, cheap energy and regulated capital to a neoliberal state attempting to lever open new arenas for commodification. In the case of the former, the state intervened to *constrain* the commodification of certain processes (electrification, rail transport) deemed essential to ensure capital accumulation and, in the case of the latter, the state intervened to *expand* the terrain of commodification.

The post-1994 social formation has certain sharp discontinuities with the above configuration. Chiefly the victory over the apartheid state has brought to an end the extra-economic intervention into wage relations based on the legal separation of white and black labour and the political exclusion of black people from citizenship. But there are many points of continuity with the Apartheid form of capital accumulation. These are:

- The racial composition of the bourgeoisie has remained the same. The capitalist class is overwhelmingly white.
- The state has championed a process called Black Economic Empowerment, which has been carried out at the behest and with the enthusiastic support of the white capitalist class. But BEE is based on the same regime of accumulation as that espoused by the white capitalist class – cheap labour power.
- The system of cheap labour power is now based on neoliberal prescriptions of labour flexibility, externalisation of labour contracts, informalisation and increased labour segmentation and these are being pursued by an interventionist state (through its promotion of greater labour flexibility in its labour laws amongst other things).
- The racial composition of the new battalions of cheap, informalised, flexibilised, segmented labour is overwhelmingly black, with black women being the most informalised and flexibilised. All indices indicate that the white employed still dominate the white-collar, the professional and the managerial strata.

---

1. The concept, racial capitalism, is associated with a body of work by what was then called 'the revisionist school' of historians and political economists in the 1970s. Analysts associated with this body of work include Frederick Johnstone (1976), Harold Wolpe (1972) and Stanley Trapido (1971). They counterposed themselves to the dominant liberal perspective, which saw apartheid as dysfunctional to capitalism and industrialisation. Instead they argued that racial segregation and apartheid were integrally linked to capitalism in South Africa.

These continuities with the Apartheid period of racial capitalism lead me to characterise the Mbeki regime as neoApartheid. The new social movements in South Africa arose as instances of social action in defence of declining living standards but with a particular focus on service delivery and the local state.

These struggles were first and foremost local in that they are about the arena in which the working class is most confronted with the class character of the ANC government. At the local level it has been the institutions of local government that have been the agents of the attacks. But while being given additional responsibilities for delivering services, the institutions of local government have had their transfers from the national fiscus drastically cut. Under the SA political dispensation, the ANC State has followed in the path of other neoliberal states in that:

- It has shifted executive power and financial decision-making outside the scrutiny of the electorate and consolidated this power in the Executive, grouped around the Office of the State President.
- It has shifted and devolved 'non-core' management of services functions to the provinces.
- In turn, the locus for delivery of services has been devolved to local government.

But the transfers of resources from the national fiscus are substantially inadequate to meet the scale of delivery required for a post-Apartheid configuration. And so cost-recovery and collecting of payments has become the leitmotif of the officers of local government. And, therefore, against the promises of a 'better life for all' and the expectations that after apartheid things would be better, living standards for the black working class have worsened. And after 20 years of local residents in working class townships boycotting service payments as a protest against the apartheid organs of local government, now it is an ANC local government attempting to force the poor to pay. And so evictions from houses, water cut-offs and electricity cut-offs have become the order of the day in the sprawling townships around Johannesburg, Durban and Cape Town.

The issue of locality is deeply bound to the experience of the urban and rural poor and the attacks on their living standards – as attacks by the institutions of local government. They have thus been defensive struggles against the immediate oppressor – the local government functionary cutting off their water, evicting workers from their houses or suspending electricity connections.

The service delivery struggles of social movements in South Africa are defensive struggles - even where they challenge service commodification for instance. They have extracted important concessions from the state – stopping evictions and cut-offs in the Western Cape in 2005/2006, stopping the pink slips, forcing the state to respond with indigent policies and engagement around alternative housing, obtaining favourable legal judgments in respect of evictions etc. They are challenging the terms of their impoverishment. But they have not as yet begun to challenge the legitimacy of current relations of accumulation in South Africa and the state institutions which reproduce poverty as a requirement for accumulation.

Challenging social movements on poverty and the poor

The principal vehicle for ensuring the conditions for accumulation is the state. The capitalist state and its set of institutions – the legislature, the army and police, the judiciary etc – is itself a product of capitalist social relations but also enforces, regulates and shapes the terms of these relations, who gets apportioned which amount of the social surplus generated, who gets exploited and how this exploitation is enforced and what forms it may take. The state uses its monopoly on violence and law-making to force the terms of its rule, but its institutions are continually engaged and contested from within the side of those who own the means of production, as well as from those are excluded from ownership. Those who own the means of production and control the terms of apportionment and distribution do so through the state, but capitalist social relations are also maintained and mediated through a whole gamut of institutions of civil society which make these relations appear natural, everyday and eternal. This appearance of the naturalness of capitalism, of the sanctity of private property, of the millions of daily acts of commodity exchange, of the natural roles of men and women, of wages being the reward for work etc is maintained through the church, the family, political parties, social clubs, schooling, and the media. But these institutions of civil society extend their influence deeply into society, into the working class and the poor themselves and establish what Gramsci called hegemony over public opinion.

Interestingly enough Nilsen and Cox (2005) refer to this shaping of public opinion/hegemony as 'social movements from above' in their schema which paraphrases Gramscian theory in the language of social movement theory. Social movements may contest the terms of accumulation by engaging the state and changing public policy, with regard to the issue of poverty as a case in point. Green and Hulme (2005) have an analysis and understanding of poverty which leads them to the notion that people need to be empowered and mobilised in order to be more effective in influencing the so-called poverty reduction programmes: "Poverty reduction does not simply require 'good' policy: it requires creating the capacity of poorer people to influence, and hold accountable, those who make policies" (Green and Hulme, 2005: 867).

But social movements can also fundamentally change public opinion about the 'normality' of capitalist relations themselves. In its most extreme form this may involve shifting the centre of gravity of public opinion so fundamentally from the capitalist state, that its rule is challenged at the level of its very legitimacy – thereby either exposing it as a force of counter-revolutionary violence or impotence.

But in order to do this, new social movements need to become more than issue-based collectives or instances of social action – local or otherwise - more than networks – national or international. They need to become counter-hegemonic forces, able to, whether collectively or otherwise, galvanise public opinion so that the normality of capitalist relations and the legitimacy of its state and institutions of accumulation are questioned in practice. They need not only contest the terms of impoverishment but become movements of the poor.

Writing on social movements is often normative, with a related tendency to celebrate the potential of movements to transform society as well as the role they play in making the political dimensions of development that much more visible. Yet movements suffer many constraints. Elsewhere I spoke about poverty being political and that the focus of poverty-eradication should be political power and political change. I also said that the fact that poverty is regarded as an issue for action by poverty specialists and state reformers indicates a relative weakness in the state of the social movements in South Africa today. Among these weaknesses are problems of representation and internal democracy within movements.

Another evident problem is the extent to which movements capture the concerns and interests of the poorest. In this sense movements suffer the same problem as other organisations – namely that the poor, and especially the very poor, lack time and resources to participate in mobilisations; and also lack capacities to make their voices heard in the debates and arguments that lead, ultimately, to the formation of movement discourses. Movements, thus, become captured by, or at the very least give attention to the most vocal or the most resourced within their ranks – in South Africa this is often English-speaking, politically-literate, urbanised men.

There are three indices of these weaknesses – firstly the current divide between the strongest of the old social movements, the labour movement, and the new social movements; secondly, the lack of immersion of the activists of the new social movements in the communities in which they are active and thereby, the lack of self-sustaining pipelines of activists which result from such an immersion; and, thirdly, the lack of explicitly feminist politics in movements which are largely female in composition but continue to be lead by male activists.

In the case of the trade union-new social movement divide, ILRIG conducted a 2002/2003 study of a Cape Town example of two movements – the older South African Municipal Workers' Union (SAMWU) and the then new Anti-Eviction Campaign (see Xali, 2004) – and found that despite the fact that both shared a commitment at leadership level to make common cause, instances of collaboration almost never occurred

The AEC and the SAMWU Cape Town branch are organisations that draw their membership from working class communities in and around Cape Town. SAMWU's membership consists of blue collar workers involved in delivering municipal services such as water and cleaning. The union has a number of current campaigns focusing on the impact of privatisation and commercialisation of public services on employment and service delivery. The Western Cape Anti-Eviction Campaign (AEC) brought together community groupings fighting the evictions of householders from both private and public sector houses in poor communities – frequently the same victims of the same policies contested by SAMWU.

Our study found, however, that there are few instances of the membership of the two formations working together and there is little knowledge of the daily struggles and campaigns of the other. Moreover, despite SAMWU members, including shop stewards, living in the very communities from which the AEC formations draw their membership, there are few instances of these members participating in AEC campaigns.

There appear to be a number of obstacles that currently stand in the way of developing the limited linkages between the trade unions and the new social movements. The obstacles referred to in this study were broadly grouped as:

- institutional – how the formations are structured and how they define membership;
- political – specifically differing attitudes towards the African National Congress and its ally, the South African National Civics Organisation (SANCO);

- organisational methods – particularly the structured membership base and negotiations culture of the union as against the campaign-based activities of the new social movement.

Compounding these were issues of composition – in terms of the differing gender, age and employment status of the membership and leadership of the organisations. The majority of people active in the social movements were unemployed, black women. In many cases they are single mothers, unemployed and running households (Despite the fact that the majority of the membership was female, the leaderships of the movements as represented through its various structures were predominantly men).

That women are being drawn into struggles and largely constituting the shock troops of the emerging social movements in South Africa can be ascribed to the attack on the living standards of the poor chiefly in the area of social services. These social services are being commodified – largely through forms of privatisation, commercialisation, outsourcing and cost recovery. The attack comes in the form of a direct attack on spheres of public life which are closest to the domestic sphere and which increase the burden on the domestic sphere. Women are therefore directly bearing the cost of the neoliberal restructuring in specific ways and are therefore directly in the firing line. But having been drawn into struggles in overwhelming numbers why do women not dominate these and have their domination reflected in leadership, in decision-making and in policies adopted?

The coming out of women in struggle is of additional significance because it also opens up the potential to challenge what takes place in the domestic sphere. It opens a possibility for the women from poor communities to think of ways to address the gender division of labour in the household. But only if the movements themselves are challenging this gender division of labour and are creating an environment in which women (and men) are able to unmask the gender power relations in the public and private spheres and the connections between these two. Women in struggle willing to stand the brutality of the police may make the link with oppressive relationships at home, but they need appropriate organisational expressions of their struggles which allow this link to be facilitated.

In many ways this composition of the new social movements in South Africa is a challenge to the willingness of the trade unions to take seriously their capacity to reflect the concerns of the poorer, unemployed or informally employed sectors of the poor. The labour movement in South Africa has a long history, what Moody (1997) and others have called 'social movement unionism', but the decline in the living standards of the poor has raised the real possibility that trade unions in their current composition and structural forms may be losing their ability to be a social movement of the poor.

In the case of the new social movements studies by Egan and Wafer (2006) on the Soweto Electricity Crisis Committee (SECC), by Greenberg (2006) on the Landless People's Movement (LPM) and others all reveal a picture of mainly poor unemployed older women as the backbone of movements in which vocal leaders were young male activists. This speaks to the fragility of the new social movements as representative forces within the poor: they still lack women's empowerment and have shallow roots in communities, beyond the courageous activists at the coal face of confrontation with the state and local authorities.

This is not a uniquely South African problem. For instance, two studies of one of the most celebrated, South-based anti-globalisations mobilisations – the water movement in Cochabamba, Bolivia, that contested the privatisation of the cities' and region's water provision system, and ultimately led to the withdrawal of the concessionaire – each refer to ways in which certain interests were squeezed out of the main platforms of the movement.

Perreault (2006: 166) comments:

> In the water war, irrigators consolidated their influence, but ... they did so in a way that largely obscured the needs of Cochabamba's urban migrant population, which has only precarious access to water and shares in few of the collective political and social benefits enjoyed by more organised sectors such as irrigators, miners, or factory workers.

A caveat related to this regards the role of alliances within movements. The likelihood that movements will affect policy and deeply-seated social structures depends greatly on the extent to which, within the movement process, alliances form that cut across social differences: urban/rural, ethnic, gender, local economic interests, nationality etc. This requires an understanding, a Gramscian understanding, of hegemony not only in respect of becoming hegemonic in respect to civil society (which is a goal which may yet be some way off), in general, but in the sense of how social movements – old and new may become a representative force of the poor.

In order to do so, they must contest with the ruling class the definition of poverty – for instance moving the measurements upwards, setting the bar higher, making poverty unacceptable because public opinion wants any existence in whatever form or measure eradicated (as opposed to wanting it hidden and disguised) etc. They must forge common struggles between the trade unions and the new social movements. They must sink roots in all sections of their communities and integrate migrant communities. They must confront patriarchy and remove obstacles to women's full participation and leadership. In short – become a hegemonic force amongst the poor. And important in establishing this hegemony, in becoming such a representative force, is the winning of public opinion of the middle class.

This means that social mobilisation and action must become so generalised that sections of the middle classes regard their own material conditions as being poor and become angry at being poor in relation to the state but proud to be part of the poor in regard to social mobilisation. This was the case with the black middle classes in South Africa until the 1980s – where poverty was seen as a mobilisation issue vis-à-vis the state but an issue of social solidarity in relation to other oppressed strata. The demobilisation of the South African mass movement after the 1980s was also an act of de-linking the black middle classes from the poor, making poverty a special interest – as a subject for disdain - and not a matter for public opinion – and so depoliticising poverty.

References

Alvarez, S. Dagnino, E. and Excobar, A. eds., 1998. *Cultures of Politics, Politics of Cultures. Revisiting Latin American Social Movements.* Boulder: Westview.

Aminul Islam, S., 2005. Sociology of Poverty: Quest for a New Horizon. *Bangaldesh Journal of Sociology,* 2(1).

Ballard, R. Habib, A. Valodia, I. eds., 2006. *Voices of Protest: Social Movements in Post Apartheid South Africa.* Pietermaritzburg: University of KwaZulu Natal Press.

Bebbington, A., 2006. Social movements and the politicisation of chronic poverty policy CPRC Working Paper, Chronic Poverty Research Centre: Manchester.

Cleaver, F., 2005. The inequality of social capital and the reproduction of chronic poverty. *World Development.* 33(6), pp.893-906.

Du Toit, A., 2004. 'Social Exclusion' Discourse and Chronic poverty: A South African case study'. *Development and Change,* 35(5).

Fine, B. and Rustomjee, Z., 1996. *The Political Economy of South Africa: From Minerals-Energy Complex to Industrialisation.* Johannesburg: Witwatersrand University Press.

Gentle, L., 2006. Black Economic Empowerment and South Africa. Paper delivered to the annual Rosa Luxemburg Conference, UKZN.

Government of RSA. 2004. *Towards 10 Years of Freedom.*

Gramsci, A., 1977. *Selections from Political Writings 1910-1920.* London: Lawrence and Wishart.

Green, M. and Hulme, D., 2005. From correlates and characteristics to causes: thinking about poverty from a chronic poverty perspective. *World Development,* 33(6), pp.867-879.

Harriss-White, B., 2005. Destitution and the poverty of its politics. *World Development,* 33(6).

Harvey, D., 2003. *The New Imperialism.* Oxford: Oxford University Press.

Innes, D., 1984. *Anglo American and the Rise of Modern South Africa,* London: Heinemann.

Jessop, B., 1998. The hollowed out state. *Economy and Society.*

Johnstone, F., 1976. Class, *Race and Gold: A Study of Class Relations and Racial Discrimination in South Africa*. London: Routledge and Kegan Paul.

Kabeer, N., 2005. Snakes and ladders and traps: Chronic Poverty Research Working paper, No 50. Manchester Institute for Development Policy and Management: Chronic Poverty Research Centre.

Kaplan, D., 1977. Class Conflict, Capital Accumulation and the State: An Historical Analysis of the State in Twentieth Century South Africa, unpublished Ph.D. Thesis: University of Sussex

Lipton, M., 1986. *Capitalism and Apartheid: South Africa, 1910 – 1986*. Aldershot: Wildwood House.

Macdonald. D. and Pape, J., 2002. *Cost Recovery and the crisis of service delivery in South Africa*. Cape Town: HSRC and Zed Press.

Meth, C., 2007. *What is pro-poor growth? What are some of the things that hinder its achievement in South Africa?* London: Oxfam.

Nattrass, N., 1989. Apartheid and Profit Rates: Challenging the Radical Orthodoxy. *Indicator SA*, 7(1).

Nilsen, G. and Cox, L., 2005. At the heart of society burns the fire of the social movements. What would a Marxist theory of social movements look like? Paper presented to the Tenth International Conference on Alternative Futures and Popular Protest, 30 March – 1 April, Manchester Metropolitan University.

Perreault, T., 2006. From the Guerra Del Agua to the Guerra Del Gas: Resource governance, neoliberalism and popular protest in Bolivia. *Antipode*, 38(1).

Trapido, S., 1971. *South Africa in a Comparative Study of Industrialisation*. University of London: Institute of Commonwealth Studies, vol. 3.

Wolpe, H., 1972. Capitalism and Cheap Labour Power in South Africa: From Segregation to Apartheid. *Economy and Society*, 1(3).

Xali, M., 2004. Trade unions and Social Movements: Obstacles to and Possibilities for collaboration. ILRIG report for the Centre for Civil Society: UKZN.

Yudelman, D., 1983. *The Emergence of Modern South Africa: State, Capital and Organised Labour on the South African Gold Fields, 1902 – 1939*. London: Greenwood.

16.
Ideologies, strategies and tactics of township protest
Trevor Ngwane

Introduction

A variety of questions are suddenly apparent, and the former certainty that critical analysts had when confronting apartheid and post-apartheid neoliberalism must now be reviewed, given the many thousands of unexpected protests that rose from townships in recent years. Why are people coming out in protest? What are their demands? Is the protest action solely about the delivery of services or does it signify a bigger dissatisfaction with the social order as such? Is there an imagined future that inspires the protesters when they wage their struggles? Or are the people only interested in getting their 'bread and butter' and their 'bricks and mortar'? What do the protesting people actually want? Do they have dreams? What are the social conditions and power relations that are necessary for the fulfillment of their demands? Do they link the struggle for satisfying their immediate needs, e.g. for water, electricity, housing, etc., with the struggle for broader social change, for a change in power relations? Do they see continuity between the anti-apartheid struggle and the struggle today? Questions of ideology and agency intertwine and the search for ways to pose these questions – rather than settle upon answers - is the *raison d'être* of this chapter.

In the pages that follow, we ask the following related questions: What is the significance of the service delivery protests in South Africa? To what extent do they contribute to policy change and development in South Africa? To what extent do they signify a renewal of working class politics and the rebuilding of a movement for radical change in the country? The context is the crisis in the provision of basic services at local government level, and we are mainly concerned with protests around the delivery of basic services such as water and electricity, as well as strikes by municipal workers insofar as they are related to the delivery of basic services.

The chapter asks these questions in order to eventually understand the protest actions, the ideology and thinking that informs the actions of the protesters, who they are in sociological terms, and the political significance of their actions in post-apartheid society. Any such research should aim to assess the actual and potential impact of the protests in changing (specific) policies and (general) power relations in favour of the protesters, and I will argue, consider how protests signify underlying processes in the development of working class politics.

In general I am inclined to conclude that the protests pose fundamental questions for emergent, dominant and residual approaches to political and social analysis. These approaches are, respectively, the postmodernist, (neo)liberal and Marxist schools of thought. Postmodernist analyses have, over the last three decades, challenged and sometimes eclipsed theoretically-inclined liberal and structuralist social scientific perspectives in the academic world. Postmodernist arguments are related in complex ways to the 'autonomist' perspective propounded by some social movement practitioners. Liberal and neoliberal approaches are dominant in that almost all the governments of the world, and hence the universities and research institutes they fund, willingly work within this paradigm, or are compelled to, given the global balance of forces. Marxist perspectives increasingly seem residual, that is, they are losing their past power and influence in the political and academic world, mainly as a result of the crisis of the global socialist project marked by the collapse of the Soviet Union and the capitalist restoration that occurred in countries once deemed socialist or communist.

I write this chapter from a Marxist perspective but in so doing I also aim to point a critical searchlight on the Marxist approach as much, if not more than, on the other perspectives. Marxism, to paraphrase Engels, is not a dogma but a guide to action. My job in this chapter will have been done if I can help us move one step towards understanding the protest action taking place in South Africa through examining the action itself and, in the process, evaluate and improve the intellectual tools we use to evaluate social phenomena.

Protest action has an important and proud history in South Africa. It was primarily working class action that drove the ruling class to discard the apartheid system and embrace democracy. Despite the fact that an 'elite transition' was ultimately brokered, the engine of change was the underlying class struggle and at the forefront of that struggle was the action of millions of ordinary working class people (Bond, 2005; McKinley, 1997; Marais, 1998). But this action was arguably inspired by a collective dream or vision of a society without apartheid, a society where all would be equal before the law, all could vote, all would have a share in the country's wealth. Although each community and group was fighting around its own demands, the anti-apartheid movement provided a common platform and forged a broader unity around the need for a struggle to abolish apartheid as a social system or form of government. In this sense it was primarily working class action that challenged and 'solved' the crisis of apartheid. This is not to discount the role of other actors and processes, but the catalyst and driving force was arguably militant mass action especially in the 1980s. Through their actions, working class people forced the apartheid state to unban the ANC and other liberation movements and to allow for majority rule.

Today, many commentators, basing themselves on government figures, note the exponential increase in the number of protest actions in post-apartheid South Africa (Harvey, 2007; Duncan and Vally, 2008, Ballard et al., 2006). What are the continuities and the breaks between the old anti-apartheid mass action and the new mass action in post-apartheid society? What is the crisis that is pushing working class people into struggle? And what is the solution that might be engendered by protest action? Are people only fighting about the delivery of basic services or is there a broader vision informing the protests just as was the case in the struggle against apartheid? During the anti-apartheid struggle the various problems and grievances of the people coalesced around the demand for ending apartheid and ushering in democratic majority rule. What are the problems today, what are the main demands and what is the unifying vision, if any?

The ANC government has not lived up to national liberation expectations. The delivery of basic services has been slow, inequality has increased, millions live miserably in shacks while still more millions lead futile lives unemployed. In addition, there are the social problems associated with poverty and inequality such as crime, alcohol and drug abuse, youth delinquency, dysfunctional families, rape, child molestation, etc. South Africa is also experiencing a health crisis with HIV/AIDS infections at record high levels while the health system is deteriorating (Buhlungu, 2007). This research will investigate the extent to which the protests are a response to these problems. Importantly, it will seek to find out from the protesters themselves: what are the reasons behind government failure and what are the possible solutions?

The protests have tended to centre on issues of service delivery at local government level. It is generally agreed even by the government that there is a crisis in the operation of local government in South Africa. This necessitated, for example, the setting up of Project Consolidate by the central government to support struggling municipalities.[1] Left scholars of local government have generally seen the crisis of local government as a crisis of neoliberal policy (Bond, 2007; Bond, 2004; Bond and Dugard, 2007; McDonald, 2002). This implies that the protests might represent a profound working class critique of neoliberalism at local government level. But if that is so, are the protesters aware of the significance of their protests? Do the protesters make demands that

---

1. *Mail & Guardian*, 'Ministers' report card, December 2005; *SA Reconciliation Barometer Newsletter*, The Institute for Justice and Reconciliation, quoted in *The Sunday Independent*, 8 December 2005.

require a change away from neoliberal policies? What are the solutions
and alternatives inherent in the protests?

But the question of service delivery goes beyond socio-economics
into politics. It brings into question the nature and quality of the post-
apartheid democracy. South Africa has a government, a Constitution and
laws that for all intents and purposes guarantee open and accessible
channels of communication between policy makers and the people.
Indeed, those who make the decisions are ostensibly answerable to the
masses. So, why are there protests? Why are the people not following the
'proper channels' to air their grievances?

Theories of contemporary participation and protest

Certain laws compel municipalities to involve communities in
'community participation' processes to enable people to influence
decisions that affect them.[2] John Williams, after studying community
participation in the Western Cape, observes,

> Most community participation exercises in post-apartheid South
> Africa are largely spectator politics, where ordinary people have
> mostly become endorsees of pre-designed planning
> programmes, [and] are often the objects of administrative
> manipulation (Williams, 2006: 197).

He concludes that the formal democratic processes that he observed at
local government level are "a limited form of democracy [that] give rise
to an administered society rather than a democratic society" since there
is no real debate of policy or of social programmes by the (working
class) electorate and government officials and leaders. (Williams, 2006)
A study of community participation in local economic development
processes in Durban by Richard Ballard, Debbie Bonin, Jennifer
Robinson and Thokozani Xaba reveals that these processes allow
ordinary people 'to demand accountability' from "their elected
representatives and sometimes quite senior officials." However, they are
'consultative rather than participatory' and "invariably... become
conspicuous for the issues they leave out, and for the voices they did not
hear" (Ballard et al., 2006). John Mavuso points out, the limitations of the
ward committee system as a mechanism to involve the people in local
government participatory democracy (Mavuso, undated).

---

2. Republic of South Africa, Municipal Structures Act No. 117 of 1998, Pretoria:
Government Printers; and the Local Government Systems Act No. 32 of 2000. Also,
Constitution of the Republic of South Africa, Act No. 108, 1996.

David Hemson, dealing with the same issues of participation, concludes that ordinary people can either participate through voting in local government elections, through official 'community participation' structures such as ward committees, and interestingly, through "social movements; the contestation of municipal policy and practice through marches, memoranda and the setting up of local alternative community structures" (Hemson, undated). For Hemson, the protests are part and parcel or an extension of the democratic process of contesting power and exerting influence. Williams more or less comes to the same conclusion when he argues that "community participation in South Africa is informed by the memory of community struggle – a radical form of participation – against the racist apartheid State" and that this must be harnessed because: "It is precisely this repertoire of radical strategies that can and should be revisited and adapted, to advance the interests of the materially marginalised communities at the local level" (Williams, 2006: 1).

In his groundbreaking research Luke Sinwell (2009: 31) distinguishes between 'invited' versus 'invented' spaces of popular participation in matters of state and governance. The former refers to formal channels of participatory democracy afforded to the masses by state authorities such as ward committees, *imbizos* and integrated development plans (IDPs). Invented spaces are those that the people create for themselves through their 'self-activity' such as community self-organisation, direct action and other non-official mechanisms of exerting pressure and effecting desired change sometimes against the wishes of the powers that be. Based on extensive research conducted in Alexandra, one of the oldest and poorest black working class townships in South Africa, he concludes that progressive change is more likely to emanate from invented rather than invited spaces.

However, Sinwell laments the extent to which community activism even in the invented spaces fails to question power relations and social structures in a fundamental way. His research findings indicate that community organisations tend to work within, for example, the budgetary constraints set by the state. As a result community groups end up competing among themselves for limited state resources rather than questioning what he regards as the state's neoliberal framework and its ideological underpinnings.

Sinwell's thesis forces all radical commentators to revisit their premises and their assessments of the protest movement in South Africa. For example, the emergence of social movement organisations in post-apartheid society around the year 2000 was heralded by many (of this ilk) as indicative of a popular critique of neoliberal policy that would presumably culminate in radical and even revolutionary change. I am among those who, from a Marxist activist perspective, advocated this position both as a wish, goal and prognosis (Ngwane, 2003). But Sinwell's findings indicate that even prominently radical social movement organisations such as the Anti-Privatisation Forum are better characterised as having a politics that looks to the state for 'delivery' rather than seeking to question the legitimacy of the state, let alone seek to replace it with a new social order and power. There is a need for further research into the actual practices and politics of a wider range of social movement organisations in order to test the accuracy or otherwise of Sinwell's argument. If he is right, many social movement practitioners and commentators will no doubt have to go back to the drawing board.

Is there continuity between protest action during apartheid days and that taking place in post-apartheid South Africa? Do the protests today represent a form of revival of the working class militancy that characterised the battles against apartheid? If so, is this desirable or must South Africa 'move on' and deal with new issues in new 'democratic' ways? The language, imagery and form of the protest action suggest continuity between the present post-apartheid and the past anti-apartheid struggles. But there is also evidence suggesting a break, for example, the fact that the present government is regarded as 'legitimate', as 'our government'. The democratic and human rights rhetoric adopted by the post-apartheid state is also a crucial factor.

Do Sinwell's critical observations reflect processes that arise out of this changed historical context? The call to overthrow apartheid seemed perfectly 'reasonable', but the same call against a democratically elected government, no matter the hardships visited on the masses by its neoliberal policies, would relegate a movement to the lunatic fringe by hostile critics. As Michael Sachs (2003: 27) put it, the new movements' "claims to be the voice of the poor will continue to sound hollow against the spectacle of 15 million working class people standing in the sun to mandate their political representatives in the state."

I am not suggesting that the call for revolutionary transformation is wrong or outdated, but rather that the ushering in of a democratic order might erode the power of this argument in the popular imagination. Furthermore, radicals during the anti-apartheid struggle tended to see racial oppression and class exploitation as two sides of the same coin. The post-apartheid order appears to belie this twinning in that the two seem to have been successfully disentangled in a manner closer to the liberal perspective on apartheid than that of the radicals (although the liberals believed this would occur gradually and through capitalism's rising success in 'lifting all boats', whereas actually it happened via capitalist crisis in the mid-1980s). Indeed, the liberals had argued that apartheid was like a fetter on capitalist development; could it be that in the new South Africa we see unleashed the full – Marx would say 'naked, brutal' – power of capital? Further thinking along these lines is necessary, and I would tentatively suggest that the Gramscian notion of hegemony might provide a good entry point in addressing this conundrum. There is evidence to suggest that during the transition from apartheid to a democratic order the leaders of the national liberation movement co-operated in the 'demobilisation' of the popular protest movement as part of the preparation for the new order (Grossman and Ngwane, forthcoming). But these thoughts require further elaboration and verification.

In his 3rd Thesis on Feuerbach, Marx wrote: "The coincidence of the changing circumstances and of human activity or self-changing can be conceived and rationally understood only as revolutionary practice."[3] In other words, by engaging in mass action, the masses change themselves. Participation in mass protest action affects the thinking of the participants and thus can be seen as contributing to the development of class consciousness and, by extension, of the workers movement. One possible implication is that despite the 'reformist' nature of the demands and politics of the present protest movement, it is possible that over time it might radicalise and the protesters develop a more radical consciousness that would disprove Sinwell's disconsolate assessment and serve as a fillip to revolutionary thought and aspiration.

There are certain commonalities between postmodernism and a strand of revolutionary thinking found in 21st century movements called 'autonomism' or what to me sometimes seems better termed 'anarcho-autonomism'. The post-modernists acknowledge the historical role of modernism but argue that the time has come to go beyond it; the autonomists acknowledge the historical role of Marxism but argue that the time has come to go beyond it. There are other more substantive similarities such as the disdain for structures, organisation and (hierarchical) leadership. There is also a common emphasis on the chaos and messiness of social phenomena rather than a focus on identifying order and patterns. In this section I want to deal with the autonomists' emphasis on the 'newness' of protest politics in the post-Soviet Union historical era, hence the deployment of terms such as 'new social movements' to refer to the current protest movement in this country.

It is noteworthy that newness is emphasised by prominent practitioners and commentators of the international 'anti-globalisation movement' or what some call the global economic justice movement, 'the children of Seattle'. A celebrated catchphrase of this movement is 'one

---

3. Marx, K., 3rd Thesis on Feuerbach, Marx Engels internet archive.

no, many yeses' (Kingsnorth, 2003). Is there a contradiction between the emphasis on the newness of struggles waged in post-apartheid South Africa by the 'new social movements' or 'service delivery' protesters, and the claim that these organisations or communities carry the mantle of the anti-apartheid struggle that has been usurped by the new government's adoption of neoliberal policies?

Marxists tend to see a continuity in struggles because then and now the struggle was and still is about attaining the goal of 'socialism'. For the autonomists the struggle for socialism is not only old hat but represents a retrogression because of the failures of the socialist experiment in the world and their principled opposition to a fight for state power or any common alternative vision of society. Such visions are regarded as grand meta-narratives that are imposed on the masses and as such must be denounced. The struggle for state power is discouraged by the autonomists because the state is seen as inherently hierarchical and undemocratic.

But this perspective is challenged by Sinwell's observation that many movements look to the state for delivery and relief rather than being anti-state. Perhaps what is new in South Africa is a legitimate democratic order which for the masses is still too early to dismiss, whereas in Europe the masses have had a long enough experience of and disappointment with liberal democracy.

Studies of contemporary politics in South Africa must now take into account the service delivery protests (Hemson and Owusu-Ampomah, 2005). Richard Ballard, Adam Habib and Imraan Valodia co-edited a seminal work dealing with the 'new social movements', that is, the various organisations such as the Treatment Action Campaign, the Anti-Privatisation Forum (APF), the Soweto Electricity Crisis Committee, Jubilee South Africa and even the South African National Civic Organisation, an organisation active during the anti-apartheid struggle but with a different orientation after apartheid (Ballard et al., 2006). In general the movements are seen as a response to the shortcomings of neoliberal policy but the editors question the notion that these movements consciously seek to go beyond the neoliberal order, notwithstanding the apparent need for this. While some leaders might state this need, the rank and file members are seen as more interested in immediate 'bread and butter' issues rather than in grand schemes to change the world. The book was published before most commentators had recognised the rise of 'spontaneous' community uprisings and riots, termed 'service delivery protests'.

Subsequent research into protests and social movements addresses the community uprisings that became notable in the small towns of the Free State in 2004, such as Harrismith (Intabazwe township), a few years after the emergence and prominence of the 'new social movements'. At first these protests were referred to as 'spontaneous' because observers were caught by surprise and could not identify a single organisation or leader that organised them. However, it is now recognised that these protests are organised and led by community organisations and leaders many of whom belong to the 'Alliance' of the ruling party, the African National Congress (Alexander 2010).

There has been some debate as to whether it is accurate to call these 'service delivery protests' given the fact that some of their demands relate to questions of good governance, accountability, corruption and community participation in local government. Some prominent community protests, such as in Khutsong, have been around the issue of demarcation. Demarcation struggles involve communities refusing to be administratively re-allocated into another province, a kind of forced removal by pencil. This controversy arose out of the attempt to 'regularise' cross-border municipalities in South Africa.

Other works on the subject tend to focus on one or two case studies, and still others deal with the service protests as an important factor or background phenomenon in the analysis of the political economy of the country or aspects of it under study (Barcheisi, 2005; Harvey, 2007; Desai, 2002). During the decade beginning around 1997, South Africa experienced an exponential rise in the number of community protests and strikes after a period of lull following independence in 1994 (Duncan and Vally, 2008).

How are we to understand these protests? In his prolific work, Patrick Bond (2002, 2003, 2004, 2007) has consistently approached the protests as representing the beginnings of a solution to the present neoliberal crisis. His revolutionary optimism requires critical assessment in the light of evidence and recent scholarship on the subject. Does Sinwell's assessment pour cold water on Bond's hopes? The jury is still out, in part because many of these struggles involve and are led by the youth. Youth learn fast and it is possible that the struggles may still evolve along radical lines. My 2009-10 research visits to Siyathemba township, Balfour, seem to indicate the existence of processes that accelerate the political development of the youth leadership's struggle ideas within a relatively short space of time. However, this research is still very much work in progress and cannot be deployed here in a definitive way.

In a study of an earlier period in South Africa's history, Jonathan Grossman usefully deploys the twin concepts of working-class mood and combativity in an attempt to explain political processes, class relations and class struggles (Grossman, 1985). Grossman asserts that an increase in mass action (strikes) and "the development of new organisations, the decline of existing organisations, and the revitalisation of old organisations" are indicators of the mood of the working class (Grossman, 1985: 20).

With the dawn of the new South Africa, mass action and protest tended to increasingly take the form of peaceful and orderly marches which invariably culminated in a banal ceremonial handing over of the memorandum. Then followed a period mainly characterised by massive one-day strikes by the unions against the privatisation of state assets. From about 2000 to 2004, a new wave or type of mass action emerged that was increasingly organised by emergent organisations called the 'new social movements', that is, campaigning organisations such as the Anti-Privatisation Forum, Landless Peoples Movement, Concerned Citizens Forum, the Treatment Action Campaign, Western Cape Anti-Eviction Campaign, etc. (Ballard et al., 2006). These were militant protests and were often ideologically scathing of the political status quo. They were often referred to by commentators as 'single-issue' campaigns.

Then, from mid-2004, an unexpected wave of protests arose that tended to involve whole communities in veritable 'community uprisings' or riots, also sometimes termed 'popcorn protests'. A noticeable feature of these protests was their sometime violent or disruptive nature captured in the emblematic burning tyre. This brief overview of the protest movement and its changes over time underline the importance of periodisation.

During the period under investigation, municipal workers also struggled memorably against Igoli 2002, a privatisation plan by the Johannesburg municipality (Barcheisi, 2005; Bond, 2002). The dynamism of the protests and strikes appear to indicate changes in the nature of the protests, the political context and possibly in the 'class consciousness' or political outlook of the protest movement and its leadership over the (post-apartheid) period under investigation. Further research and analysis is necessary.

Despite the localism of the service delivery protests, some scholars have pointed out the national and international dimensions of these struggles. They note that national government sets the policy and budgetary parameters for the operation of local government. They also note that, in the context of globalisation, national policies are sometimes a result of external influences such as the need for countries to follow the policy recommendations of the World Bank, the World Trade Organisation and other international agencies. Bond, for example, has argued that the World Bank acted as an advisor to the new ANC administration in the 1990s, a role that culminated in the bank's officials co-authoring the country's macro-economic policy GEAR (Bond, 2005).

This suggests that we need to locate our understanding of protest action in South Africa within an international context in order to account for influences that exist outside our borders. Some protesting organisations receive support from organisations abroad.

What is the relationship between the development and contestation of social and economic policies at international, national and local level? To what extent and in what ways do the protesters see themselves as contributing to the global struggle against neoliberalism? How are they, if at all, influenced by the global movement? Is 'localism' a constraint on struggles that challenge processes that are national and international in character or origin?

The interpretation of social movements

Various scholars, activists and unionists have explored and criticised the shift of the ANC government from pushing a redistributive agenda assumed to be beneficial to the majority to implementing trickle-down macro-economic policies that primarily benefit big business and related social interests (Barchiesi, 1005; Bond, 2005; Harvey, 2007). This is often characterised as the shift from the Reconstruction and Development Programme (RDP) to the Growth, Employment and Redistribution programme (GEAR). Some of this work has focused on the provision of municipal services with some of it showing how neoliberal policies have led to a slowing down or abandonment of programmes that would allow more working class people to access services (Ruiters and Bond, 1999; Roome, 1995). Some of this work has zeroed in on privatisation and cost recovery as policies that jeopardise access to basic services for millions of ordinary South Africans (McDonald and Pape, 2002; Municipal Services Project Special Report, 2002).

Ebrahim Harvey has investigated the implementation of neoliberal policies in the sphere of local government where Johannesburg municipality enforced the installation of pre-payment meters in a working-class area in Soweto (Harvey, *op cit*). Some writers in this genre have gone further to explore and suggest alternative policies that would be more likely to guarantee access to basic services to most South Africans. The underlying principle in such solutions involves calls for the 'decommodification' of basic services and a Constitutional-legal reminder that these are enshrined in the country's Constitution as rights (Bond, 2003). However, some analysts (like Bond and Karen Bakker) have criticised the discourse of human rights, and they prefer to conceptualise the struggle as a fight for declaring basic services as part of the 'commons' (Bakker, 2007). This is an important debate at a conceptual level, and needs grounding in reality and in the lived experiences of people who must live with the consequences of policy choices such as the protesters.

Harvey's study leads him to make some general observations about the struggle and the politics of protest. He argues that organisation is key in the building of any movement, and particularly an anti-neoliberal counter-movement. In contrast, he argues, social movements have tended towards spontaneous and *ad hoc* mobilisation around single issues and not towards a focus on building organisation with a broader vision and programme in mind. He sees the way forward as necessitating the forging of links between different organisations such as between social movements and unions (Harvey, 2007: 250).

Franco Barchiesi (2005) also bemoans the failure of municipal unions to support and link up with the community in the struggle against privatisation. This contrasts with experiences of unity during the anti-apartheid struggle.

Are social movements intrinsically good for democracy? Do protests undermine or strengthen democracy? In a study of the Soweto Electricity Crisis Committee, Fiona White argues that in general social movements do contribute to strengthening democracy but may undermine it if they use illegal methods on a long-term basis (White, 2008). This criticism necessitates self-reflection by members of this organisation and other movements assessing, to what extent their strategies advance or undermine their cause. The question of legality, rule of law and the constitutionality of struggle strategies are very important given South Africa's relatively young democracy. How do the protesters justify themselves when they burn down a government building, as sometimes happens?

This question is related to a general critique that is emerging in 'democracy studies' in post-colonial societies. For example, a survey of democracies and democratisation in Asia reveals that there is a rolling back of substantive democracy using 'culture-centric [Asian] exceptionalism' as a justification because of (an elite) "fear of mass participation in representative democracy" (Cho et al., 2008: ix). Analysts of developments in South Korea, Taiwan, Thailand and the Philippines indicate that there are many ways in which democracy can be subverted such that regimes "hold elections in order to provide a representative façade for undemocratic governance" (Surendara, 2008: 25).

Could it be that the mass protests are provoked by a perceived failure of democratic processes in South Africa? Or should they be considered, as Williams and Hemson argue, part of the democratic process? How do the protesters justify themselves in post-apartheid South Africa?

Marxist answers to social movement questions

Government, (neo)liberal and pro-establishment commentators tend to view the protests as an aberration and a problem that needs to be sorted out. But if we start from Karl Marx's assertion, "The history of all hitherto existing society is the history of class struggles," instead of seeing the turmoil and disruptions caused by the service delivery protests and the strikes as somehow 'dysfunctional', we might conclude that it is exactly these struggles that ultimately drive history forward. Policy changes arise out of the sometimes adversarial interaction between the policy makers and those who are objects of that policy. The tension arises from the contradictory class interests represented by the authorities *vis-a-vis* those of the masses.

This materialist interpretation of history requires systematic review and updating given class formation and differentiation processes taking place in South Africa today and their intersection with race and racial identities. For example, there is arguably a burgeoning 'underclass' that leads precarious lives in shacks without steady employment and social security and a black middle class, sections of whom live fabulous lives of newfound riches and privileges. Gender is another important variable that needs to be factored in our analysis. The fact that some protests become xenophobic needs exploration in order to combat this. In what follows, I will consider some writers whose ideas might help in developing an enhanced theoretical understanding of protest politics in South Africa.

David Harvey provides a Marxist theoretical framework to explain how government services that were heretofore assumed to be the birthright of citizens are turned by the neoliberal regime into commodities that can be bought and sold on the market. 'Commodification' of basic services is what the World Bank, IMF and WTO recommend to local governments throughout the world. This arises out of the profitability crises facing world capitalism, and the attempt by the capitalists to obviate this by seeking new avenues to make profits through taking over services that traditionally fell under the ambit of the state; what others call 'public goods'. He has termed this process "accumulation by dispossession" (Harvey, 2000; Harvey, 2005).

Ashwin Desai wrote *We are the Poors,* a seminal work on post-apartheid grassroots struggles, from a participant-observer point of view. His theory is that class eclipses race in the struggle for basic services in South African working class townships. "We are not Indians, we are the poors" (Desai, 2002). This research seeks to explore questions of agency and identity on the part of those acting collectively in defence of their interests. In this respect the relationship of class, race and gender is important. The work of Manuel Castells is important in that it focuses on the sphere of the community as a site of struggle and of reproduction and consumption; a corrective to the customary Marxist focus on the workplace (Castells, 1978; Castells, 1983).

George Rude (2005) provides us with a theory of 'popular ideologies of protest' that can help in understanding the motivations and ideas of people participating in collective actions such as strikes and service delivery protests. He distinguishes between 'received' and 'inherent' ideologies and makes the point that ordinary people integrate formal ideologies into their daily thinking when they are engaged in making history. Antonio Gramsci's (1971) concept of 'hegemony' and 'counter-hegemony' helps us understand the role of dominant ideologies in society and how these are sometimes challenged leading to monumental social change. Do the protesters represent aspects of a counter-hegemonic project in South Africa?

Michael Addison (2002) helps us to understand the role of 'violent politics'. His concept covers riots, terrorism, insurrection and civil war. Its relevance is that a significant number of the community protests turn violent. Addison's concept helps us to understand the eruption of violence in an analytic way locating it in a historical-social context rather than following the mass media's sensationalism, the government's denunciation or indulging in moralistic repugnance or indeed uncritical support.

The escalating protests seem to give credence to the Marxist perspective of class struggle, that class society is always involved in a fight with itself. Postmodernists and autonomists can and will legitimately proffer their own profound insights and truths based on their perspectives. The difference is that for Marx (and the Marxists) the solution is socialism and communism and for these to occur what is required is active commitment to progressive social change. Scholars and commentators need to put words into action, to turn analysis into programme, understanding into vision. In his words: 'The philosophers have interpreted the world in various ways, the point is to change it.'

Conclusion

Critical research cuts through surface appearances by analysing the backdrop of their historical and structural contexts. It gives a voice to imposed silences and explores hitherto unexplored areas. It introduces new and fresh perspectives even on issues that have been well researched by other scholars. Unlike crude positivism that seeks to explain social reality from an indifferent perspective, critical research strives to change the world for the better.

However, the researcher must also be able to sift through social reality systematically and with honesty, without being blinded by preconceptions and moral preferences. Social research is a social activity like any other; hence it can take a side, since it serves a social purpose. It should declare its moral-political position to the scholar community so that it can be judged accordingly (Thompson, 1995; Bailey, 1982).

In this chapter I have endeavoured to pose some critical questions about the genesis and prognosis of protest politics in post-apartheid society and, as expected, have managed to raise more questions than providing any definitive answers. This unsatisfactory outcome is unavoidable because often half the battle in the quest to understand complex social-historical phenomena is to pose the correct questions in the first place. More research, thinking and debate are necessary to shed better light on the subject matter of this chapter. I hope my attempt, inspired by and building on the work of others, has advanced the debate a little.

Let me conclude on a general and conceptual note and observation. It seems to me that all three major theoretical approaches considered here provide an inadequate framework for tackling the questions raised. The neoliberal, the postmodern/autonomist and the Marxist schools of thought all suffer shortcomings.

Neoliberalism represents the ideology of the ruling class and as such needs to be understood, dissected and, I would argue, transcended. In South Africa there is simply too much evidence to indicate that this approach is an essential part of the problem of increasing human suffering, rather than part of the solution.

Autonomism, which is related in complex ways to postmodernist and sometimes anarchist thought, is an approach that is legitimately deployed to advance the interests of subaltern classes. However, in the South African context, autonomism has struggled to inspire and guide the protest movement in a significant way due to certain theoretical and strategic weaknesses this chapter has generally, if inadequately, pointed to.

Lastly, as a Marxist scholar and movement activist, I admit to the challenges facing Marxist revolutionary thought including the burden of a historical legacy of failure in the practical implementation of this ideology. But for some reason, Marxist thought is still taken seriously by scholars and mass movement activists in this country, perhaps more so than in many other countries.

This is a gift to Marxists and we must courageously bear the brunt of reviewing this intellectual approach, identify its weakness, update it to suit the changing times and strive to re-unite its emancipatory ideas to the real mass protest movement of change. The hallmark of this work should be the unity of theory and practice and a willingness, in the spirit of Marx himself, to criticise everything existing, including our own shibboleths.

References

Addison, M., 2002. *Violent Politics*. Oxford: Palgrave.

Alexander, P., 2010. Rebellion of the poor: South Africa's service delivery protests – a preliminary analysis. *Review of African Political Economy*, 37(123), pp.25–40.

Bailey, K. D., 1982. *Methods of Social Research*. New York: The Free Press.

Bakker, K., 2007. The commons versus the commodity: Alter-globalisation, anti-privatisation and the human right to water in the global south. *Antipode,* 39 (3), pp.430-455.

Ballard, R. et al., 2006. Development and New Forms of Democracy in Durban. Paper presented at 'The place of participation in a democratising South Africa: Decentralisation, local councillors and civil society in post-apartheid cities.' Colloquium organised by the HSRC, IFAS and CUBES, 20-21st November WITS, Johannesburg.

Ballard, R. et al. eds., 2006. *Voices of Protest: Social Movements in Post-Apartheid South Africa*. Pietermaritzburg: University of KwaZulu-Natal Press.

Barchiesi, F., 2005. Social citizenship and the transformation of wage labour in the making of post-apartheid South Africa, 1994-2001. Ph.D. thesis, University of the Witswatersrand, Johannesburg.

Bond, P., 2002. *Unsustainable South Africa: Environment, Development and Social Protest*. Pietermaritzburg: University of Natal Press.

Bond, P., 2003. Against Global Apartheid: South Africa meets the World Bank, IMF and International Finance. Johannesburg: Zed Books.

Bond, P., 2004. South Africa's Resurgent Urban Social Movements: The Case of Johannesburg, 1984, 1994, 2004. Lecture presented to the Centre for Civil Society, Durban.

Bond, P., 2005. *Elite Transition: From Apartheid to Neoliberalism in South Africa*. Pietermaritzburg: University of KwaZulu-Natal Press.

Bond, P., 2007. Johannesburg: Of gold and gangsters. In Davis, M. and Betrand, D. eds. *Evil Paradises: Dreamworlds of Neoliberalism.* New York: New Press.

Buhlungu, S. et al., 2007. *State of the nation 2007*. Cape Town: HSRC Press.

Castells, M., 1978. *City, Class and Power*. London: Macmillan.

Castells, M., 1983. *The City and the Grassroots*. Berkeley: University of California Press.

Cho, H. et al. eds., 2008. States of Democracy: Oligarchic Democracies and Asian Democratisation. Mumbai: Earthworm Books.

Desai, A., 2002. We are the Poors: Community struggles in post-apartheid South Africa, New York: Monthly Review Press.

Duncan, J. and Vally, N., 2008. National Trends Around Protest Action: Mapping Protest Action in South Africa, Power Point presentation, Centre for Sociological Research, University of Johannesburg.

Gramsci, A., 1971. *Selections from the Prison Notebooks of Antonio Gramsci*. Translated and edited by Q. Hoare and G. Nowel Smith, New York: International Publishers.

Grossman, J., 1985. Class relations and the policies of the Communist Party of South Africa: 1921-1950. Ph.D. thesis, University of Warwick.

Grossman, J. and Ngwane, T., 2005. Social Movements and the Revival of the Workers' Movement in South Africa. Unpublished paper.

Grossman, J. and Ngwane, T., (to be published). Looking back moving forward: legacies of struggle and the challenges facing the new social movements. In *Searching for South Africa*. UNISA: Pretoria.

Harvey, D., 2000. *Spaces of Hope*. Edinburgh: Edinburgh University Press.

Harvey, D., 2005. *The New Imperialism*. Oxford: Oxford University Press.

Harvey, E., 2007. The Commodification of water in Soweto and its implications for social justice. Ph.D. thesis, University of the Witswatersrand, Johannesburg.

Hemson, D. and Owusu-Ampomah, K., 2005. 'A Better Life For All?' Service Delivery and Poverty Alleviation. In J. Daniel, R. Southall and J. Lutchman, eds. *State of the Nation: South Africa: 2004 – 2005*. Cape Town and Michigan: Human Sciences Research Council and Michigan State University Press.

Hemson, D., nd. Can participation make a difference? Prospects for people's participation in planning. Cape Town: URED, HSRC.

Kingsnorth, P., 2003. *One No, Many Yeses*. London: The Free Press.

Marais, H., 1998. *Limits to Change Vol. 1: The Political Economy of Transition*, London, Zed Books.

Mavuso, J., nd. Challenges facing the ward committee system – Managing diversity within demarcated ward boundaries, IDASA paper.

McDonald, D., 2002. The Bell Tolls for Thee: Cost Recovery, Cutoffs and the Affordability of Municipal Services in South Africa. *Municipal Services Project Special Report*.

McDonald, D. and Smith, L., 2004. From apartheid to neoliberalism in the mother city. *Urban Studies*, 41(8), pp.1461-1484.

McDonald, D. and Pape, J., 2002. Cost Recovery and the Crisis of Service Delivery in South Africa in South Africa. Cape Town: HSRC Press.

McKinley, D., 1997. *The ANC & The Liberation Struggle: A Critical Political Biography*. London: Pluto Books.

Municipal Services Project Special Report. 2002. The Bell Tolls for Thee: Cost Recovery, Cutoffs and the Affordability of Municipal Services in South Africa.

Ngwane, T., 2003. The Anti-Privatisation Forum. *Labour Bulletin*, 27(6), pp. 31-32.

Roome, J., 1995. Water Pricing and Management: World Bank Presentation to the SA Water Conservation Conference. Unpublished paper, South Africa, 2 October.

Rude, G., 1980. *Ideology and Popular Protest*. London: Lawrence and Wishart.

Ruiters, G. and Bond, P., 1999. Contradictions in Municipal Transformation From Apartheid to Democracy: The Battle over Local Water Privatisation in South Africa. *Working Papers in Local Governance and Democracy*, 99(1).

Sachs, J., 2003. We don't want the fucking vote: Social movements and demagogues in South Africa's young democracy. *Labour Bulletin*, 27(6).

Sinwell, L., 2009. Participation as Popular Agency: The Limitations and Possibilities for Transforming Development in the Alexandra Renewal Project. Ph.D. thesis, University of the Witwatersrand, Johannesburg.

Surendara, L., 2008. Democratising Democracy –Beyond Representative Politics to the Politics of Inclusion. In Cho et al., *States of Democracy: Oligarchic Democracies and Asian Democratisation*. Mumbai: Earthworm Books.

Thompson, E. P., 1995. *The Poverty of Theory*. London: Merlin Press.

White, F., 2008. Strengthening Democracy? The Role of Social Movements as Agents of Civil Society in Post-Apartheid South Africa. Ph.D. thesis, University of London.

Williams, J., 2006. Community Participation: Lessons from post-apartheid South Africa. *Policy Studies*, 27(3), pp.197-217.

17.
Rethinking poverty and assistance in Southern Africa
James Ferguson

Introduction

In reflecting on the large and rapidly expanding literature on neoliberalism, I am struck by how much of the critical scholarship on the topic arrives in the end at the very same conclusion - a conclusion that might be expressed as: "neoliberalism is bad for poor and working people, therefore we must oppose it." It is not that I disagree with this conclusion. On the contrary. But I sometimes wonder why I should bother to read one after another extended scholarly analysis only to reach, again and again, such an unsurprising conclusion.

This disappointment in recent progressive scholarship strikes me as related to a parallel problem in progressive politics. For over the last couple of decades, what we call 'the Left' has come to be defined by a series of gestures of refusal, which I call 'the antis'. Anti-globalisation, anti-neoliberalism, anti-privatisation, anti-Bush, perhaps even anti-capitalism – but always 'anti', not 'pro'. This is good enough, perhaps, if one's political goal is simply denouncing 'the system' and decrying its current tendencies. And many, it must be said, seem satisfied with such politics. In my own discipline of anthropology, studies of state and development tend, with depressing predictability, to conclude (in tones of shocked indignation) that the rich are benefiting and the poor are getting screwed. The powerless, it seems, are on the losing end of things. This is not exactly a surprising finding, of course (isn't it precisely because they are on the losing end of things that we call them 'powerless' in the first place?). Yet this sort of work styles itself as 'critique', and imagines itself to be very (as we say) 'political'.

But what if politics is really not about expressing indignation or denouncing the powerful. What if it is, instead, about getting what you want? Then we progressives must ask ourselves: What do we want? And this is really a quite different question than: What are we against? *What do we want?* Such a question brings us quite directly to the question of government. Denunciations of government as power sometimes seem to imply that it is some sort of scandal that people should be governed at all. But unless one finds anarchist alternatives convincing (which I certainly do not), a progressive answer to the question "what do we want?" will have to involve an exploration of the contemporary possibilities for developing genuinely progressive arts of government.

New arts of government

I therefore wish to begin by pointing out two reasons (no doubt not the only two) why such arts of government will have to depart in significant ways from those that the left came to rely upon in the 20th century (and that characterised, in different ways, both socialist and social democratic or 'welfare state' regimes). The first reason is the increasing prominence (especially in Africa, but not only there) of urban masses who are not, and are not likely to become, formal wage labourers. Such people (variously, and inadequately, described as 'the informal sector', 'the lumpen', the youth, and so on) now constitute the majority of the population in many African cities, and a very substantial proportion in much of the rest of the world, as Mike Davis (2007) has recently pointed out, in his usual alarmist style. The twentieth century social democracies, on the other hand (and still more so the state socialist regimes), were built on the putatively universal figure of 'the worker'. The Keynesian welfare state, as we know, was founded on a pact between capital and organised labour, and the domain we have come to know as 'the social' was constructed on the foundation of the able-bodied worker. Indeed, the list of those requiring 'social' intervention (the elderly, the infirm, the child, the disabled, the dependent reproductive woman) sketches a kind of photographic negative of the figure of the wage-earning man.

Today, however, the question of social assistance is transformed in societies where young, able-bodied men look in vain for work, and are as much in need of assistance as everyone else. A compact between capital and organised labour, meanwhile, even were it politically possible, risks leaving out most of the population. New approaches to distribution, and new approaches to the question of social assistance, will need to be based on a fundamental rethinking that gives a new prominence to those hard-to-categorise urban improvisers who have for so long been relegated to the margins both of society, and of social analysis.

The second challenge to progressive thought and politics that I would like to identify is the rise of transnational forms of government, and philanthropic funding of what we used to call 'the social'. Much has been written about the governmental role played by international organisations like the IMF and the World Bank. But the last couple of decades have also seen an explosion in *de facto* government carried out by an extraordinary swarm of NGOs, voluntary organisations, and private foundations. The Gates Foundation in Mozambique, to take just one example, is carrying out a wide range of projects (in health, hygiene, education, sanitation, etc.) that looks something like the 20th century 'social' of the social welfare state.[1] But there is obviously a very different relation to the nation-state here, and to the national political arena. Policy and state are, in very significant ways, decoupled, in ways that we are only beginning to find ways to think about.

More generally, technical prescriptions for 'making poverty history' often seem almost irrelevant because they presume the central actors to be states – and certain sorts of states at that: well financed, bureaucratically capable, poverty-fighting states that resemble nothing so much as 20th century European welfare states. Couldn't the Democratic Republic of the Congo solve all its problems, reformers seem to say, if only its government would start to behave like that of Sweden? Well, maybe so, but it's the sort of ahistorical and asociological formulation that is worse than useless. Yet what happens when states of the imagined, poverty-fighting kind are simply not present? How can poverty policy be effective where states are (as the political scientists, rather misleadingly, say) 'weak', or even actively anti-developmental? Where financial capacity is tiny and needs are enormous? What happens when the key implementers of poverty policy are not national states at all, but transnational NGOs, or private transnational foundations? What would count as progressive politics here?

One response here – understandable in the wake of neoliberalism – is to call for the reinstating of old-style developmental states, effectively undoing neoliberalism and going back to the 1970s. I am sceptical that this is an adequate response – partly because the supposedly developmental states I know from the 1970s in Africa were pretty awful, and partly because I doubt that you can run history backward (as if you could just hit the rewind button and try again). The world has changed, and simply re-asserting third world sovereignty will not get us very far in dealing with a fundamentally reconfigured politico-spatial world order. Imperialism is undoubtedly alive and well. But I don't think we have a good analysis of, say, the Gates Foundation, or the Soros Foundation, if we see them simply as the imperial tools of the global rich, undermining the sovereignty of African governments. It is much more complicated than that – and perhaps also more hopeful. Can we find ways of thinking creatively about the progressive possibilities (and not only the reactionary dangers) of this new terrain of transnational organisation of funds, energies, and affect? Can we imagine new 'arts of government' that might take advantage of (rather than simply fighting against) recent transformations in the spatial organisation of government and social assistance?

---

1. I refer here to the remarkable Ph.D. research now being carried out by Ramah McKay (Department of Anthropology, Stanford University).

Most broadly, can we engage with these new configurations of governmental power in a way that goes beyond the politics of denunciation, the politics of the 'anti'? Can we develop new ways of thinking through the problem of government that are genuinely progressive, but that don't take for granted the absolute solidity or centrality of those two figures of twentieth-century left common sense: the worker and the nation-state?

It is here that we have to look more carefully at the 'arts of government' that have so radically reconfigured the world in the last few decades, and I think we have to come up with something more interesting to say about them than just that we're against them. With respect to poverty and social policy, for instance (my particular interest here), it is simply not the case (as is often suggested) that neoliberal government ignores poverty, or leaves it to 'the market'. (Later in this essay, I will discuss a range of welfare-like interventions and social payments that coexist with – and may, in fact, be necessary complements to -- neoliberal economic models).

Twentieth-century democracy and social policy

At the same time, there is sometimes room (in part because of the political spaces opened up by 'democracy' as the characteristic mode of legitimation of neoliberal regimes) for social movements and 'pro-poor' organisations to have some real influence on matters of 'social policy'. (Hence my current interest in the 'Basic Income Grant' (BIG) campaign in South Africa, which I'll discuss in a moment.) To understand the political possibilities and dangers that such emergent phenomena contain, we will surely need empirical research on the actual political processes at work. But beyond this, there is a palpable need for conceptual work, for new and better ways of thinking about practices of government and how they might be linked in new ways to the aspirations and demands of the economically and socially marginalised people who constitute the majority of the population in much of the world.

In matters of 'social policy', Foucault's 1983 observation remains true more than a quarter century later: "We are still bound up with an outlook that was formed between 1920 and 1940, mainly under the influence of Beveridge, a man who was born over a hundred years ago. For the moment ... we completely lack the intellectual tools necessary to envisage in new terms the form in which we might attain what we are looking for." (Foucault, 1988: 166).

It is in this spirit, then, that I want to consider what I am calling 'the uses of neoliberalism'. I begin with a consideration of 'uses in the literal sense of semantic usage, as the wide variation in the way the term is used requires some clarification before we can begin to ask some new questions that might bring to light the surprising affinity of some aspects of what we call 'neoliberalism' with certain forms of progressive politics.

As even a cursory inspection reveals, there is a huge variation in the way the word, 'neoliberalism' is used in contemporary scholarship. In perhaps the strictest sense, neoliberalism refers to a macroeconomic doctrine (and is, in this sense, a true -'ism'). The key elements of the doctrine have been variously described, but all accounts include a valorisation of private enterprise and suspicion of the state, along with what is sometimes called 'free-market fetishism' and the advocacy of tariff elimination, currency deregulation, and the deployment of 'enterprise models' that would allow the state itself to be 'run like a business'. (See Peck 2008 for an illuminating review of the rise and dissemination of this doctrine.)

A related usage would have 'neoliberalism' refer to a regime of policies and practices associated with or claiming fealty to the doctrine referenced above. Such a regime of practice is obviously different from the doctrine itself. Indeed, as David Harvey (2005) has argued, this divergence is, in fact, necessary, since neoliberal doctrine, if applied consistently, implies a world that could never, in fact, exist (which leads Harvey to term it 'utopian'). Rather than purely applying the utopian neoliberal doctrine, Harvey points out that dominant groups around the world have used neoliberal arguments to carry out what is in fact a class project. 'Neoliberalism', in this sense, has become the name for a set of highly interested public policies, only partly consistent with neoliberal doctrine, that have vastly enriched the holders of capital, while leading to increasing inequality, insecurity, loss of public services, and a general deterioration of quality of life for the poor and working classes.

But the policies of neoliberal regimes have often diverged from neoliberal doctrine for other reasons, as well – reasons which have less to do with straight-forward power grabs by the rich than with the contingencies of democratic politics. This no doubt helps to account for the otherwise paradoxical fact that a number of regimes pursuing undoubtedly neoliberal macroeconomic policies have also seen substantial recent rises in social spending (examples include India, Brazil, and South Africa, among others). Neoliberal policy is thus much more complicated than a reading of neoliberal doctrine might suggest.

The neoliberal label

It is perhaps also worth mentioning, if only very briefly, some other common uses of the term. One is as a sloppy synonym for capitalism itself, or as a kind of shorthand for the world economy and its inequalities. In much current anthropological usage, for instance, 'neoliberalism' appears in this way, as a kind of abstract and malevolent causal force that comes in from outside (much as 'the world system' was reckoned to do at an earlier theoretical moment) to decimate local livelihoods. Another, more interesting, usage sees 'neoliberalism' as the name of a broad, global cultural formation characteristic of a new era of 'millennial capitalism' -- a kind of global meta-culture, characteristic of our newly de-regulated, insecure, and speculative times (e.g., Comaroff and Comaroff, 2000). And finally, 'neoliberalism' can be indexed to a sort of 'rationality' in the Foucauldian sense, linked less to economic dogmas or class projects than to specific mechanisms of government, and characteristic modes of creating subjects. (I will have more to say about this last usage shortly.)

It is, then, possible to identify many quite distinct referents for the same widely-used term. This has some obvious dangers, of course. There is plainly a danger of simple confusion, since the meaning of the term can slip in the course of an argument being passed from author to reader (or, indeed, even in the course of an argument made by a single author). There is also another danger, only slightly less obvious, which is that such an all-encompassing entity can easily come to appear as a kind of gigantic, all-powerful first cause (like the mega-categories like 'Modernity' or 'Capitalism' have often done before it) -- that malign force that causes all manner of bad things to happen. This yields empty analysis (since to say that all our problems are caused by 'neoliberalism' is really not to say much), and may also lead to an ineffectual politics -- since all one can do with such a gigantic, malevolent 'thing' as 'neoliberalism' conceived in this way is to denounce it. (And that, the evidence suggests, doesn't seem to do much good).

One response would be to stop using the word altogether. This is indeed very tempting. If the word is so ambiguous and imprecise, perhaps we should just be careful to be more specific, and use less all-encompassing terms. When the term 'neoliberalism' is used as sloppily as it is in many texts, one is tempted to pencil one's objections in the margins as one might in reading a student paper: "What do you mean by 'neoliberalism' here? Do you mean the liberalisation of trade policies? Then say so! Do you mean techniques of government that work through the creation of responsibilised citizen-subjects? Then say that! The two don't necessarily go together. Say what you mean, and don't presume that they are all united in the giant package called 'neoliberalism'. Such insistence on specificity and precision would undoubtedly improve the analytical clarity of many of our discussions.

But there is also some utility in words that bring together more than one meaning. As long as we can avoid the mistake of simply confusing the different meanings, the word can be an occasion for reflecting on how the rather different things to which it refers may be related. In particular, I would like to use this confusing, conflating word as an occasion for thinking about the relation between the following two things:

First, we may consider the new governmental rationalities that emerged through the Thatcher-Reagan assaults on the North Atlantic, post-war welfare state. Key here was the deployment of market mechanisms and 'enterprise' models to reform government, restructure the state, and pioneer new modes of government and subjectification, as discussed in the pioneering works of what are sometimes referred to as the 'Anglo-Foucauldians'. (See, e.g., Barry, Osborne and Rose, 1996, Rose, 1999, Cruikshank, 1999, Miller and Rose, 2008.) There is a clear analysis in this literature of what it is that distinguishes 'neoliberalism' from liberalism. Liberalism, in this account, was always about finding the right balance between two spheres understood as properly distinct, if always related: state and market, public and private, king and merchant. Neoliberalism, in contrast, puts governmental mechanisms developed in the private sphere to work within the state itself, so that even core functions of the state are either subcontracted out to private providers, or run (as the saying has it) 'like a business.' The question of what should be public and what private becomes blurred or irrelevant, as the state itself increasingly organises itself around 'profit centres', 'enterprise models', and so on. Rather than shifting the line between state and market, then, neoliberalism in this account involved the deployment of new, market-based techniques of government within the terrain of the state itself. At the same time, new constructions of 'active' and 'responsible' citizens and communities were deployed to produce governmental results that did not depend on direct state intervention. The 'responsibilised' citizen, in the ideal scheme at least, comes to operate as a miniature firm, responding to incentives, rationally assessing risks, and prudently choosing from among different courses of action.

Against this understanding of the neoliberal, consider what we might call neoliberalism in the African sense. Here, neoliberalism has meant first of all the policy measures that were forced on African states in the 1980s by banks and international lending agencies, under the name of 'structural adjustment'. Reforms focused on removing tariffs, deregulating currency markets, and removing the state from production and distribution (via dismantling of state marketing boards and parastatals). This did involve privatisation, and an ideological celebration of markets. But the development of new technologies of government, responsibilised prudential subjects, and so on (all the things that Nikolas Rose and the other 'Ango-Foucauldians' tend to emphasise) was very limited. Neoliberalism here, in fact was (in these terms) not very 'neo' at all. It was, in fact, largely a matter of old-style laissez-faire liberalism in the service of imperial capital. And it had disastrous and wildly unpopular results (especially, the selling off precious state assets to foreign firms at fire-sale prices, massive deindustrialisation, and increased unemployment). Across much of the continent, indeed, it has raised the spectre of a kind of recolonisation. The result is that 'neoliberalism' in Africa refers to a quite fundamentally different situation than it does in Western Europe and North America. The hasty and uncritical application of ideas of neoliberalism-as-governmental-rationality to Africa is thus clearly a mistake, based on a confusion (an art of government versus a crude battering open of third world markets).

But bringing these two different referents together can be more interesting, if we don't just equate them, but instead reflect on the conceptual themes they share (broadly, a technical reliance on market mechanisms coupled with an ideological valorisation of 'private enterprise' and a suspicion of the state), and use such a reflection to ask if the new 'arts of government' developed within first-world neoliberalism might take on new life in other contexts, in the process opening up new political possibilities.

Can the left follow the right's lead in developing new arts of government? And (perhaps more provocatively) are the neoliberal 'arts of government' that have transformed the way that states work in so many places around the world inherently and necessarily conservative? To ask such questions requires us to be willing at least to imagine the possibility of a truly progressive politics that would also draw on governmental mechanisms that we have become used to terming 'neoliberal'.

I have been led to these questions by my current interest in anti-poverty programmes in southern Africa that seek to provide cash support for incomes, and thus (in theory) harness markets to the task of meeting the needs of the poor. This is happening in several African countries, but also in a great many other postcolonial states – from Brazil and Venezuela to Mexico and Bangladesh – where leftist and rightist regimes alike have seen fit to introduce policies that transfer cash directly into the hands of the poor. (See Fiszbein and Schady, 2009, Standing, 2008 for reviews.) The South African Basic Income Grant campaign is the example I will focus on here. The proposal, which I'll discuss in some detail in a moment, is to deal with a crisis of persistent poverty by providing an unconditional minimum monthly payment to all. The argument goes like this: Markets aren't working for poor people because they're too poor to participate in them. Government programmes aren't working because the state is inefficient. So: provide income support directly, in the form of cash, and then say to the poor: "you are now empowered to solve your own problems in the way you see best."

In contrast to older forms of 'welfare' assistance, the claim is that such grants rely on poor people's own ability to solve their own problems, without imposing the policing, paternalism, and surveillance of the traditional welfare state. More broadly, similar new lines of thought are calling for an increased role for direct cash transfers in many forms of social and humanitarian policy (e.g. famine relief, which will be briefly discussed shortly). The reasoning here often includes recognisably neoliberal elements (including the valorisation of market efficiency, individual choice, and autonomy; themes of entrepreneurship; and scepticism about the state as a service provider). But the politics are avowedly (and, I think, on balance, genuinely) 'pro-poor' (as the phrase has it). 'Pro-poor' and neoliberal – it is the strangeness of this conjunction that is of interest here. For the sorts of new progressive initiatives I have in mind seem to involve not just opposing 'the neoliberal project', but appropriating key elements of neoliberal reasoning for different ends. We can't think about this (or even acknowledge its possibility) if we continue to treat 'neoliberal' simply as a synonym for 'evil'. Instead, I suggest (and this is a deliberate provocation) that some innovative (and possible effective) forms of new politics in these times may be showing us how fundamentally multivalent the neoliberal arts of government can be.

Let me emphasise that to say that certain political initiatives and programmes borrow from the neoliberal bag of tricks doesn't mean that these political projects are in league with the ideological project of neoliberalism (in David Harvey's sense) – only that they appropriate certain characteristic neoliberal moves (and I think of these discursive and programmatic moves as analogous to the moves one might make in a game). These moves are recognisable enough to look 'neoliberal', but they can, I suggest, be used for quite different purposes than that term usually implies. In this connection, one might think of statistical techniques for calculating the probabilities of workplace injuries. These were originally developed in the 19th century by large employers to control costs (Ewald, 1986), but they eventually became the technical basis for social insurance, and ultimately for the welfare state (which brought unprecedented gains to the working class across much of the world). Techniques, that is to say, can 'migrate' across strategic camps, and devices of government that were invented to serve one purpose have often enough ended up, though history's irony, being harnessed to another. Might we see a similar re-appropriation of 'market' techniques of government (which were, like workplace statistics, undoubtedly conservative in their original uses) for different, and more progressive sorts of ends? Maybe not -- one should remain genuinely open-minded about this – but it is perhaps worth at least considering.

The Basic Income Grant proposal

My principal example is the Basic Income Grant campaign in South Africa. For historical reasons, South Africa came to democratic independence in 1994 with a quite well developed system of social grants and pensions (which I will not be able to describe here for reasons of space). In recent years, as neoliberal restructuring has led to widening inequality and very high rates of unemployment, these social grants have substantially expanded, and have been instrumental in holding together what might otherwise be an explosive situation (a fact of which the ANC government appears to be acutely aware). But planners have been bothered by the patchy and arbitrary spread of the coverage, and the inefficiency and cost of administering a host of cumbersome and bureaucratic targeted programmes.

In this context, the government appointed, in 2000, a Committee of Inquiry (the Taylor Committee) to recommend measures to rationalise the system of social assistance. When the Taylor Committee issued its report in 2002, it surprised many by calling for a far-reaching new comprehensive system of income support, anchored by a 'basic income grant' (BIG) to be paid to all South Africans (Department of Social Development 2002). (This idea had first been raised by COSATU in 1998 [at the Presidential Jobs Summit], and has been advocated from 2001 onward by a formal coalition of church groups and labour, the BIG Coalition).[2]

The proposal was for a modest payment of about R100 (at that time, about $16) per person per month, to be paid to all South Africans, irrespective of age or income. (The amount may seem so small as to be of little use, but the theory was that the sum of many per-person payments would put a larger household on a footing similar to that of a household with a member receiving a pension under the current system). The commission argued that such a universal system of direct payments was the most efficient way to direct assistance to all poor South Africans.

---

2. Barchesi (2007) gives a detailed and illuminating account of the origins of the BIG campaign and the Taylor Committee report.

Better off South Africans would also receive the grant, but the funds they received (and then some) would be recuperated through the tax system. Since South Africa currently has both effective mechanisms of taxation and comparatively low tax rates (as a percentage of GDP), BIG advocates argue (e.g., Standing and Samson, 2003), the measure could be funded through increases in either the income tax or the VAT, as well as by savings created by rationalising the existing system of pensions. The proposal has been endorsed as fiscally viable by some reputable economists, and promoted in recent years by a wide-ranging alliance of backers, including church groups, NGOs, and the powerful Congress of South African Trade Unions (COSATU); and a watered down version has even been endorsed by the main (and historically white) opposition party, the Democratic Alliance. It appears to enjoy support from some significant forces within the ANC (including the former Minster for Social Development, Dr Zola Skweyiya), but has been emphatically rejected by the top leadership.

My interest in the campaign is not driven by a strong sense of personal support for or opposition to it. As a piece of public policy, I find it both very attractive and potentially problematic; and I don't presume that it will be implemented (indeed, I would guess that it probably will not be). I am interested, rather, in the logic of argument that is deployed in its advocacy – a way of thinking about persistent poverty, the 'informal sector', the market, and the state.

It is important to recognise that the arguments that have been made in favor of the BIG have been many-sided and complex, and they are not reducible to a single logic or rationality (neoliberal or otherwise). These arguments do include recognisably neoliberal elements (as I will emphasise below). But BIG proponents certainly do not all, or always, make a radical or unconditional break with the older language of social democracy. On the contrary, a reading of pro-BIG documents shows that traditional welfare-state arguments are regularly deployed. These include themes of social solidarity and moral obligation; the advantages of social cohesion and dangers of class war; Keynesian arguments about stimulating demand; and labour-rights arguments about giving workers the security to say no to dangerous and demeaning work.[3] Yet these lines of argument lie side by side with others, which are markedly different from social democratic reasoning, and surprisingly similar to the neoliberal reasoning that we more usually associate with anti-welfare

---

3. As Barchiesi (2007) has noted, some more conservative formulations of the BIG have also made the contrary argument, that it would help move unemployed people into very low wage jobs. He also points out another important theme that I do not explore here: the implicit or explicit moralism of much of the discussion around 'the social question' in South Africa.

discourses. The intermingling of these different themes speaks to the complex political struggles around the BIG, which have been discussed by others (e.g., Mattisonn and Seekings, 2003 and Barchiesi, 2007). My interest here, though, is not in analysing these politics, but in identifying some surprising ways in which certain discursive 'moves' that we can readily identify as neoliberal are being put to work in the service of pro-poor and pro-welfare political arguments. To make this process visible, it is useful to pull some of these neoliberal 'moves' out of the broader mix of BIG arguments so that we can see the work that they are doing.

Consider the following distinct arguments that are presented in pro-BIG discourse:

1. Perhaps unsurprisingly (in these times), the social democratic theme of social obligation is largely replaced in BIG rhetoric by the theme of 'investment in human capital'. The poor individual is explicitly conceptualised as a micro-enterprise. The BIG would (as the coalition web site claims) "enable working families to invest more of their incomes in nutrition, education and health care – with corresponding productivity gains" (Tilton, 2005). So, hungry people, for instance might appear to need to eat, but really what they need is "to invest more of their income in nutrition" in order to build up their "human capital", with "corresponding productivity gains." Pro-BIG arguments are generously seeded with this sort of language that recasts social spending as 'investing' in a kind of 'capital' (see Fine, 2000 for a useful critique of 'social capital' theory).

2. A second theme is a critique of dependency (one that neatly reverses the usual right-wing arguments against social payments). It is the existing 'safety-net', the BIG promoters argue, that breeds dependency. Today, any economically productive poor person is surrounded by dependents who must be supported. This dependency constitutes a 'tax' on the productivity of the poor, which both creates a disincentive to work, and degrades human capital. The 'dependency' of absolute poverty is a drag on productivity, and it makes workers unable to be economically active, to search for better jobs, etc. What is more, insecurity breeds passivity, and inhibits entrepreneurship and 'risk-taking behaviours'. A poor South African thinking of starting a small business, for instance, under present circumstances must consider the terrible risk of falling into destitution and hunger in the event of failure. The same person with a monthly BIG payment would be empowered to be much bolder. Providing basic income security for all, it is claimed, will enable the poor to behave as proper neoliberal subjects (i.e., as entrepreneurs and risk-takers); the status quo prevents it, and promotes 'dependency'.

As the report of the Taylor Committee put it, "By providing ... a minimum level of income support people will be empowered to take the risks needed to break out of the poverty cycle. Rather than serving as a disincentive to engage in higher return activities, such a minimum (and irrevocable) grant could encourage risk taking and self-reliance. Such an income grant could thus become a springboard for development" (Department of Social Development 2002: 61). In this way, the BIG would provide not a 'safety net' (the circus image of old-style welfare as protection against hazard) but a 'springboard' – a facilitator of risky (but presumably empowering) neoliberal flight.

3. Pro-BIG arguments also borrow from established neoliberal critiques of welfare paternalism (such as the old Thatcherite complaint about the 'nanny state' that tries to run everybody's life in the name of the needs of 'society'). The existing social assistance system, BIG advocates point out, makes moralising judgments about 'the undeserving poor', and requires surveillance, normalisation, and so on, which is both objectionable in itself, as well as expensive and inefficient. What is more, recipients are publicly labelled as such, and thus set apart from the general population; in this way, they may be subtly stigmatised. The BIG, on the other hand, would be paid to everyone; citizens would access their funds (in the ideal scheme) by simply swiping their national identity cards in an ATM. They would use the funds (as good rational actors) in the way they saw best. There would be no policing of conduct, no stigmatising labels, no social workers coming into homes – and no costly bureaucracy to sort out who does or doesn't qualify. Through the radical step of eliminating means testing (and, in some versions, replacing documents with biometric technology [Breckenridge, 2005]), it is proposed that the 'formalities' of social assistance might be streamlined in a way that might make social payments catalytic of, rather than contrary to, the vital economic logic of informality. The state is here imagined as both universally engaged (as a kind of direct provider for each and every citizen) and maximally disengaged (taking no real interest in shaping the conduct of those under its care, who are seen as knowing their own needs better than the state does).

4. Perhaps the most striking (and in some ways, disturbing) change from traditional social democracy is the explicit rejection of formal employment as the 'normal' frame of reference for social policy (let alone as an entitlement to which all have rights). The Taylor Committee Report notes that "High unemployment, including the massive net loss of formal sector jobs, and a growing shift towards so-called 'atypical' work, has reduced the incomes of the poor" (Department of Social Development, 2002: 32). And it sees no prospect for an end to this shift away from formal employment. Indeed, the report goes on:

In developing countries, where stable full-time waged formal sector labour was never the norm, it is increasingly unlikely that it will become the norm. (2002: 38)

The reality is that in the developing world formal sector employment may never become the norm that it is in Europe" (2002: 154).

The need for assistance, then, is not about being 'between jobs' or correcting for dips in the business cycle. Formal employment is not (and never will be!) the normal state of affairs. Social assistance is here radically decoupled from expectations of employment, and, indeed, from 'insurance' rationality altogether. Instead: the Taylor Report re-understands the condition of unemployment not as a hazard, but as the normal condition (most people, most of the time will, for the foreseeable future, live that way), and seeks not to prevent that condition, but to make it productive.

5. How can unemployment be productive? Here, the 'informal sector' appears in a newly central role, appearing not as it did through most of the 20th century as a problem to be solved, but instead as the solution itself. To be economically productive, BIG advocates point out, does not require formal sector employment; social payments are most significant not as temporary substitutes for employment, but as a way of promoting greater productivity, enterprise, and risk-taking in the 'informal' domain within which more and more South Africans are expected to make their living. BIG payments, then, are understood neither as temporary relief nor as charity, but as a means of enhancing production by enabling both job-seeking and, crucially, entrepreneurial activity.

I hope to have identified some recognisably neoliberal motifs here. But I hope it's also clear that this is not the neoliberalism we love to hate, the so-called 'neoliberal project' identified by David Harvey (2005). It's something else – a set of much harder to place arguments that link markets, enterprise, welfare, and social payments in a novel way. It leaves us neither with something to hate, nor something to love, but rather something to ponder.

Farmers and food prices

It may be helpful to briefly discuss one additional example, to help suggest something that I am increasingly convinced is the case: that the BIG campaign is part of a much wider, worldwide shift in thinking about poverty and social and humanitarian assistance. The example I have in mind is the increasingly influential argument that hunger is best dealt with by boosting the purchasing power of those at risk, rather than by distributing food aid.

The traditional international food aid system involves taking excess grain (produced under subsidised conditions in rich countries) and transporting it to places (largely in Africa) where people are at risk of hunger. Following Amartya Sen, critics have long noted the perverse effects of this: depressing producer prices for local farmers, and damaging the local institutions for producing and distributing food crops. Once food aid has arrived, local food production often never recovers, and the 'temporary' crisis becomes permanent.

As an alternative, Sen's followers have pushed for cash payments to be made directly to those at risk of food deficit. People with money in their pockets, Sen points out, don't starve. And the economic chain of events that is set in motion by boosting purchasing power leads (through market forces) to increased capacity for local production and distribution.

A number of pilot projects have been launched putting these principles into practice in recent years. Among the best known is the Cash for Relief Programme in Ethiopia, which used cash payments to enable households that had been hit by crop failure to rebuild their assets and regenerate their livelihoods (and not only to eat). Another widely discussed project has been the Kalomo Social Cash Transfer Scheme in Zambia. Here, too, cash took the place of food aid, with the result that recipients were able to meet non-nutritional as well as nutritional needs, including education, transportation, and health care (Schubert and Goldberg, 2004). An impressive range of similar projects is reviewed in Standing (2008) and Farrington and Slater (2006). (See also the review of the potential for cash transfers in 'unstable situations', recently done by Harvey and Holmes (2007) for the UK Department for International Development.)

The arguments made by the increasingly numerous promoters of such programmes are in many ways similar to those made on behalf of the South African Basic Income Grant. Dispensing cash, they insist, is in the first place more efficient and less expensive than other sorts of assistance, and often requires less infrastructure and institutional capacity. In any case, they argue, why should bureaucrats decide on behalf of recipients what their needs are? Cash transfers provide hungry people with the flexibility to access a broad range of goods and services available on the market to meet their needs, and their enhanced demand stimulates the provision of needed services through market mechanisms.

And poor people, in this conception, are the best judges of what their needs are, and how they should be met – perhaps using money to go to the clinic this month, to pay school fees for a child the next, to buy a bag of maize meal the next, and so on. Rather than wasting the money on frivolous expenditure, advocates insist, the research shows that recipients generally apply their scant cash resources very rationally, and even make canny small investments. As one power-point presentation on the Kalomo project put it: "The 'grannies' turned out to be excellent economists!"

Top-down, state-planned attempts to directly meet nutritional needs through trucking in food, in this view, are bound to be clumsy, inefficient, wasteful, and destructive of local markets. Cash transfers, on the other hand, put more decision-making power in the hands of those who know their predicament best (the hunger-afflicted themselves), and enable them to use the flexibility and efficiency of markets to help solve their own problems. Much more than direct food aid, cash transfers can have a catalytic effect on many other income-gaining activities, thereby contributing powerfully to the 'multiple livelihood strategies' that are so important in keeping the poorest households afloat.

Such arguments recall Jane Guyer's groundbreaking work on feeding African cities (1989). Consider, Guyer suggests, how food ends up finding its way to consumers' plates in the vast megacities of West Africa such as Lagos. The logistical task of moving thousands of tons of food each day from thousands of local producers to millions of urban consumers would be beyond the organisational capacity of any state (to say nothing of the less-than-exemplary Nigerian one). Here, market mechanisms, drawing on the power of vast self-organising networks, are very powerful, and very efficient. Such forms of organisation must appear especially attractive where states lack capacity (and let us remember how many progressive dreams in Africa have crashed on the rocks of low state capacity).

Why should relying on this sort of mechanism be inherently right-wing, or suspect in the eyes of progressives? The answer is, of course, not far to find: markets serve only those with purchasing power. Market-based solutions are thus likely to be true 'solutions' only for the better-off, whose needs are so effectively catered to by markets. But the food aid example shows a way of redirecting markets toward the poor, by intervening not to restrict the market, but to boost purchasing power. I have become convinced that (at least in the case of food aid) this is probably good public policy.

Is it also neoliberal? Perhaps that is not the right question. Perhaps we should rather ask: Are there specific sorts of social policy that might draw on characteristic neoliberal 'moves' (like using markets to deliver services) that would also be genuinely progressive? That seems like a question worth asking, even if we are at this point not fully ready to answer it.

Conclusion

I want to emphasise that none of the examples discussed here are (in my view) unequivocally good (or unequivocally bad, for that matter). Instead, they leave us feeling uneasy, not sure of our moorings. They leave us less with strong opinions than with the sense that we need to think about them a bit more. They do not permit the simple denunciations (Aha! Neoliberalism!) that have become so familiar a part of the politics of the 'anti-', even as they clearly require us to turn a thoughtfully critical and sceptical eye toward their dangers and ambiguities.

I also want to emphasise as clearly as possible that none of these examples is a matter of 'leaving it to the market'. All require major non-market interventions (either by states or by state-like entities such as foundations or international agencies), and all are premised on the principle that public policy must play a redistributive role. But they are interventions that create a situation where markets can arguably serve progressive ends, in ways that may require us to revise some of our prejudices that automatically associate market mechanisms with the interests of the well-to-do.

By way of concluding, let me be clear: we need to be sceptical about the facile idea that problems of poor people can be solved simply by inviting them to participate in markets and enterprise. Such claims (which often ascribe almost magical transformative powers to such unlikely vehicles as 'social entrepreneurship' or 'microcredit') are almost always misleading, and often fraudulent. But it would be a mistake to dismiss the coupling of avowedly pro-poor social policy with market mechanisms out of hand, out of a reflexive sense that the latter are 'neoliberal' and thus 'bad'. Again, the interest here is in the potential mobility of a set of governmental devices. These devices originated within a neoliberal project that deserves all the criticism it gets. But they may be in the process of being redeployed in creative and potentially powerful ways.

If so, some emergent political initiatives that might appear at first blush to be worryingly 'neoliberal' may, on closer inspection, amount to something a good deal more hopeful. To be able to spot such developments, we will need to forgo the pleasures of the easy, dismissive critique, and instead turn a keen and sympathetic eye toward the rich world of actual social and political practice. That is a world still full of invention and surprise, where the landscape of political possibility and constraint that we have come to take for granted is being redrawn, even as we speak.

References

Barchiesi, F., 2007. South African Debates on the Basic Income Grant: Wage Labour and the Post-Apartheid Social Policy. *Journal of Southern African Studies,* 33(3), pp. 561-575.

Barry, A. Osborne, T. and Rose, N. eds., 1996. *Foucault and Political Reason: Liberalism, Neo-liberalism and Rationalities of Government.* Chicago: University of Chicago Press.

Comaroff, Jean and John L., 2000. Millennial Capitalism: First Thoughts on a Second Coming. *Public Culture,* 12(2), pp.291-343.

Cruikshank, B., 1999. *The Will to Empower: Democratic Citizens and Other Subject.* Ithaca: Cornell University Press.

Davis, M., 2007. *Planet of Slums.* New York: Verso.

Department of Social Development. 2002. Transforming the Present – Protecting the Future: Report of the Committee of Inquiry into a Comprehensive System of Social Security for South Africa. Pretoria: Government Printer.

Ewald, F., 1986. *L'etat Providence.* Paris: Bernard Grasset.

Farrington, J. and Slater, R., 2006. Introduction: Cash Transfers: Panacea for Poverty Reduction or Money Down the Drain? *Development Policy Review,* 24(5), pp.499-511.

Fine, B., 2000. *Social Capital Versus Social Theory: Political Economy and Social Science at the Turn of the Millennium.* New York: Routledge.

Fiszbein, A. and Schady, N., 2009. *Conditional Cash Transfers: Reducing Present and Future Poverty.* Washington, D.C.: The World Bank.

Foucault, M., 1988. *Politics, Philosophy, Culture: Interviews and Other Writings.* New York: Routledge.

_____ 2008. *The Birth of Biopolitics: Lectures at the College de France, 1978-1979.* Translated by Graham Burchell. New York: Palgrave MacMillan.

Guyer, J.I. ed., 1989. *Feeding African Cities: Studies in Regional Social History.* Manchester: Manchester University Press.

Harvey, D., 2005. *A Brief History of Neoliberalism.* New York: Oxford University Press.

Harvey, P. and Holmes, R., 2007. The Potential for Joint Programmes for Long-term Cash Transfers in Unstable Situations: A Report Commissioned by the Fragile States Team and the Equity and Rights Team of the UK Department for International Development. London: Humanitarian Policy Group, Overseas Development Institute.

Mattisonn, H. and Seekings, J., 2003. The Politics of a Basic Income Grant in South Africa, 1996-2002. In G. Standing and M. Samson, eds. *A Basic Income Grant for South Africa.* Cape Town: University of Cape Town Press.

Miller, P. and Rose, N., 2008. *Governing the Present.* Malden, Massachusetts: Polity Press.

Peck, J., 2008. Remaking laissez-faire. Progress. *Human Geography,* 32(1), pp. 3-43.

Rose, N., 1999. *Powers of Freedom: Reframing Political Thought.* New York: Cambridge University Press.

Standing, G., 2008. How Cash Transfers Boost Work and Economic Security. DESA Working Paper No. 50. New York: United Nations Department of Economic and Social Affairs (ST/ESA/2007/DWP/58).

Standing, G. and Samson, M., eds., 2003. *A Basic Income Grant for South Africa.* Cape Town: University of Cape Town Press.

Tilton, D., 2005. BIG Fact Sheet #1, BIG Coalition web site. Available at: http://www.big.org.za/index.php?option=articles&task=viewarticle&artid=5.

Afterword:
World Cup™ profits defeat the poor
Patrick Bond, Ashwin Desai and Brij Maharaj

Introduction

Sport, once viewed as a form of entertainment, has now emerged as an important political, social and economic force (Cochrane et al., 1996; Hillier, 2000; Smith, 2005; O'Brien, 2006). South Africa's sacrifices to host the 2010 Soccer World Cup™ - and possibly the 2020 Olympic Games – are illustrative. What can we learn from the 2010 experience? Was it a roaring success, or instead, yet another example of Jacob Zuma's own-goal approach to poverty and inequality, i.e. squandering a golden opportunity and instead making matters worse through careless regression backwards on the field?

We begin the review of South Africa's experience in June-July 2010 by providing context. We tend to view soccer within the parameters set by neoliberal globalisation, which first and foremost requires countries and cities around the world to compete for illusory direct foreign investments and portfolio capital flows. Prominent promotional strategies include stimulating investment in businesses through the provision of incentives and marketing the country and city as a tourist and sporting destination. For the latter, which we experienced intensely in Durban, the consensus seems to be that major sporting events offer the "possibility of 'fast track' urban regeneration, a stimulus to economic growth, improved transport and cultural facilities, and enhanced global recognition and prestige," as Chalkley and Essex (1999) argue. Although such events do produce benefits, the international experience suggests that the privileged tend to benefit at the expense of the poor, and that socio-economic inequalities tend to be exacerbated (Andranovich et al., 2001; Rutheiser, 1996; Owen, 2002). These concerns were borne out when South Africa hosted the 2010 World Cup.

Peter Alegi (2010: 128) argues that in South Africa, the

> social and political significance of rugby and soccer ... entrenched a desire among increasingly self-confident ... leaders to host sporting megaevents for the purpose of bolstering the quest for national unity and triggering faster economic growth.

The government committed itself to spending R40 billion from the public purse to prepare the country for the 2010 Fifa World Cup™, largely in constructing/upgrading 10 stadiums, fast-tracking a fast-train from OR

Tambo Airport to Sandton and a new airport outside Durban, improving roads and building associated infrastructure. The obvious question, in the wake of the discussion in previous pages, is, can SA afford such expenditure against the competing demands of housing/services, health care, welfare and education?

This Afterword raises the following concerns relating to the hosting of the 2010 mega event in South Africa: Fifa super-profits and political corruption; dubious priorities and overspending; repatriation of profits; suspension of democratic freedoms and sovereignty; protest and defiance; and xenophobia. Until very recently, Fifa was relatively unknown in the SA public domain, and the organisation was implicitly presented as a benign, if not philanthropic, organisation. That changed in mid-2010.

Fifa mafia, dubious priorities and overspending

The Fédération Internationale de Football Association (Fifa) was established in Paris on 21 May 1904. Initial membership comprised countries from Western Europe. Present membership comprises football associations from 208 countries, exceeding that of the UN (192 members). In its quest to increase membership, Fifa often turned a blind eye to the undermining of democracy and the violation of human rights in member states, on grounds that sports and politics should not intermingle. There were allegations that senior Fifa officials were close to corrupt governments and ignored the influence of drug cartels on the game in Latin America.

But politics and sport do mix. In the early 1960s, Fifa implicitly espoused apartheid when its British president Sir Stanley Rous supported the Football Association of South Africa and its racially segregated teams and matches. It was only in 1976 that the apartheid team was thrown out, thanks to lobbying led by the late Dennis Brutus. During this period, there was another dramatic turn as the commercial/business arm of Fifa grew exponentially, ostensibly in response to the development needs of football in Africa, Asia and Latin America. However, there were concerns that Fifa had become part of the 'capitalist entertainment business'; that it had turned football into a 'millionaire's gambling casino'; and that there was a lack of transparency and accountability about how its funds were spent; and especially payments made to senior officials. There have also been controversies and allegations of corruption relating to how Fifa sells its TV rights, elects its President and chooses the hosts for the World Cup™. Before a ball was kicked, Fifa already earned R25 billion from TV broadcast rights for 2010.

World Cup™ visitors did not fail to comment upon degenerate conditions in the Cape Flats and the Soweto shacklands, while in contrast, the new R4.5 billion Green Point stadium in Cape Town and R2.3 billion refurbished Soccer City in Johannesburg received vast subsidies thanks to rulers from both the white-liberal-dominated Democratic Alliance and the black-nationalist African National Congress, respectively. Cape Town's is especially obnoxious given that an upgrade of the Newlands rugby pitch (in a white suburb) or of Athlone's stadium (in a black neighbourhood) would have been far cheaper. The latter was reportedly rejected, according to a representative of Fifa, because "A billion television viewers don't want to see shacks and poverty on this scale."[1]

The second-largest city, Durban, boasts the most memorable new sports facility (R3.1 billion worth, overrun from an original R1.8 billion budget), as well as the country's highest-profile municipal sleaze and chutzpah, exuding from a city manager, Mike Sutcliffe, who tried – but failed – to gentrify a century-old Indian/African market for Fifa's sake, and who regularly bans non-violent demonstrations. Durban's 70,000-seater Moses Mabhida stadium is delightful to view, so long as we keep out of sight and mind the city's vast backlogs of housing, water/sanitation, electricity, clinics, schools and roads, and the absurd cost escalation. Harder to keep from view is next-door neighbour Absa Stadium, home of Sharks rugby, which seats 52,000 and which easily could have been extended. The Sharks have said they cannot afford to make the move to Mabhida because of high rental costs, and a titanic battle lies ahead over destruction of the older stadium to force the issue. Trevor Phillips, former director of the South African Premier Soccer League, asks,

> What the hell are we going to do with a 70,000-seater football stadium in Durban once the World Cup is over? Durban has two football teams which attract crowds of only a few thousand. It would have been more sensible to have built smaller stadiums nearer the football-loving heartlands and used the surplus funds to have constructed training facilities in the townships.[2]

The local winners in the process are not footballers nor even rugby teams that municipal officials fruitlessly hope will one day fill the white-elephant stadia. They are the large corporations and politically-

---

1. 'Table Mounain or Bust'. *The Antidote*, 18 January 2007.
http://theantidote.wordpress.com/2007/01/18/fifa-table-mountain-or-bust/.
2. http://www.guardian.co.uk/sport/2007/jun/03/newsstory

connected black 'tenderpreneurs' (who win state tenders thanks to affirmative action, if linked to established white firms) especially in the construction sector. Asking if Mabhida's legacy is an 'arch of hope' or instead a 'yoke of debt', journalist Sam Sole named Durban's beneficiaries: primary contractor Ibhola Lethu supported Craig Simmer (whose previous employers were the crashed bus privatiser, Remnant Alton and Point development flop, Dolphin Whispers); the Broederbonder firm Bruinette Kruger Stoffberg; and Group 5/WBHO with Tokyo Sexwale's and Bulelani Ngcuka's Mvelaphanda group subcontracting a major electricity deal to Vivian Reddy's Edison Power (Sole, 2010). This tenderpreneurship strategy was profoundly corrupt, according to Moeletsi Mbeki, brother of former president Thabo: "It was a matter of co-option, to co-opt the African nationalist leaders by enriching them privately."[3]

The macro-implications will be felt over many years, because the World Cup™ has worsened South Africa's world-leading income inequality and set the stage for future economic calamities once debt payments become due. The overspending on new stadiums (in Durban, Cape Town, Port Elizabeth, Nelspruit and Polokwane) plus extravagant refurbishment expenses for Soccer City brought the state subsidy to over R25 billion, not to mention spending on associated infrastructure. It will be exceedingly hard for nearly all the stadiums to even cover their operating expenses after the final World Cup™ game.

An excess portion of the stadium bill came from unnecessary imports, at a time the SA foreign debt rose from the $24 billion Nelson Mandela inherited from apartheid to more than $85 billion today. Paying interest on the debt plus dividends to the huge, formerly South African, but now overseas-based multinational corporations – Anglo American, BHP Billiton, DeBeers, Old Mutual, SAB-Miller beer, Liberty Life, Didata, Investec Bank – pushed the country to the very bottom of the emerging markets rankings. South Africa's sixth post-apartheid currency crash (of more than 15 per cent over a month's time) will occur sooner than later, as a result.

Other indirect costs to the economy are also important to count. The World Cup™ was partly responsible for the country's construction bubble, which drove the economy at 5 per cent GDP increase per year from 2004-08, just as happened in the US prior to its crash. With the World Cup™ as justification, the state's investment in new luxury transport infrastructure soared. The R25 billion Gautrain rapid rail costs riders five times more than previously advertised, gambles on shifting rich people's behaviour away from private cars, but it probably won't

3. http://www.dw-world.de/dw/article/0,,4434689,00.html

dislodge Johannesburg-Pretoria commuters, thanks to traffic jams and parking shortages at the new stations. As labour leader Zwelinzima Vavi, put it, Gautrain "does nothing for those who really suffer from transport problems – above all, commuters from places like Soweto and Diepsloot. Instead, it takes away resources that could improve the lives of millions of commuters."[4]

And was a new R8 billion King Shaka International Airport wise for Durban, given that the old one had excess capacity until 2017, and given the doubling of distance and taxi fares from central Durban? The closure of Durban International prematurely proved the single biggest embarrassment for Local Organising Committee leadership and the Airports Company of South Africa, when King Shaka could not cope with VIP private jets that jammed the airport on July 7, the day of the semi-final, leaving more than 1000 furious soccer fans in planes that had to be rerouted.

At least one auditing firm, Grant Thornton, disagrees, arguing that more than R50 billion in spin-offs can be expected, including 415 400 jobs, with tourists spending about R.5 billion. [5] But this appears to be pie-in-the-sky, as government's statistics office reported the first quarter of 2010's losses of 71 000 jobs, with no prospect for improvement in sight, bringing to nearly a million those shed since the world crisis hit hard in 2008. In this context of economic contraction, another dose of xenophobia is feared, from both the state and society, as noted at the end. But the state's own power to regulate multinational capital itself came into question during the World Cup™.

Loss of sovereignty and democratic rights

British sports journalist Andrew Jennings, author of *Foul!* has documented in painful detail Fifa's abuse of host countries. According to Jennings (2006) a third of Fifa's executive "are involved in bribery and corruption, ticket rackets and diversion of funds." No one has uncovered explicit fraud in South Africa, in spite of a combination of a corruption-riddled Fifa and a corruption-riddled government. To illustrate, during the World Cup,™ South Africa's leading police official of the 2000s (at the same time he was serving as president of Interpol), Jackie Selebi, was judged guilty of sufficient fraud to warrant a 15-year jail sentence. Suspicions of Zuma's personal and family corruption also continued

---

4.http://amadlandawonye.wikispaces.com/COSATU+GS+Z+Vavi,+Input+to+Red+October+Transport+Campaign
5. http://www.gt.co.za/News/Press-releases/Strategic-solutions/2010/2010eia.asp

through mid-2010, as did concerns about the ruling party's youth leader, Julius Malema. The man Zuma chose as ambassador to the US, Ebrahim Rasool, was unveiled in July 2010 by a Cape Town journalist as a politician who spent cash to buy favourable newspaper coverage, and yet the appointment went ahead unhindered.

But setting aside deals – or the awarding of huge cost escalations on construction contracts - that might have been lubricated with backhanders, the most pernicious corruption associated with the World Cup was actually above board, in formal legal contracts that were kept secret until a judge ordered them opened to public scrutiny in June 2010. As Jennings concluded, "South Africa bent over and let Fifa have their way. Officials and the government have sold South Africa down the river: 'Bye Africa, bye suckers!'" 6

There are many ways in which South African sovereignty was violated by those contracts. Major geographical spaces, especially those around which the poor engage in the informal economy, have been legislated as local business Exclusion Zones (or Fifa zones), in which the South African Constitution would be temporarily suspended. Instead, the South African Government was obliged to enforce Fifa's laws, including the curtailing of democratic rights such as peaceful marches and protests. The national security apparatus told Parliament it would throw a 10km 'cordon' around the stadia, replete with "air sweeps by fighter jets, joint border patrols with neighbouring countries, police escorts for cruise ships and teams of security guards with 'diplomat' training." The aim, according to safety and security Minister Nathi Mthethwa, was to "prevent domestic extremism, strike action and service delivery protests." 7

To serve Fifa, Durban gave up a great deal of its own power as well as common sense. To illustrate, a few dozen metres away from where poor people were denied their source of fishing and income, expensive imported (German) marquee tents apparently required erection by a German construction company. And Fifa took sole occupation of Moses Mabhida Stadium, even on the 75 percent of days that soccer wasn't played over the month, keeping the facility off-limits to visitors. According to Wits journalism professor Anton Harber, this was part of a general takeover: "Fifa has banished those people who try to make a living around the stadiums, they have made us divert development

---

6.   http://www.timeslive.co.za/opinion/article461110.ece/The-underbelly-of-world-football

7.   http://www.news24.com/SouthAfrica/News/Police-unveil-SWC-security-plan-20100507

money into fancy stadiums, and we have had to give up all sorts of rights for the month they will be in control of our cities." [8]

Most chilling is that not only did Fifa get full indemnity "against all proceedings, claims and related costs (including professional adviser fees) which may be incurred or suffered by or threatened by others." In addition, confirmed one official agreement, SA will provide police specifically "to enforce the protection of the marketing rights, broadcast rights, marks and other intellectual property rights of Fifa and its commercial partners." [9] (One author, Bond, learned this first hand on July 2 when he was detained by police for circulating an anti-xenophobia flier at the Fan Fest.) [10]

Journalists getting Fifa accreditation also pledged not to throw the World Cup™ 'into disrepute' while reporting, at the risk of being banned. Hence, press freedom was compromised. With such pressure, no wonder that the superb documentary film *Fahrenheit 2010* was turned down by the three major SA television networks in the period before the World Cup. Refusing to screen it, SA Broadcasting Corporation spokesperson, Kaiser Kganyago, confirmed: "Our job is obviously to promote the World Cup and flighting anything that can be perceived as negative is not in our interest."

Rhodes media professor Guy Berger called Fifa's power an "artificial and autocratic fiat. It is simply stupid to regulate for information scarcity in an age that has unprecedented information potential -- potential even for Fifa itself. Such authoritarian backwardness is hardly surprising, however. It comes from a body that in 2010 is still forcing journalists to agree not to bring it into disrepute as a condition for getting accreditation." [11] Fifa's definition of "disrepute" is writing anything that "negatively affects the public standing of the Local Organising Committee or Fifa." [12]

Fifa also received special judicial treatment, with 24/7 prosecution of several dozen criminal incidents, including a three-year jail term for a man whose only crime was holding 30 Fifa game tickets 'without explanation', as Fifa tried to cut down on the black market. Two Dutch 'ambush marketers' were arrested as 36 women wore orange dresses, representing Bavaria brewery, to the Holland-Denmark game, though the firm's logo was tiny.

8.http://www.timeslive.co.za/specialreports/Our2010/article524269.ece/Blatter-threatens-to-gag-FIFA-reporters
9. http://www.mg.co.za/article/2010-06-04-fifa-called-the-shots-and-we-said-yes
10. http://www.pambazuka.org/en/category/features/65597
11.http://www.mg.co.za/printformat/single/2010-05-14-no-one-wants-to-air-2010-documentary
12. http://www.bizcommunity.com/Article/196/147/44260.html

Cases of this sort made Fifa seem extremist. The loss of state sovereignty to Fifa surprised observers, given the enormous experience that former president Thabo Mbeki and his negotiating team amassed in world economic policy negotiations since apartheid ended in 1994. Yet Mbeki allowed Fifa and multinational corporate sponsors full access to 'exclusion zones' with no taxes, no exchange controls and no security worries.

Trickle-down promises broken

Other logistical support, access control, and protection were provided to Fifa's corporate partners (Adidas, Sony, Visa, Emirates, Coca Cola, Hyundai-Kia, McDonalds, local phone giants Telkom and MTN, First National Bank, Continental Tyres, Castrol, McDonalds, and Indian IT company, Satyam). Only Fifa-endorsed items were advertised within a one kilometre radius of the stadium and along major roads.

Little money trickled down and most evaporated. Crafts, tourism and township soccer facilities were all meant to benefit. But as SA Football Association Western Cape provincial president, Norman Arendse, confessed, Fifa's 'fatal' top-down approach left grassroots soccer with merely 'crumbs'. [13] Aside from ear-splitting vuvuzela plastic trumpets, the much-vaunted 'African' feel to the World Cup™ will be muted, as women who typically sell 'pap' (corn meal) and 'vleis' (inexpensive meat) just outside soccer stadiums will be shunted off at least a kilometre away. According to leading researcher, Udesh Pillay of the SA Human Sciences Research Council, in 2005, one in three South Africans hoped to personally benefit from the World Cup™, but this fell to one in five in 2009 and one in 100 by the time the games began. [14]

Danny Jordaan, CEO of the World Cup™ Local Organising Committee, predicted in 2005 that the games would be worth as much as R50 billion profit to South Africa, even after 2010-related infrastructure expenses. But current estimates have been approximately halved (or more). The hospitality industry's market was glutted in many areas, after a third of rooms booked by Fifa's Match agency were cancelled in May.

Likewise, ordinary workers were misled into thinking they would benefit from manufacturing opportunities associated with World Cup™ paraphernalia, but as Congress of SA Trade Unions spokesperson Patrick Craven ruefully concluded, "Local companies have lost out, Chinese

---

13. http://www.mg.co.za/article/2010-05-20-a-tale-of-two-stadiums
14. http://www.project2010.co.za/2010_World_Cup_interview_Udesh_Pillay.asp, http://dispatch.ug/2010/06/16/is-it-really-africas-world-cup/

companies have emerged as big winners." [15] Workers lost insofar as they failed to gain local production rights for the Zakumi doll mascot, which was instead produced in what the trade union movement alleged were Chinese sweatshops where teenagers were paid $3/day. The man who arranged the deal was ANC Member of Parliament Shiaan-Bin Huang, whose home district in KwaZulu-Natal, Newcastle, had many idle factories which could have produced Zakumi.[16]

Residents, too, suffered, especially if they were working class and needed treatment at local hospitals. As *Times* journalists observed,

> Fifa's guidelines for designated hospitals around the country - which include keeping wards half empty - will result in long-term patients removed from their beds and shifted to facilities elsewhere. Routine referrals to major specialist hospitals have already been curtailed, if not stopped, until after the World Cup, leaving hundreds of patients without care for the next two months. [17]

Protest and defiance

The mood of poor and working people remained feisty in the run-up to the big event, with several dozen protests each day according to police statistics, most over 'service delivery' shortcomings. Several protests were aimed explicitly at the way the World Cup was being implemented.

For example, more than a thousand pupils demonstrated against the Mbombela stadium (Nelspruit) when schools displaced in the construction process were not rebuilt. Other World Cup™-related protests were held by informal traders in Durban and Cape Town, against Johannesburg officials by Soccer City neighbours in impoverished Riverlea township, against construction companies by workers, against the stadium construction by disabled people, and against national officials by four towns' activists attempting to relocate the provincial borders to shift their municipalities to a wealthier province.

Just a month before the first kick and during the competition, strikes were threatened, raging or had just been settled over national electricity price increases, Eskom and transport sector wages and municipal worker grievances. The SA Transport and Allied Workers Union won a

---

15. http://www.sportsillustrated.co.za/category/soccer/world-cup-2010/page/34/
16. http://www.cosatu.org.za/show.php?include=docs/pr/2010/pr0202.html&ID=2872 &cat=COSATU%20Today
17.   http://www.timeslive.co.za/sundaytimes/article464252.ece/World-Cup-hospitals-face-crisis

wage increase double the inflation rate, while the mineworkers and metalworkers demanded and won an increase 50 per cent higher than inflation.

Fifa had insisted on a protest-free zone, with regular police bannings of attempted marches – even an innocuous education-for-all rally on June 7 (even though Fifa had sponsored the group, One Goal, requesting permission to march) – until sufficient resistance emerged to overcome the harassment. A few other victories were recorded along the way. Thousands of stadium construction workers fought for higher wages and often won. And AIDS activists prevented from distributing condoms at stadiums objected and won that right.

On 13 June 2010 in Durban, several hundred security workers at Durban's Moses Mabhida Stadium began revolting after the Germany-Australia game, demanding payment of a promised bonus. They only received R190 for 12 hours' work; outsourcing and super-exploitation have soured employee relations in the often dangerous security sector. Police tear-gassed and stun-grenaded 300 to break up the protest and promised that the ringleaders would be arrested. But half the ten stadia suffered this fate, as workers downed tools against the security labour brokers, leading to mass firings and compelling more expensive policing to come to Fifa's aid as internal security.

The most successful protest explicitly against the World Cup™ was by hundreds of Durban informal traders facing displacement from the century-old Early Morning Market. Were it not for sustained resistance over a year-long period, including a pitched battle with police in mid-2009, their space would have been transformed into a shopping mall, without them.

Some of the most impressive mobilisations were on the hardest front, perhaps: pop culture. To illustrate the challenge, Somali-born Toronto-bred musician K'naan had used his hit, 'Wavin' Flags', to promote the notion that a young boy on a dusty soccer field could simply drink a Coca Cola and become a world-class player. His remixed tune for Fifa self-censored all his earlier version's harder, anti-war lyrics:

> *many wars, settling scores*
> *bringing us promises, leaving us poor...*
> *but look how they treat us*
> *make us believers, make we fight their battles*
> *then they deceive us...*
> *... violent prone, poor people zone...*
> *out of the darkness, in came the carnage*
> *threatening my very survival*
> *fractured my streets, and broke all my dreams*

Explaining why he remixed (without ideas like broken promises), K'naan explained: "It's about the one time that we all get together and the world forgets its conflict and its problems and we focus on this unity and celebration. That moment is connected now to 'Wavin' Flag'." Added Coca Cola entertainment marketing chief, Joe Belliotti: "He has the connection to Africa, he is not a fly-by-night pop star, and his song is very indicative of celebration."[18]

This kind of tragic commercialisation and depoliticisation called for a culture jam, readily provided in the tune 'Wavering Flag' by the Playing Fields Connective, whose lyrics included:

> When they are older
> Our children might wonder
> Why we sold out
> In the name of the FIFA flag...
>
> When I get sober
> From all the soccer
> There will go FIFA, and
> guess who'll be making cash?
>
> They don't put back?
> They never put back?
> They don't put back? nooo
>
> The enemy's balls,
> the penalties scored
> The LOC had the key,
> let in own goals
>
> I heard them say
> "World Cup is the way"
> But what about later?
> How long will we pay?[19]

Then there were the Chomsky AllStars, whose 'Beautiful Gain' rip-off of the World Cup was advertised as follows: "Blending punk, blues, dub and Afrobeat, 'The Beautiful Gain', with its infectious melody and sublime rhythms, is set to become the 'Free Nelson Mandela' of the 21st century."

---

18. http://www.songfacts.com/detail.php?id=17880
19. http://www.youtube.com/watch?v=KP1sh-csauA

[20] Yet more ripping protest music was released by a network of artists who came together to publicise Khulumani Support Group, the anti-apartheid victims' network which is suing corporations in the United States courts for taking away profits and interest when they should have been observing sanctions. Durban's Iain Robinson (Ewok) contributed the tune 'Shame on the Beautiful Game'[21] which soon joined a whole CD of hip-hop protest tunes produced by the Grahamstown-based group Defboyz: "The core message of this CD is that social justice should never be subordinated in the pursuit of profits... The artists represented on this CD come from all over the world and in a variety of languages – put one message across – that the powers that be must be held accountable for their actions! Peace."[22]

Finally, 15 artists from across the world were gathered virtually by Nomadic Wax, Dj Magee and Dj Nio to produce a song they describe as follows:

> Legendary South African emcee Emile YX (Black Noise Crew) used the 'World Cup' track as an opportunity to respond to what is currently happening in his hometown of Cape Town, rapping "We'll foot the bill just so they can foot the ball." Emile and 15 other artists from a range of nations, including Italy, Brazil, South Africa, Morocco, and Trinidad-Tobago, among others, rap their verses in French, Spanish, Portuguese, English, and Arabic and explore many of the controversies, benefits, and pitfalls of the historic 2010 World Cup in South Africa.[23]

But there were many aggrieved by Fifa and its South African government allies who did not fare so well. Durban's subsistence fisherfolk unsuccessfully fought a forced removal from piers at the World Cup™ Fan Fest park on the main beach. Johannesburg and Cape Town traders also lost their battle for space, due to the exclusion zones. And Cape Town housing displacees were shuttled into a bizarre, apartheid-style 'temporary' transit camp, Blikkiesdorp. Other losers included environmentalists concerned about the World Cup's™ vast carbon emissions – twice the 2006 record – and the South African government's attempt to 'offset' these through 'greenwashing' strategies such as the Clean Development Mechanism and inappropriate tree planting.

---

20. http://chomskyallstars.bandcamp.com/track/the-beautiful-gain-full-version
21. http://redcardcampaign.wordpress.com/tag/shame-on-the-game
22. http://en.wordpress.com/tag/music-4-justice
23. http://nomadicwax.bandcamp.com/track/world-cup

Most troubling, the networks of independent leftists which normally mobilise against large international events – the World Conference Against Racism (12,000 protesters on 31 August 2001) and the World Summit on Sustainable Development (30 000 marched on 31 August 2002) – were simply unable to generate enthusiasm for two attempted marches: in Soweto against Fifa's headquarters, by the Anti-Privatisation Forum; and from Blikkiesdorp by the Western Cape Anti-Eviction Campaign. In Durban, a June 16 protest march to City Hall gathered more than 1000 to demand a 'World Cup for All', On July 3, several hundred rallied at City Hall against what might be regarded as the greatest failing of South Africa's subaltern classes: xenophobia.

Xenophobia threats

A crisis began to emerge as the World Cup wound down, one that terrified progressives here and everywhere: xenophobic violence where sore losers adopt right-wing populist sentiments, and frame the foreigner. The FaceBook pages of hip young Johannesburg gangstas exploded with xenophobic raves after Uruguay beat Bafana Bafana. Wrote Khavi Mavodze, for example, "Foreigners leave our country, be warned, xenophobia is our first name." [24]

Even the ordinarily defensive African National Congress national executive committee and the Cabinet both expressed initial concern in May 2010 about a potential repeat of the violence two years earlier, that left 62 people dead and more than a hundred thousand displaced.

But denialism was another common reaction by those in power. Recall that in late 2007, the Africa Peer Review Mechanism panel of eminent persons issued a warning that went unheeded: "Xenophobia against other Africans is currently on the rise and must be nipped in the bud." Thabo Mbeki replied that this was "simply not true." [25]

So when Jacob Zuma, told his party executive in May that "The branches of the ANC must start working now to deal with the issue of xenophobia,"[26] it was depressing when another politician combined denialism and stereotyping. Replying that "There is no tangible evidence," Police General Bheki Cele added, a few days later: "We have

---

24.
http://www.facebook.com/profile.php?id=100001215301464&ref=search#!/profile.php?id=100001215301464&v=wall&ref=search
25 SA Press Association (2007) 'Mbeki critical of crime issues in APRM report', Pretoria, 6 December.
26.
http://www.politicsweb.co.za/politicsweb/view/politicsweb/en/page71654?oid=177542&sn=Detail

observed a trend where foreigners commit crime - taking advantage of the fact that we have an unacceptable crime level - to tarnish our credibility and image." [27]

Cele's finger-pointing at immigrants for crime is just one of the scapegoat strategies. The Consortium for Refugees and Migrants in South Africa called xenophobia a 'credible threat' in part because "some perpetrators appear to believe they have the tacit support of local political actors." [28]

In addition to increasing its moral suasion, prosecuting those guilty of xenophobic attacks, resolving local leadership turf battles that have xenophobic powerplays, and establishing emergency response mechanisms, the state has an obligation to address root causes for the social stress which is often expressed as xenophobia: mass unemployment, housing shortages, intense retail competition in townships and South Africa's regional geopolitical interests which create more refugees than prosperity.

Conclusion

The World Cup™ is a formidable spectacle, not least because it attracts the world's largest sports audience. South Africa's hosting has gone off nearly flawlessly, contrary to predictions by Afropessimists. According to Fifa general secretary Jerome Valcke, "It's been a perfect World Cup. The number of foreign visitors and tickets sales were beyond expectations." [29] Fifa's profit increase over the 2006 games in Germany was at least 50 per cent, he reported. Yet it is equally evident that aside from the unparalleled – albeit temporary - psychological boost, the rewards to society are outweighed by the burdens.

The international experience suggests that mega-sporting events were organised largely by the private sector, with little or no accountability to citizens or elected officials, although its decisions were likely to have major public policy implications. As Jennings has emphasised, Fifa's "unaccountable structure ... is honed to deliver the game to the needs of global capitalism - with no checks or restraints. Just cheques." The nature of urban governance associated with these events is "characterised by less democratic and more elite-driven priorities" (Swyngedouw et al., 2002: 542).

---

27.   http://www.sport24.co.za/Soccer/WorldCup/NationalNews/SAs-Cup-courts-fast-track-law-20100620
28. http://ipsnews.net/africa/nota.asp?idnews=51919
29.   http://www.timeslive.co.za/local/article520522.ece/Jordaan--Brother-not-cashing-in-on-2010

The South African experience was no different. The Fifa 2010 World Cup™ paid rhetorical lip service to reducing the socio-economic inequalities in the region; addressing the needs of the poor; was largely driven by corporate interests; and underwritten with public funds, with limited or no public participation; and undermined sovereignty and democratic rights. Mega sporting events should create zones of opportunity for those who have been historically disadvantaged; integrate the city so that urban resources are accessible to all citizens; and ensure popular participation in the planning process (Khan and Maharaj, 1998). Greater emphasis should be placed on policies that sustain growth through redistribution. This will also require a more direct intervention by the state than that currently envisaged.

In South Africa, as soccer hype fades and social protests become more insistent, local elites may realise their mistake in hosting these games in such a wasteful, arrogant manner. They may learn what we already know: profiteering by business and genuine joy associated with the world's most loved sport are mutually incompatible. The question for Brazilian soccer-lovers (2014 hosts) and for critics of multinational corporate rule is whether they will have greater success establishing countervailing pressure and reversing Fifa's power. Only with an antidote to commercialisation and foreign control can we truly call soccer the beautiful game.

References

Alegi, P., 2010. *African soccerscapes – How a continent changed the world's game*. Athens: Ohio University Press.

Andranovich, G. Burbank, M. and Heying, C., 2001. Olympic Cities: Lessons learnt from mega event politics. *Journal of Urban Affairs*, 23, pp.113-131.

Chalkley, B. and Essex, S., 1999. Urban development through hosting international events: a history of the Olympic Games. *Planning Perspectives*, 14, pp.369-394.

Cochrane, A. et al., 1996. Manchester plays games: Exploring the local politics of Globalisation. *Urban Studies*, 33, pp.1319-1336.

Hillier, H., 2000. Mega-Events, urban boosterism and growth strategies: an analysis of the objectives and legitimations of the Cape Town 2004 Olympic Bid. *IJURR*, 24, pp.439-458.

Jennings, A., 2006. *Foul!: The secret world of FIFA*. London: Harper Collins.

Khan, S. and Maharaj, B., 1998. Restructuring the Apartheid City: Cato Manor, 'A Prime Urban Reconstruction Opportunity'? *Urban Forum*, 9, pp.197-223.

O'Brien, D., 2006. Event Business Leveraging: The Sydney 2000 Olympic Games. *Annals of Tourism Research*, 33, pp.240-261.

Owen, K.A., 2002. The Sydney Olympics and Urban Entrepreneurialism: Local variations in urban governance. *Australian Geographical Studies*, 40, pp.323-336.

Rutheiser, C., 1996. *Imagineering Atlanta: The politics of place in the city of dreams*. London: Verso.

Smith, A., 2005. Reimagining the city: The value of sport initiatives. *Annals of Tourism Research*, 32, pp.217-236.

Sole, S., 2010. Durban's Moses Mabhida Stadium: Arch of hope or yoke of debt? In C. Herzenberg, ed. *Player and referee: Conflicting interests and the 2010 FIFA World CupTM*. Pretoria: Institute for Security Studies.

Swyngedouw, E. Moulaert, F. Rodriguez, A., 2002. Neoliberal urbanisation in Europe: Large scale urban development projects and the new urban policy. *Antipode*, 34, pp.542-577.